Crime and Criminal Justice Policy

Longman Criminology Series

Series Editor: Tim Newburn

Crime and Criminal Justice Policy

2nd Edition

Tim Newburn

Harlow, England • London • New York • Boston • San Francisco • Toronto
Sydney • Tokyo • Singapore • Hong Kong • Seoul • Taipei • New Delhi
Cape Town • Madrid • Mexico City • Amsterdam • Munich • Paris • Milan

Pearson Education Limited
Edinburgh Gate
Harlow
Essex CM20 2JE
England

and Associated Companies throughout the world

Visit us on the World Wide Web at:
www.pearsoned.co.uk

First published 1995
Second edition published 2003

© Pearson Education Limited 2003

The right of Tim Newburn to be identified as author
of this work has been asserted by the author in accordance with
the Copyright, Designs and Patents Act 1988.

All rights reserved. No part of this publication may be
reproduced, stored in a retrieval system, or transmitted
in any form or by any means, electronic, mechanical,
photocopying, recording or otherwise, without either the
prior written permission of the publisher or a licence
permitting restricted copying in the United Kingdom
issued by the Copyright Licensing Agency Ltd,
90 Tottenham Court Road, London W1T 4LP.

ISBN: 978-0-582-36955-9

British Library Cataloguing-in-Publication Data
A catalogue record for this book is available from the British Library

10 9 8 7 6 5 4 3 2
08 07

Typeset in 10/12pt New Baskerville
Printed and bound in Malaysia
The publisher's policy is to use paper manufactured from sustainable forests.

Contents

For Mary

Introduction

As the title indicates, this book is about criminal justice policy. The criminal justice system is that conglomeration of institutions and agencies that respond to – and on occasion attempt to prevent – 'crime'. It is wider than the penal system, which is concerned with punishment or other responses to offenders. Thus, the focus of this book is not only on the courts, probation and prison services, but also, for example, on the work of the police and the treatment of victims in the criminal justice system. In taking such a broad focus, there are inevitably areas that receive somewhat less attention than others.

The text is designed as an introduction to the recent history of criminal justice policy, though with considerable attention paid to longer-term historical transformations. It opens with an overview of the emergence of the modern penal system. The introductory Chapter, together with the first sections of Chapters 3 and 6 – which cover the growth of the new police and the development of the probation service – chart the birth of the modern criminal justice system. With Chapter 1 focusing on punishment in the eighteenth, nineteenth and early twentieth centuries, Chapter 2 looks at the developments in post-War Britain, focusing specifically on the growing prison 'crisis' of the last 25 years.

After looking at the nineteenth-century origins of the modern police, Chapter 3 examines the development of British policing up until the 1980s. The early 1990s, examined in Chapter 4, saw a number of inquiries into policing, including the appointment of a Royal Commission on Criminal Justice (which examined areas of police powers and procedures), the Sheehy Inquiry (which considered rank structure, remuneration and conditions of service in the police) and a White Paper (focusing on accountability). The pace of change was swift in the 1990s and the Chapter concludes by examining the continuing scrutiny of policing that has occurred in the wake of the Stephen Lawrence Inquiry, the Patten Inquiry and the Police Reform Act.

Though originally thought to be a central part of their mandate, crime prevention has generally been relegated to the margins of police activity. Chapter 5 examines the growing visibility of, and emphasis on, crime prevention and, more recently, 'community safety' in criminal

justice policy-making. Chapter 6 focuses on the changing role and functions of the probation service. It begins with the emergence of probation
around the turn of the twentieth century and its development into a
fully professional service. It closes with the 'nationalisation' of the service in the early twenty-first century. Following on from this, Chapter 7
examines the enormous expansion of 'alternatives to custody' that has
taken place since the Second World War. The chapter then focuses on
the passage of the Criminal Justice Act 1991, the quick retreat from it,
and the increasing politicisation of sentencing policy.

Juvenile courts only came into being after the Children Act 1908, and
Chapter 8 examines the developments leading up to the Act and the
operation of the 'juvenile justice system' since that period. The key
points in this history include: the Children and Young Persons Act 1933,
which required magistrates to have regard to the welfare of the child
when sentencing; the Criminal Justice Act 1948, which introduced
detention and attendance centres; the Criminal Justice Act 1982 and the
introduction of several new disposals (youth custody, care orders and
community service); intermediate treatment; the development of the
policy of diversion in the 1980s; and the return to penal populism in the
1990s and since.

Chapter 9 looks at the position of victims of crime. It has become something of a cliché in writing about victims of crime to note that they were
once the forgotten party in the criminal justice process. However, great
changes have taken place in criminal justice policy with regard to victims
in the past 30 years, though not necessarily as a result of the development
of a coherent policy for the treatment of victims. The United Kingdom
was at the forefront of change with the setting up of the Criminal Injuries
Compensation Scheme in the mid-1960s, and that, together with the
increasing use of court-based compensation order by the criminal courts
and the emergence and growth of a voluntary Victim Support movement,
means that victims have become a central facet of the avowed policies of
both the major political parties – an aim recently reinforced in the latest
government White Paper, *Justice For All.*

Since the first edition of this book was written, almost a decade ago,
certain features of criminal justice policy that were fairly dominant then
have become even more visible. In particular, the highly politicised
nature of the terrain is now the most inescapable feature of criminal justice policy-making. The utilisation of crime issues by politicians for narrowly political ends continues unabated. As a consequence, the recent
history of policy-making is profoundly depressing. I feel somewhat like
the children's author, Lemony Snicket, who, in his books *A Series of
Unfortunate Events,* warns readers that should they be looking for a happy
tale, with an optimistic ending, then they would do well to put the book
down now and search elsewhere. The same applies here, for there is little in the recent history of criminal justice and penal policy to make one
optimistic for the future. The prison population is rising at an almost

exponential rate – with politicians showing little concern about it – and punitive rhetoric still dominates the landscape, and serves to mask the few more enlightened aspects of policy in this area. It is difficult to see what is going to shake us from these punitive trends. Churchill once noted that 'the mood and temper of the public in regard to the treatment of crime and criminals is one of the most unfailing tests of the civilization of any country'. There is a growing body of research evidence that suggests that, provided with an opportunity to think constructively about 'crime and criminals', the public are actually significantly less punitive than is often believed to be the case. The sad truth appears to be that it is the political climate, and our politicians, that are the dominant feature in the punitive cycle.

As ever, there are a large number of people that have contributed in some way or other to what follows. My criminological colleagues at the LSE – Stan Cohen, David Downes, Rod Earle, Janet Foster, Stephanie Hayman, Niki Lacey, Mario Matassa, Jill Peay, Coretta Phillips, Declan Roche, Paul Rock, Robert Reiner, Judith Rumgay, Mike Shiner and Anna Souhami provide the most stimulating and challenging of environments in which to work. I began rewriting this when I was at Goldsmiths' College and I am grateful to Frances Heidensohn, Geoff Pearson and Carole Keegan for their friendship, support and encouragement. A number of colleagues have read parts of the text in draft, and I am particularly grateful to Adam Crawford, Trevor Jones, George Mair, Rod Morgan and Ken Pease for advice and constructive criticism. Most of all I would like to thank my family – Mary, Gavin, Robin, Lewis and Owen – for their continuing love and support.

Chapter 1

The emergence of the modern penal system

> According to one line of contemporary thought on penal matters the eighteenth
> century criminal law was insufficiently severe to afford adequate protection
> against crime. Death, which . . . was then the appointed penalty for a large – and
> growing – number of offences, was considered too mild a punishment for a
> great many of them.
>
> (Radzinowicz, 1948: 231)

Generally speaking, historical studies of punishment tend to focus on the
emergence of the prison and on the changes that took place in the nineteenth century and that have taken place since (for an exception, see
Beattie, 1986). As a consequence, relatively little attention has been paid to
the medieval prison which, although primarily a means of containment of
those awaiting trial rather than a source of punishment itself, can
nevertheless be seen as the precursor to the modern prison (Sharpe, 1988).
The death penalty was the focus of the penal system in medieval times, and
though it appears that levels of capital punishment were high – say by
Victorian standards – from about the mid-sixteenth century, they had
actually been significantly lower in the two centuries before that (Bellamy,
1973). The rate of imprisonment declined significantly towards the end of
the seventeenth century, as did the use of public shaming rituals such as the
use of the ducking stool and the parading of prostitutes.

In the century or so after 1688, approximately 200 new capital offences
were placed on the statute books, many of which were property crimes,
and this body of legislation has since been referred to as the 'bloody
code'. Indeed, given that the major burden of law enforcement fell upon
the shoulders of the voluntary constable, 'the wide range of capital sanctions served . . . to enforce the law through terror' (Harding et al., 1985: 57).
Nevertheless, the numbers of public executions appear to have fallen
fairly consistently throughout the eighteenth century (Beattie, 1986;

Sharpe, 1990). There was a developing debate during the course of the 1700s about crime and punishment in general and about capital punishment in particular. The bloody code came under increasing attack and one historian suggests that 'what is really remarkable about the century's penal policy is the almost constant search for viable secondary punishments' (Sharpe, 1990: 40). Transportation was one of the other major forms of judicial punishment in the latter half of the seventeenth century, but by the turn of the century a number of colonies were beginning to refuse to receive any further convicts. However, the Transportation Act 1718 once again increased the numbers, and between that date and the suspension of transportation to America in 1775, 30,000 convicts were transported from England.

Prior to 1775 then, prison was used sparingly as a punishment. When it was used, sentences were generally short and generally confined to those found guilty of offences such as manslaughter, commercial fraud and rioting. By contrast, for other major felonies like murder, highway robbery and arson the most usual punishment was the death penalty. That said, although in theory the criminal law was intended to be rigidly applied, in practice a significant element of judicial discretion was present. Thus, for example, Ignatieff (1978) notes that judges in the Home Circuit in the 1750s commuted a third of the death sentences they had imposed and sentenced the offenders concerned to transportation instead. The use of such judicial discretion together with the introduction of new legislation during the eighteenth century meant that the use of transportation grew quickly. By the 1760s, transportation to the American colonies accounted for at least 70 per cent of all sentences at the Old Bailey (see Table 1.1).

Hanging at this time was, like whipping, a public ritual carried out by a local official, generally with a sense of ceremony or theatre designed to maximise what was believed to be the deterrent potential of the spectacle.[1] However, during the course of the century, the celebratory elements of the spectacle grew and it lost some its earlier solemnity, leading some to question its deterrent effects.

Table 1.1: Distribution of punishments, Old Bailey, 1760–94

Year	Death sentence %	Transported/ hulks %	Whip/brand/ fine %	Imprisoned %
1760–64	12.7	74.1	12.3	1.2
1765–69	15.8	70.2	13.4	0.8
1770–74	17.0	66.5	14.2	2.3
1775–79	20.7	33.4	17.6	28.6
1780–84	25.8	24.1	15.5	34.6
1785–89	18.5	50.1	13.2	13.3
1790–94	15.9	43.9	11.7	28.3

Source: Ignatieff (1978: 81)

Imprisonment was, as noted above, used sparingly as a punishment before 1775. It was used by local justices to punish summary offences such as vagrancy, bastardy, embezzlement and various forms of theft. The fact that relatively few offenders were in prison at this time was, it is suggested, not a function of an absence of sentencing powers on behalf of the local justices, but more a reflection of the relative absence of police to enforce such summary powers (Ignatieff, 1978). The emergence of the 'new police' in the early nineteenth century is covered in Chapter 3.

There were three basic types of prison in use at this time: debtors' prisons, such as the Dickensian Marshalsea; the county or borough gaol, of which there were more than 50 in existence in the middle of the century; and houses of correction or bridewells, where the poor were supposed to be put to work. The system was under strain, however, and in 1750 a crisis of numbers and an outbreak of typhus focused attention on the prisons and began the process of reform. John Howard, a wealthy Bedfordshire businessman, is the person most closely associated with reform, though commentators have also pointed to the role played by such figures as Henry Fielding and Thomas Gibson (Gatrell, 1980; Sharpe, 1990).

Howard was, among many things, a sheriff, one of whose functions was to visit the local prison. Appalled at many of the practices and conditions he witnessed at Bedford gaol, in 1774 he began visiting all the prisons in England and Wales. At each institution he recorded its size, the nature of its population, the quality of the food served, the weight of the chains used and many of details of the day-to-day life of the incarcerated. Whilst he was by no means alone at this time in condemning the conditions in the prisons, the 'originality of Howard's indictment [lay] in its "scientific", not in its moral character' (Ignatieff, 1978: 52). His report, *The State of the Prisons*, contained many proposals for reform and had a significant effect on the public. Crucially, there was an emerging belief among the reformers that punishment had lost much of its authority because of the degree of discretion that had been allowed those who imposed it. In prison, not only was there an incredible level of squalor, but corruption flourished.

Pressure on the system increased markedly with the outbreak of the American War of Independence and the suspension of transportation to the colonies in 1775. The suspension was only ever intended to be temporary, and the first practical alternative that was put into practice was the employment of two floating prisons or 'hulks' – the *Justitia* and the *Censor* – which were moored on the Thames. Within two years the hulks contained over 2,000 convicts. The consequence of the War was far more fundamental, however, than merely forcing the state to use adapted warships as temporary prisons in place of the colonies. In fact, 'almost overnight, imprisonment was transformed from an occasional punishment for felony into the sentence of first resort for all minor property crime' (Ignatieff, 1978: 81, and see Table 1.1 above).

Although at first many of the prison sentences that were handed out for these minor offences were relatively severe, the conditions in many of the prisons meant that many did not survive the sentence. Within a few years, the average length of sentence had been reduced significantly. For seven years or so the system held up, but with the widespread outbreak of fever in 1783, together with the end of the War and a major increase in crime, there was a vast increase in the number of offenders being committed for trial. It was estimated by Howard that the prison population increased by almost three-quarters in the decade from 1776. The increases were accompanied not only by a deterioration in general conditions, but also by sporadic rioting in a number of gaols.

Contemporaneously with the changing balance of punishment from transportation to imprisonment, there occurred a decline in confidence in public rituals surrounding the punishment of the body. Branding had been abolished in 1779, whipping was declining markedly, Howard was campaigning vigorously against corporal punishment in prison and the frequency and nature of public executions was changing. The Tyburn processional, for example, in which offenders were taken by cart from Newgate prison to be publicly hanged at the Tyburn gallows, had become particularly rowdy, and was officially stopped in 1783. Executions thereafter took place by the walls of the prison itself. Moreover, the level of pardons was increasing and only a relatively small proportion of those sentenced to death were actually hanged (Radzinowicz, 1948). This whole movement Ignatieff (1978: 90) argues:

> . . . indicates a loss of confidence in the morality and efficacy of ritual
> punishments, a growing resistance to the idea that the state should
> share the infliction of the punishment with the community assembled at
> the foot of the gallows or around the whipping post. Withdrawing the
> gallows under the shadow of Newgate and increasing the use of
> imprisonment denied the offender the opportunity for public defiance
> and the crowd the chance to turn the ritual to its own purposes.
> Compared to ritual punishment, imprisonment offered the state
> unparalleled control over the offender, enabling it to regulate the amount
> of suffering involved in any sentence, free of the jeers of the populace.

The one other alternative was once again to use transportation as a means of responding to the rise in crime. The Americas were no longer a possibility and Africa proved unworkable. By the mid-1780s, Australia was the preferred option. There was, however, a significant amount of resistance at home to the full-scale resumption of transportation and although it once again took its place as a major method of dealing with the most serious crimes (though it was used less frequently than before), minor property offences were no longer dealt with in this way. By the end of the decade imprisonment was taking the place of transportation as the punishment of 'first resort'.

In 1779, the Penitentiary Act was passed, which would have provided for the building of two penitentiaries to house those who would otherwise have been sentenced to transportation. The intention was that such convicts should be made to undertake hard and servile labour during the day and be kept in solitary confinement at night. A reasonable diet was specified and clothes were to be provided. In this way, 'the imperatives of deterrence were harmonised with those of humanity' (Ignatieff, 1978: 94). Though the original plan for two penitentiaries was never acted upon, the idea of a national or central penitentiary finally got underway in 1816. By that time the deterrent value of transportation and of public hanging was being seriously questioned (though they had been subject to criticism for at least a century by this point), and some reformers wished to explore the idea of long-term imprisonment. Sited by the Thames at Millbank, the penitentiary, with its harsh regime, presaged a new austere period in British penal history.

In addition to the penitentiary, the other highly influential attempt to create a new model on which imprisonment could be organised was Bentham's 'Panopticon': a circular building in which cells were organised around, and visible from, a central observation or inspection tower. It was to be organised in such a way as to prevent communication between the incarcerated, but to facilitate their constant supervision. Bentham went to great lengths to persuade the authorities of the efficacy of his plans for a penitentiary, but by 1810 it had been rejected, in part, because of the very significant emphasis Bentham placed on the importance of labour as the basis of punishment, and his plans to run such institutions on a similar basis to the way in which factories themselves were run (Melossi and Pavarini, 1981).

In the late eighteenth and early nineteenth century, the penitentiary system came under attack from a number of sources. First, the fact that they had been used to house political prisoners, such as John Wilkes, resulted in the growth of a popular campaign against the regimes in the penitentiaries, and especially against solitary confinement. Second, in the wake of the largely evangelical prison reform movement in the late 1800s there came a new philanthropic movement associated with Quakers such as Elizabeth Fry. By 1820, the prison system was desperately overcrowded and with too few staff to attempt to enforce discipline (Ignatieff, 1978). Outside the penitentiaries, the 'hulks' were still operating – almost 50 years after their introduction as a temporary measure – and were the scene of widespread disorder and great danger.

The third source of pressure was a campaign for reform led by the Prison Discipline Society. One of the consequences of this campaign was the Gaols Act 1823. Although the legislation had little effect on either the nature of regimes or on general conditions, by requiring magistrates to submit annual reports on their prisons to the Home Secretary it set in motion the process that eventually led to centralised control of the prison system. Crime was rising quickly at this point, as were the numbers sent to prison (Emsley, 1987). It was relatively petty offenders, however, that were filling up the gaols and there was widespread concern about the perceived rise of indiscipline among the agricultural classes and the metropolitan poor that provided the majority of these new inmates. New measures in prison were felt to be necessary and as the regime at the main convict prison, Millbank, became increasingly austere, so local prisons began to tighten the nature of the regimes. One of the most significant developments first occurred at Coldbath Fields House of Correction in London, where complete silence amongst inmates was introduced in the 1830s. The banning of all communication, the use of the treadmill (which had started some time earlier) and the introduction of a much more austere diet for inmates were the hallmarks of the new system of discipline which was in place around the country from the 1830s onwards. It was not only the penal system that was affected by the widespread concern about crime and disorder. This was also the point at which the 'New Police' emerged in an attempt to provide a more effective method of enforcing the summary powers that were available (see Chapter 3).

In the penal sphere, 'the opening of Pentonville in 1842 represents a point of culmination in the tightening up of social controls underway since 1820' (Ignatieff, 1978: 193). Whitworth Russell and William Crawford, the prison inspectors, began lobbying in the mid-1830s for the construction of a new model prison. Crawford had been to America to look at two models there: one organised around solitary confinement based in the Western Penitentiary in Philadelphia, the other a silent regime used in Auburn and Sing Sing. It was a prison along the lines of the Philadelphia model that the two inspectors pressed for, though they wished to modify the regime in a number of ways. Its essence nevertheless remained solitary confinement. What the nature of the regime was to be was the focus of one of the major debates of penology at the time. There were two basic schools of thought: one which believed in permitting association between inmates (though not necessarily allowing them to speak) and one which believed that association of any kind would lead to the development of an inmate subculture and moral harm. It was believed that separation was 'not only morally beneficial, by preventing contamination and providing an opportunity for reflection and self examination, but greatly facilitated the task of security and control' (Home Office, 1979: para. 2.6). It was such beliefs which underpinned the development of the new convict prison, Pentonville.

In 1850, central control was formalised with the establishment of the Convict Service. This included the convict prisons, Millbank and Pentonville, two public works prisons (Portland and Dartmoor) one prison for juveniles (Parkhurst), the hulks and cells for separate confinement that were rented in certain local prisons. Transportation to Australia finally ceased in 1868, though it continued to Gibraltar until 1875, (Braithwaite, 2003), and this gave further impetus to the increasing use of imprisonment for serious crimes, and not merely the summary offences and petty felonies which had been its primary focus in the previous period. The consequence was an increasing emphasis on long sentences of imprisonment. Those who would otherwise have been transported spent a period in solitary confinement in either Pentonville or Millbank and were then transferred to one of a number of centrally run public works or 'invalid' prisons where they engaged in 'hard labour' – usually quarrying. At the end of this period, the convicts were released on parole – what was then known as 'a ticket of leave' – though public confidence in the system was extremely low, and those on ticket of leave were often harassed (Tobias, 1972). The eventual consequence was the introduction of photographing those paroled in such a manner, in order to make their identification easier should their ticket need to be revoked, and indeed specific officers in the Metropolitan police were given the task of supervising such ticket of leave men in the capital. Though the probation service has its roots largely elsewhere (see Chapter 6), the use of police officers in this manner marked the beginning of community-based oversight of offenders.

By the mid-nineteenth century, then, incarceration had become the major sanction for dealing with adult offenders. In essence, it took two forms: 'imprisonment' where sentences of up to two years were served in a local prison; and 'penal servitude' where sentences were five years or more and were served in a convict prison such as Millbank or Pentonville. The Penal Servitude Act 1865 restricted the use of remission with the intention that the general level of severity should be increased once more. Although the new measures 'were intended to increase the deterrence value of penal servitude, their ironic effect was to curtail the use of penal servitude and to make imprisonment in local prisons the mainstay of the whole system' (Garland, 1985: 7).

Despite the new measures, there was concern at this time that penal servitude remained insufficiently severe. From the 1860s, the convict system came under the control of Sir Edward Du Cane, who during his working life was to have a profound effect on the whole of the prison system. The Prisons Act 1877 transferred justices' penal powers to the Home Office, and created the Prison Commission which was to be responsible for the organisation and administration of the new service, though assisted by the inspectorate which had been set up by the Gaol Act 1835. In addition to his control of the convict system, from 1877, Du Cane also became Chairman of the Prison Commissioners. Radzinowicz and Hood (1990) describe his philosophy as being based on the belief that the aim of punishment was both to deter and to reform, but that deterrence should always come before reformation. Under Du Cane, the regimes at Millbank and Pentonville became significantly more austere. In addition, the use of flogging which had happened infrequently under his predecessor, Joshua Jebb, increased in frequency and severity.

During the period of Du Cane's Chairmanship, 1869–95, the numbers sentenced to penal servitude more than halved, as did the number confined in both convict and local prisons. By the end of the period, anyway, it was no longer possible to sustain a system based on large-scale public works. In 1893, a major public debate about the prison system began in the press. The system, it was suggested, was failing in its objective of deterring criminals whilst simultaneously being too harsh, and the focus of the attack was Du Cane himself, who was criticised for being autocratic and secretive. As a response to the campaign, a Departmental Committee under the Chairmanship of Herbert Gladstone was set up in 1894. The Gladstone Report, which reported within a year, is widely considered to be a landmark in British penal history, and it contained a number of far-reaching proposals.

The Report was critical of the failure to pay sufficient attention to 'the moral as well as the legal responsibility of the prison authorities'. Crucially, it placed the reform or rehabilitation of prisoners, with deterrence, as the 'primary and concurrent objects' of the system. For the first time, deterrence did not take priority over reform. The Committee's desire to reinforce the rehabilitative role of regimes led to the recognition of individual inmate's needs. As a result the Committee stated:

> We think that the system should be made more elastic, more capable of being adopted [sic] to the special cases of individual prisoners; that prison discipline should be more effectually designed to maintain, stimulate, or awaken the higher susceptibilities of prisoners, to develop their moral instincts, to train them in orderly and industrial habits, and whenever possible to turn them out of prison better men and women, both physically and morally, than when they came in.
>
> (quoted in Radzinowicz and Hood, 1990: 577–8)

In addition, they recommended the introduction of a new form of classification of prisoners, of a measure of associated labour and of a new system of penal reformatories for young offenders. Although the Report paid credit to the efficiency with which Du Cane had reorganised the prison system since the Prison Act 1877, the legitimacy of his administration had been fatally wounded and he resigned three days after its publication. He was replaced by Sir Evelyn Ruggles-Brise.

The Gladstone Report is viewed by many as ushering in an age of penal optimism (Sharpe, 1990) and, in part, this was underpinned by a fall in the prison population (see Figure 1.1).

The report did not, however, prompt quick action and it was 1898 before new legislation was passed. Even then the Prison Act had an extremely stormy passage, and the government was forced to state that there was no intention of 'revolutionising the present code; the alterations . . . will be few' (quoted in Radzinowicz and Hood, 1990: 581). As Garland (1985) points out, it was only the issues that were the source of immediate concern that were acted upon at this stage and more than a decade passed before the more fundamental restructuring took place. Nevertheless, the next two decades saw a major transformation in the penal system; one which has been described as resulting in the construction of a new system of 'penality' (Garland, 1985).

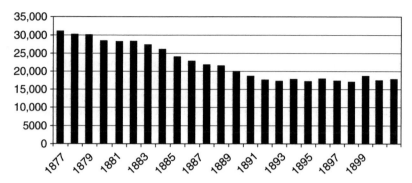

Figure 1.1   Prison population, England and Wales, 1877–1900
Source: Prison Statistics England and Wales, London: Stationery Office

The emergence of a new penal system?

> England and Wales entered the twentieth century with a system of judicial
> punishments which showed, in embryo at least, a number of differing trends.
> At the centre of the system, practically and symbolically, stood the prison.
> Hardly thought of as a dominant form of punishment for the serious offender
> in 1800, by 1900 the prison was firmly established in both the popular
> consciousness and the practice of the courts as the most potent means by
> which the generality of offenders might be punished.
>
> (Sharpe, 1990: 88)

One of the changes made after the passage of the Prison Act 1898 was
the introduction of a new system of classification. This separated
younger convicts from older, and first offenders from recidivists.
Crucially, it was not merely a system of administrative classification, but
a method of distinguishing the needs of individual prisoners. Whilst
from a present day perspective this may not seem a revolutionary alter-
ation, it signalled a significant shift from Victorian penal practice in
which uniformity was seen as the key. This is illustrated in the views of Du
Cane written in 1885:

> A sentence of penal servitude is, in its main features, and so far as it concerns
> the punishment, applied on exactly the same system to every person subjected
> to it. The previous career and character of the prisoner makes no difference
> in the punishment to which he is subjected.
>
> (quoted in Garland, 1985: 14)

In addition to a growing emphasis on individualisation under Ruggles-Brise,
regimes began to change. Privileges for the well-behaved were introduced
after the turn of the century; there were increases in the number and
frequency of letters and visits, a broader selection of books became available

and occasional entertainments were allowed. Privileges can be withdrawn, of course, as well as given, and as the old controls of separation and silence were gradually eroded, new micro-forms of control, which sought conformity through the use of privilege, were extended. In addition, the imposition of corporal punishment declined markedly, though demands that the penalty be abolished altogether were not acted upon. Significantly, however, the 1899 Prison Rules stated that it was the duty of all prison officers 'to treat prisoners with kindness and humanity . . . the great object of reclaiming the criminal should always be kept in view by all officers, and they should strive to acquire a moral influence over the prisoners by performing their duties conscientiously, but without harshness'.

In the aftermath of the resignation of Du Cane, when the implications of the Gladstone Report were still being digested, two well-known literary figures had, in very different ways, a major impact on the penal debates of the period. The first, Oscar Wilde, was imprisoned for gross indecency in 1895. His sentence of two years was spent in Pentonville, Wandsworth and Reading. The harsh conditions in prison quickly took a heavy toll on Wilde and, as a result of some campaigning on his behalf, a number of improvements were made to his conditions. Although on release Wilde made some largely unsuccessful attempts to become involved in prison reform, the impact that incarceration had had upon him kept the question of prison conditions in the minds of some of the key actors.

The second literary figure was the author John Galsworthy. A visit to Dartmoor Prison prompted him to begin campaigning to bring an end to solitary confinement. As we have already seen, the resistance to permitting association among convicts was strong and the new Commissioner of Prisons, Ruggles-Brise, was only willing to reduce the period of separate confinement rather than abandon it altogether. This in itself was quite a significant victory for Galsworthy. By 1910, however, Galsworthy had written a play about penal servitude, *Justice*, and both Ruggles-Brise and Churchill, the Home Secretary, attended the opening night. At least partly as a result, the period of separate confinement was further reduced to one month for the less serious offenders and to three months for 'recidivists'. As Radzinowicz and Hood (1990: 593) argue, to have conceded to the demands that were being made to end separate confinement 'would be to admit to unjustified practices in the past'. It was 1922 before separate confinement was abolished altogether.

On what basis then does Garland argue that the period between the Gladstone Report and the First World War saw the emergence of a new system of penality? In fact, it is on the basis of a broad series of changes, the vast majority of which occurred outside the prison system. First of all, the range of sanctions available to the criminal courts increased enormously at this time. There was, for example, the formalisation of probation and the introduction of probation orders as a result of the Probation of Offenders Act 1907 (see Chapter 6). Borstal training was introduced by the Prevention of Crime Act 1908 (see Chapter 8). This sentence, which was available for offenders aged between 16 and 21, was semi-determinate and was to be followed by a period of licensed supervision. The same Act introduced a sentence of 'preventive detention' with a maximum of ten years' for 'habitual criminals', again followed by supervision. In addition, new measures were also introduced – in 1898 and 1913 – to provide detention in an inebriate reformatory or in an institution for the mentally defective. Finally, new restrictions were introduced. The Children Act 1908, for example, abolished penal servitude for children and young offenders, and imposed restrictions on the use of imprisonment of 14–16-year-olds.

Second, in addition to the increased range of sanctions available, Garland (1985) points to the increased range of agencies working in the penal field. Thus, as has already been suggested, the first decade of the century saw the emergence of the basis for a formal, national probation service, though it was some years before this was fully realised. A few years later, an association was established to organise and regulate the supervision of convicts on release.

Third, there was the establishment of a number of new institutions in this period. From 1908, for example, the juvenile court had jurisdiction over all cases involving people under the age of 16. Other new institutions which were introduced included the Borstals – with a regime based on reformation and training – and preventive detention institutions, such as that at Camp Hill, which were 'secure, but less rigorous than those of regular prisons' (Garland, 1985: 22). The common feature of these agencies was the fact that they were targeted at specific populations of offenders; this was the beginnings of a system based on 'specialisation' and 'classification'. Garland sums up the developments thus:

> Although most . . . took place outside the prison system, involving extraneous agencies and institutions, these changes clearly had a large impact upon the prison and its functioning. Many of these new sanctions . . . were conceived as direct alternatives to imprisonment, while others functioned to remove certain classes of offender out of the domain of the prison and into specialist institutions. The consequence was that the prison was *decentred* – shifted from its position as the central and predominant sanction to become one institution among many in an extended grid of penal sanctions. Of course it continued to be a sanction of major importance, but it was now deployed in a different manner, for a narrower section of the criminal population, and often as a back-up sanction for other institutions, rather than the place of first resort.
>
> (Garland, 1985: 23)

Within this new penal complex, reform occupied a primary place. Whereas in the Victorian penal system it had clearly been placed behind deterrence as an aim of penal practice, in the period in which Ruggles-Brise was in charge of the prison system, the emphasis shifted towards reformation. Probation supervision, after-care, borstal training, even the prison itself, were all reoriented towards a new emphasis upon the possibilities of 'saving' rather than 'hating' criminals. As Garland describes in great detail, it would be inaccurate to suggest that there was a radical rupture between previous practices and those in evidence by 1914. As with many major historical transformations, there were many visible elements of continuity as well as change. Nevertheless, he argues, there was an overriding element of discontinuity; one resulting in increasing diversity of penal practice. 'There has been a move from *a calibrated, hierarchical structure* (of fines, prison terms, death), into which offenders were inserted according to the severity of their offence, to *an extended grid of non-equivalent and diverse dispositions*, into which the offender is inscribed according to the diagnosis of his or her condition and the treatment appropriate to it' (Garland, 1985: 28).

The inter-War years

In addition to Ruggles-Brise, the other major figure of the period was Sir Alexander Paterson. Early in life he was involved in voluntary social work and, in particular, with the care of borstal boys and discharged prisoners. In 1922, he became a member of the Prison Commission and spent the next two decades working for the reform of the prison system. There was significant optimism in penal circles at this time, and it was by no means unrelated to the decline in the prison population that had taken place since 1908. Although the prison commissioners anticipated a rise after the First World War, it did not materialise, and the prison population remained at around 12,000 up until the Second World War (see Figure 1.2).

A mood of scepticism about the efficacy of prison, which is often felt to originate with Churchill's tenure at the Home Office before the First World War (Rutherford, 1986b) was carried over into the inter-War

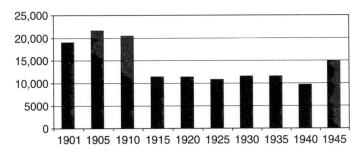

Figure 1.2   Prison population, England and Wales, 1901–45
Source: Prison Statistics England and Wales, London: Stationery Office

period. Two books published in the 1920s gave expression to this mood and reinforced the sense of scepticism. Sidney and Beatrice Webb's *English Prisons Under Local Government* viewed prison as 'demoralising and dangerous', and Hobhouse and Brockway's *English Prisons Today* argued strongly for greater use of existing alternatives to prison. The end-point of this optimism was perhaps the Criminal Justice Bill, which was introduced to Parliament in 1938. The Bill included new restrictions on the use of custody, and would have introduced residential hostels – to be known as 'Howard Houses' – had the War not interrupted its progress in the House.

The increased variety of penal institutions and the emphasis on reform combined in this period to bring about the establishment of the first open prison. An experimental open prison had been established as early as the 1890s in Switzerland, and a number of open institutions were in operation in the United States in the early 1930s. The first open prison in Britain was established at New Hall Camp near Wakefield Prison in 1933. The fact that such an experiment could even be mounted in the 1930s illustrates how much change had taken place since the Gladstone Report less than 40 years previously.

Perhaps the other major change – and one that had its origins in the Gladstone Report – was the already-mentioned borstal system that was closely associated with Ruggles-Brise and later Paterson. Once again, it was a foreign example that was crucial in bringing about change – this time the reformatory at Elmira in New York State. The aim was to provide a strict regime based on discipline, hard work and physical exercise. Indeed, the borstal regimes in many respects sought to emulate and recreate an ethos similar to that found at the time in the public schools, and the house system was introduced in the 1920s. There was, however, some opposition to the introduction of the borstal system and it was actually fairly slow to get off the ground. It was only by the late 1920s/early 1930s that it was seen as a core method of dealing with young offenders.

All this change did not take place, however, without significant grievances being felt and expressed. As the May Report noted, looking back on twentieth-century penal policy, although many commentators have suggested that the Gladstone Report represents a new, liberal trend in English penal policy, one saw it as 'the source of many of the problems which have affected the prison system and its staff ever since'. This is a reference to J.E. Thomas, who argued (1972) that the reformulation of the central aims of the prison service to put reformation on a par with deterrence caused confusion of purpose for prison officers. Staff became uncertain whether their control and discipline function was really central to the objectives of the prison system. Furthermore, he argued that the increased association between inmates actually made the control function more difficult.

Perhaps not surprisingly, many prison officers felt that the increased demands being made upon them were not being met with better pay and conditions. From the turn of the century onwards, prison officers began to develop a collective outlook. The establishment of the *Prison Officer's Magazine* in 1910 provided an outlet for discontent within the service. A union – the National Union of Police and Prison Officers (NUPPO) was formed in 1913 and a Prison Officers' Federation in 1915. The Federation and NUPPO amalgamated in 1918, after the latter had apparently established the right to strike. As a consequence, a number of prison officers became involved in the police strike of 1919. All of those who participated lost their jobs, and though the *Magazine* was resurrected in the 1920s (it had been suspended in 1918), it was not until 1938 that The Prison Officers' Association (POA) was established.

The substantial increases in police pay which had been recommended by the Desborough Committee in 1919, after the police strike, led to further claims by prison officers. The claim was rejected by a Committee of Inquiry, under the Chairmanship of Earl Stanhope, on the grounds that the tasks and responsibilities of prison staff were less than those of the police and that actual incidence of serious injury was markedly lower. Indeed, certainly as far as the latter was concerned, this did appear to be the case. Although there were a small number of relatively minor disturbances, most of the prison system appears to have been relatively calm for the majority of this period. As the prison population rose after the Second World War, and even outstripped the increased capacity provided by the largest ever prison-building programme, so the frequency and violence of prison disturbances increased. So severe did things become in 1990 that numerous authors have described the modern penal system as being in 'crisis' (see, for example, Cavadino and Dignan, 1992). The changes in the prison system since 1945 are covered in Chapter 2.

Notes

1. Perhaps most powerfully captured in the opening pages of Foucault's (1979) *Discipline and Punish*, in which he describes the death of Damiens the regicide.

Chapter 2

Prisons and imprisonment in post-War Britain

> There is a major 'geological fault' in the prison landscape . . . the 'fault' is the unpredictable and volatile size of the prison population.
>
> (Sir Brian Cubbon, former Permanent Secretary, Home Office, quoted in Morgan, 1992a: 236)

As we saw in Chapter 1, the prison population in England and Wales dropped from a high of over 30,000 in 1877 – when the Prison Act was passed – to a low point of a little over 9,000 at the end of the First World War. Thereafter, the population rose slightly, but generally hovered between 10–12,000 in the years up to the Second World War (see Figure 1.2). It is the period since then that is the focus for this Chapter.

The expectation after the War was that crime levels would at worst remain stable and, given the anticipated improvements in living standards and the development of the welfare state, might even drop (Bottoms, 1987). This, we know of course, is quite the reverse of what happened. Indeed, so significant have the changes been, that it is hard to credit that it was only half a century ago that only half a million indictable crimes were recorded each year, and the prison population remained under 15,000.

The story since has been one of expansion. The trend has not been unilinear and there are important lessons to be learnt from the falls as well as the rises. Nevertheless, it is the growth in the prison population, indeed, what has been referred elsewhere to as the 'crisis in prison numbers' (Cavadino and Dignan, 1992), that has set the tone for much that has happened in criminal justice policy-making since 1945.

By 1953, the average daily prison population exceeded the 1908 level for the first time (see Figure 2.1). Substantial increases in recorded crime after the War led to a fairly conservative response by the government, somewhat in contrast to the relatively radical overhaul that was going on

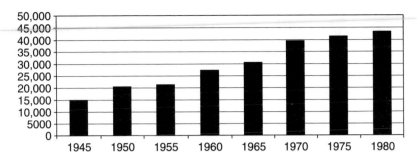

Figure 2.1 Prison population, England and Wales, 1945–80
Source: Prison Statistics England and Wales, London: Stationery Office

in other areas of social life. The reformist tradition that held sway in the decades leading up to the Second World War, and that was associated with Paterson, did not survive for long. Paterson died in 1947, and the Criminal Justice Act passed in 1948, which contained many reforms that had been close to the statute books a decade earlier, was by no means a uniformly liberalising piece of legislation.

Although the 1948 Act restricted the use of imprisonment in several ways, the pre-War idea of 'Howard Houses' for juvenile offenders was dropped, whereas pressure from the Magistrates' Association for a new short-term, military-style, custodial sentence was successful. The 1948 Act thus included a new detention centre order which was intended to be a short but firm sentence that would 'deter' certain hard-core young offenders. That said, arcane ideas of hard labour and penal servitude were done away with by the Act and this led the May Report 30 years later (Home Office, 1979) to describe the legislation as being 'firmly in the liberalising tradition' (para. 2.22).

The period from the Second World War until the early 1970s represents the time in which the 'rehabilitative ideal' (Allen, 1981) was at its height. In 1949, the English Prison Rules introduced for the first time the formula of 'a good and useful life' as being the primary aim of the 'treatment and training' to be provided in prison. The Chairman of the Prison Commissioners at the time, Sir Lionel Fox, explained the official purpose in greater detail:

> [We seek] to provide a background of conditions favourable to reform, and where necessary and possible to foster this delicate and very personal growth by personal influences. . . . Then, leaving deterrence to speak for itself, [training] concentrates on the social rehabilitation of the prisoner, so as to remove as many obstacles as possible to the maintenance, after discharge from prison, of such will to do right as may have become established or incipient therein. . . . The protection of society is not well served if [the prisoner] comes back to it unfitted rather than fitted to lead a normal life and earn an honest living, or as an embittered man with a score against society that he means to pay off
>
> (Fox, 1952, quoted in Bottoms, 1990b: 4)

In the early years after the War, however, the numbers being imprisoned were already putting the system under immense strain. Although placing more than one prisoner in a cell designed for one happened extremely rarely up until this point, its frequency started to increase in the late 1940s, at one stage reaching a peak of 6,000 prisoners incarcerated three to a cell, though this was down to 3,000 by 1955 (Ryan, 1983).

It was, as has already been suggested, the significant and sustained rise in recorded crime that was the primary motor behind the rise in the average size of the prison population in this period. Crime rose relatively consistently throughout the late 1940s, levelled off slightly in the early 1950s and then doubled between 1955 and 1964 (Maguire, 1994). It was to be some time before continued increases on this scale laid siege to positivistic assumptions that individuals could and would be reformed by the identification and application of a variety of forms of treatment. Nevertheless, the increasing numbers incarcerated in gaols in England and Wales put considerable pressure on the system.

Such pressure was increased within the system by the escalation of long-standing industrial relations problems. Decreasing numbers of staff during the War years increased the burdens on officers, and this was exacerbated by the increasing expectations that were placed on staff as a result of the emerging emphasis on rehabilitation and the sheer weight of numbers entering prison. The feeling amongst staff was that the increased responsibilities were not being matched by increased pay levels, and disputes over pay went to arbitration in 1950, 1952, 1954, 1956, 1957 and 1959. Indeed, in late 1957, the Wynn-Parry Committee was set up to look into remuneration and conditions of service; a Committee which made few changes of lasting consequence to officers' conditions of service, but did eventually settle on a pay formula – linked to civil service salaries – which allowed agreements to be reached for very nearly the next 20 years.

In response to mounting public concern about levels of crime, especially among young people, a White Paper – *Penal Practice in a Changing Society* – was published in 1959. Though much of it concerned proposals about police operations and for 'tightening up' the criminal law, it also focused on penal policy. A great deal was said about the size of the prison population, and particularly about the degree of overcrowding in detention centres. Details of a prison building programme were outlined and, despite the increasing evidence that was available about the relative ineffectiveness of custodial sentences as a method of rehabilitating offenders, the White Paper affirmed the government's commitment to the use of prison. As we will see in Chapter 6, this was the point at which the diagnosticians held sway within the probation service, and a similar medical model underpinned official faith in the prison system. The White Paper included, for example, the announcement that work was to begin on the first purpose-built psychiatric prison at Grendon Underwood. Thus, at the end of the 1950s, tough talking on crime and penality was combined with a faith in rehabilitation that was largely undiminished.

As Lord Windlesham (1993) describes in some detail in his analysis of penal policy in this period, although there was considerable public concern about rising crime, and much government attention devoted to responding to the difficulties associated with rising crime and increasing prison numbers, there was one other issue which commanded the bulk of public attention: capital punishment. There was an attempt to include a clause abolishing capital punishment in the 1947 Criminal Justice Bill. The Labour Home Secretary, Chuter Ede, was against including such an amendment but, largely through backbench pressure, he was forced to accept a debate over a motion that the death penalty be suspended for five years. The vote was won in the Commons, but lost in the Lords and eventually, under pressure of time, the clause was dropped from the Bill.

Significant elements of the government were unenthusiastic about abolition and this was reflected in the terms of reference of the Royal Commission set up in 1948 to 'consider and report whether liability under the criminal law in Great Britain to suffer capital punishment for murder should be limited or modified'. Reporting in 1953, it recommended that juries should have the power to assess the appropriateness of the death penality as against life imprisonment in individual cases. If anything changed the parliamentary mood during the course of the 1950s, it was a series of cases in which either the guilt of the offender or the appropriateness of the death penalty was called into question. The cases of Derek Bentley, Timothy Evans, James Hanratty and Ruth Ellis reinforced the abolitionists' case, though the Conservative government remained resistant to the idea of changing the law during most of the 1950s. Further pressure enabled a Private Members Bill to be introduced, and once again passed in the Commons in 1956 but, predictably, the House of Lords once again voted against the Bill by a huge majority. Public opinion was, however, changing, and there was widespread support for the Homicide Act, passed in the following year, which limited the death sentence to certain types of murder, such as killing a police or prison officer and killing with a firearm. Nevertheless, it was not until the election of a Labour government in 1964 that abolition appeared a realistic possibility.

The 1960s were the scene of one of the periodic, yet very significant, crises that grip the prison system from time to time. On this occasion it was a 'security crisis' (Rutherford, 1986b) or 'crisis of containment' (Cavadino and Dignan, 1992), and the response to that crisis has had a profound impact upon the prison system ever since. Up until the early 1960s, issues of security had not been considered to be especially important, though the increasing numbers of prisoners convicted of the most serious crimes and sentenced to very long terms of imprisonment was beginning to put the issue of security on the agenda.

Table 2.1: Escapes and attempted escapes from penal establishments (male)

Year	Daily ave. population	Escapes and attempts	Escapes and attempts per 1,000 of the prison population
1895	14,954	9	0.6
1928	10,305	73	7.3
1938	10,388	211	21.1
1946	14,566	864	57.6
1956	19,941	932	46.6
1964	28,718	2,090	72.0

Source: Thomas and Pooley (1980)

As can be seen from Table 2.1, there was a significant increase in both the absolute number of escapes and attempts and in the proportion of the prison population involved in escapes or attempts. Moreover, there were a number of highly publicised escapes by notorious criminals in the mid-1960s. Public attention had been focused on crime by such cases as the Great Train Robbery in 1963 and the imprisonment of the spy, George Blake, in 1964. In August 1964, however, accomplices of one of mail train robbers, Charles Wilson, broke into Birmingham prison and helped him escape. He had served only four months of his 30-year sentence. In July 1965, another of the gang, Ronald Biggs, also serving 30 years, escaped from the exercise yard at Wandsworth prison. Perhaps most embarrassingly of all, and certainly the final straw as far as the government was concerned (Stern, 1989), was the escape one year later of George Blake from Wormwood Scrubs.

The Home Secretary's response was to form a Committee, under the chairmanship of Lord Mountbatten, to examine why the escapes had taken place and to make recommendations for improvements to prison security. This immediate reaction was in stark contrast to the response to security problems in the 1930s, when, on that occasion, the Prime Minister deemed it practicable merely to attempt to ride out the worst of the disquiet (Mountbatten Report, 1966; Home Office, 1979; Thomas and Pooley, 1980).

The Mountbatten Committee's diagnosis was that the central problem lay in the insufficiently secure accommodation for the small number of very high-risk prisoners, together with overly secure regimes for the rest. The major recommendations made by the Mountbatten Committee were that a system for categorising inmates should be introduced. The categories ranged from those requiring the highest possible degree of security, whose escape would pose a major threat to the safety of the public or the security of the realm, down to those in the fourth category who could reasonably be entrusted to serve their sentence in open conditions. The Committee also proposed that those in the top-security category should be housed together in a new purpose-built, top-security prison, and this was given the name 'Vectis' and was to be located on the Isle of Wight, rather than in the currently existing maximum security blocks. 'Vectis' was to house approximately 120 prisoners and, if necessary, a second top-security prison would also be built. In 1967, the Prison Department compiled a list of all category A prisoners, which ran to a total of 138 (Cohen and Taylor, 1972). The intention behind the 'concentration' policy (Cavadino and Dignan, 1992) was that it would not only ensure that category A prisoners were kept in secure surroundings, but that security could be relaxed in other regimes.

The May Inquiry, set up over a decade later, reflected on the impact of the Mountbatten Committee's Report and noted that it was: 'hard to evaluate just how much of a change in ethos the Mountbatten report did initiate, but there is certainly a widespread belief that it ushered in an era in which concern with security became, and has remained, central to large parts of the system.' Sim (1991: 110–11) has argued that Mountbatten's recommendations 'led directly to a major intensification in the levels of security and control experienced by prisoners as well as to a significant increase in the number of prison officers employed to manage the system'. The Committee's recommendation that prisoners should be categorised on reception was quickly accepted and acted upon, but the Vectis proposal was rejected. Instead, the Home Secretary asked a sub-committee of the Advisory Council on the Penal System to consider what type of regime would be appropriate for category A prisoners (those 'who in no circumstances must be allowed to get out').

The sub-committee, chaired by Professor Leon Radzinowicz, reported in 1968 (Advisory Council on the Penal System, 1968). It completely rejected the idea of concentrating high-risk prisoners. It did so on the basis that providing adequate work and recreational facilities in an establishment catering for such a small number of category A prisoners would be problematic, and that those inmates who were unsettled or unsettling others could not be transferred. They concluded therefore that 'the chances of creating a tolerable and constructive regime in an establishment known to all involved as the end of the road, would be minimal' (Home Office, 1979: para. 2.33) What they proposed was a policy that has since become associated with the term 'dispersal'.

By this is meant that category A prisoners are dispersed amongst a number of *training prisons* designed for that purpose, with upgraded security. The thinking behind this was that in such institutions a relaxed regime could be created, as long as the perimeter walls were secure, and that it would then be possible to treat high-risk prisoners very much like everyone else in the prison. As one member of the Committee put it, the aim was to disperse the category A prisoners 'into liberal prisons rather than concentrating them into an oppressive fortress that would cast a shadow over [the] whole prison system' (Leo Abse, quoted in Rutherford, 1986b: 79).

At first, there were three 'dispersal' prisons; by 1970 there were five; and by 1980, seven. The degree to which such prisoners were actually dispersed, then, was more than somewhat limited and the policy was widely felt not to have been a success. As the May Report (Home Office, 1979) put it: 'The history of the seven "dispersal" prisons that . . . cater for this class of inmate within the system has not generally been a happy one.' Controversy has since raged over whether it is the dispersal policy itself which has led to inmate unrest, or factors connected more generally with the growth in the proportion of difficult offenders within the system; similarly it is alleged that the dispersal system entails the devotion of excessive amounts of security to categories of inmate who do not require it. Put crudely, the argument advanced by critics of this policy is that although dispersal largely solved the problem of perimeter security, it exacerbated the problems of internal control.

In essence, the consequence of adopting the policy of dispersal was to subject a very large number of prisoners to a degree of security deemed to be necessary, in fact, for very few. In terms of resources, it was the commitment of huge resources 'providing top security for thousands of people, for the benefits of hundreds' (Stern, 1989: 125). Thus, Stern (1989) estimated that in 1988, 390 convicted prisoners deemed to be Category A were housed in prisons with room for 2,968.

Downes and Morgan (1994: 219) conclude that 'the unwanted side effects of these directives were to heighten security across the system, prioritise control and surveillance at the expense of other objectives (such as work, training, education, recreation, and better rights and conditions) and in combination with the impact of adverse research findings halt the spread of therapeutic regimes while leaving intact the differentiation between local and training prisons based upon that ideology'. Similarly, Sim (1991), in addition to noting the move towards the use of control units and segregation blocks as part of the dispersal policy, also identifies two other major sets of changes resulting from the Mountbatten and Radzinowicz Reports. First, he argues that the emphasis on blanket security and technological control was such that they increasingly dominated managerial thinking. Second, he suggests that the enforcement of the Prison Rules intensified, and even petty regulations began to be enforced more vigorously.

The control of category A prisoners never really ceased to be a problem. At one of the dispersal prisons, Parkhurst, there was a high level of discontent at the level and methods of prison security used, and in 1969 over 150 prisoners barricaded themselves in association rooms, together with a number of hostages. A petition signed by 120 prisoners was made public and the Home Secretary immediately ordered an inquiry. The report of the inquiry was, however, never made public and only a small number of staffing changes were made (for some details see Home Office, 1984b). Within a few months the worst prison riot for nearly 40 years erupted at Parkhurst, in which 28 prisoners and 35 prison officers were injured (Ryan, 1983).

The response of the prison authorities to the control problems that arose at least partly because of the new emphasis given to security was oppressive. Three major approaches were employed: an increasing emphasis on physical force, including the deployment of tactical intervention squads; the segregation of prisoners under 'Rule 43'; and the reallocation of prisoners considered to be disruptive. The recent history of prison disturbances illustrates the fact that none of these tactics alone or in combination were particularly effective.

Although officially, Prison Rule 1 still encapsulated the primary function of the prison service at this time, a White Paper, *People in Prison*, published in 1969, placed 'treatment and training' behind the aim of holding 'those committed to custody and to provide conditions for their detention which are currently acceptable to society' (quoted in King and McDermott, 1989). The White Paper included the term 'humane containment' for the first time in an official document, and the use of the term signalled the beginnings of a major shift in emphasis in penal policy.

Although numbers had been rising fairly steadily since the Second World War, the proportionate use of imprisonment had been decreasing. As Bottoms (1987) shows, however, it was not probation that was the main alternative, but the fine that was being used increasingly frequently. This trend toward declining proportionate use of custody came to an end in the mid-1970s (see Chapter 7) – in 1974 the proportion of adult males given a custodial sentence had dropped as low as 15 per cent. As Brake and Hale (1992: 144) argue, 'since 1974 not only have the absolute numbers being sent to prison increased but the courts have become more punitive'.

The Criminal Justice Act 1967

By this stage, the relentless rise in prison numbers had been forcing the hand of policy-makers for some years. One method of attempting to influence the size of the population is through executive measures such as remission and parole. In theory, they may provide one possible safety valve when the pressure of numbers seems too great. The practice of early release began with the 'ticket of leave' system in the nineteenth century, followed by unconditional remission at the turn of the twentieth. Although remission has most often been justified in terms of its effects on individual prisoners, there are a number of instances where it has been used by politicians to attempt to control overall numbers.

Perhaps the most clearly visible illustration of the impact of prison numbers on policy-making lies in the introduction of parole in 1967. Although its introduction was defended on rehabilitative grounds (Home Office, 1965a; Morgan, 1983), the increasing size of the prison population also gave a strong political and pragmatic impetus to the change (Bottomley, 1984; Fitzmaurice and Pease, 1986; Maguire, 1992).

Parole was introduced during the period when the rehabilitative ideal was still relatively untarnished. The White Paper, for example, argued that 'a considerable number of long-term prisoners reach a recognisable peak in their training at which they may respond to generous treatment but after which if kept in prison they may go downhill'. (para. 5). However, if alleviating prison overcrowding was the central aim, there was a fundamental problem with the way parole worked in practice. It is simply that crowding in the prison system has always been concentrated in the local prisons and remand centres, rather than in the training prisons where those most likely to be eligible for parole are accommodated.

The system of parole was subject to widespread criticism, the most far-reaching, and effective in the longer-term, came from Roger Hood. Maguire (1992: 182) summarises his critique, saying that Hood questioned:

> the key premises underpinning its introduction and operation. He pointed out that there was simply no evidence of a 'peak in training', or that, even if such a thing existed, it could be identified by the Board: indeed, it was questionable if any meaningful training at all took place in many prisons. The system encouraged manipulation and dissimulation by prisoners and was profoundly unfair. Above all it was wrong in principle for what were *de facto* sentencing decisions to be taken by a secret and unaccountable executive body, which gave no reasons for its decisions and which was not subject to appeal.

The other major change brought about by the 1967 Act was the introduction of the suspended sentence of imprisonment. This was, as Bottoms (1977) has noted, the first completely new sentence since the introduction of statutory probation in 1908. By the mid-1970s, it was the second most commonly used sentence for adult males in the Crown Court. Such a sentence had been proposed as early as 1950, but was rejected by the Advisory Council on the Treatment of Offenders in both 1952 and 1957. Two theories have been used to justify the suspended sentence: the first Bottoms calls the 'special deterrent theory' (offenders would be deterred from further offending by the knowledge that if caught prison would result), and the second the 'avoiding prison theory' (allowing courts to signal the gravity of the offence without having to resort to a custodial sentence). It has, however, only ever been the latter which has formed the basis for official justifications and defences of the sentence. The effect of the introduction of the suspended sentence is considered in greater detail in Chapter 7; for now it is enough to note that although it was conceived of as an alternative to custody, the aim being to reduce the prison population, it only succeeded in that aim in a very temporary and very minor way.

Grievances among the incarcerated

Although, as a result of the changes brought about by the Criminal Justice Act 1967, there was a reduction in the prison population in 1968, by 1970 it was beginning to rise quickly. Overcrowding was becoming a problem again (see Table 2.2) and it was the growing remand population that was bearing the brunt of the worst conditions. With the increasing pressure within the system, some form of disturbance was not unexpected and in 1972 that is what happened at Brixton prison, which was the main remand prison for London. It was at this time that the prisoners' rights movement took off. PROP (Preservation of the Rights of Prisoners) was formed, mainly by ex-prisoners, but supported by academics, and a *Prisoners' Charter* was drawn up. This made very broad demands, including, among many others, the right to institute legal proceedings without the permission of the Home Office; the right to legal representation at disciplinary hearings; and the right to receive reasons from the Parole Board when applications were rejected. Later in the year, a national demonstration was organised and it is estimated that between 5,000 and 10,000 prisoners took part in sit-down strikes in prisons around the country (Ryan, 1983; Rutherford, 1986b).

One of the responses to this was the threat of action by prison staff, including the possibility of a work to rule. The possibility of negotiations between PROP and the POA was rejected by the Home Office, who said that further demonstrations would be dealt with severely. The importance of this is perhaps twofold. First, the demonstrations brought about further clampdowns in the prison system. Control units, for example, were introduced and the treatment meted out to some of the men segregated in such units, together with the use of an increasingly

Table 2.2: Prison overcrowding in England and Wales, 1969–79

Year	Three in a cell	Two in a cell
1969	7,653	2,886
1970	9,288	4,886
1971	8,238	6,212
1972	6,609	7,128
1973	4,221	8,388
1974	4,122	10,024
1975	5,298	10,342
1976	5,709	10,726
1977	4,950	11,040
1978	5,082	11,016
1979	4,833	11,752

Source: Fitzgerald and Sim (1982: 16)

paramilitary response to disorder, led to a new and bitter phase in the history of disturbances in British prisons. The regime in control units was informed by the idea of sensory deprivation. The cells were windowless and sound-proofed, lights were kept on at all times, association between prisoners was not permitted and prison officers were trained to minimise their communication with inmates and provided with footwear that muffled the sound of their approach (Coggan and Walker, 1982; Sim, 1991).

Second, and equally importantly, the prisoners' movement had quite a profound politicising effect on the prison officers themselves. The militant stance adopted by staff did not disappear in the early 1970s and Rutherford (1986b: 82) has argued that by the end of the decade 'it was not prisoners but unionised custodial staff that posed the greatest challenge to the Home Office control of the prison system'.

The disturbance at Brixton in 1972 was followed later that year by further disturbances at Gartree and at Albany, although the most serious riot in the period happened four years later at Hull. Hull, originally a local prison, was reclassified as a training prison in 1966 and as a dispersal prison in 1969. The riot, which lasted for four days, resulted in damage to the prison estimated then at £725,000 (Thomas and Pooley, 1980), a large number of injuries to prisoners as order was restored and prosecutions of prison officers for assault. Similar brutality, it was claimed, was used in quelling another disturbance at Gartree in 1978, and the following year saw the introduction (their existence had never been officially mentioned) of the paramilitary Minimum Use of Force Tactical Intervention squad (MUFTI) to bring a disturbance at Wormwood Scrubs to an end. Rutherford (1986b) notes that the role of the POA was especially interesting after the end of the disturbance. He quotes the official inquiry as saying that in the particular wing of the prison involved in the disturbance: 'the local branch of the POA . . . sought to prevent a return to anything like the former regime in D Wing, and there were strong indications that the Governor came under pressure so severe that some of the policy decisions . . . he made at that time were against his own better judgement' (1986b: 84). Indeed, Rutherford concludes that the POA, at both a local and national level, challenged 'the authority and administration of the prison system'. By 1978, over 60 branches of the POA were involved in over 100 separate disputes (Ryan, 1983).

In the 1970s, then, the primary concerns within the prison system were concerns about control. Initially, these concerns were focused on prisoners, on the largely peaceful demonstrations associated with the prisoners' rights movement and on the more violent disturbances that occurred at a small number of prisons. Later on, however, the concerns became just as much, if not more, about the control of staff. Although no officers were prosecuted for assaults on inmates in Wormwood Scrubs – despite a two-year police investigation – it was clear that something fairly urgent had to be done. By 1978, the prison service was in almost continual dispute with the POA over staffing levels, over pay and conditions and about overtime. As is almost always the solution in such cases, the response of the Home Office was to set up a Departmental Committee.

The May Report

The Committee, under the chairmanship of a High Court judge, Mr Justice May, was instructed by Merlyn Rees to inquire into the state of the prison services in the United Kingdom; and to have regard to the size of the prison population and the capacity of the prison service to accommodate it; the responsibility of the prison service for control, security and treatment of inmates; and the pay and conditions for staff. However, the Committee decided to interpret its terms of reference broadly because although 'it seemed inevitable to us that we should concentrate on the organisational, resources, pay and industrial relations issues, it was equally plain we could not ignore wider criminal justice matters . . . because we could not . . . make credible and worth-while recommendations about the resources required for the prison system without an adequately informed view on the size and nature of the future prison population, including the possibility of reducing it' (Home Office, 1979: para. 1.5).

The Home Secretary had impressed upon the Committee the urgency of the inquiry and initially it was hoped that it would report within six months, but it eventually took a year. If anything, the delay probably heightened expectations of the Report at a time when concern was high anyway.

Lord Windlesham (1987: 241) describes the Report as: 'the most comprehensive account available on the state of British prisons – their populations, organisation, and staffing. Set up by a government of one complexion and reporting to that of another, it is free from political bias and is an invaluable repository of factual information.' On the other hand, for Fitzgerald and Sim (1980: 84), it 'was an opportunity not simply to review but to change fundamentally the 100-year old recipe of more prisoners and more prisons. In the event, it passed up that opportunity, preferring, like so many Inquiries before it, to represent the recipe for prison crisis as a recipe for prison salvation. It simply won't work'.

As part of its broad interpretation of its terms of reference, the Committee took evidence and made recommendations on the fundamental penal objectives and, in particular, on the future for Rule 1. Two criminologists, Roy King and Rod Morgan (1979), in their evidence to the Committee argued, successfully as it turned out, that the rhetoric of 'treatment and training' had had its day. They went on to argue that it should be replaced by a system based on the notion of 'humane containment', and underpinned by the principles of minimum use of custody, minimum use of security, and the 'normalisation' of the prison. Though accepting that 'treatment and training' was outmoded, the Committee rejected humane containment as a 'means without an end', resulting in prisons becoming human warehouses for inmates and staff. Consequently, they recommended that Rule 1 be rewritten and in rejecting 'treatment and training' introduced the idea of 'positive custody':

> The purpose of the detention of convicted prisoners shall be to keep them in custody which is both secure and yet positive, and to that end the behaviour of all the responsible authorities and staff towards them shall be such as to:
>   (a) create an environment which can assist them to respond and contribute to society as positively as possible;
>   (b) preserve and promote their self-respect;
>   (c) minimise, to the degree of security necessary in each particular case, the harmful effects of their removal from normal life;
>   (d) prepare them for and assist them on discharge.

Some critics, however, were sceptical about the degree to which this represented anything much more than warehousing itself. Fitzgerald and Sim (1980: 82) suggested that the proposed new Rule 1 simply represented a move from 'warehousing' to 'zookeeping' 'where some limited consideration is given to the state of the stored'.

Following its recognition that imprisonment should be used as little as possible, the May Committee backed policies to reduce the prison population, but felt that there was little chance of their being successful. As a consequence, it therefore recommended a massive building and refurbishment programme to end enforced cell-sharing and end slopping out, and this was acted upon without delay (King and McDermott, 1989). In 1982, the biggest prison building programme undertaken in the twentieth century began, in which 25 new prisons were to be built at an estimated capital cost of over £1,300 million (Cavadino and Dignan, 1992).

The idea of 'positive custody' never garnered much support and during the 1980s considerable emphasis continued to be placed by campaigners on prisoners' rights and on timetables for the introduction of minimum standards and conditions (Morgan, 1994b). The Committee's proposals to end cell-sharing and slopping out, for example, were linked to the European Standard Minimum Rules and, as King and McDermott (1989) argue, it looked for a while as though the government might respond to outside pressure by publishing a draft code of standards for the prison system. In 1982, the Home Office even undertook to do so, but no such code ever appeared. The question of standards remains (see, for example, Casale, 1984, 1994; King and McDermott, 1989) but, as in other areas of criminal justice such as policing and probation (see Chapters 4 and 6), government has actually placed much greater emphasis on financial management and on economy, efficiency and effectiveness; prisons had 'entered the Thatcher era' (Morris, 1989).

The prison crisis escalates

William Whitelaw, the Home Secretary when the May Committee reported, was replaced by Leon Brittan, who in 1983 announced new restrictions on the use of parole. This, together with the prison building programme that was by now underway, led Brittan at the party conference that year to say 'the measures that I have outlined . . . will put us on course for ending prison overcrowding by the end of the decade' (quoted in Morris, 1989: 138).

Parole, as we have seen, was introduced in 1967 and, at the very least, there has always been an element of pragmatism underpinning its use. The element of pragmatism has become more evident as time has passed. After 1967, the first major change to parole was made in 1975 by the then Home Secretary, Roy Jenkins. Prompted by a desire to reduce the number of minor property offenders in prison, he encouraged the Parole Board to relax their policy in such cases, the assumption being that such offenders would be unlikely to commit serious offences on parole (Maguire, 1992). The effect was an almost 50 per cent rise in the proportion of licences granted between 1976 and 1980. '*De facto*, therefore, parole began to shift from being an occasionally granted privilege towards, if not a right, at last a reasonable expectation, particularly on the part of prisoners sentenced to between 18 months and three years' (Maguire, 1992: 183).

Prison numbers, however, were still a major problem, and in 1981 the government seemed to be looking favourably on the proposals contained in the Home Office's *Review of Parole in England and Wales* (1981). This would have meant that prisoners serving between six months and three years would have been entitled to automatic release under the supervision of a probation officer after only one-third of their sentence had elapsed (Cavadino and Dignan, 1992). There was considerable resistance in some quarters, and it has been argued that the judiciary threatened to undermine the policy by changing their sentencing practices (Ashworth, 1983) and, as a consequence, it was never introduced.

In 1983, however, using powers introduced by the Criminal Justice Act 1982, Leon Brittan announced a number of changes to sentencing and to the parole system. Maximum sentences for carrying firearms were increased, for example, and the power to refer 'over-lenient' sentences back to the Court of Appeal was introduced. It was the changes to the parole system, however, that were the most contentious. He announced that the threshold of eligibility for parole would be reduced from 12 months to six months – a largely liberal measure. However, he went to say that in future ministers (and not the joint committee of Parole Board and Home Office officials as it had been previously) would set a minimum tariff period to be served by life-sentence prisoners, related to the circumstances of their offence and that some categories of prisoner serving life (particularly those who had murdered prison or police officers or children) would not be released until they had served a minimum period of 20 years. In addition, drug traffickers sentenced to more than five years would 'be treated with regard to parole in exactly the same way as serious violent offenders – they should not get it' (quoted in Scraton et al., 1991: 137).

The Brittan rules were underpinned by a policy of 'bifurcation': the adoption of a relatively liberal approach in relation to those prisoners considered to be unlikely to commit particularly serious offences, whilst simultaneously adopting a tough approach to the treatment of more serious offenders, especially those convicted of crimes of violence. This policy of bifurcation has had a number of consequences. First, it has meant that there has been a considerable increase in the size of the long-term prison population. Second, it has been seen as unjust by prisoners who have suffered as a consequence of it. Both of these have contributed to the increasing problems within prisons over the past decade.

Changes in sentencing practice and in parole have had a marked impact not only on the size, but also on the nature of the prison population. In the years after the Second World War, life sentences were relatively rare. In 1945, approximately four-fifths of offenders sentenced to custody were serving six months or less. Of the daily average prison population, fewer than 20 per cent of sentenced prisoners were serving 18 months or more (Morgan, 1994b). Now fewer than two-fifths of offenders sentenced to custody serve sentences of six months or less, and whereas in 1957 there were a total of 140 lifers in the prison system, by 1987, 250 a year were receiving such sentences (Scraton et al., 1991). Furthermore, one of the consequences of the bifurcatory influences on sentencing and parole has been that although the proportions of sentences for property and violent offences has not changed all that markedly over the past three decades, the proportion of the prison population that is there because of a violent offence has increased significantly.

It was abundantly clear by the early 1980s that the dispersal policy in relation to the long-term prison population was not succeeding in terms of control. Disturbances continued, and only two of the eight dispersal prisons had not been the site of a major disturbance by 1983 (see Home Office, 1984b: Annex D; and Bottoms and Light, 1987). In 1983, Leon Brittan announced the establishment of the Control Review Committee (CRC), an internal working party made up of civil servants and prison governors. The Committee, in its report, suggested that there was a 'disruptive population' of between 150 and 200 inmates who presented a major control problem, and it recommended the introduction of five or six 'long term prisoner units' to relieve the problem. It also argued for the construction of two 'new generation' prisons in which the 300–400 top-security prisoners could be housed. A small number of special units have been established, but the idea of building 'new generation' prisons, though it also found favour with Woolf, has always proved too expensive an option. A powerful argument against the view that it is a small minority of 'dangerous' or 'disturbed' prisoners that are the root of the control problem was made by King (1985: 189):

> Probably the most widely held view, both inside and outside the Prison Department, is that the worst control problems have been generated by comparatively few peculiarly difficult, recalcitrant and dangerous prisoners, some of whom may be psychologically disturbed. These prisoners are typically thought of as including terrorists, strong-arm men and leaders of criminal gangs, serving very long sentences of imprisonment; men who are as dangerous inside prison as they are outside . . . . It would be irresponsible and naive to deny that such men exist. Of course they do. But I do wish to argue that conceptualising the control problem as the product of 'difficult' or 'disturbed' individuals, and developing a reactive policy towards them, has been both partial and self-defeating. Partial in that it ignores all the structural, environmental and interactive circumstances that generate trouble, reducing it to some inherent notion of individual wilfulness or malfunction. Self-defeating in that the policy itself becomes part of those very circumstances that generate the trouble; it is likely that among those who get defined as troublemakers there are some who are made into troublemakers as a result of the way they are dealt with in prison. Just as there are some who come to prison as troublemakers.
>
> (quoted in Scraton et al., 1991: 143)

In the four years following the CRC's report, there were a number of disturbances of a quite serious nature in prisons in England. Among the dispersal prisons, Gartree and Parkhurst experienced protests in 1985, and then in the full range of institutions there were, from 1986 to 1988, 22 separate disturbances, 42 acts of concerted indiscipline, 25 roof-climbing incidents and 245 escapes (Scraton et al., 1991).

In addition to these disturbances there were, once again, a significant number of disputes involving prison staff. From the POA's position, these disputes were about the conditions in which their members were working, the dangers they faced and the pay and general terms and conditions of employment experienced. From the Home Office's perspective, and the Home Office and the POA had now been locked in almost constant dispute for a decade, the key issue was overtime and how it might be reduced. In 1985 alone, prison officers took action at Wormwood Scrubs, Bedford and Parkhurst and the Home Secretary was booed at the POA conference (Sim, 1987).

Officers were in dispute, disturbances by the incarcerated showed no signs of diminishing, even though the building programme was in full swing the prison population was continuing to rise and there appeared to be little evidence of the trend changing. The prospect of the government's vision of an 'end to overcrowding' becoming a reality seemed slim (Morgan and Jones, 1992). There remained considerable disagreement about the objectives of the service, and there was no commitment to enforceable standards. Indeed, evidence comparing conditions in the early 1970s and the mid-1980s showed that although there had been some improvement in sanitary facilities, 'on most measures, including access to those facilities, [the research] revealed consistently worse regimes ... in spite of major improvements in staff:-prisoner ratios' (King and McDermott, 1989: 107). This represents a fairly comprehensive critique of the effectiveness of the May Inquiry.

A study undertaken by the Prison Department and a team of management consultants in 1986 presented, according to the Home Secretary, Douglas Hurd, 'a telling indictment of the complementing and shift systems and the working practices that surround them' (McDermott and King, 1989: 161). In a bid to resolve some of the problems related to staffing and working practices, the Home Office introduced what it called the 'Fresh Start' package, which sought to buy out overtime working, albeit at the cost of still further increases in staffing. The basic idea was that the improved working practices that were proposed would produce cost savings, and a proportion of these savings would be reinvested to enhance regimes. Fresh Start abolished overtime, it reduced prison officers' working hours and, according to one observer, through its creation of a modern management structure, 'has moved the Prison Service from the 1950s to the 1980s organisationally' (Stern, 1989: 158). Research conducted in five prisons in the immediate aftermath of the introduction of Fresh Start painted a rather more gloomy picture – certainly as far as the nature of the regimes was concerned (McDermott and King, 1989), and the Woolf Report (1991) records examples of officers continuing to work many extra hours per week. Thomas (1994: 116) concludes that: 'The results of Fresh Start were, to put it mildly, disappointing. To begin with it was not long before staff felt cheated. Woolf reports that staff felt "misled" and that "they do not believe that the Prison Service has delivered what it promised".' One consequence of this was that grievances among prison officers remained high, and therefore one source of tension within prisons remained largely unchecked.

One other source of tension was the conditions faced by remand prisoners. Historically, it has been the local prisons in which overcrowding has been at its most extreme, these also being the institutions in which remand prisoners are generally held. It was King and Morgan's (1976) study which first highlighted the particularly poor conditions faced by untried prisoners. Morgan (1994a) has argued that it is the 'treatment and training' philosophy which underpins the 'historical marginalisation' of prisoners on remand (at the time the philosophy was first employed there were relatively few prisoners on remand or awaiting sentence). His argument is that the adoption of that philosophy forced all prisoners into two categories: trainable or untrainable: 'Those deemed trainable – sentenced prisoners except those serving very short sentences (for whom there was held to be insufficient time) and the recalcitrant (for whom the time had apparently passed) – were to be classified and allocated to the "training" prison whose regime was best fitted to meet their needs. Untrainable short-term sentenced prisoners (which included most fine defaulters) were to remain in the "local" prisons where those prisoners morally and legally ineligible for training, the untried and the unsentenced, were also to be housed' (1994a: 145).

As we have seen, during the course of the 1980s, not only did the anticipated fall in the prison population not occur, but the numbers steadily increased. Facing the prospect of increased overcrowding rather than an end to overcrowding, the government began to pursue alternative means of limiting the prison population. These included the introduction of bail information schemes (see Chapter 5), the Prosecution of Offences Act introduced time limits for bringing cases to trial, guidelines for the committal of cases to the Crown Court were introduced, and advice was issued to sentencers to use remands in custody less frequently. There is some evidence that these measures had a levelling effect from about 1987 onwards (the overall prison population exceeded 50,000 in 1987) up until 1991, whereupon the level once again rose. Prior to 1987, the huge increase in the number of prisoners on remand or unsentenced accounted for a very significant proportion of the overall increase in the prison population. For example, Morgan and Jones (1992) show that whilst the increase in the overall prison population between 1975 and the early 1990s was 22 per cent, the number of untried prisoners increased by 142 per cent. Ironically, it was in the midst of the period when a degree of check appeared to have been placed on the level of remand and unsentenced prisoners that the major prison disturbances at Strangeways and elsewhere took place. In fact, as Morgan (1994a) points out, five of the six most serious disturbances at this time occurred either in remand establishments or in places where remand prisoners played an important part in the disturbances.

Strangeways and the Woolf Report

The disturbance that occurred at Strangeways in April 1990 was not only the most serious of all the disturbances that year, but was the longest and most serious riot in British penal history. It began on 1 April and continued until 25 April. At the time Strangeways was the largest prison in England and Wales and, indeed, one of the largest in Europe. It was built in 1868 and 'was a fine Victorian building' (Woolf, 1991: para. 1.19). The prison, not unusually for a local prison, was extremely overcrowded. Its certified normal accommodation was 970 and on 1 April 1990 it was holding 1,647 prisoners. Fewer than 700 of those prisoners were sentenced.

The Woolf Report (para. 1.22) noted that although improvements had been made to the living conditions in the prison in the three years prior to the riot, 'on 1 April 1990, the physical conditions, in addition to being grossly overcrowded, were still insanitary and degrading'. The disturbance began during a service in the prison chapel, the officers who were present quickly having to withdraw. During the ensuing disturbance and siege, the inside of the prison was gutted, a total of 147 officers and 47 prisoners received injuries (including those affected by smoke or fumes) and one prisoner received injuries which it was thought may have contributed to his death. At the end of the disturbance, the prison was entirely uninhabitable and the estimated cost of repair and refurbishment (though much of the refurbishment, it might be argued, was necessary anyway) was £60 million.

What happened in Manchester led, by one means or another, to protests and disturbances in other parts of the country, including at Dartmoor prison, at Pucklechurch youth remand centre, at Glen Parva YOI, and at Bristol and Cardiff prisons. April 1990, Ryan (1992: 51) has suggested, 'was perhaps the worst month in the history of the modern prison system'.

An immediate departmental inquiry was set up, and was to be conducted by Lord Justice Woolf. The eventual terms of reference[1] were: 'To inquire into the events leading up to the serious disturbance in Her Majesty's Prison Manchester which began on 1 April 1990 and the action taken to bring it to a conclusion, having regard also to the serious disturbances which occurred shortly thereafter in other prison establishments in England and Wales.' The Home Secretary, in announcing the Inquiry, made it clear that it would be up to Lord Justice Woolf to interpret the terms of reference as he saw fit and, with one notable exception, the interpretation was a broad one. Morgan (1992a: 232), himself an assessor to the Inquiry, noted that: 'On one vital issue, however, Woolf refused to embark. He decided that sentencing policy lay outside his terms of reference.' The Inquiry was carried out with great speed and the Report was published on 25 February 1991 to considerable acclaim.

In a number of respects, the Report pulls no punches. It identifies a number of problems with the prison service in general and, in relation to the riot at Strangeways, Woolf concluded that: 'The disturbance could have been avoided. When it occurred it should not have been allowed to engulf the whole prison. The disturbance should have been brought to an end earlier' (para. 1.16). The Deputy Director of Prisons in London was severely criticised in the Report, as were the governors then in charge at Bristol and Dartmoor.

Central to Woolf's understanding of the disturbances is the recognition that 'there is no single cause of riots and no simple solution or action which will prevent rioting' (para. 9.23) and the identification of three requirements which he suggests must be met if the prison system is to be stable. They are *security, control* and *justice*. Each, Morgan (1992a) suggests, are equally important and must be balanced. Security refers to the obligation of the Prison Service to prevent inmates escaping; control to the obligation to prevent prisoners being disruptive; and justice the obligation to treat them with humanity and 'to prepare them for their return to the community in a way which makes it less likely that they will reoffend' (para. 9.20). Woolf argues that sufficient attention must be paid to all three of the requirements and that the three must be kept in balance. A lack of balance is likely to lead to disruption and disturbance and, as Morgan (1992a: 233) notes, 'It is apparent that, in Woolf's view, the Prison Department has overemphasised security, given insufficient weight to justice and often adopted inappropriate control measures'. What then is Woolf's solution?

The Woolf Report, which runs to almost 600 pages of analysis and documentation, culminates in 12 major proposals. The first recommendation is for closer co-operation between the different parts of the criminal justice system. To facilitate this, Woolf proposed the establishment of a central Criminal Justice Consultative Council, supported by a series of regional committees. The second recommendation is for more visible leadership of the Prison Service by a Director General 'who is, and is seen to be, the operational head and in day to day charge of the Service'. This should be achieved through the establishment of a 'compact' or 'contract' between ministers and the Director General of the Prison Service. The Director General should be responsible for the performance of the 'contract' and publicly answerable for the operations of the service.

The third and fourth recommendations are for increased delegation of responsibility to governors of establishments and an enhanced role for prison officers. 'Compacts' or 'contracts' appear once again in recommendation five. Woolf suggests that there should be a compact for each prisoner setting out the prisoner's expectations and responsibilities in the prison in which he or she is held.

Sixth, Woolf recommended the setting up of a national system of accredited standards with which, in time, each establishment would be required to comply. The Report also encourages the increased use of alternatives to custody, particularly the use of probation and bail hostels. Seventh, in a more concerted attempt to restrict future overcrowding, Woolf recommended a new Prison Rule which would prevent an establishment holding more prisoners than is provided for in its certified normal level of accommodation. Parliament would have to be informed if, under exceptional circumstances, the rule were to be departed from.

Woolf's eighth recommendation was for a public commitment by ministers for a timetable to provide access to sanitation for all prisoners not later than February 1996. The ninth recommendation was for better prospects for prisoners to maintain their links with families and the community, through more visits and home leaves and through being located in community prisons as near to their homes as possible. Recommendation ten, that prisons should be divided into small and more manageable and secure units, reinforces the thrust of the previous recommendation.

Woolf's eleventh recommendation was for a separate statement of purpose, separate conditions and generally a lower security categorisation for remand prisoners. The final recommendation was for improved standards of *justice* within prisons. These include the giving of reasons to prisoners for any decision which materially and adversely affects them, a grievance procedure and disciplinary proceedings which ensure that the governor deals with most matters under his present powers, relieving boards of visitors of their adjudicatory role (Shaw, 1992).

The response to Woolf

The genius of the Woolf report lies in its ability to locate a grave breakdown in law and order in the context of the long-standing problems of the prison system – overcrowding, decrepitude, poor management, a lack of justice and humanity. The full history of the Woolf inquiry has yet to be written, but it was clear to observers that Waddington and his senior civil servants were appalled by the breadth of approach which Woolf immediately brought to his task. It would have been easy, safe even, for Woolf to have concentrated on the locks and bars aspects of security and control. It is to his very considerable credit that, with one or two exceptions, he avoided such an approach.

(Shaw, 1992: 164–5)

The expectations that awaited the publication of the Report were high. Nevertheless, 'to a considerable extent [Woolf] confounded the sceptics and produced a document which met with approval across the political spectrum and was acclaimed by penal pressure groups as the most important examination of the prison system this century' (Player and Jenkins, 1994: 10). Some of the government's responses to the Woolf Report were announced by the Home Secretary in February 1991, though the major response came in a White Paper, *Custody, Care and Justice* (Home Office, 1991), in September 1991. The more immediate response by the Home Secretary was that provision would be made for more generous visiting allowances, an increase in the number of telephones available to prisoners and an acceleration of the timetable for an end to slopping out, the revised plan being that no prisoner should be slopping out after the end of 1994.

The White Paper, it is fair to say, received a mixed reception. However, several important commentators have admitted that it was more faithful to the spirit of Woolf than they had expected (see, for example, King, 1994). On the positive side, for example, the White Paper accepted the recommendation that a Criminal Justice Consultative Council be created, together with local area committees, though both the Woolf and White Paper proposals fall short of recreating a body along the lines of the previously influential Advisory Council on the Penal System, or the more recent suggestion of a Sentencing Council (Ashworth, 1992). The national Council came into operation in late 1991 and the area committees in 1992. Although the then Lord Chief Justice, Lord Lane, resisted having the judiciary chair the Council or be represented on area committees (Morgan, 1992a) his successor, Lord Justice Taylor, reversed this decision and, although the new arrangements were not ideal, they were probably 'the best that could be achieved for the time being (Roberts, 1994: 241).

The references in the Woolf Report to a 'structured stand-off' between ministers and the Director General of the prison service, together with the establishment of some form of contract between the parties to govern the running of the system, was essentially in line with extant government policy anyway, and the subsequent transferral of the prison service to agency status has underlined the general process that was already underway. The White Paper also accepted the need for standards, and committed the government to introducing a code of standards focused on the service to be provided for prisoners, though there was continuing resistance to introducing *legally enforceable* standards (Casale, 1994).

Where outright rejection came, however, was over the proposals to introduce a new prison rule to eliminate overcrowding. Woolf had even suggested that the Home Secretary might use his powers of executive release rather than allow serious overcrowding, and had recommended that a statutory limit be placed on the length of time that prisoners could be kept in police cells. The response in the White Paper, *Custody, Care and Justice* (Home Office, 1991), accepted that there was a need to reduce overcrowding (para. 1.34), but did not see this as the priority that Woolf had done, and certainly seemed to sense no urgency in the matter. Part of the reason for this was a surrounding sense of optimism about population levels. Numbers had fallen from over 50,000 in 1988 to below 45,000 in 1990 and, given the large number of additional prison places resulting from the prison-building programme, it seemed likely that an end to serious overcrowding was near.

Indeed, the White Paper commented that 'the prison system is in sight of providing sufficient places to match the average size of the prison population', though it recognised that this was dependent upon the sentencing trends of the courts and the impact of the Criminal Justice Act 1991. The prison population continued to fall, and sharply, during 1992, particularly after the introduction of the Criminal Justice Act 1991 in October, but this was short-lived, as indeed were many aspects of the Act (a brief history of the 1991 Act is contained in Chapter 7). By the spring of 1993, the population once again started to rise and, with the Home Secretary making plain his faith in the deterrent effect of the prison system at the Conservative Party conference that year, 'Let us be clear. Prison works. It ensures that we are protected from murderers, muggers and rapists – and it makes many who are tempted to commit crime think twice', it continued to rise.

So steep was the rise that a Home Office projection of future trends in 1993, which suggested that the population would rise to 51,600 by the year 2001 (Home Office Statistical Bulletin 6/93), was within a year shown to be far too conservative in its estimates. The prison population once again exceeded 50,000 in October 1994. By 1997, the average population in custody was 61,100, greater than at any time before (Home Office, 1998c). The rise in the prison population between 1993 and 1997 was over one-third. Home Office projections in 1997 suggested that the prison population was expected to break the 70,000 mark by 2002, and to reach almost 83,000 by 2005 (Home Affairs Committee, 1998). As we shall see, these projections were once again something of an under estimate.

Woolf, as we have seen, placed considerable emphasis on the role of overcrowding in the issue of control in prisons, yet he also made some very specific recommendations about discipline and grievance procedures within prison. Over 1,200 prisoners wrote to the Woolf Inquiry with complaints about the disciplinary system (Morgan and Jones, 1991). In many respects, Woolf reiterated the view taken by the Prior Committee (Home Office, 1985) which had been strongly critical of the role of the Board of Visitors in disciplinary proceedings. In the event, Woolf concluded that it was not 'possible or reasonable to expect a Board of Visitors to act as both watch-dog and as an adjudicatory body' (para. 14.390) and recommended that they cease to have a disciplinary function. He rejected the idea of a specialist Prison Disciplinary Tribunal and, instead, proposed that disciplinary and criminal offences should be separated, and that governors should hear the former and that the latter should be referred to the Crown Prosecution Service (CPS) (Livingstone, 1994). In relation to complaints, Woolf recommended the addition of an independent element in the form of Complaints Adjudicator. The majority of these recommendations were accepted by the government and, although it took a significant length of time for the Prisons Ombudsman (as the Adjudicator became called) to be appointed, the post became operational in 1994. The Prisons and Probation Ombudsmen merged in 2001.

The final element of the Woolf Report that it is necessary to focus upon here is the emphasis upon community and, specifically, the recommendation in relation to community prisons. Stephen Shaw (1992) has suggested that Woolf's use of the term 'community prison', whilst perhaps the most significant phrase in the whole report, is also rather vague about what it might mean. The vagueness arises from the fact that two separate notions are actually employed: first, the notion of prison and community being integrated (something close to what King and Morgan (1980) referred to as 'normalisation'). Second, is an idea that has been characterised as 'comprehensive prisons' (Shaw, 1992) where prisoners of very varying types (different classifications, remand and sentenced, adult and young, perhaps even male and female) are held on one site but are housed in separate units. Woolf proposed that prisons should accommodate no more than 400 inmates, separated into units housing 50–70 prisoners each.

The White Paper, though recognising the length of time that such a policy might take to implement, nevertheless commented positively on the idea of multi-functional community prisons. In particular, it stated that the government would: 'identify a number of existing and new local prisons which might be replanned as multi-functional community prisons; consider whether there are existing prisons which could be more directly linked to a local prison so that prisoner's sentence plan could provide for the prisoner to progress mainly through that cluster of establishments' (para. 5.16). Observers have, however, pointed out that the White Paper appeared to contain a very limited conception of the role and nature of the community prison. In particular, the Prison Service 'appears wedded to single-purpose prisons and sees the shifts that have occurred in different sections of the population as an obstacle in the way of Woolf's ideas' (Roberts, 1994: 237).

As King and McDermott (1995: 326) observe, had Kenneth Clarke, the man who appointed Derek Lewis as Director General of the Prison Service, 'remained at the Home Office, [he] would have been content to let well enough alone'. Not so his successor, Michael Howard. Cracks in the relationship between Howard and Lewis surfaced fairly early on. In particular, the Home Secretary requested a paper from the Director General 'setting out the ways in which prison might be refocussed to become a more austere experience', having carefully leaked the fact that the Director General's original paper had not met with approval. Indeed, Lewis (1997) suggests that at the initial point at which Howard's plans to overturn *Custody, Care and the Community* were leaked to the press, the Home Secretary had not actually read the White Paper. Howard swiftly issued a statement saying that he did not disagree with the White Paper, but the damage – certainly in relations with staff within the Home Office and, according to Derek Lewis, with relations with the Prison Service – had already been done. Michael Howard's 1993 Conservative Party conference speech, having only been Home Secretary for five months, set the tone for penal policy for much of the rest of the decade. 'Prison works', he famously announced. He went on: 'This may mean that more people will go to prison. I do not flinch from that. . . . We shall build six new prisons. They will be built and managed by the private sector.' Such a statement about private prisons would have been pretty much unthinkable even five years previously.

Privatisation and penal policy

Although private sector involvement in prisons may be traced back a century or more (Ryan and Ward, 1989), there has been a major revival of interest and activity in this area since the late 1980s. From approximately 1982 onwards, the government began vigorously to pursue its 'Financial Management Initiative' (FMI), designed to encourage efficiency and cost savings by applying private sector management methods to the public sector and imposing market disciplines on them. The 1980s also saw the emergence of an issue that had begun to threaten other public services: privatisation. Privatisation and the FMI were, of course, linked, for increasing restrictions on staff levels and resources in the public sector increase the opportunities for competitors from the private sector.

In fact there was relatively little interest shown in the idea of prison privatisation up until 1986–87. In 1984, the Adam Smith Institute, perhaps the most forceful proponents of privatisation, had advocated full-scale privatisation of the prison system (Adam Smith Institute, 1984), whereas milder proposals were offered in 1985 by two academic Social Democrats, and in 1987 by Lord Windlesham, the then Chairman of the Parole Board (for details see Ryan and Ward, 1989; Rutherford, 1990). Crucially, however, in 1986, the Home Affairs Committee had recommended experimentation with private sector construction and management of custodial institutions, and that such experiments should be based in remand establishments.

Following the 1987 election, a Home Office junior minister visited the United States to examine private prisons there and, at approximately the same time, a new consortium of two British firms and the Corrections Corporation of America – a leading player in private prisons there – was formed actively to campaign for prisons privatisation in the United Kingdom. Nevertheless, by the end of the decade little progress appeared to have been made and Rutherford (1990: 62) concluded, for example, that 'in the immediate future, the private sector's role in prison management in Britain is likely to be marginal at most'.

Things, however, changed quite quickly. The Criminal Justice Act 1991 contained a provision which allowed the management of any prison, not just remand centres, to be contracted out to any agency the Home Secretary considers appropriate. In April 1992, Group 4 Security won the contract to manage a new purpose-built institution for remand prisoners, the Wolds, and a second prison, Blakenhurst, opened in 1993 under the management of UK Detention Services. The government's Private Finance Initiative, launched in 1992, encouraged all departments to explore increasing the private financing of public services. It was feared that the transfer of the Prison Service to agency status was part of a process of wholesale privatisation, though this naturally was denied by the Home Office. Nevertheless, the private sector is playing an increasing role in providing services within prisons generally, together with what appeared to be plans to extend significantly the private management of prisons. In 1993, tenders were invited for the running of existing as well as new prisons, including Strangeways (where the contract was eventually awarded in-house).

As James et al. (1997: 157) put it, 'this new ethos' was also reflected in the appointment of Derek Lewis, previously chief executive of Granada, as Director General of the Prison Service in 1993. During the 1990s, a whole series of other prisons passed over to, or were opened under, private management including Doncaster, Blakenhurst and Buckley Hall.

The Secure Training Centres, first introduced by Michael Howard (see Chapter 8), were privately run, and those that will be opened under the New Labour administration will also be so. The Conservative government made a number of claims as to the efficiency and cost-effectiveness of privately run prisons. The early signs were that high standards were being delivered at some of the privately run institutions (Morgan, 1994a; James et al., 1997). James et al., in their study of the Wolds prison, concluded that it: 'provided a much-improved environment for prisoners than that which prevailed in other local prisons in the region at that time' (1997: 177). Although the practical concerns of many of the opponents of the contracting out of the management of prisons have not, as yet at least, been necessarily warranted, some private prisons, notably Buckley Hall, Doncaster and Blakenhurst, suffered considerable operational difficulties in the early years of their operation. What certainly could not be assumed is that extending the process of privatisation would speed up the types of changes in regimes recommended by Woolf. On the contrary, 'one obvious danger is that, as ministers distance themselves from the operational concerns of the new Prison Agency, debates about resources will be increasingly defined in terms of internal good husbandry and relegated from the political agenda' (Player and Jenkins, 1994: 27).

The mixed-economy of penal provision is now with us to stay. Some observers expected that the election of a Labour government in 1997 would lead to a change of policy in this area – given their long-standing opposition. However, Jack Straw, by then Home Secretary, announced that 'if there are contracts in the pipeline and the only way of getting the [new prison] accommodation in place very quickly is by signing those contracts, then I will sign those contracts' (Nathan, 1998). The U-turn was completed less than a year later, when Straw, in a speech to the Prison Officers' Association, said that following two internal prison service reviews, all new prisons in England and Wales would be privately constructed and run.

The aims of imprisonment?

It is clear from an examination of the history of imprisonment that differing theoretical answers to the fundamental question 'What is prison for?' can in fact have important consequences for daily life in prisons. Experience therefore suggests that, without an adequate statement of aims, we shall not develop the best practicable kind of daily regime in prisons.
(Bottoms, 1990b: 3)

As we have seen in this and the previous chapter, the prison has been viewed in different ways at different times and, accordingly, has been perceived as performing a different function within the penal system. Crudely speaking, it moved from being merely a repository for those awaiting trial, sentence or death in the sixteenth and seventeenth centuries to a site where punishment was inflicted on an increasingly wide range of offenders during the course of the eighteenth and nineteenth centuries. As the end of the nineteenth century neared, so the emphasis upon the reform and rehabilitation of offenders grew, and the primacy of this role was reinforced by the Report of the Gladstone Committee in 1895. From the mid-twentieth century, for almost 30 years – perhaps the high point of penal optimism – the notion of 'treatment and training' became the explicit guiding principle of the prison system.

With the emergence of research which questioned the effectiveness of treatment (Brody, 1976; Lipton et al., 1975) the rehabilitative ideal began to collapse and faith in the efficacy of treatment and training diminished. In their evidence to the May Inquiry in 1979, King and Morgan were critical of Prison Rule 1 on grounds far broader than merely some form of penal pessimism. Morgan (1994b: 895) describes their position as rejecting Rule 1 because it was 'so vague that it had never been operationalised. Indeed, it was inspired by aspirations incapable of fulfilment, something the prison staff had always known. Moreover, it quite arbitrarily excluded remand and trial prisoners from view' (Morgan, 1994b: 895). King and Morgan (1980: 31–2) suggested that it would be better to attempt to turn the practical and prosaic concept of 'humane containment' into a reality:

> Humane containment refers explicitly to the prison system, which forms only a part of the wider criminal justice system. We believe that what we regard as humane containment is most compatible with what has come to be called the 'justice' or 'due process' model for dealing with offenders generally. Taken together they best fit the state of current knowledge about law and order and the effectiveness of criminal sanctions. They therefore offer the best basis at this time for the development of a coherent policy for the future of the prison system.

Humane containment was to be underpinned by three principles: the minimum use of custody; the minimum use of security; and the 'normalisation' of the prison. The May Committee, however, rejected the idea of 'humane containment', though it did accept that Rule 1 needed to be rewritten and, in attempting to do so, it introduced the notion of 'positive custody'. This in turn, however, has not been adopted. In Bottoms' (1990b) view, it is the humane containment formula that has been the more influential on debates about prison since 1980, particularly because of its 'congruence' with the demands for improved rights and standards for prisoners which dominated much of this period. Nevertheless, 'there has remained a persistent unease within the prison service about the starkness' of this simple phrase, leading Bottoms (1990b: 9) to suggest that the central problem with the notion is that it is perceived to be *ontologically insufficient*.

At least for a period, the question of the aims of imprisonment dropped off the agenda and, largely because of the increasing emphasis upon financial management, the penal debate became more and more influenced by questions of economy, efficiency and effectiveness. A statement of tasks of the prison service was set out by the Director General in 1983, and it began 'The task of the Prison Service is to use with maximum efficiency the resources of staff, money, building and plant made available to it by Parliament in order to fulfil', four functions, which include keeping untried and unsentenced prisoners in custody until it is time to bring them to court; keeping sentenced prisoners in custody; to provide 'as full a life as is consistent with the facts of custody'; and, to help prisoners keep in touch with the community. This led Stern (1989: 50) to comment:

> It may seem a sad decline from the high ideals of changing human beings and sending them back out into the world crime-free to aspirations of giving prisoners a regular bath and ensuring they get their visits from their families. However, since we are still a long way from realizing even these modest ambitions for a good proportion of our prisoners, it at least has the advantage of being both measurable and achievable.

We have moved then from a position in which at least some emphasis was placed upon a moral mission to one dominated by what Garland (1990) characterises as institutionally defined managerial goals, and Rutherford (1993) calls 'expedient managerialism'. Expedient managerialism, he says, gives priority to narrowly defined performance measures and to short-term trouble-shooting over any articulation of purposes and values. This, as we shall see in subsequent discussions of, for example, policing and probation, can just as well be applied to other parts of the criminal justice system.

Since the publication in 1983 of the statement of tasks, there has subsequently been the report of the Control Review Committee (Home Office, 1984b) which, like the statement of tasks adopted by the Scottish Prison Service in the same year, distanced itself in some important respects from the 1983 formulation. In 1985, the ex-Governor of Wormwood Scrubs published a report entitled *A Sense of Direction*, in which he stressed the principles of 'individualism, relationship and activity' (Dunbar, 1985: 84). In 1988 and 1989, the English and Scottish Prison Services issued mission statements, the former characterised by Bottoms (1990b: 15) as containing a 'humane containment plus' formula, the latter improving upon this somewhat by adding the aim of providing 'prisoners with all possible opportunities to help them to lead law-abiding and useful lives'.

Where, then, does Woolf come into all this? As one of the assessors to the Inquiry has noted: 'At first glance the Woolf Report is disappointingly thin when it comes to a discussion of the purposes of imprisonment. No history of the debate is provided and there is no radical critique of the Prison Service's current statement of purpose. However, Woolf's brief criticism of existing formulations – the absence to any reference to justice and the failure to provide specifically for unconvicted prisoners – unlocked a process of logic with radical implications' (Morgan, 1994a: 111).

Woolf's formulation, as we have seen, rested on the suggestion that a balance needed to be created between security, control and justice. Security and control had dominated the debate for some years, and it is the addition of 'justice' which has influenced the debate. Whilst the Woolf formula falls well short of a new statement of aims, it does at least recognise that even though the primary purpose of prison is not positive for those incarcerated, some form of moral duty must be placed upon the prison service to ensure that inmates' and officers' sense of dignity is maximised and that their sense of injustice is minimised. This, together with increasing the opportunities for prisoners' to take responsibility for their behaviour, lies at the heart of Woolf's recommendations for reducing reoffending.

Nevertheless, and as has effectively been the case throughout the history of the modern prison, much is going to depend on how many people are actually incarcerated. If the prison population continues to rise, as it is predicted to do, then the chances of further major disturbances being avoided cannot be great. The sense of grievance and injustice which is documented at length in the Woolf Report will not be tackled until there is a radical diminution in the numbers held in prison. When the first edition of this book was written in 1994, the outlook appeared bleak. In early 2003, the situation, as we will see, has in many respects deteriorated significantly. Vivien Stern's overview, written in 1989, now appears unusually percipient:

> The history of Britain's prisons since 1945 has not been a happy one. It is a story of many dedicated people trying to make things better, and continually trapped by what can only be called 'the system' – the system in which the sentencers produce a steadily rising prison population; the system that fears political embarrassment and revelations in newspapers about prisoners enjoying themselves watching colour videos more than it fears revelations about prisoners locked up for twenty three hours a day and having no access to sanitation; the system where the processes, procedures, rules, Standing Orders and Circular Instructions take on a life of their own, and gradually blot out the consciousness that it is people not numbers being locked up.
>
> (1989: 247)

The 1990s and beyond: the spectre of mass incarceration

> The problem of overcrowding is a cancer eating at the ability of the Prison Service to deliver. Many inmates should not be in jail, the most significant group being those jailed for less than 12 months. . . . There is an opportunity now for a different approach, a holistic approach, which recognises that all parts of the justice system need to pull together.
>
> (Lord Woolf, 30 October 2002)

Lord Woolf's speech was delivered against the background of a prison population at record levels, and one rising at a rate that appeared likely to outstrip even the building of new prisons. Successive Labour Home

Secretaries had been forced to take emergency measures to release prisoners towards the end of their sentences in order to relieve pressure on the system, yet despite Woolf's assertion that people on all sides of crime argument now understood that continued prison expansion was not the answer to the problem, the numbers keep on rising.

What has happened to the prison population in the past ten years is, by any standards (except possibly those of the United States), extraordinary. In 1990, the prison population stood at roughly 45,600. By 1993, it had dropped by approximately 1,000. At the time of writing, early 2003, the prison population is over 73,000 and rising. The pace of change is easier to grasp graphically (see Figure 2.2). Despite broad concern about both the size of the prison population, and the general trend in its growth, little has been done to stem its overall growth (though the home detention curfew was used at one point of crisis). The most recent projections, published in December 2002, suggest that the prison population may exceed 100,000 by 2009. Indeed, the Home Office's most extreme projections, and recent increases in the prison population have generally outstripped most projections, suggest that by June 2009 there will be at least 109,000 people in prison in England and Wales (Councell and Simes, 2002). This projection was based on the assumption that custody rates increase annually at 2.5 per cent for males and double that for females to 2005, and slightly quicker than that thereafter. To put this in context, the rate of increase in 2002 was 7 per cent. We may assume therefore that in the absence of radical policy change in the direction of more limited use of custody, even these dramatic projections may underestimate the penal future that awaits us.

What are the dynamics behind this spectacular rise in the number of people in prison? Without doubt the climate of the times has played an important role. The populist punitiveness espoused by politicians of all hues fuelled the initial 'bidding war' between Michael Howard and Jack Straw in the mid-1990s. Since that time there have been a number of policy changes that, directly or otherwise, have led to further prison

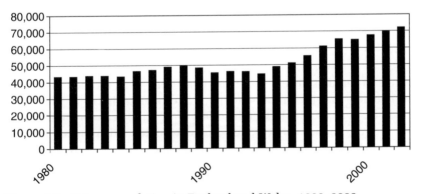

Figure 2.2 Prison population in England and Wales, 1980–2002
Source: Prison Statistics England and Wales. London: Stationery Office

expansion. Though New Labour Home Secretaries have stayed clear of the crude 'prison works' rhetoric employed by Michael Howard, they have nonetheless, as Morgan (2002) argues, taken the view that the problem of crime as currently configured may, once analysed and understood, actually require the incarceration of more offenders or the incarceration for longer of serious and/or persistent offenders. Thus, 'the sotto voce message reflected in this is that imprisonment plays a central strategic role in the management of crime – and, thus, in that sense, prison works' (2002: 1114). As David Garland (2001: 204) concludes, 'we face the real possibility of being locked into a new "iron cage"' of punitive justice.

Moreover, we are living in times when there appears to be relatively little political pressure to reverse these changes. Clearly, there are financial and administrative constraints on prison population growth, but there remains little sense within government that there is any principled objection to penal expansion. The bulk of recent policy initiatives seem more likely to lead to further population growth rather than any decline. The one obvious exception has been the increasing use of the early release 'safety valve'. The electronically monitored Home Detention Curfew (HDC) was introduced as part of the Crime and Disorder Act 1998. According to the Home Secretary:

> The case for introducing an element of tagging into the last part of a short-term prison sentence is very strong . . . but it has been reinforced by the recent rise in the prison population. No-one wants to see an unnecessarily overcrowded prison system, and it would be the height of irresponsibility not to take advantage of modern technology to help prevent that. The alternatives are bound to be at the expense of constructive prison regimes, and at the expense of improving the prisoner's prospects for resettlement – in other words, at the expense of the law-abiding public.
>
> (quoted in Leng et al., 1998: 126)

Prisoners serving a sentence of three months or more and less than four years are eligible to be considered for the scheme, and prisoners would be tagged for between 15 days and two months depending on the length of their sentence. In the first 16 months (the HDC went live in January 1999), a total of 21,400 prisoners were granted early release under the scheme. Of these, 1,100 were recalled to prison: two-thirds because of breach of curfew conditions and the bulk of the remainder because of a change of circumstances. Less than 1 per cent were recalled because it was deemed that they represented a risk of serious harm to the public (Dodgson et al., 2001). In October 2002, the Home Secretary announced that the maximum curfew period would be extended from the existing 60 days to 90 days. Though there had been some controversy over the numbers reoffending whilst on curfew, of the 59,000 prisoners released under the HDC by end of 2002, fewer than 3 per cent offended while on curfew. Despite the apparently impressive numbers, the HDC has only a marginal effect, albeit potentially important one, on overall prison numbers. Other policy initiatives look set to have a more substantial impact. Both the 'custody plus' and 'custody minus' sentences, proposed by the Halliday Review (see Chapter 7), have the potential to lead to further increases in custodial sentencing. Other elements of the Criminal Justice Bill, published in November 2002, such as the proposed scrapping of the 'double jeopardy' rule, the restriction of the right to jury trials, the introduction of 'indeterminate' sentences for sex offenders and greater use of previous convictions in determining sentence, all move in the same direction. Indeed, even the Home Office Minister at the time, Lord Falconer, admitted that the reform of sentencing incorporated into the Criminal Justice Bill would likely lead to a 'modest increase' in the prison population (*Guardian*, 22 November 2002). Under such circumstances, the tenor of the times is likely to be particularly important.

Recent political rhetoric has remained largely punitive and, occasionally, mystifyingly confused. Lord Woolf, quoted at the top of this section, has been an unlikely contributor to this confusion. In January 2002, during a period when there was considerable public and political concern about street crime (see Chapter 4), the Lord Chief Justice announced that mobile phone thieves should expect jail sentences of up to five years, and occasionally more. The day after his speech a 23-year-old man, convicted of just such a robbery, received a jail sentence of four years. By contrast, one year later, the Lord Chief Justice caused considerable controversy when he announced guidelines advising trial judges that first-time burglars should generally receive non-custodial sentences. With a national press generally uninterested in anything beyond the headlines created by 'crime' stories, the apparently mixed messages emanating from such usually safe hands as Lord Justice Woolf opened up further space in which both critical journalists and politicians could pander to public fears. With the prison population predicted to smash the 100,000 barrier under current policy initiatives, the introduction of new legislation and the continued recourse to penal populism by the majority of front line commentators mean that the predictions are almost certainly underestimates, and possibly quite dramatic ones at that. Where five years ago, mass imprisonment United States-style still appeared only a dystopian vision, in the early twenty-first Century it is looking more and more likely.

Notes

1. When the Inquiry was first set up on 5 April, its terms of reference were limited, for obvious reasons, to the disturbance at Strangeways. Revised terms of reference were issued on 10 April.

Chapter 3

The new police and the emergence of policing policy

Until relatively recently, the image of PC George Dixon (of *Dixon of Dock Green*) was so all-pervasive that it was easy to persuade ourselves that we had only just emerged from a 'golden age' of policing in which there had been general respect for, and consensus about, the role of the constabulary. Whilst this would certainly be a gross overstatement, it would also be wrong to characterise the history of British policing as one beset by conflict. After a period of quite intense resistance to the introduction of the 'new' police, the period from perhaps the 1870s to the late 1950s was one of relative acceptance and general calm in relation to policing. This is not to suggest, of course, that conflict – sometimes of a quite serious nature (see Morgan, 1987) – did not occur; simply that in relative terms there would appear to have been, in this period, broad acceptance of the legitimacy of the police. This situation has, quite clearly, changed, and it is a brief history of this process of change – particularly in recent decades – that is outlined in this and the following chapter. It is important to consider the history of the police in England and Wales and, accordingly, this chapter is divided into three main sections. The first looks at policing in England and Wales prior to the establishment of the Royal Commission on the Police in 1960. The second takes the period from 1960 to the election of the Thatcher government in 1979, and the third, police and policing policy from 1979 up until the end of the 1980s. Chapter 4 examines policing policy from that period to the present day.

The emergence of the modern police service

While the principal duty of the new police when they were first established in London in 1829 was declared to be the prevention of crime, as the nineteenth century wore on, English policemen found themselves carrying out a variety of tasks which fitted the older definitions: they regulated traffic, ensured that pavements were unimpeded, kept a watchful eye for unsafe buildings and burning chimneys, administered first aid at accidents and drove ambulances, administered aspects of the Poor Law, looked for missing persons, licensed street sellers and cabs, and supervised the prevention of disease among farm animals. Such tasks rarely figure prominently in police histories or police memoirs, and some of these tasks have subsequently been yielded to specialist agencies; yet the fact remains that since their creation the police have become more and more responsible for the smooth running of a variety of different aspects of society and not simply for the prevention and detection of crime and the maintenance of public order.

(Emsley, 1991: 3)

The term 'constable' originated in Norman times, and by the thirteenth and fourteenth centuries there were a variety of posts with this title, the majority of which were linked to manors or parishes. The medieval constable was responsible for making regular reports to the local court leet and with maintaining the King's peace. It is suggested by some police historians that the emergence of the office of justice of the peace in the fourteenth century usurped the position hitherto occupied by the constable and led to the decline of this office from this point to the emergence of the new police 400 years later (see Critchley, 1978). The extent of the declining importance of the office of constable is disputed by Emsley (1991) and others, though he accepts that it may have been in decline from the late seventeenth century onwards.

Eighteenth-century England was characterised by increasing concerns about crime. Though there is also dispute as to the extent to which there was any real basis for such fears (see Reith, 1938; Emsley, 1991), outbreaks of disorder such as the Gordon Riots certainly gave the impression of increasing lawlessness. By the mid to late eighteenth century, crime and disorder was perceived to pose a threat to social stability. One consequence, at least in London, was the emergence of the 'trading justice' – the man who 'probably because he lacked sufficient estate, opted to profit from the fees paid for performing judicial tasks' (Emsley, 1991: 18) – and professional thief-takers who profited from the existence of rewards for bringing offenders to justice. The most famous of these thief-takers were the Bow Street Runners, employed by Henry Fielding, who, whilst probably not as corrupt as others working at the same time, were certainly not 'above suspicion' (Emsley, 1991: 19). By the end of the eighteenth century, Fielding's operation, which had begun with the Runners, had expanded to include a variety of patrols, including armed patrols.

It was around this time that proposals started to emerge for a co-ordinated police service for London – the word 'police' being quite common currency by this point. It was not until 1829, however, that Robert Peel was successful in getting legislation through Parliament to introduce the Metropolitan Police. Though many of the more traditional histories of the police have presented this development as a logical and successful progression from earlier arrangements, Emsley (1991: 23), for example, suggests that the new police constables were 'initially at least, probably less efficient than several of the old night watches'. Crime prevention was, as has been noted, the primary responsibility of this new force. Emsley (1983) in his historical study of the emergence of the modern service quotes from the Metropolitan Police's first instruction book that indicated that 'every effort of the police' was to be directed at the prevention of crime. It went on:

> The security of person and property, the preservation of the public tranquillity, and all other objects of a police establishment will thus be better effected than by the detection and punishment of the offender after he has succeeded in committing the crime. This should constantly be kept in mind by every member of the police force, as the guide for his own conduct. Officers and police constables should endeavour to distinguish themselves by such vigilance and activity as may render it impossible for any one to commit a crime within that portion of the town under their charge.

Though such a short description implies a myriad of responsibilities (the prevention of crime, the maintenance of order, and the detection and punishment of the offender) the 'New Police' actually possessed relatively limited functions and powers. Crime prevention – the supposed core of the role – was actually fairly narrowly conceived at the time, largely as a 'scarecrow' foot patrol function. There has been a long and protracted academic debate about the reasons for the introduction of the Metropolitan Police in the 1820s, though the control of what was perceived to be a markedly rising crime rate and the maintenance of social order are accorded a central role in both the 'traditional' and the 'radical' histories (see Critchley, 1978; and Silver, 1967, for differing histories; and Reiner, 2000, for an overview and synthesis).

Though the Metropolitan Police was the first, and remains the largest and best known of the constabularies, forces were set up in the provinces within a matter of years of the establishment of the new police in London. Though the Metropolitan Police was a major influence on the development of forces outside London, the Metropolitan model was experimented with in other areas and was by no means uncritically adopted. Although the central tasks of these forces were similar to those outlined by Rowan and Mayne (Emsley, 1991), a wide variety of other duties were soon acquired by the police. Many of these – inspectors of nuisances, of weights and measures, inspectors under the Diseases of Animals Acts; the inspection of dairies and shops, contagious diseases, explosives, bridges, even in the case of some borough forces running both fire and ambulance services (Critchley, 1978), together with informal services such as 'knocking up' people for work (Emsley, 1983) – were what would most accurately be described as 'service' functions. Though never important enough to form the defining characteristic of the police, such functions were nevertheless one element in the process of legitimisation of the police during the course of the nineteenth century (Reiner, 1992). Nevertheless, it was in general the law enforcement and order maintenance functions that continued to be considered to be the core activities of police officers.

That this was the case is illustrated quite well in Reiner's (1992) discussion of the process of increasing legitimisation of the police in this period. He argues that one of the elements of police policy which contributed towards their legitimation was the appearance that the police were 'effective'. The criteria by which this effectiveness was judged are illuminating:

> By the 1870s then, the police had come to be seen as offering an effective law enforcement service to the middle and upper classes, who complained when its quality seemed to decline. The working class too made use of it, but the less respectable sections of this class were predominantly at the receiving end of law and order campaigns.
>
> (Reiner, 1992: 72)

There were, by this point, three types of police authority in existence. Peel's Metropolitan Police Act 1829 established a new 'police office' at Westminster, and two justices, responsible to the Home Secretary, were to be responsible for control over the new force. The Act made the Home Secretary responsible for approving the size of the force and gave him the power to command the two justices (later Commissioners) to execute specific duties. Although the power of the Home Secretary over the police generally, and not just the Metropolitan Police, has come in for increasing criticism, Lustgarten (1986) argues that, given that in 1829 the electorate consisted of only a tiny fraction of the male population and that monolithic party government underpinned by the whip system did not exist, the arrangements for the governance of the capital's police were 'designed to ensure the maximum accountability that the political system was capable of constructing at the time'.

Until recently, the broad parameters of the system of accountability for the Metropolitan Police remained largely unchanged from its time of inception. The establishment, for example, of elected local representative government for London in 1888 did not prise control away from the Home Office. As has been suggested above, although the Metropolitan Police was the first of the forces to be established, the arrangements for its governance were not copied when other forces were set up. With the growth of provincial police forces there developed two alternative systems of local accountability. The Municipal Corporations Act 1835 established Watch Committees that possessed the power to appoint officers and establish regulations for the running of the town forces. Following this, the County Police Act 1839 gave justices of the peace the power to appoint a chief officer of police, who held statutory office and could only be dismissed at Quarter or General Sessions. The standing of the county force chief constable was much greater than that of the borough chief; at the same time, the county forces were much more closely tied to the Home Office. The 1839 Act stated that all county forces were subject to rules concerning 'government, pay, clothing and accoutrements of constables' to be promulgated by the Home Secretary (Lustgarten, 1986).

The establishment of police forces did not become compulsory until the County and Borough Police Act 1856, which reinforced the power of the Watch Committee and of the justices. The Act did, however, introduce the first provision for central inspection of police forces, empowering the Crown to appoint three inspectors of constabulary to assess the efficiency of all forces. The power of the centre was at this point, and for some years to come, 'limited in both character and amount' (Critchley, 1978), but tended to grow thereafter. The Local Government Act 1888 established the administrative pattern for policing for almost the next 100 years. It established county councils and, under their aegis, standing joint committees consisting of two-thirds elected councillors and one-third local magistrates to be the police authority for county forces, an arrangement which was applied to all police authorities by the Police Act 1964.

There were a number of well-publicised disputes between chief constables and Watch Committees around the turn of century, each of which revolved around, though none resolved, the question of whether a chief is entitled to act independently in enforcing the law. At the turn of the century, practices varied greatly from force to force, with some chief constables being largely subservient to their Watch Committee and others acting quite independently on occasion (Brogden, 1982; Spencer, 1985).

By the time of the First World War, over 50,000 men were employed in constabularies across England and Wales. The War, however, both depleted police numbers and added a layer of duties that had not been present in peacetime. Dissatisfaction over pay and conditions – which also affected the prison service at this time (see Chapter 1) – led to the establishment of the Police and Prison Officers Union in 1913. A dispute over the legitimacy of union membership resulted in a police strike for about a week in London in 1918 and spurred on unionisation outside the capital. Fears about unionisation grew apace and in 1919 the Home Secretary introduced a Bill which sought to implement the Desborough Committee's recommendations on police pay – which was to be substantially increased – and on unionisation – which was to be outlawed.

The First World War, and the police strikes that almost immediately followed its conclusion, were the source of the next important set of structural changes to policing and its governance. The Home Office had begun, via Her Majesty's Inspectorate of Constabulary (HMIC), to oversee the activities of all police forces, and growing central control and supervision was made possible through the Police (Expenses) Act 1874, which increased the Exchequer grant to local police forces from one-quarter to cover one-half of police expenditure. (It was not until the Local Government Act 1985 that it was increased, this time to the 'symbolic' figure of 51 per cent.) During the War, the government began to assume the role of a co-ordinating body, setting up committees and issuing Circulars and instructions under the emergency regulations (Critchley, 1978), thus forging the first links between senior officers and the Home Office.

The Police Act 1919 gave the Home Office increased powers over the regulation of pay, conditions and discipline in all police forces, and also set up an advisory body before which such regulations were to be laid (Critchley, 1978; Jefferson and Grimshaw, 1984). At the same time, a police department was set up in the Home Office which, similarly, had responsibility for provincial police forces as well as the Metropolitan Police.

From this point onwards, the history of police accountability is one dominated by increasing central control, generally at the expense of local police authorities (Jefferson and Grimshaw, 1984; Lustgarten, 1986). Lustgarten in fact suggests that from the 1920s two trends were visible. The first was increasing Home Office influence through legislation and through less formal means, and the second was increasing freedom of action on the part of chief constables, eventually enshrined in the 'principle of constabulary independence'. In both cases, local police authorities were the 'losers'. The next major piece of legislation was the Police Act 1946, which gave the Home Secretary power compulsorily to amalgamate police forces with populations below 100,000.

Within a decade-and-a-half, a Royal Commission was sitting and was about to propose some of the most far-reaching changes to British policing for a century-and-a-half. What were the reasons for such a development? Interestingly, although the period 1955–64 has rightly been described by Stevenson and Bottoms (1989) as a 'decade of transition' as far as the politics of the police were concerned, they also show that, in official documents at least, the Home Office actually painted quite a positive picture of policing in the latter half of the 1950s. However, there was increasing concern shown by the Home Office at increases in recorded crime at this time, and by chief constables about the more visible developments in youth culture which were held to be indicative of declining morals (Newburn, 1991).

Behind the public presentation of official confidence in the police, by the mid to late 1950s there was increasing concern about their effectiveness, and towards the end of the decade a number of well-publicised disputes between police authorities and their chief constables threw the issue of the accountability of the police into sharp relief. In 1958, for example, the Nottingham Watch Committee requested that the chief constable report on an investigation he had instituted in connection with corruption charges involving members of the City Council. The chief constable refused and the Watch Committee used their power to suspend him. The Home Secretary ruled that such an action interfered with the chief constable's duty to enforce the criminal law free from political control and reinstated him. In 1959, the House of Commons debated a motion censuring the Home Secretary for making £300 of public money available to settle an action brought against a Metropolitan Police constable as the result of an alleged assault. These, and a number of other causes célèbres, put the issue of accountability high on the agenda – though the focus was on individual officers rather than on force policies – and led to the establishment of a Royal Commission on the Police.

The police and policing after the Royal Commission

The Royal Commission on the Police 1960

A number of very small-scale scandals in the late 1950s, together with a steadily rising crime rate, prompted the establishment of a Royal Commission on the Police, which examined many issues which continued to be high on the political agenda in the 1990s: police pay, police accountability and the possibility of a national police force. The latter was rejected, although a number of arguments in favour were advanced in a minority report, many of which are resonant of the effectiveness and efficiency arguments that continue to be deployed in support of such a move. Stevenson and Bottoms (1989: 10–11) concluded that: 'Overall, one is left with the clear impression of a Commission impressed with some of the logic of the nationalisers' case, but regarding it as simply too radical in the context of the times.'

The recommendations made by the Royal Commission in its final report (1962) formed the basis for the Police Act 1964, which is the primary statute defining the responsibilities of the three main bodies responsible for the police: the police authority, chief constable and the Home Office (now consolidated with other legislation in the Police Act 1996). More particularly, the Royal Commission, set up in 1960, was given the central task of reviewing:

> the constitutional position of the police throughout Great Britain, the
> arrangements for their control and administration, the principles that should
> govern remuneration of police officers and, in particular, to consider:
> (1) the constitution and functions of local police authorities;
> (2) the status and accountability of members of police forces, including
>   chief officers of police;
> (3) the relationship of the police with the public and the means of
>   ensuring that complaints against police are effectively dealt with.
> (Royal Commission on the Police, 1962)

Spencer (1985) makes the important observation that the Royal Commission, although tasked with examining the issue of accountability, did not have among its objectives 'ensuring that policing policies reflected the needs and priorities of the communities they served' and, as a consequence, their recommendations did not cover such ground. The recommendations that the Commission did make with regard to accountability were, in the main, implemented by the Police Act 1964 and they have formed the basis for practice for most of the period since. Once again, the general trend brought about by the Royal Commission and the Act was to reinforce the powers of chief constables and the Home Office at the expense of local authorities (Marshall, 1978).

The Royal Commission began from the position that 'the problem of controlling the police can . . . be restated as the problem of controlling chief constables' – a statement which has been much contested since. It went on to note that chief constables were accountable to no one, nor subject to anyone's orders for the way in which they settle general policies in relation to law enforcement and that, therefore, with regard to establishing more effective supervision, 'the problem [was] to move towards this objective without compromising the chief constable's impartiality in enforcing the law in particular cases' (Royal Commission on the Police, 1962: para. 92).

The Police Act 1964

This Act replaced the old system of Watch Committees and joint standing committees with a single system of police authorities. The Watch Committees had been composed entirely of councillors, whilst half of the members of the joint standing committees were magistrates. The new authorities were to consist of two-thirds councillors and one-third magistrates and, outside London, these authorities took two basic forms – though a third emerged as a consequence of the abolition of the Metropolitan authorities. The most common was the police authority which covered one county. This was a committee of the county council, usually referred to as the police committee, and was like other council committees except that none of its decisions, other than financial ones, could be overruled by the full council. The second type was the combined police authority for police forces that serve more than one county, consisting of councillors and magistrates from each county, and wholly independent of each and all of the constituent councils.

Police authorities were placed under a duty to secure the maintenance of an 'adequate and efficient' force for their area, though these terms were undefined. In the event, the Police Act 1964 empowered police authorities to:

1. appoint a chief constable, his deputy and assistants, subject to the approval of the Home Secretary;
2. determine the overall establishment, and number of each rank, of the force;

3. provide vehicles, clothing and equipment;
4. determine the overall budget of the force, subject however to the requirement that costs incurred under authority of central government Regulations, or any statute, must be met; and
5. require its chief constable to submit a report in writing on matters connected with the policing of the area.

Consequently, the only statutory duty owed by the chief constable to his police authority was the submission of an annual report, though the authority could 'require' that he also provide a written report on any matter related to policing of the area. This was, then, a form of what Marshall (1978) has termed 'explanatory' accountability, wherein the police are required *post hoc* to explain the policies they have followed or actions they have taken. Though potentially powerful, this provision in the 1964 Act provided little actual leverage, for a chief constable could refuse to make such a report if he believed it would contain information 'which in the public interest ought not to be disclosed, or is not needed for the discharge of the functions of the police authority'. Furthermore, police authorities had no powers to instruct chief constables to change any policies set out in the reports provided them. The 'unsatisfactory, indeed somewhat ludicrous result' according to Lustgarten (1986) was 'that police authorities are dependent on their chief constable for information, making their ability to offer effective criticism subject to the co-operation of its primary target. And the position of the Home Secretary as ultimate arbiter quietly emphasises the power of central government in policing matters'.

One of the major changes made by the Act was the enshrining in statute of the fact that supreme responsibility for local policing lay with chief constables, each force thenceforward being 'under the direction and control' of its chief officer. In order to do this, he was empowered by the Act to appoint, promote and discipline all officers up to the rank of chief superintendent. The Act also required chief constables to investigate complaints against the police and to submit all complaints that reveal that a criminal offence has been committed to the Director of Public Prosecutions.

The third pillar of what has since become known as the 'tripartite structure' is the Home Secretary. Many of the powers conferred on the police authority are only exercisable with the approval of the Home Secretary. Thus, although the chief, deputy and assistant chief constables are appointed by the police authority, such decisions must not only be approved by the Home Secretary, but they are subject to regulations promulgated by him. In addition, the Home Secretary could require a police authority to retire its chief constable 'in the interests of efficiency', though this provision has never been formally invoked.

Although a number of changes were made during the 1970s and 1980s, this was the basic structure that underpinned the process by which the police in England and Wales were made accountable for their general policies (the complaints procedure for dealing with allegations of individual misconduct is considered below) up until the passage of the Police and Magistrates' Courts Act 1994. Although there was an initial acceptance of the new arrangements brought about by the 1964 Police Act, together with continuing support for the police, this changed significantly, and perhaps irrevocably, during the following decade. A number of factors contributed to this change, and two key elements are considered here: the move to Unit Beat Policing and a series of corruption scandals which tarnished the image of the Metropolitan Police, in particular, but perhaps policing in general.

The introduction of Unit Beat Policing

In August 1967, the Home Office issued a Circular which encouraged police forces to adopt a new system of policing which reduced the number of officers on foot patrol and put them into cars. This was felt to have the advantage of allowing much wider geographical areas to be covered on a 24-hour basis and, together with the personal radios that were to be issued, of enabling officers to respond much more quickly to calls from the public. According to its proponents, Unit Beat Policing (UBP) was going to enable a better service to be offered to the public in all the major areas of police work: in the maintenance of public order, in the detection of crime, and in the prevention of crime, whilst also improving relations with the public. This is now widely presented as being the polar opposite of what has happened in practice, partly, it is suggested, because the whole idea was fundamentally misconceived, but also because it was undermined by a combination of insufficient resourcing and a police culture which played down the 'service' element of the system and exploited the opportunities it provided for 'action' (Holdaway, 1983). One of the unintended consequences of the reorganisation was to highlight the 'crime fighting' aspects of police work, and to devalue the service role. Reiner (1992: 76) suggests that with the transformation of patrol into a 'fire brigade' service, the emphasis was placed on 'technology, specialisation and managerial professionalism as the keys to winning the fight against crime'.

The crucial change brought about by UBP, it is argued, was the move away from foot patrol and into panda cars. Although there was never any systematic evaluation of the impact of UBP (Weatheritt, 1986), a general consensus has nevertheless emerged, which blames many of the perceived modern ills at its door. On one level, the absence of evidence is irrelevant, for the fact is that the universal criticism of the new system reveals a great deal about where things are *believed* to have gone wrong irrespective of when and why they actually went wrong:

> The pandas were, it is widely agreed, a disaster. They distanced the police
> from the public and, it has been suggested, encouraged policemen to see
> themselves in uncomplicated terms as knights-errant in the war against crime
> rather than as members of the community fully bound up in all aspects of its
> life and so lessening the likelihood of crime occurring in the first place.
>
> (Manwaring-White, 1983; quoted in Weatheritt, 1986: 96)

The main charge laid at the door of UBP is that, albeit unintentionally,
it was partly responsible for a sea-change in the style and image of British
policing, a new style that not everyone was entirely comfortable with. As
Chibnall (1977) described it: 'The "British bobby" was recast as the
tough, dashing, formidable (but still brave and honest) "Crime-Buster"'
(quoted in Reiner, 1992: 76). However, just around the corner were a
series of well-publicised cases that would challenge the reputation for
honesty.

The uncovering of corruption in the 1970s

In the space of less than ten years, at least four separate corruption
scandals involving Metropolitan Police officers were uncovered. It all
began with journalists from *The Times* tape-recording conver-
sations between detectives and criminals in which the covering-up of
serious crimes was being discussed. Equally as shocking as these
revelations was the subsequent apparent inability of those tasked with
investigating these abuses to secure co-operation within the force and to
discipline those officers involved. This pattern continued with other
allegations against officers from the Drug Squad and the Obscene
Publications Squad (Cox et al., 1977). There were even allegations
towards the end of the decade that detectives had been involved in
major armed robberies. Once again, even after the appointment of a
new Commissioner – Sir Robert Mark – to tackle the problem, these
scandals proved stubbornly resistant to successful investigation. The
huge and heralded *Operation Countryman* (an inquiry into alleged
Metropolitan Police corruption headed by the chief constable of
Dorset), for example, set up by Mark's successor, Sir David McNee, also
petered out in an unseemly exchange of allegations and counter-
allegations of malpractice, incompetence and corruption. If the general
public had ever accepted the image of George Dixon at something
approximating face-value, they were unlikely to do so after this.

Although there was growing concern about police effectiveness and
honesty during the 1960s and 1970s, there remained for most of this
period a striking lack of political controversy about policing. Whilst the
emergence of the 'new' police in the 1820s was the subject of considerable resistance and political debate, much of the history of British
policing has been characterised by an absence of political controversy,
and a deliberate avoidance of 'politicking' by police representatives. This

situation began to change in the 1960s, initially with campaigns for better pay. More recently, however, the Police Federation has become a vocal and influential pressure group, even going so far as to place an advertisement in the national newspapers in the run-up to the 1979 General Election, linking rising crime with the failure of the Labour administration's policies, and recommending a series of changes that were far from dissimilar to those being proposed by the then Conservative opposition (McLaughlin and Murji, 1998). The crucial development which saw the police thrust into the centre of political controversy was the election of the radical Thatcher government. The Thatcher administration was preparing for a period of radical and controversial change which, it was anticipated, would lead to conflict, and in which the police would need to play, or be persuaded to play a central role.

A changing political context: policing after 1979

Soon after the 1979 General Election, the new Conservative government honoured its pledge to implement in full the Edmund-Davies Committee's far-reaching recommendations on increasing police pay. Up until this point there had been a large measure of agreement between the two main political parties in relation to the police and policing. However, the increasing political profile of senior officers and other representatives, together with a series of significant public disagreements with Labour Party spokesmen (over the policing of the Grunwick dispute, rising crime rates in the late 1970s and the policing of the riots in the early 1980s) led to the end of this bipartisan consensus. The policing of the Miners' Strike in 1984 brought the relationship between the police and the Labour Party to an all-time low.

It would be wrong, however, to create the impression that some form of straightforward party political alignment has developed in recent decades. The reality has been that despite Mrs Thatcher's 1985 conference promise that 'the government will continue steadfastly to back the police. If they need more men, more equipment, they shall have them', police criticism of government policy has increased rather than decreased (Rawlings, 1992). There are a number of quite specific reasons for this. These are: the ending of the police's apparent immunity from the government's public expenditure cuts as the equation 'more money equals less crime' began to look increasingly untenable, the problems that were perceived to stem from the Police and Criminal Evidence Act 1984 and the introduction of the Crown Prosecution Service; and the ever more visible spectre of privatisation. The relationship between the police and the incumbent government was also lastingly affected by the urban riots of the early 1980s and the way in which the police were deployed during the miners' dispute later in the decade.

Urban unrest and policing the riots

During the 1980s, the Conservative government introduced what has been described by one commentator as the 'single most significant landmark in the modern development of police powers': the Police and Criminal Evidence Act 1984 (PACE). The following year it also removed the police's prosecutorial role with the introduction of the Crown Prosecution Service (CPS), and in 1986 passed legislation to alter significantly the public order laws (via the Public Order Act 1986). All of these developments can, at least in part, be traced back to the urban unrest of 1981.

Although it is the Brixton disorders which are most often remembered, the first 'riot' in 1981 occurred in central London as violence broke out during a protest march organised by the New Cross Massacre Action Committee. Three months later, on 10 April 1981, an hour-long riot occurred in Brixton. This was the prelude to a full weekend of disorder in which over 400 police officers were reported injured, over 250 people arrested and over 7000 police officers involved in attempting to restore order (Scarman Report, 1982: paras. 3.79–3.94). Further serious disorder occurred in Liverpool, and later in the cities of Birmingham, Sheffield, Nottingham and Hull, among others. Following a police raid on houses in Railton Road, rioting again broke out in Brixton in July, and then, briefly, again in Liverpool.

In the aftermath of the 1981 riots, Lord Scarman was appointed to inquire into the causes of the unrest in Brixton in April and to make recommendations. From the inception of the 'new' police onwards, there has been disagreement about the main or central functions of the police, and this was an issue that Scarman also tackled and which has continued to be the subject of vigorous debate since. For Sir Robert Peel, the main task for the police was 'crime prevention', though this was extended by Sir Richard Mayne in his 1829 instructions to the 'New Police of the Metropolis' in which he singled out 'the prevention of crime . . . the protection of life and property, the preservation of public tranquillity' as the core policing duties (Emsley, 1983). Scarman, too, was in favour of this formulation, though in the event of a conflict of aims, he felt that the maintenance of public tranquillity was the primary responsibility – i.e. he recognised that there would inevitably be situations in which the enforcement of the law would have to come second to the maintenance of the public peace.

Beginning from this position, Scarman was critical of the policing of Brixton and especially the heavy-handed 'Swamp 81' operation. In response to high levels of street crime, a saturation exercise had been planned in which large numbers of police officers patrolling the streets and using 'stop and search' powers, would attempt to 'detect and arrest burglars and robbers' (Scarman Report, 1982: para. 4.39). During the operation, the officers in the Brixton area made almost 950 'stops', which resulted in 118 arrests. More than half the people stopped were black. A total of 75 charges were brought, though only one was for robbery, one for attempted burglary and 20 for theft or attempted theft. As a result of his inquiry, Scarman concluded that the lack of consultation with community representatives prior to 'Swamp 81' was 'an error of judgement' (Scarman Report, 1982: para. 4.73), that the whole operation 'was a serious mistake, given the tension which existed between the police and local community' (Scarman Report, 1982: para. 4.76) and that 'had policing attitudes and methods been adjusted to deal fully with the problems of a multi-racial society, there would have been a review in depth of the public order implications of the operation, which would have included local consultation. And, had this taken place, I believe . . . that a street "saturation" operation would not have been launched when it was' (Scarman Report, 1982: para. 4.77).

Scarman's recommendations as a result of the inquiry were wide-ranging and took in such diverse areas as recruitment of ethnic minorities to the police, increasing consultation through the introduction of statutory liaison committees, the introduction of lay visiting to police stations, the independent review of complaints against the police and the tightening of regulations regarding racially prejudiced behaviour by officers. The Report emphasised the need for change and 'was the trigger for a reorientation of policing on a wide front. Indeed by the late 1980s, [Scarman's] ideas had become the predominant conception of policing philosophy amongst Chief Constables' (Reiner, 1992). Before this took place, however, there was one other major policing operation which was to have a major effect on the future of the service.

Policing the miners' strike

The tactics employed during this dispute had a profound effect not only on the nature and style of public order policing in this country (Waddington et al., 1989), but also on public perceptions about the police more generally. With respect to the former, Jefferson (1990: 1–2), although using a degree of hyperbole, suggests that the new image of public order policing is: 'not one of a line of bobbies defensively "pushing and shoving", but of "snatch squads": menacing teams of officers, unrecognizable in visored, "NATO-style" crash helmets and fireproof overalls, advancing behind transparent shields being banged by drawn truncheons, making "search" sorties into crowds of fleeing demonstrators for the purpose of arrest, or a spot of retributive "destruction".' Despite the rather colourful language, this picture of public order policing accords with what many people will have seen on television over the past 20 years.

The turning point in the policing of the 1984–85 miners' strike is widely regarded as being what has since become known as the 'battle of Orgreave'. New training and tactics for public order policing had been instituted in the early 1980s, and the new style which was formulated in the then unpublished Association of Chief Police Officers (ACPO) *Public Order Manual of Tactical Options and Related Matters*, was first unveiled at Orgreave. Perhaps the most controversial of the manoeuvres adopted was that of using mounted officers to charge into the ranks of the pickets followed by sorties of officers with long shields, short shields and batons, all organised in a highly militaristic manner. The drift towards the type of paramilitarism first evident at Orgreave and later used at many other disputes and demonstrations (Northam, 1989) has led to an extended debate about the likely long-term impact of the use of such tactics.[1]

What is uncontestable, though, is that the public image of the police has changed. Although militaristic public order policing and 'individualistic' mainstream policing are diametrically opposed, equally they cannot be fully separated (Morgan and Smith, 1989). Waddington (1991) concluded in relation to the strike, the 'television pictures of a police officer apparently hitting a prostrate picket repeatedly with his truncheon at the Orgreave coke works during the miners' strike did immense damage to the police reputation for restraint'. In addition, however, as Morgan and Smith (1989) suggest, 'the change in public order policing has created conditions in which the legitimacy of the police is bound to be examined and questioned more closely than in the past'.

The Police and Criminal Evidence Act 1984

The changing climate within which the police were operating was also signalled by the proposals contained in the draft Police and Criminal Evidence Bill published in 1982, much of which arose out of a report by the Royal Commission on Criminal Procedure (RCCP) published during the previous year. The RCCP focused on the rights of suspects, an issue that had been debated vociferously for some time, but which had been brought to a head by the 'Confait case' in which, it was eventually found, three boys had been convicted of murder on the basis of false confessions. The Judges' Rules, which at that time formed the basis for suspects' rights, were identified by many commentators as being inadequate, and were examined closely by the Royal Commission. The RCCP's report had been controversial when it was published, receiving support from the police, but being widely criticised by left and liberal spokespeople inside and outside Parliament. The Police and Criminal Evidence Bill which was first introduced in late 1982 went through a number of phases before it reached the form that we now recognise as the Police and Criminal Evidence Act 1984 (PACE), and was itself widely criticised by almost all groups that had an interest in it, though there now appears to be a measure of agreement as to its worth. The Act was enacted at the end of 1984, and not only extended police powers in a number of important ways, but also introduced far-reaching procedural safeguards (many of which have been revised since) to guard against abuses of these powers. There is not the space here to go into great depth about the content of the legislation, but it is worth considering three areas of change in a little detail.

Police investigation

PACE replaced a variety of statutory and common law rules which had previously regulated police investigative powers. Thus, one of the core aims of the Act was to attempt to balance police powers with protection for the arrested person. PACE, which extended police powers of arrest, detention and stop and search, was therefore accompanied by four codes of practice which replaced the extant Judges' Rules that laid down procedures for the questioning of suspects. The four codes of practice were contained in s. 66 of the Act and covered police statutory powers to stop and search; the search of premises and the seizure of property; the detention, treatment and questioning of persons by the police; and identification procedures. A fifth code covering tape-recording of interviews with suspects was introduced subsequently, and in 1991 revised codes of practice, directed primarily at reinforcing the suspect's right to legal advice, came into operation. It appears this may have had quite a significant impact, for there is some evidence that the judiciary have adopted a stricter attitude towards infringements of the PACE codes of practice than they did towards the old Judges' Rules (Feldman, 1990). Research on the impact of PACE and the revised codes of practice has, however, been equivocal, with clear gains and continuing problems with regard, for example, both to suspects' rights and complaints against the police (see *inter alia*, Brown, 1989; Brown et al., 1992; Maguire and Corbett, 1991; McConville et al., 1991). There can be little doubt, however, that the Act has had an impact on the behaviour of police officers, and on the culture of policing, and the worst fears of its critics should certainly have been allayed (Benyon and Bourn, 1986).

Police accountability

Lord Scarman's chief recommendation on accountability was that local community consultative committees should be set up. In Scarman's view, there had been insufficient formal liaison between the black community and the police in and around Brixton, and the absence of such communication was both a symptom and a cause of the 'withdrawal of consent' that underpinned the policing problems in the area (Morgan, 1992c). He concluded that 'a police force which does not consult locally will fail to be efficient'.

Scarman dashed the hopes of many critics of the existing arrangements by endorsing the 'tripartite' structure. He did, however, suggest that police authorities could act more effectively and vigorously if there were better arrangements for local consultation in areas considerably smaller than those covered by whole forces. He favoured the introduction of a statutory duty to make such arrangements 'at police divisional or sub-divisional levels'. This, as Morgan (1992c) concludes, 'was the participative mechanism on which he pinned his faith that policing would in future be more congruent with the wishes of people locally'.

Scarman's recommendation that local consultative committees should be established was quickly followed by a Home Office Circular (54/1982) supporting such arrangements and, as an illustration of the influence of Home Office Circulars in the area of policing generally, a large number of police authorities, in the main supported by their chief constables, established such committees in their regions. Statutory provision for the making of arrangements 'in each police area for obtaining the views of the people in that area about matters concerning the policing of the area and for obtaining their coopera-tion with the police in preventing crime in the area' were introduced under s. 106 of PACE.

On the basis of his analysis of the varied political and administrative statements, oral and textual, issued by ministers and civil servants since 1981, Morgan (1992c) suggests that police community consultative groups (PCCGs) have, at least in the minds of officials, four major objec-tives. The first is as a forum in which consumers of police services may articulate and communicate to the providers of the service what it is they want. This is related to Scarman's view that effective policing can only be maintained if the police are aware of public concerns and priorities. The second aim is the perceived need to educate the public. This arises from the simple observation that, given that police resources are finite, they need to be rationed in some fashion. Consequently, one way of avoiding the widespread alienation that would follow from the police continually failing to meet public expectations is to persuade the public, through education, to temper the demands they make on the police. The third function of PCCGs, he suggests, is to resolve conflict. Given that policing involves coercive powers and, indeed, that the communities being policed may impose conflicting demands on the police (Smith, 1987), it is neces-sary to have forums in which disputes can be resolved. Finally, he suggests, the hope was that PCCGs would form the basis for police-public co-operation for crime-preventive activities.

The Scarman Report was widely criticised for having recommended statutory consultation rather than control by some form of elected police authority, and whilst the latter might not have been the solution to the problem of accountability, the available evidence does not suggest that the consultative committees have been particularly successful either. Research by Morgan and colleagues (Morgan, 1987; Morgan, 1989; Morgan and Maggs, 1985) found that PCCGs were, in the main, dominated by police and police authority members, and that they seldom contained people who were, or were likely to be, critical of the police. Consequently, police accounts tend to dominate proceedings and tend to be accepted by the committees. Morgan concludes that in terms of accountability PCCGs have achieved little other than legitimising current practices and arrangements.

One further development which also arose out of recommendations made by Lord Scarman in his report on the Brixton disturbances also needs to be described here. He suggested that there 'should be random checks by persons other than police officers on the interrogation and detention of suspects in the police station' (Scarman Report, 1981: para. 7.10). The Home Office issued a guideline document in 1983 and pilot schemes were established in six police authorities and one Metropolitan Police district. There was considerable delay before the Home Office subsequently issued a Circular (12/86) which commended the introduction of lay visiting schemes 'wherever local wishes and circumstances might make them appropriate'. Arrangements for schemes are left to individual police authorities, and their objectives are stated to be 'to enable members of the local community to observe, comment and report upon the conditions under which persons are detained at police stations and the operation in practice of the statutory and other rules governing their welfare, with a view to securing greater understanding of, and confidence in, these matters' (quoted in Kemp and Morgan, 1990).

Lay visitors were to be allowed access to areas of police stations where 'persons are detained pending interview, release or production in court, including the cells, charge areas, detention rooms and medical rooms . . . [but] not CID or other operational areas'. They were to be allowed to speak to detained persons, including remand prisoners, examine documents such as custody records which relate to their detention and treatment whilst in the station, but not records which relate to the investigation of any offences it is believed they may have committed. However, the police retain considerable control over access to prisoners. Thus, seeing detained persons or their custody records requires the written consent of the detainee, and it is the responsibility of the officer in charge of the station to obtain that consent. Permission can be withheld by the police in 'exceptional circumstances', and interviews in progress may not be interrupted.

The rights of suspects in police stations had been a central concern of PACE, though the arrangements for lay visiting were not, unlike PCCGs, made statutory under the Act. The creation of PCCGs, the introduction of lay visiting and new rules governing the treatment of suspects in police stations were all, at least to an extent, part of a general process of increasing the visibility of police activities with a view, as Circular 12/86 outlining lay visiting suggested, to increasing public confidence in such work.

Finally, under this section on accountability it is important to mention one further development although, strictly speaking, it does not relate to PACE. As has been suggested, the early 1980s were a time in which policing in general and the tripartite structure in particular came under increased scrutiny (Reiner, 1993). In the local government elections in 1981, radical Labour councils were returned in all the Metropolitan areas, and the police authorities in those areas gradually began to attempt to exercise some of their powers. There were a number of major clashes between authorities and chief constables, and such conflict contributed to the overall disenchantment with which the government viewed these particular councils. The Local Government Act 1985 abolished these authorities and replaced them with joint boards, which, it has been argued, have proved more accommodating to police influence than their predecessors (Loveday, 1987; Reiner, 1993). Joint Boards were made up of nominees of constituent district councils and, as far as practicable, membership reflected the local party political balance. In general, this meant a move away from Labour domination or control in the metropolitan areas (Loveday, 1991) and, additionally, resulted in an increased profile for the magistrate members of police authorities.

Police complaints

Largely as a result of the pressures stemming from the corruption scandals of the 1970s, the government set up a part-time lay body, the Police Complaints Board (PCB) in 1976 to monitor the investigation of complaints against the police. The PCB achieved remarkably little, however, and was replaced by the Police Complaints Authority (PCA) after PACE. The PCA is a full-time body with the power to supervise investigations of any serious complaint – those in which it is alleged that the actions of an officer led to the death of or serious injury to a member of the public or any other case it deems to be in the public interest. Procedures for the informal resolution of minor complaints were also introduced. Research contained both positive and negative conclusions about the operation of the system. On the one hand, it was suggested that the system was staffed by committed and able police investigators; that police officers responsible for complaints and discipline were increasingly impressed by it; and that the 'informal resolution' procedure appeared promising (Maguire and Corbett, 1991). On the other hand, it was suggested that there were an overwhelming majority of 'dissatisfied customers' – be they officers or complainants (Maguire and Corbett, 1991). The subject of police complaints has always aroused considerable debate, and there would seem to be continuing suspicion by the public of any system that involves the police investigating themselves, and suspicion by officers themselves of bureaucracies which they feel are unsympathetic to the job they are faced with. Widely known by officers as the 'Prosecute Coppers Association', the PCA attracted a motion of no confidence at the Police Federation's Annual Conference in 1989 (Rawlings, 1992) and, as we will see below, reform has been back on the agenda more recently.

Financing the police

Not only did the Conservative Party use the issue of 'law and order' as one of the central planks of its platform in 1979, but as has been suggested, the Thatcher administration moved quickly once elected to put some of its financial promises into practice. The recommendations of the Edmund-Davies Committee were implemented almost immediately, and, in addition, police staffing levels increased by just over 6 per cent in the period 1979–84. More remarkably, in the same period public expenditure on the police doubled from £1,644 million to £3,358 million. Recorded crime continued to rise, however, despite this increased financial commitment. The total number of notifiable offences stood at just over 2.5 million in 1979, but had risen by approximately 37 per cent to almost 3.5 million by 1984. In addition, the official clear-up rate for notifiable offences declined from 41 per cent in 1979 to 35 per cent in 1984. What is more these trends continued throughout the 1980s: expenditure on the police rose a further 20 per cent by 1987, whereas notifiable offences rose a further 6 per cent to over 3.7 million and clear-ups fell to 33 per cent (*Social Trends* vols 11–19).

Perhaps not surprisingly against this background, as noted in Chapter 2, from approximately 1982–83 onwards, the government began vigorously to pursue its 'Financial Management Initiative' (FMI), designed to encourage efficiency and cost savings by applying private sector management methods to the public sector, and imposing market disciplines on them. Although initially it looked as if the police might be safe from such scrutiny, the publication of Home Office Circular 114/1983 (and later the even tougher 106/1988), largely without consultation with police representative bodies, signalled that the financial climate had changed. The Circular outlined potential new management strategies for the police – now generally referred to as 'Policing by Objectives' (PBO) – many of which had influential supporters within the police. Kenneth Newman, for example, had introduced very similar initiatives into the Metropolitan Police before the Circular was published. Nevertheless, both ACPO and the Police Federation were, on occasion, very hostile to the new emphasis on 'value for money'. The core issue in this conflict was summed up by Rawlings (1992: 46) as the government's view that 'PBO will lead to a more efficient and effective use of resources and, almost as a by-product, will tend to hold down the numbers of police officers and so reduce costs; police organisations regard its primary objective as being the cutting of expenditure through a reduction in the number of police officers without any real concern about the effect this may have on policing'.

In addition to the problem that crime continued to rise inexorably despite the increase in resources, one of the key reasons that the Conservative government felt able to adopt such a stringent financial policy, particularly in its second term of office, was that recorded levels of public satisfaction with the police had been declining for some years.

Although public confidence remained high, with 85 per cent of the public who had an opinion rating the performance of the police as either 'good' or 'very good' in 1988, the trend was nevertheless in a downwards direction. Thus, for example, 92 per cent of the public had rated the police in that manner in 1982, and other data from the three British Crime Surveys conducted in the 1980s showed that the proportion of the public who gave the police the highest possible rating dropped from just over one-third in 1982 to under a quarter in 1988 (Mayhew et al., 1989). Furthermore, this decline in confidence was observed in most major social groups and communities including those non-Metropolitan areas traditionally supportive of the police (Skogan, 1990; Tuck, 1989).

The spectre of privatisation

The 1980s also saw the emergence of an issue that had begun to threaten other public services: privatisation. Privatisation and the FMI were, of course, linked, for as police representatives were quick to point out, restrictions on human and financial resources increase the opportunities for competitors to provide services hitherto the preserve of the police. Recent years had seen considerable increases in the size and significance of the private security sector, increasing civilianisation (and use of 'specials') within the police, the emergence of plans to privatise the Police National Computer and to formalise a customer-contractor relationship between police forces and the Forensic Science Service, each of which gave some credence to police fears.

The impact of both financial constraint and the spectre of privatisation was to open up a debate about the future shape of policing in Britain. Throughout the 1980s, as the Conservative Party increasingly turned its attention to the police, so the ACPO and the Federation became ever more visible in public debate, and the Labour Party belatedly entered the fray with a range of proposals for policing, many of which were very close to the opinions being expressed by senior officers (Reiner, 1992; Sheerman, 1991). The apolitical stance of senior officers and the previously existing bipartisan consensus on policing had both disappeared, but had not been replaced by an easily identifiable alignment between police representatives and one or both of the major political parties. The accord in the early 1980s between the police and the Thatcher government was undermined by the FMI and the threat of increasing privatisation, together with an attempt from the centre gradually to increase control of the police through Home Office Circulars, the expansion of the Common Police Services budget and the National Criminal Intelligence Service. Indeed, Reiner (1991; 1992) has suggested that this process effectively created a *de facto* national police force.

It was, in part at least, the increased scrutiny of the police by the government pursuing its FMI, and the inability of the police to control local crime rates, together with declining public confidence in the police, that was the driving force behind a renewed evaluation of the police function, and a desire by some senior officers to reassess the role and function of the service. One consequence of this was increasing attention on the idea of the prevention of crime, and a growing emphasis on the role of the 'community' in the prevention and detection of crime.

Crime prevention and community policing

Although crime prevention has since the inception of the new police been thought of as a key function of the service, there has generally been a lack of clarity about exactly what this is to mean in practice. Indeed, it was not until after the publication of the report of the Cornish Committee on the Prevention and Detection of Crime (Home Office, 1965b) that specialist crime prevention departments began to come into being in any number. The Committee recommended, *inter alia*, the need for specialist police officers who would be experts in crime prevention technology; that an officer of at least the rank of inspector take the role of force crime prevention officer, and that a more professional approach was needed in respect of the publicity material used by the police.

Perhaps anticipating one of the potential problems with this approach, the Committee pointed out that the creation of the specialism should not be taken to imply that the responsibility of other officers with regard to crime prevention had lessened. Furthermore, in what has by now become a standard crime prevention argument, it emphasised the importance of building relationships with organisations outside the police, and as part of this process of eliciting such support it recommended the setting up of 'crime prevention panels' (see Chapter 5).

Such panels have no formal status and have generally been chaired by the police themselves (Home Office, 1971). Their purpose is to consider crime prevention proposals and to help in the process of publicising campaigns and initiatives aimed at improving (usually physical) security measures. Because of their lack of status and the fact that there has never been any requirement to set them up in local areas, crime prevention panels developed in a largely ad hoc way and, following the lead taken by the nascent crime prevention departments which exercised a strong influence over them (Home Office, 1971), tended to focus fairly narrowly on physical security (Gladstone, 1980).

Despite the apparent rise in the stock of crime prevention with central government, responsibility *within* police forces for crime prevention work remains the domain of specialist crime prevention units and crime prevention officers (CPOs). It is worth considering briefly what it is that these officers do. In the main, crime prevention is a small-scale police specialism, with CPOs usually representing less than 1 per cent of a force's establishment (Harvey et al., 1989) and rarely occupying ranks higher than chief inspector. Crime prevention officers have usually been located within departments with 'community' in their title (community liaison, community involvement and so on) or within CID. Whatever the location, crime prevention work tends to remain fairly marginal, rarely permeating 'the force much beyond the designated officers, whatever the line of responsibility upwards' (Harvey et al., 1989: 88).

The relatively narrow focus of crime prevention panels has largely been replicated within police forces, and research tends to suggest that the tasks actually undertaken by CPOs have, in practice, been very limited. Harvey et al. (1989) found that although a broad range of officers within community liaison departments or their equivalents felt that they were engaged in crime prevention work, there was a tendency for force CPOs to demarcate very clearly between crime prevention work and 'community' work. Particular emphasis, for example, was placed on the need for technical or hardware expertise, and this 'bias' was reinforced in the training CPOs received at the then Crime Prevention Centre in Stafford.

In a similar vein, research on the work of CPOs in London (Johnston et al., 1993), based on observation and worksheets, concluded that the majority of work undertaken by the officers fell into the following ten categories: residential surveys, commercial/industrial surveys, alarm problems, firearms, displays, talks, designing out crime, initiatives, crime panels and training. Although, once again, this is quite a broad list, the research suggests that the vast majority of CPOs' time was devoted to surveys and to meetings about firearms and alarms. The bulk of the work was of a technical variety, largely concerned with target hardening, surveillance, entry/exit screening and access control – all standard techniques of 'situational prevention' (Clarke, 1992).

Johnston et al. (1993) also argued that because much of the work is of a fairly narrow technical kind, most police 'crime prevention activity [is] largely *reactive*, responding to the demands of the public to do surveys . . . or responding to the need of the service in general to try to reduce the time spent on false alarm calls' (Johnston et al., 1993: 5). The work of crime prevention design advisors was more proactive, but little connection was found between this work and local crime problems. They concluded that although the work was justifiable in that it was largely done in response to public demand, the delivery of the service 'was not co-ordinated with the rest of the policing service, nor was it necessarily planned to focus on the Division's main priorities for crime prevention'.

Where more socially based or 'community' initiatives were undertaken, it was generally unclear on what basis they were being encouraged. Thus, Harvey et al. (1989: 90) suggest: 'In the plethora of activities initiated and encouraged – soccer, netball, youth clubs, "Cops, Kids and Carols" concerts, shooting [*sic*], and schools liaison – the common good seems to be the encouragement of friendly relationships between police and juveniles. Work described as crime prevention sometimes appears, in fact, to be principally public relations with no clearly articulated connection between a good press and crime preventive effects.'

As crime continued to rise, despite the increase in resources devoted to policing in the early 1980s, one of the key messages emanating from the police was they could not be expected to carry responsibility for the prevention of crime unaided. As a result, increasing emphasis came to placed upon the 'community', both in relation to policing and criminal justice generally and, more specifically, in relation to crime prevention (cf. Willmott, 1987; Crawford, 1997). Indeed, the impetus for this began even earlier, crucial in this regard being a Home Office Circular (211/1978, which became known as the Ditchley Circular). This recommended improved co-ordination between criminal justice agencies, together with community-based initiatives, as a solution to what was perceived at that time to be the piecemeal approach to dealing with juveniles.

The so-called 'community-policing' approach that developed is most closely associated with John Alderson, the one-time Chief Constable of Devon and Cornwall, who emphasised the importance of close relationships between police and public and, consequently, the broad service role of his constabulary (Alderson, 1979). The emphasis upon community and upon what has since become known as 'inter or multi-agency co-operation', broadened the focus of crime prevention from its previous preoccupation with technology, 'target-hardening' and opportunity reduction, to the social conditions which provide the context of, and the social organisations which are involved in regulating, that behaviour defined as criminal. Such an approach has been quite widely referred to as 'social crime prevention' (Clarke, 1981) to distinguish it from 'situational crime prevention' (Clarke and Mayhew, 1980; Clarke, 1992), and whilst this distinction is not necessarily always helpful (Bottoms, 1990a), it nevertheless retains considerable currency within criminology. The changing emphasis within crime prevention was also reflected, for example, in the curriculum at the Home Office Training Centre which, according to Laycock and Heal (1989), moved away from 'the previous locks and bars emphasis towards community involvement, crime pattern analysis and inter-agency work' (see Chapter 5).

Community-focused policing initiatives were many and varied during the 1980s, and although little rigorously collected evidence is available, there is little to suggest that much success was achieved. Thus, research on, *inter alia*, community constables (Brown and Iles, 1985), directed patrolling (Burrows and Lewis, 1988), focused patrolling (Chatterton and Rogers, 1989), neighbourhood policing (Irving et al., 1989) and Neighbourhood Watch (Husain, 1988; Bennett, 1990; McConville and Shepherd, 1992) illustrated the difficulties in planning, implementing and evaluating community-focused crime prevention measures. *Implementation* is perhaps the important word here, for the majority of problems that have been identified have stemmed from programme failure (Hope, 1985) rather than, it is argued, fundamental flaws in the philosophy that underpins them.

Though initially treated as a peripheral specialism of low status and interest when placed alongside crime fighting (Graef, 1989), the 1980s saw an increasing emphasis placed on crime prevention, with a concomitant rise in the visibility of such work (or, at least, the publicity given to the work) within the police, to the point at which Reiner (1992: 99) even felt able to assert that crime prevention departments became the 'belles of the ball'. Though this is a considerable overstatement, a number of very significant changes did take place during the 1980s, and in his review of these developments, Bottoms (1990a) highlights the setting up of the Crime Prevention Unit in the Home Office in 1983, the issuing of the 1984 inter-departmental Circular on crime prevention (Home Office and others, 1984, followed by Scottish Office, 1984), the two seminars on crime prevention held at 10 Downing Street in 1986 – one chaired by the Prime Minister, the other by the Home Secretary – the 'Five Towns Initiative' launched in 1986, followed by the Safer Cities Programme in 1988 and the launch of the charity *Crime Concern*. To this list one might add the reconstituting of the Home Office Standing Conference on Crime Prevention, the second Home Office Circular (44/1990) which updated 8/84, and the formation of the ACPO sub-committee on crime prevention. Bottoms (1990a, p. 19) concluded that:

> By any standards, this is a formidable list of developments. The 1980s, we can safely assert, has put crime prevention firmly on the map: a conclusion which is true not only in Britain, but also, at a minimum, in France, in the Netherlands and in the Council of Europe.

During the course of the 1990s, the stock of what is now generally referred to as 'community safety' rose and pressure increased on government to establish clear lines of accountability. Within police forces themselves, mixed messages about crime prevention continued. Successive governments have stressed the importance of crime prevention initiatives and programmes and, at least at a rhetorical level, argued that the prevention of crime should be considered to be a central part of the standard policing function. Similarly, the police themselves have generally been quick to support the idea that this area of work remains fundamental. By contrast, however, research has shown that the reality within the police is rather different. Both Harvey et al. (1989) and Johnston et al. (1993) reported that CPOs and the departments within which they work remain fairly marginal within most police forces, and crime prevention work remains a fairly narrowly defined specialism. With the passage of the Crime and Disorder Act 1998 (see Chapters 4 and 5), and the fact that police forces and local authorities are jointly tasked with taking lead responsibility in crime prevention and reduction initiatives, it is possible that this may all change. In the process, the police will once again be forced to attempt to define, and possibly rethink, what it is they are principally there to do (Newburn, 2002b).

Notes

1. See, for example, the debate between Jefferson and Waddington which started with their articles in the *British Journal of Criminology* (1987) 27(1), and has led to numerous other articles and to two books: Jefferson, 1990; Waddington, 1991.

Chapter 4

Policing: the 1990s and beyond

The renewed scrutiny of the police which followed the period after the miners' strike and the introduction of PACE was, in this case, stimulated by the continuing increase in levels of crime and the uncovering of a large number of miscarriages of justice. The release of the Guildford Four, the Birmingham Six, the Maguires, the acquittal on appeal of the 'Tottenham Three' and the widespread allegations concerning the West Midlands Serious Crimes Squad led, directly or otherwise, to a situation in which public confidence in the police fell to an all-time low. Calls for a new Royal Commission on the Police have been staunchly resisted by successive Home Secretaries, but the seriousness of the Birmingham and Guildford cases made some form of review inevitable, and the Home Secretary responded by appointing a Royal Commission on Criminal Justice, to be chaired by Lord Runciman.

Successive Commissioners of Police have instituted major programmes of reform aimed at improving police-public relations, and a largely 'service-based, consumerist' view of policing is now espoused by police managers' (Reiner, 1992). It had looked for some time, however, that internal reorganisation and re-presentation was going to prove insufficient, and the possibility of even more significant change was signalled by the appointment of a reformist Home Secretary, Kenneth Clarke, after the 1992 General Election. Those who had followed the career of Mr Clarke through the Departments of Health and Education expected swift and far-reaching action, and they were not disappointed, for within six months of his taking office he had instituted two reviews of different aspects of policing. Three inquiries which were in whole or in part focusing on policing were therefore set in train. It is worth considering here both the remits of these inquiries and the broad recommendations coming from each.

The White Paper on Police Reform

The chances of there being radical reform increased with the announcement by Clarke to the Home Affairs Committee that he was considering the possibility of reforming the structure of policing and of the structure of accountability of the police. This review, which was conducted entirely within the Home Office, had no official terms of reference. Despite, or perhaps because of, this lack of official profile, it managed to cause at least as much controversy as the other inquiries put together. The furore – in which it was reported that Mr Major had stepped in to chair a Cabinet sub-committee meeting on the review in order to calm a row, ironically, between Clarke and the then Environment Secretary, but subsequently Home Secretary, Michael Howard – was apparently caused by a proposal to remove some elected members from police authorities and to replace them with businessmen. The course of the inquiry was accompanied by a succession of leaks to the press, and the 'kites which were flown' included the possibility of reducing the number of police forces by up to half; the privatisation of a number of current policing functions; the removal of any local funding of the police; and the abolition of local police authorities and their replacement with government appointed boards.

When in June 1993 the Home Secretary eventually made a statement in Parliament, the plans he suggested and incorporated in a White Paper (Home Office, 1993d) did indeed contain many of the proposals that had been discussed in the press in the previous months. They included:

1. Altering the composition of elected police authorities so that the 16-person committees would comprise eight local councillors and three magistrates being joined by five members appointed by the Home Secretary 'for their management or financial experience and local knowledge'.
2. Introducing an advisory body for London to help the Home Secretary 'oversee the performance' of the Metropolitan Police.
3. Introducing national league performance tables utilising approximately six key performance indicators such as response times to emergency calls and clear-up rates.
4. Giving chief constables greater financial control over local budgets, but also introducing strict cash limits.
5. Moving the focus of policing from force headquarters to local or basic command units.
6. Encouraging the recruitment of up to an extra 10,000 specials, and extending their role to include beat duties.
7. At some stage in the future, an as yet unspecified number of forces will be amalgamated, but this is unlikely to happen until some of the other major reforms have been implemented.

Reactions from the police staff associations were mixed. The Police Federation was critical of the proposal to redesign police authorities, their chairman, Alan Eastwood suggesting that it was a blow for local democracy. The Superintendents' Association opposed the proposal for the introduction of national league tables on the grounds that there was a risk that they would simply measure quantity, rather than quality, and might fail to take account of local differences. By contrast, John Barrow, the President of ACPO, welcomed elements of the Report – particularly the proposals for greater financial freedom for senior officers and for the new pay formula, though he too was critical of the plans for police authorities. We will return to the Police and Magistrates' Courts Act 1994 below.

The Sheehy Inquiry

Announced to general surprise at the Police Federation conference in May 1992, the terms of reference of the Inquiry were 'To examine the rank structure, remuneration, and conditions of the police service in England and Wales, in Scotland and in Northern Ireland, and to recommend what changes, if any, would be sensible'. It was chaired by Sir Patrick Sheehy, the chairman of BAT industries, and its other members were Mr John Bullock (Joint Senior Partner, Coopers Lybrand), Professor Colin Campbell (Vice Chancellor, Nottingham University), Mr Eric Caines (Director of Personnel, NHS) and Sir Paul Fox (former Managing Director, BBC Television). It was intentional that none of the members of the Inquiry had any experience of policing.

The Inquiry eventually reported on 1 July 1993 (*Inquiry into Police Responsibilities and Rewards*) just two days after the publication of the White Paper and, once again, given the level of discussion in the press prior to its publication, contained little in the way of surprises. It made 272 recommendations in all, designed, it was suggested, to 'reward good performance and penalise bad'. Some of the major recommendations included:

1. New recruits to the police to be hired on ten-year, fixed-term contracts which would be considered for renewal subsequently every five years.
2. Abolition of the ranks of deputy chief constable, chief superintendent and chief inspector.
3. The introduction of a severance programme to enable the termination of the contracts of up to 5,000 middle-ranking and senior officers.
4. The introduction of performance-related pay, with up to 30 per cent of the salaries of chief constables and their assistants being linked to performance-related bonuses.
5. The reduction of starting pay and the linking of pay rates to non-manual private sector earnings.
6. The ending of many forms of overtime payment and the freezing of housing allowances.

Reactions to the Sheehy Inquiry Report were varied. The Police Federation reacted negatively, arguing that the recommendations would remove the vocational aspect of the work, turning it into a 'job like any other job' ('Police threaten "open conflict"'. *Financial Times*, 1 July 1993). The Superintendents' Association echoed this sentiment suggesting that recruitment, retention and motivation would all be hit by the proposals, though there was cautious approval from some quarters for the financial and structural reorganisation heralded by the Report.

In the main, the proposals contained in both the Sheehy Inquiry Report and the White Paper were discussed together by the national press, and one academic commentator suggested that 'though separate, these two initiatives must be regarded as a single centralising package' (Waddington, 1993). His argument was that the White Paper's proposal to reduce local authority representation on police authorities and the Sheehy Inquiry's support for the introduction of fixed-term contracts that would be reviewed by the Home Office was merely another element in a century long process involving the 'gradual accretion of central control over the police'. This was certainly the implication drawn in relation to the White Paper by *Police Review* (2 July 1993), whose editorial comment concluded: 'This White Paper is committed to devolving command to basic units while it creates a strong central control system. It could be named the "Home Office Rules"'.

The Royal Commission on Criminal Justice

Set up in the aftermath of the release of the Birmingham Six in March 1991, the first Royal Commission to consider the police since that appointed in 1960 was given wide terms of reference, but not wide enough, according to some critics. Sir John May had been appointed in October 1989 to lead an inquiry into the circumstances surrounding the convictions of the Guildford Four and the Maguires, and the eventual overturning of the convictions for Birmingham pub bombings prompted a broad review of criminal justice.

The Home Secretary, Kenneth Baker, announcing the appointment of the Royal Commission under Lord Runciman, said that the aim of the review would be to 'minimise so far as possible the likelihood of such (miscarriages of justice) happening again. The review was to cover all stages of the criminal justice process: the investigation and pre-trial stages (the management of the investigation by the police and the role of the prosecutor); the role of expert witnesses and, in particular, that of forensic scientists and the reliability of scientific evidence; the place of the right to silence in criminal proceedings; the possibility of a role for investigating magistrates; the conduct of criminal trials and the duties and powers of the courts. In addition, the review was to examine appeals procedures, the powers of the Court of Appeal, and the investigation of alleged miscarriages of justice once appeal rights have been exhausted – including the functions at present carried out by the Home Secretary' (*Hansard*, HC Deb, 14 March 1991).

The Commission reported on Tuesday 6 July 1993, and its report included a total of 352 recommendations (Royal Commission on Criminal Justice, 1993). Many of these focused upon court procedures – such as the right to trial by jury, the right of silence and the introduction of an element of formal plea bargaining – although some were directed at the police, though they were largely uncontroversial and were perhaps not as far-reaching as some commentators had expected. Thus, the Commission, in deciding that it would not be necessary to have supporting evidence for confessions in order to secure a conviction, recommended that police investigations should not be closed down after a confession is made. Interviewing training should be given to all officers, it suggested, and training in the supervision of investigations is also necessary, the Commission argued, as is improved management and supervision of 'specialist squads'. Continuous video-taping of police custody suites should also be brought in, and the taping of witness statements should be increased. It also recommended that custody records should be computerised and that all forces should have a helpline that officers could use to report any concerns that they had about malpractice of fellow officers. The Commission defended the retention of the right to silence. Some commentators have suggested that this defence was rather 'half-hearted' (Sanders and Young, 1994: 374) and, as we shall see, legislation has been passed since which significantly amends this 'right'. Finally, the Commission suggested that the acquittal of an officer in criminal proceedings should not be bar to disciplinary proceedings with possible dismissal, and that the standard of proof should not be the same as that in a criminal court.

The Home Office Review of Core and Ancillary Tasks

In addition to the Royal Commission, the Sheehy Inquiry and the internal Home Office review which led to the White Paper, a further inquiry – known as the Review of Core and Ancillary Tasks – was also set in train. The terms of reference of the review were: *To examine the services provided by the police, to make recommendations about the most cost-effective way of delivering core police services and to assess the scope for relinquishing ancillary tasks.* The starting point for the review team was the observation that demands on the police continue to grow at a rate that outstrips increases in police resources and places a strain on the service. They suggested, therefore, that 'some of the resources needed to improve performance in core areas of work supporting key and national objectives will have to be found by releasing resources currently absorbed by peripheral non-essential tasks or by finding more cost-effective ways of delivering core tasks'. The Inquiry was, in essence, a further step along the road towards privatisation of certain police functions. Although the initial aims of the Inquiry were modified as work progressed, the under-lying rationale continued to be the desire to limit public expenditure in this area. An Interim Report from the Inquiry was published late in 1994 (Home Office, 1994b) and a Final Report in 1995 (Home Office, 1995a).

The Home Office Review of Core and Ancillary Tasks (the Posen Inquiry) explicitly looked for ways to extend one particular form of pri-vatisation – contracting-out – to the police service. Although few would advocate a wholesale 'hiving off' of policing, there are organisations, such as private security firms, carrying out functions which overlap with police activities (Jones and Newburn, 1998). When policing is seen in its broad symbolic sense, it is much easier to portray it as a public good which must be provided by the state (Loader, 1997). But when it is broken down into its constituent functions, it is possible to identify tasks which could be, and sometimes already are, undertaken by organisations other than the police. Hiving off these functions to private organisations would arguably allow the police to concentrate on their 'core' activities without under-mining their position. In the event, the Final Report of the Inquiry seemed a damp squib, merely recommending the contracting-out of a small number of peripheral duties, such as escorting wide loads, though it did also suggest that a national crime reporting system should be estab-lished and that force crime pattern analysis should be standardised. Signalling, at least for the time being, the end of the threat of large-scale contracting out, the Home Secretary, Michael Howard, said that the government had 'looked hard at the current role of British policing. It is the right role. This government will not change it'.

The Police and Magistrates' Courts Act 1994

Following on from the White Paper on police reform, and its other inquiries into policing, the government introduced its Police and Magistrates' Courts Bill – a Bill that was to cause considerable controversy both inside and outside Parliament. Much of the controversy surrounded differing interpretations of the likely implications of the Bill for the gov-ernance of the police. Thus, for example, Sir John Smith, then President of the ACPO, took the view that 'we are witnessing a move, perhaps unin-tended, for national control of the police by central government'. Such an interpretation was stoutly resisted by government spokesmen, with Lord Mackay, who introduced the Bill in the House of Lords, saying: 'This is not the centralisation of policing, as is often suggested. It is precisely the reverse. It is giving away to police authorities and to chief constables various powers which the Home Secretary presently has. It is making those local police authorities stronger, more independent and more influential. It is enabling policing to be done locally, to be the responsi-bility of local people, and for policing to be accountable to local people.'

Initial proposals included the idea that the Home Secretary have the power to appoint the chairmen of the authorities, and also that all authorities be limited to 16 members. In the event, authorities were able to choose their own chairmen. The selection of independent members was more complicated. Police authorities had a local selection panel, consisting of one person appointed by the Home Secretary, one by existing members of the police authority and the third chosen by the other two, which selected a shortlist of 20 candidates, from which the Home Secretary chose ten to go forward to the final round, from which the councillor and magistrate members selected the final five appointees.

The newly constituted police authorities were required to determine objectives for the policing of the authority's area during the forthcoming financial year; to issue a plan setting out the proposed arrangements for the policing of the authority's area for the year (the 'local policing plan'); to include in the local policing plan a statement of the authority's priorities for the year, of the resources expected to be available and of the intended allocation of those resources; and that a draft of the local policing plan 'shall be prepared by the chief constable for the area and submitted by him to the authority for it to consider'.

These proposals, together with a degree of financial devolution, formed the basis of the government's claim that the new police authorities would be independent, strengthened bodies, with powers to hold local chiefs to account. With regard to finance, in the Lords debate, Lord Mackay said that the new police authorities would 'be free-standing with their own money and their own standard spending assessments. Decisions about policing will be taken by the police authority. They will not be taken by a committee of a local authority which can be over-ruled by the local authority' (*Hansard* 18 January 1994). The police authorities are therefore independent of local councils, yet subject to significant oversight by the Home Office, a situation which prompted Vernon Bogdanor to claim that 'the Bill establishes a national police force under the control of the Home Secretary' (*The Times*, 19 January 1994). What then are controls that may be exercised by the Home Office?

The Act enables the Home Secretary to set objectives for policing and to require police authorities to set performance targets for measuring the achievement of those objectives. It also enables him to issue codes of practice relating to the exercise of police authority functions. Reinforcing the importance of national objectives, Lord Mackay said in opening the debate on the Bill in the Lords that 'the primary duty of each police authority will be to secure the maintenance of an efficient and effective police force . . . this small but important change will ensure that police authorities give priority not only to achieving value for money with the resources available, but also to ensure that the results are consistent with the objectives that have been set' (*Hansard*, 18 January 1994).

What is contained in the Act goes beyond setting targets for the police. First of all, the Home Secretary determines a set of objectives, and following that he may then direct individual police authorities to establish performance targets. A variety of individually tailored conditions are added to these, depending on his view of the force and the authority. Police authorities, therefore, have to follow a set of objectives established annually by the Home Secretary to establish targets and formulate a local policing plan, but cannot do this independently. The local objectives have to be consistent with national ones. Furthermore, the Home Secretary can issue codes of practice for the new authorities, and local policing plans are governed by these codes and by directions issued by the Home Secretary. Thus, as one commentator has argued, the context of the functions of police authorities is to be substantially different, for it may reasonably be inferred that part of HMIC's function in future will include reporting on the performance of the authority's duties as well as those of the force (Grenyer, *Police Review*, 24 December 1993).

The Act also gave the Home Secretary powers to order force amalgamations. Because the proposals over the constitution of local police authorities dominated the political debate at the time, the issue of force amalgamations – touted so strongly prior to Sheehy – was largely overlooked. The Home Secretary said that he had no immediate plans for amalgamating forces and yet the Police and Magistrates' Courts Act 1994 (PMCA) includes striking new powers. It gives the Home Secretary power to amalgamate forces without having any form of local inquiry as would be the case under the Police Act 1964, and contains no requirement on him to justify his plans before an independent inspector, or even to do more than give reasons to those that have objections to his proposals. This certainly represented a remarkable concentration of power centrally over decisions about the structure of local forces.

Finally, the Act replaced the existing provisions on police grant under which the Home Secretary refunds 51 per cent of police expenditure. Under the terms of the Act, each police authority receives a cash-limited amount of police grant. The new police authorities also receive funding through revenue support grant, non-domestic rates and the council tax. The Act established new police authorities as major precepting bodies for local government finance purposes. In terms of financial devolution, the Home Secretary no longer decides how many police officers a police force will have. That is decided by the chief constable and the police authority.

One crucial new power contained in the Act was that enabling the Home Secretary to direct police authorities to spend above a certain amount in total – that is, to increase any precept that is made. It seems likely that such a measure was introduced at least partially after the experience of Derbyshire Constabulary in the early 1990s, which was twice refused a certificate of efficiency after local disagreements over a realistic budget for the force. The new powers allow the Home Office to dictate, where it considers necessary, increased expenditure on policing against the will of the local police authority.

One of the issues not resolved by the Act was the anomalous position of the Metropolitan Police. At the time of the Act, the Home Secretary was set to remain the police authority for the capital despite his predecessor's view that 'London needs a police authority, and the arrangement whereby the Home Secretary is in theory the police authority for London is not adequate if we are to hold the Metropolitan Police to account, and if we are to assist them by giving clearer guidance on priorities' (Kenneth Clarke, 1993, quoted in *Hansard*, 18 January 1994). Thereafter, it was agreed that a body be appointed to advise the Home Secretary on the running of the Metropolitan Police, but this fell some way short of a full-scale police authority for London. The situation was changed in 2000 as a result of the Greater London Local Authority Act 1999, which introduced an independent police authority for the capital.

There was little doubt in most commentators' minds about the potential for centralisation under the arrangements brought about by the PMCA. A key factor in the extent of centralisation in practice was always likely to be determined by the ways in which the new police authorities and chief constables adapted to the new arrangements. One possibility would have been for local government to campaign for a reversal of the changes and a restoration of the old arrangements. Although a 1994 Association of Metropolitan Authorities discussion paper on quangos recommended that 'the changes of the Police and Magistrates Courts Act 1994 should be reversed and the pre-1994 situation restored' (Association of Metropolitan Authorities, 1994: 17) critical voices declined relatively quickly after the Act came into force.

What then are we to make of the impact of the PMCA? Research by the Policy Studies Institute (PSI) (Jones et al., 1994) on the pre-PMCA arrangements suggested that one reason for the relative lack of influence of police authorities was their size and structure. Police authorities tended to be too large to be effective decision-making bodies, and covered large areas with a range of local communities within them. A vital component of the 1994 reforms was therefore the restriction of the size of police authorities. Although still clearly covering large areas, and the smaller size bringing problems for political representation of certain areas, early research suggested that the new police authorities are generally more effective and streamlined discussion and decision-making bodies than their predecessors (see Jones and Newburn, 1997).

Depoliticisation was one of the most visible consequences of the PMCA. The influence of party politics generally, and the political complexion of authorities in particular, has clearly diminished significantly in most areas. Surveys of police authority clerks by Jones and Newburn (1997; Newburn and Jones, 2000) found that the majority appeared to feel that the new police authorities had increased their levels of influence and effectiveness compared with their predecessors. However, this feeling was mainly restricted to the shire areas, and metropolitan police authority clerks were less likely to view the changes in such terms. This may well reflect the finding from other research (Jones et al., 1994; Loveday, 1987) which suggested that metropolitan police authorities tended to be more active and 'hands-on'.

The introduction of independent members – one of the most controversial of the reforms – appears to have been experienced in generally positive terms. Although there is little evidence in support of Kenneth Clarke's proposition that independent members would bring a range of experience to police authorities that had not previously been available to them, most police authority clerks suggested that the contribution being made by the new members at least equals what would have been expected from the elected and magistrate members already in place (Jones and Newburn, 1997). In terms of broad occupational and professional categories, the largest group was taken up by people whose background was commercial enterprise or the professions (approximately 45 per cent). However, significant minorities of independent members come from other backgrounds (accountants/lawyers/doctors – 20 per cent; academics/teachers – 15 per cent; armed/emergency services – 7 per cent; civil service – 6 per cent: see Jones and Newburn, 1997 for details).

A number of studies found that an important source of the lack of influence of pre-1994 police authorities was that police authority members and officers took a very limited view of the police authority role, and did not use the limited statutory powers available to them (Morgan, 1992c). The lack of motivation and awareness among police authority members was a major target of the 1994 reforms, although clearly the government wished to encourage a particular kind of activism, focused on performance review and increasing effectiveness and efficiency. The PSI research suggested that this was beginning to occur in many, although not all police authorities. It is the case that the main impact of the changes upon police authority business was the introduction or reinforcement of business and commercial perspectives, and the diminution of party politics in police authority business. In part, this process reflects the continuing spread of the philosophy of new public management (Hood, 1991), encouraged no doubt by the presence of non-councillor police authority members, but also in part because of the reduced size of the police authority, and has seen the focus on objectives (local and national) and performance measurement move increasingly to the fore. To this extent, 'managerialism' appears to have tightened its grip on police authority business.

Previous research has shown that most chief constables go to some lengths to develop good working relationships with their police authorities (Reiner, 1991). However, it has been argued that 'when push comes to shove' the chief constable will always prevail (Reiner, 1992). The first two years following the PMCA saw a gradual bedding down of the new arrangements, and few clear examples of tensions between chief constables and police authorities, including over what should go into local policing plans. Subsequently, however, clear tensions emerged leading, in the case of Sussex and after the intervention of the Home Secretary, to the resignation of the Chief Constable. Nonetheless, this is the exception rather than the norm and is, in part, no doubt, a product of what one clerk called the continuing 'compliance culture' which exists in many authorities, where members find it difficult, or are simply unwilling, to challenge the chief constable or other senior officers. Reflecting not only the dominance of forces in the drafting of plans, but also the difficulties associated with using local consultative mechanisms for such a purpose, there appears to have been little in local policing plans which has come via PCCGs and other similar groups. Partly as a result of this, and partly because of the emphasis on consultation within the legislation, most police authorities have reviewed their arrangements for local consultation (Elliot and Nicholls, 1996). It remains the case, however, that PCCGs are generally regarded as an inappropriate vehicle for consultation about strategic issues. A minority of police authorities are taking the lead in setting up new forms of consultation, such as focus groups and specially designed public attitude surveys, independently of those now routinely undertaken by most police forces.

It is still difficult to assess precisely what changes to the shape of the 'tripartite triangle' of police governance have been brought about in recent years. Whilst, ideologically, the triangle is generally presented as an equilateral one – representing a relationship between three equal players, all the evidence points to it being an isosceles triangle, with the local police authority as the least powerful participant. The PMCA strengthened the hand of the local police authority by formalising its power to set objectives. Simultaneously, however, the Act dealt an extra card to the Home Secretary in the shape of national objectives, as well as giving chief constables an 'opt-out' by allowing them merely to have 'regard to' the policing plan. There remains much to be played for.

Other aspects of centralisation

As was suggested above, one of the new powers available to the Home Secretary as a result of the PMCA, was the ability to order the amalgamation of police forces without formal public consultation. The reason for the introduction of this power was the long-held belief that economies of scale could be achieved through amalgamation and, moreover, that the changing nature of much criminal activity meant that old, local geographical areas were less and less relevant to the day-to-day realities of contemporary policing. The new power has not, as yet, been utilised by any of the Home Secretaries to whom it has been available, though talk of possible mergers and amalgamations of forces regularly recurs in both policing and policy circles.

There were, however, a number of changes in the mid-1990s that further 'centralised' certain aspects of policing in modern Britain, most of which concerned the creation or reinforcement of national policing bodies. Of course, some of this is not new at all. The Police Act 1964 provided the basis for the establishment of Regional Crime Squads (RCSs) and within a year, nine RCSs had been established. The Squads grew in size significantly during the 1970s and 1980s, though their number was reduced from nine to six in the early 1990s. At that stage, each of the RCSs covered an area comprising several forces and was staffed by (over 1,000) officers on secondment from forces around England and Wales. The main functions of RCSs were: to identify and arrest persons responsible for serious criminal offences which transcend force and regional boundaries; to co-operate with regional intelligence offices in generating intelligence; and, where appropriate, to assist in the investigation of serious crime.

Since the time of the establishment of the RCSs, in addition to the increasing pressure to create more specialist national units to combat various forms of criminal activity which, it is argued, cannot effectively be countered by existing force, there has also been pressure for increasing international co-operation as a result of the developing European Union. In 1989, the Home Affairs Committee of the House of Commons, as part of their investigation of drug trafficking and related serious crime, heard evidence from several senior police officers that there was need for greater national co-ordination of certain policing activities. Plans for a National Crime Intelligence Service (NCIS) got underway in 1990, the intention being to integrate the work of the existing National Football Intelligence Unit, the Art and Antiques Squad, the National Drugs Intelligence Unit, the regional criminal intelligence offices and a variety of other bodies. NCIS was established in 1992.

At the 1995 Conservative Party conference, the Home Secretary announced that he intended creating an operational National Crime Squad to deal with serious crimes, a proposition implicitly endorsed by the Home Affairs Committee in its 1995 report on organised crime. The White Paper, *Protecting the Public*, published in March 1996, confirmed the government's intention of forming a National Crime Squad (NCS) and announced that it would be led by a co-ordinator with 'executive power to direct its resources from a national and international perspective'. This was put into effect by the Police Act 1997 and the NCS came into operation on 1 April 1998. The Director General of the NCS effectively takes control of the RCSs, which are absorbed into the structure of the NCS. The Service Authority which oversees the NCS comprises 17 members, of whom ten (core members) also sit on the NCIS Service Authority, and is not expected to have a particularly influential or hands-on role.

There is considerable debate as to the implications of these developments and other related reforms of policing in the United Kingdom. In particular, it is suggested by some that what we are witnessing is the progressive nationalisation of policing, and Reiner (1991) has argued that we have a *de facto* but not a *de jure* national police force (see also Uglow and Trelford, 1997; Wall, 1998). Notwithstanding the creation of new national policing bodies, the increasing visibility of a national senior police officer elite (Savage et al., 2000), the increasingly powerful and vocal role taken by the ACPO, the differences between individual forces in relation to the most basic aspects of policing, such as crime recording (Her Majesty's Inspectorate of Constabulary, 1996) and levels of patrol service (Audit Commission, 1996), should make one sceptical of the claims made for the creation of a national force by default. In fact, alongside the centralising tendencies in contemporary policing, there have been simultaneous pressures towards localisation and fragmentation: the PMCA, for example, supported by advice from the ever-influential Audit Commission, encouraging forces to devolve budgets and decision-making down to the level of Basic Command Units.

Policing under New Labour

Political debate about 'law and order' in the 12–18 months prior to the 1997 General Election was characterised by significantly more heat than light. In the competition to appear 'tough on crime', Michael Howard and his Shadow, Jack Straw, each sought to persuade the electorate that he and not the other could be entrusted with pursuing policies which would 'protect the public'. Most rhetorical attention was paid to prisons and to youth crime, with relatively little political discussion being devoted to the subject of policing. For a brief period, after a series of visits to the United States by members of the Shadow Cabinet and their advisors, including one to assess the policing experiments in New York City, New Labour came out in favour of what became known as 'zero tolerance' policing. In the three years from 1994–97 there was a 37 per cent drop in New York City's crime rate, a 50 per cent drop in the homicide rate (Bratton, 1997) and a drop of almost two-thirds during the course of the decade. One of the key figures in the New York experiment was former NYPD Commissioner, Bill Bratton, who, among others, claimed that the most significant reason for the decline in the homicide rate and in recorded crime was changes in policing strategies during this period.

Jack Straw visited Bratton during 1995 and was clearly impressed by what he heard. Within a short period, Straw was making speeches based, loosely, on a version of the Wilson and Kelling 'Broken Windows' thesis and using the imagery associated with what he took to be the essence of 'zero tolerance policing' in New York (Wilson and Kelling, 1982). Indeed, spokespeople from both major political parties made frequent references to 'zero tolerance' in their pre-election speeches. In practice, there have only been limited experiments with 'zero tolerance policing' in the United Kingdom. The Metropolitan Police in King's Cross undertook a vigorous and, they allege, successful campaign to 'clean up' the area by focusing as much on minor infractions and incivilities as on major crimes. One of their operations, entitled Operation Zero Tolerance, ran for six weeks in late 1996 and involved 25 police officers 'who have been instructed to clamp down on all crime in the area, however apparently trivial or irrelevant'. The only major explicit attempt to introduce a form of zero-tolerance policing was that in Hartlepool under the guidance of then Detective Superintendent Ray Mallon, one of the few British police officers of any seniority to have embraced the idea. The term 'zero tolerance' appeared twice in the Labour 1997 election manifesto, once in relation to petty criminality and once in relation to educational underperformance. Since that time, however, talk of zero tolerance has lessened, particularly since the unfortunate experience of Ann Widdecombe. Ms Widdecombe, as Shadow Home Secretary, used her speech at the Conservative Party Conference 2000 to propose a new policy of zero tolerance in relation to drug use. She said:

> Today I am able to announce a new policy. Earlier this year, I visited New York, where under Mayor Giuliani crime has plummeted. Although we can't replicate exactly what I saw there, we can learn the lessons. And so, from the possession of the most minimal amount of soft drugs right up the chain to the large importer, there will be no hiding place. There will be zero tolerance.

Reaction to the speech was both immediate and almost universally condemnatory (though the reasons for this were undoubtedly as much a matter of internal party politics as they were of policy or principle). Ms Widdecombe, who had not long previously been touted as a possible leader of her party, saw not only any ambitions she may have had in that direction dashed, but also her position as Shadow Home Secretary almost fatally undermined. Politicians have generally treated the term 'zero tolerance' with greater caution since that time.

As with all new governments, but particularly in the case of a party that had not formed a government for the best part of two decades, there was considerable speculation as to what New Labour planned to do in relation to policing. The pre-election zero tolerance rhetoric, and the desire to occupy the 'law and order' territory, led many to suspect that major changes might be on the cards. The new Home Secretary was said to be in favour of radical reform. In the event, it was not until the second Labour term, and the arrival of David Blunkett in the Home Office, that police reform reached the top of the agenda. This is not to say that Straw's time was not marked by any important events. One of his first, and bravest, acts as Home Secretary was to do what his Conservative predecessors had signally failed to do – instigate an official inquiry into the murder of Stephen Lawrence.

The Stephen Lawrence Inquiry

On 22 April 1993, 18-year-old Stephen Lawrence was stabbed to death in Eltham, South London. Stephen Lawrence was by no means alone in being subject to a vicious racist assault. There were numerous other cases at the time and, of course, they continue (Bowling, 1999). However, partly because of the way in which the case was handled, and partly because of the public campaign that was subsequently mounted by family and supporters, the case focused attention on racist victimisation and, once again, on the attitudes and behaviour of the police.

Stephen Lawrence was standing at a bus stop with a friend, Duwayne Brooks, when they were approached by a small group of clearly hostile and abusive white youths. Though Brooks was able to escape and call for help, Stephen Lawrence was stabbed twice and died within a short period of time. To date (early 2003), no one has been successfully charged with Stephen Lawrence's murder. As the Macpherson Inquiry put it (para. 2.1), 'those violent seconds in 1993 have been followed by extraordinary activity, without satisfactory result'.

The police investigation found no witnesses to the attack other than Duwayne Brooks and 'other sound evidence against the prime suspects [was] conspicuous by its absence' (para. 2.2). A private prosecution was launched against five suspects in 1996, but failed because of lack of evidence (two suspects were discharged at the committal stage and the other three, who went to trial, were acquitted). Ominously, the verdict of the Inquest jury was that 'Stephen Lawrence was unlawfully killed in a completely unprovoked racist attack by five white youths'. The Macpherson Inquiry (para. 2.10) concluded:

> There is no doubt whatsoever but that the first MPS investigation was palpably flawed and deserves severe criticism. Nobody listening to the evidence could reach any other conclusion. This is now plainly accepted by the MPS. Otherwise the abject apologies offered to Mr and Mrs Lawrence would be meaningless.

The Home Secretary had met with Mr and Mrs Lawrence in June 1997 and afterwards said that 'it is not an option to let this matter rest. I recognize that a strong case has been made by Mrs Lawrence for some form of inquiry and I am actively considering what she put to me' (Macpherson, 1991: Appendix 1). The decision to establish an Inquiry, chaired by Sir William Macpherson of Cluny (formerly a High Court judge) was announced on 31 July, the terms of reference of which were to be: 'To inquire into the matters arising from the death of Stephen Lawrence on 22 April 1993 to date, in order particularly to identify the lessons to be learned for the investigation and prosecution of racially motivated crimes.'

The Inquiry reported in February 1999 and memorably said that:

> The conclusions to be drawn from the evidence in connection with the investigation of Stephen Lawrence's racist murder are clear. There is no

doubt but that there were fundamental errors. The investigation was marred by a combination of professional incompetence, institutional racism and a failure of leadership by senior officers. A flawed MPS review failed to expose these inadequacies. The second investigation could not salvage the faults of the first investigation.

(para. 46.1)

The 'professional incompetence' included a lack of direction and organisation in the hours after the murder, little or no pursuit of the suspects, insensitive treatment of both the Lawrence family and Duwayne Brooks, inadequate processing of intelligence, ill-thought out surveillance and inadequate searches. At least as damningly, if not more so, the Inquiry concluded that incompetence could not alone account for the failure of the Metropolitan Police. Rather, it suggested that the very fact that the victim was black led directly to less competent behaviour on the part of officers, in particular, with regard to their actions at the scene of the crime, in connection with family liaison, the treatment of Duwayne Brooks and in the use of inappropriate and offensive language. The Service, the Inquiry suggested, was 'institutionally racist'. This it defined (para. 6.34) as:

> The collective failure of an organisation to provide an appropriate and professional service to people because of their colour, culture or ethnic origin. It can be seen or detected in processes, attitudes and behaviour which amount to discrimination through unwitting prejudice, ignorance, thoughtlessness, and racist stereotyping which disadvantage minority ethnic people.

The Inquiry made 70 recommendations which covered: the monitoring and assessment of police performance; the reporting and recording of racist incidents and crimes; the investigation and prosecution of racist crime; family liaison; the treatment of victims and witnesses; first aid; training; employment, discipline and complaints; stop and search; and recruitment and retention. These recommendations amounted 'to the most extensive programme of reform in the history of the relationship between the police and ethnic minority communities' (Bowling and Phillips, 2002: 16). At the centre of the recommendations was a proposed Ministerial Priority for the police to seek to 'increase trust and confidence in policing among minority ethnic communities'.

The vast majority of the Inquiry's recommendations were accepted by the Home Office (56 were accepted in full, five in part and seven were referred to the Law Commission for further examination) and the Home Secretary published an action plan for their implementation and has subsequently published two Annual Reports detailing the progress that has been made. The climate of policing has changed since Lawrence. The HMIC *Thematic Inspection on Police and Community Relations* (1999a: 9), for example, found evidence 'on this inspection that many officers partly due to publicity around Sir William Macpherson's Inquiry have race issues in the forefront of their minds'. However, the thematic also reported 'that whilst a number of forces are at the cutting edge of progress in this field, the approach by a large section of the police service is less than satisfactory' (HMIC, 1999a: 3). Though the pace of change within the police service may be relatively slow, the Lawrence case did have an appreciable impact on the political climate. As Reiner (2000: 211) notes, 'the Macpherson Report . . . has transformed the terms of the political debate about black people and criminal justice . . . what had not [previously] featured in public awareness and political debate was the disproportionate rate at which black people suffered as victims of crime'. In this, the Macpherson Inquiry achieved something that Scarman hadn't. Moreover, as Bowling and Phillips (2002: 18) note:

> Where Scarman was hesitant on the question of accountability, Macpherson was strident. Since the Lawrence Inquiry had concluded that the failings of the police were systemic and the result of insufficient accountability, it recommended the introduction of lay oversight into all areas of police work, and the creation of a fully independent complaints system. Crucially, the Inquiry recommended bringing the police into the ambit of race relations law, a proposal that had been roundly rejected two decades earlier.

The Crime and Disorder Act 1998

In the aftermath of the murder of Stephen Lawrence, the then Home Secretary, Michael Howard, had rejected calls to introduce a new criminal offence of 'racial violence' arguing that 'all violent crimes, regardless of motivation, can already be dealt with properly under existing legislation' (*Hansard*, HC Deb, vol. 235, col. 32, 11 January 1994). The Labour Party took a different view and in their 1997 General Election manifesto (Labour Party, 1997) committed themselves to introducing a new offence of racial harassment and a new crime of racially motivated violence. In the event, the Crime and Disorder Act 1998 introduced 'racially aggravated offences'. Racial aggravation is defined as occurring when 'at the time of committing the offence, or immediately before or after doing so, the offender demonstrates towards the victim of the offence hostility based on the victim's membership (or presumed membership) of a racial group' or where 'the offence is motivated (wholly or partly) by hostility towards members of a racial group based on their membership of that group' (see Malik, 1999 for a discussion).

As we will see in greater detail in Chapter 5, the Labour Party made it clear in its pre-election documents that community safety and crime prevention were to be key elements in its criminal justice strategy once elected. There was a manifesto commitment to implement the Morgan Committee recommendations (Labour Party, 1997). In fact, what was included in the Crime and Disorder Bill was a variant on the Morgan proposals, the compromise being a provision to give local authorities *and* the police new duties to develop statutory partnerships to help prevent and reduce crime.

The Crime and Disorder Act received Royal Assent in July 1998 and, in addition to placing a statutory duty on chief police officers and local authorities, in co-operation with police authorities, probation committees and health authorities to formulate and implement a 'strategy for the reduction of crime and disorder in the area', it requires them to:

- carry out a review of the levels and patterns of crime and disorder in the area (i.e. what is now generally referred to as an 'audit');
- prepare an analysis of the results of that review;
- publish in the area a report of that analysis; and
- obtain the views on that report of persons or bodies in the area (including police authorities, probation and health and any others prescribed by the Home Secretary) whether by holding public meetings or otherwise.

The final element in the Act which is of particular relevance here is s. 17, which imposes on all local authorities a duty 'to exercise its various functions with due regard to the likely effect of the exercise of those functions on, and the need to do all that it reasonably can to prevent, crime and disorder in its area'. The consultation paper preceding the new legislation, *Getting to Grips with Crime*, described this new duty in the following manner: 'The proposals are not about requiring local government to deliver a major new service, or to take on substantial new burdens. Their aim is to give the vital work of preventing crime a major new focus across a very wide range of local services. . . . It is a matter of putting crime and disorder considerations at the heart of decision-making' (Home Office, 1997b: 6).

Under New Labour, the idea of 'joining up' has become a key organising idea in how social policy should be designed in response to the challenge posed by contemporary levels of crime and disorder. There are two fairly simple ideas at the heart of this formulation. First, there is the assumption – supported by a wealth of rigorous academic research – that the problems that the government has to tackle are multidimensional in character (Farrington, 1996). Whatever the problem – unemployment, poverty, crime, social exclusion – its causes are various and unlikely to fall solely within the remit of one government department or to be amenable to a single 'solution'. The second assumption, which follows logically from the first, is that the responses to these problems need, equally, to be multidimensional and multi-agency in character. Community safety is a good example.

As an approach, community safety has three key elements. It tends to be localised, to have a broad focus on social problems beyond simply crime and disorder and to be delivered via 'partnership' (Crawford, 1998). The Crime and Disorder Act 1998 reforms raise a host of issues for policing, and how it is to be delivered (for a review see Newburn, 2002b). Perhaps the most important – even though it is not a simple or direct consequence of the Act – concerns the implications for the 'role' of the police in the delivery of 'policing'. Crucially, it appears that the logic of the Crime and

Disorder Act 1998 is such that, in tandem with other changes that are taking place in the United Kingdom, local policing is set to become increasingly pluralised. There are a number of reasons for this. First, it is the case that the 1998 Act places a significantly increased emphasis on the identification of local problems and local responses to them. Second, it encourages local choice and is likely therefore to stimulate competition. Third, it explicitly encourages partnerships between public, private and municipal providers and, additionally, 'Best Value' requirements will further reinforce this 'marketisation' of criminal justice. Perhaps crucially in this regard, Best Value requires reviews of service provision to be undertaken according to what are known as the 'Four Cs': *challenge* why and how a service is being provided; invite *comparison* with others' performance across a range of relevant indicators, taking into account the views of both service users and potential suppliers; *consult* with local taxpayers, service users and the wider business community in the setting of new performance targets; and embrace fair *competition* as a means of securing efficient and effective services. Together, therefore, the Crime and Disorder Act 1998 and Best Value not only make explicit the impossibility of a 'police solution' to policing, they are likely to stimulate competition and change.

The 'plural' nature of the provision of policing and security is increasingly clear in the United Kingdom early in the twenty-first century. This pluralisation raises a number of questions about the nature and delivery of services. For government, however, one of the most pressing has been the issue of the governance of security networks. Numerous authors have already given some attention to the question of how such networks might be governed (see, for example, Jones and Newburn, 1998; Blair, 1998; Johnson, 2000; Loader, 2001). Of all these, it is the case put forward by Ian Blair that has received the greatest discussion. Focusing on the opportunities provided by the Crime and Disorder Act 1998, Blair argued that plural policing and, in particular, plural patrolling, should be provided within what he calls a 'police-compliant system', i.e. a system in which many providers are possible, but where standards, training and accreditation would be overseen by the public police. Such views have clearly been influential, as will be clear when the latest police reform programme is discussed below. Before that, however, there has been one further review of policing in the United Kingdom that addresses similar issues and which is also set to be an important influence in years to come: the review of policing in Northern Ireland conducted by the Chris Patten.

The Patten Inquiry

The Independent Commission on Policing in Northern Ireland (the Patten Inquiry) was set up as part of the Good Friday Agreement (10 April 1998). The Inquiry first met in June 1998, and reported in September 1999 (Patten, 1999). The Good Friday Agreement stated that:

The participants [in the negotiations] believe it essential that policing
structures and arrangements are such that the police service is professional,
effective and efficient, fair and impartial, free from partisan political control;
accountable, both under the law for its actions and to the community it
serves; representative of the society it polices, and operates within a coherent
and co-operative criminal justice system, which conforms with human
rights norms.

(para. 1.9)

Taking account of these principles, the Commission's role was to examine
policing in Northern Ireland and to make proposals for future policing
structures and arrangements, including means of encouraging widespread community support.

There is not the space here to consider the Inquiry's recommendations
in detail. Rather, it is those on accountability that have perhaps the clearest relevance to policing policy more broadly. The Inquiry recommended
a radical overhaul of accountability structures. At the heart of this was the
recommended introduction of a Police Ombudsman and a new Policing
Board (not *Police* Board) to replace the largely discredited Police
Authority, whose role would be to supervise the broad range of issues in
policing and the 'contributions that people and organizations other than
the police can make towards public safety'. Most notably, the Inquiry
examined the so-called principle of 'constabulary' or 'operational independence' and suggested that 'operational responsibility' was a more
useful and appropriate term. The Inquiry went on:

Operational responsibility means that it is the Chief Constable's right and
duty to take operational decisions, and that neither the government nor
the Policing Board should have the right to direct the Chief Constable as to
how to conduct an operation. It does not mean, however, that the Chief
Constable's conduct of an operational matter should be exempted from
inquiry or review after the event by anyone. That should never be the case.
But the term 'operational independence' suggests that it might be.

(para. 6.21)

Beneath the Policing Board should be established District Policing
Partnership Boards (DPPB) as a committee of the District Council with a
majority elected membership. In particular, it was envisaged that these
Boards would have responsibility for promoting partnership of community
and police in the collective delivery of community safety. Perhaps most radically in this regard the Inquiry recommended that District Councils should
have the power to contribute an amount initially up to the equivalent of a
rate of 3p in the pound towards the improved policing of the district. This
could enable DPPBs to purchase additional services from the police or
other statutory agencies, or indeed from the private sector. Critics suggested that this would be exploited in such a way as to enable services
involving, or even controlled by, paramilitaries to be purchased by DPPBs.

Though by no means enacted in full in Northern Ireland (McEvoy et al., 2002), and unlikely to be enacted on the mainland in the near future given the police reform programme that is underway, nonetheless the Patten Inquiry outlined an approach to policing and to police accountability that has the potential to transform policing in England and Wales in important ways, and may yet be seen as a model for reform in the future.

Police reform programme

As was noted above, when New Labour came to power in 1997 it was widely expected, and rumoured, that the new Home Secretary, Jack Straw, would seek to undertake major reform of policing. It is not clear why such reform did not occur, though there is much evidence of previous reform attempts being successfully resisted by the police service (Jones and Newburn, 1997). At the beginning of the second Labour term, Straw's successor, David Blunkett, announced that he planned to set up a Standards Unit for the police along the lines of a similar unit that had been established during his time in the Education Department. The core objective of the Unit was said to be to identify and disseminate best practice in the prevention, detection and apprehension of crime in all forces in order to reduce crime and disorder as well as the fear of crime. Its remit was to:

- work with forces and basic command units (BCUs) to ensure the most effective use of intelligence, detection and successful prosecution procedures;
- identify BCUs or forces performing below their best, based on HMIC reports, statistical information or particular cases of concern;
- engage directly with the BCU or force to establish the nature of the problems, the extent to which best practice may be lacking and the remedial action required;
- engage similarly with other local agencies to ensure their effective contribution, including through Crime and Disorder Reduction Partnerships, where it is apparent that this is the key to police success in tackling crime and disorder at force level and below; and
- draw validated best practice from HMIC, National Police Training, the Crime Reduction College and other agencies, spread its use through local engagement, and identify for professional evaluation any new examples or techniques it comes across.

The Home Secretary summarised the purpose of the Unit as being to:

> Identify where good practice is working and work out where and how standards can be raised by spreading best practice. The heart of its task will be to identify and remove the barriers to success, identify solutions and help forces cut down on bureaucracy. It is not about publishing league tables or

'naming and shaming'. It is about providing real, practical help based on what works, through tailored and targeted operational training.

In addition to the Standards Unit (PSU), he let it be known that a White Paper containing proposals for reform of various aspects of the police service would also shortly be published.[1] Released in early December 2001, the White Paper, *Policing a New Century: A Blueprint for Reform* (Home Office, 2001) focused on police performance, police numbers, bureaucracy and 'red tape', pay and conditions, occupational health, and the possible introduction of community support officers and accredited organisations to undertake patrol activities and tackle low-level crime. The major proposals contained in the White Paper are summarised in Figure 4.1.

The White Paper was followed by the Police Reform Act, passed in the summer of 2002. The Act introduced an Annual Policing Plan, provided powers to promote consistency across police forces through the introduction of statutory codes of practice, introduced new powers to require police forces to take remedial action where they are judged to be inefficient or ineffective by HMIC and strengthened police authorities' powers to suspend or terminate the contract of a chief constable. The Act introduced 'Community Support Officers' and created new arrangements for the accreditation of civilian neighbourhood and street wardens and other members of the so-called 'extended police family'.

The reform programme now underway builds on, and significantly extends, the managerialist thrust of many of the reforms set in train during the 1990s. At the heart of the latest changes lies a concern with police performance and accountability. This was illustrated most recently in what became known as the 'street crimes initiative'. Recorded crime statistics had shown a 13 per cent rise in street crime in 2000–01, and further rises in 2001–02 appeared to generate a high level of concern within government that, despite repeated reforms and increased investment, the police service were failing in this crucial area of crime reduction. The response was as dramatic as it was unusual. There was, in effect, direct government intervention in local policing strategies. A 'summit' on street crime involving politicians and police representatives was held in Downing Street and, subsequently, a cross-government initiative was announced that involved the identification of the ten forces in which the greatest street crime problems existed, and which would be the focus of attention in the coming months. For the following six months these ten forces provided weekly crime figures to a designated government minister.[2] Considerable extra resources, £31 million in all, were devoted to enhanced police operations within those forces, and a range of new initiatives, including video ID parades, a 'premium' CPS service to speed-up appearances in court and the funding of extra prison places for young offenders, were set in train to attempt to meet the Prime Minister's promise to have street crime 'under control by September' [2002] (*Police Review*, 26 July 2002). By October, the Home Office was announcing success, with the number of offences

1. Improvements to police leadership:
    - improvements to selection and training of senior officers;
    - possible increase in delegation to BCU level;
    - the development of the standards unit, a national policing plan, and a national policing forum.

2. The overhaul of police training at all levels:
    - increased training and support for BCU commanders;
    - development of a national competency framework.

3. Improvements to detection and conviction rates:
    - establishment of the National Centre for Policing Excellence;
    - introduction of civilian senior investigating officers;
    - implementation of the National Intelligence Model.

4. Introduction of police support staff with powers to carry out many of the functions in the custody suite and elsewhere:
    - the use of case managers and support staff to interviews suspects, take statements, process and document prisoners, including finger printing and DNA testing, security evidence and exhibits, preparing case files for the CPS, investigating bail applications;
    - provision of powers to gaolers (civilian detention officers) regarding search and use of reasonable force.

5. Introduction of police support staff with powers to enable them to carry out a basic patrol function:
    - the introduction of community support officers, under the formal direction and control of the chief officer, to provide a visible presence in the community;
    - the accreditation, by the police, of other community safety organisations, including private security, as part of the extended policy family;
    - the extension of limited powers to community support officers and accredited organisations.

6. Reform of police pay and conditions of service:
    - reform of overtime, rest day and public holiday working;
    - increases to starting salaries;
    - measures to aid recruitment and retention;
    - changes to the rules governing ill-health retirement.

7. Strengthening crime and disorder partnerships (CDRPs), particularly to support developments in the extended police faimly:
    - closer linking of the work of CDRPs and Drug Action Teams;
    - development of policing priority areas.

Figure 4.1:   The White Paper: *Policing a New Century*

apparently having dropped by 16 per cent since the initiative began in April 2002. According to the Home Secretary: 'Much of what has been done through the street crime initiative has been about step by step practical improvements; better working between police and CPS, improved facilities for victims and witnesses, video ID parades that cut delays. These sometimes small steps have meant real improvements – a greater proportion of suspects charged and taken to court and fewer out on bail to re-offend' (Home Office press release, 14 October 2002). Although unstated by the Home Secretary, it seems rather that the street crimes initiative was primarily about the continued struggle between central government and chief constables over the management and direction of police performance. In this case, considerable control in an unusually hands-on manner was exercised by central government, and by the Prime Minister in particular. The acquiescence of chief constables, to the extent it existed, was encouraged, as so often, with the promise, and delivery, of extra resources.

In this manner, the police reform programme has further centralised control over British policing. Police authorities have always been the poor relation in the tripartite structure for the governance of the police introduced by the Police Act 1964; the triangle was always more isosceles than equilateral. This position was reinforced by the increasingly interventionist stance taken by the Home Office since that time, and by the increasing power of chief constables, especially as exercised collectively through ACPO. The managerialist reforms introduced by the PMCA sought to enhance the role of police authorities and, to a degree, did so. If anything, however, New Labour has been even more centralising than its Tory predecessors. The direct involvement of the Prime Minister and colleagues in the street crimes initiative, the Police Reform Act, the creation of the PSU, and the issuing of the first National Policing Plan in November 2002 are illustrative, on the one hand, of New Labour's view that the police service is inefficient and in need of modernising and, on the other, its unwillingness to invest real responsibility in local police authorities.

Conclusion

The day-to-day practice and the public face of policing in Britain have changed significantly in the past 30 years. The escalation of official crime rates up until the mid to late 1990s and the precipitous decline in public faith in the police, particularly in the 1980s, coincided with reformist governments determined to overhaul public services, particularly by applying private-sector management strategies and increasing competition through privatisation. Beginning in the 1980s and gathering pace since, the twin prongs of centralisation and managerialism have been key themes in contemporary policing.

It is in the area of policing that what has been referred to as 'market-based criminal justice' (McLaughlin and Muncie, 1993) in England and Wales has perhaps been most visible over the past two decades. The bipartisan consensus that existed, certainly up to the mid-1970s and perhaps to the end of the decade, was abandoned by a 'law and order'-espousing Conservative government that poured significant resources into policing in the hope that this would have a noticeable impact on crime rates. Not only were crime rates not lowered, however, but they continued to rise at an ever increasing rate. The party of law and order manifestly failed to increase the general populace's sense of safety and security and the 1979 manifesto promise to 'spend more on fighting crime whilst we economise elsewhere' started to look like a fairly unsound investment. They appeared quick to blame the police for failing to deliver, though other favourite folk devils were also invoked to explain why crime continued to increase. One of the enduringly popular scapegoats was always the 'permissive society' (Newburn, 1991); Norman Tebbit, for example, suggesting that the aetiology of crime could be found in 'the post-war funk which gave birth to the permissive society, which in turn generates today's violent society' (quoted in Rawlings, 1992: 43).

By the mid-1980s, the police had lost their apparent immunity from the managerial imperatives that were being imposed on the rest of the public sector. From about 1982–83 the government began to pursue its Financial Management Initiative, using private sector management methods to impose market disciplines upon the police. During the 1980s, Her Majesty's Inspectorate of Constabulary gradually increased its financial scrutiny of individual forces and, by the late 1980s, the Audit Commission began to investigate not only the financing of the police, but also its organisation and management. This process continued into the 1990s with the Sheehy Inquiry and the Police and Magistrates' Courts Act 1994. In the event, direct privatisation of policing functions has been more of a threat than a reality. Nonetheless, the mixed economy of policing is now with us. The private security industry is huge and expanding quickly (Jones and Newburn, 1998). Closed-circuit television has, since the mid-1980s, been growing at an extraordinary rate, and is now present in the majority of town centres (Norris et al., 1998; Newburn, 2001).

Increasing managerialism has been accompanied by a process of growing centralisation of control over the police. This process has gathered pace in the twenty-first century with the interventionist New Labour administration attempting to micro-manage policing both from the Home Office and from Downing Street. The police are being pulled in a number of directions simultaneously. There are centralising and globalising pressures that are stretching policing organisations up to, and beyond, state boundaries, side by side with localising tendencies that increase the emphasis on small-scale units of policing. Managerialism itself reflects this, being able both to stress the potential economies of scale achievable through the creation of larger and larger forces, as well as the suggested organisational benefits of devolved budgets and management to basic command unit (BCU) level. The National Policing Plan (Home Office, 2002b) requires police forces to work flexibly across geographical and institutional boundaries whilst also outlining the work that the PSU will be undertaking in experimenting with further devolution of responsibilities to BCUs.

These pressures on public policing are no doubt set to continue. Indeed, there are those who believe that we are witnessing a sea-change in the organisation of policing. Thus, Bayley and Shearing (1996) have recently argued that: 'modern democratic countries like the United States, Britain and Canada have reached a watershed in the evolution of their system of crime control and law enforcement. Future generations will look back on our era as a time when one system of policing ended and another took its place' (but see Jones and Newburn, 2002 for a critical response). It is certainly the case that contemporary policing appears both more diverse and more fragmented. The language of 'community', of 'partnership' and the apparently remorseless expansion of surveillance and private security are leading to a gradual process of redefinition of public policing in the United Kingdom. The increasing talk about, and visibility of, the 'extended police family' raises both the functional questions of who does what (and, more particularly, what do the police do) and issues of accountability and governance (who regulates and controls what policing bodies do). This remains the area in which the big debates in the future of policing will occur.

Notes

1. At the same time, a police reform website was launched with the aim of encouraging dialogue between ministers and officers. This can be found at www.policereform.gov.uk.
2. Avon and Somerset (Baroness Blackstone); Greater Manchester (Lord Falconer); Lancashire (Hazel Blears); Merseyside (Yvette Cooper); Metropolitan Police (John Denham); Nottinghamshire (Ruth Kelly); South Yorkshire (Stephen Twigg); Thames Valley (Barbara Roche); West Midlands (Lord Rooker); and West Yorkshire (Harriet Harman).

Chapter 5

Crime prevention and community safety

The primary reason for following a chapter on policing with a chapter on crime prevention is that, as Crawford (1998: 30) notes, 'an understanding of crime prevention is intrinsically linked to the history of modern policing'. There are a number of ways in which this is so. First, as we saw in Chapter 3, crime prevention has generally been considered to be one of the key functions of the police since the formation of the Metropolitan Police at the beginning of the nineteenth century. The second reason is that changes in modern policing have had a significant impact on what is understood by crime prevention. Despite the centrality of crime prevention to the mandate of the new police in the early nineteenth century, it was not until the 1970s and 1980s in Britain that crime prevention became a prominent part of central government criminal justice policy – and even then it was largely at the level of rhetoric rather than practice. The focus of this chapter is, therefore, largely on the period since the late 1970s and upon the increasing emphasis that has been placed by successive governments on crime preventive strategies, culminating in the central place accorded to 'community safety' in the Crime and Disorder Act 1998.

The 'rise' of crime prevention represents, according to some, a paradigm shift in criminal justice (Tuck, 1988). The emerging paradigm emphasises 'partnership', 'community' and 'prevention', and in doing so places decreasing emphasis upon the role of formal criminal justice agencies and on the power of the 'sovereign state' to solve the problem of crime (Garland, 1996): 'In contemporary appeals to "community" and "partnerships", crime control is no longer conceived of as the sole duty of the professional police officer or other criminal justice agents. Rather, it is becoming more fragmented and dispersed throughout state institutions, private organisations and the public. Responsibility for the crime problem, according to current governmental strategies, is now everyone's. It is shared property' (Crawford, 1997: 25).

Defining crime prevention

As is standard practice on these occasions (Graham and Bennett, 1995; Gilling, 1997; Crawford, 1998), we need to begin by briefly defining our terms. There are a number of different ways of classifying crime prevention initiatives or approaches. We will briefly consider two here. The first distinguishes primary, secondary and tertiary activities; the second separates 'situational' from 'social' crime prevention. Primary prevention generally refers to action that is targeted at a general population and which aims to prevent (crime) before it occurs. Secondary prevention is action targeted at a more specific 'at risk' population. Finally, tertiary prevention tends to be targeted at known offenders in order to reduce offending and/or the harms associated with offending (Brantingham and Faust, 1976).

The best known, and most widely used of all the means of distinguishing models of crime prevention, is that between 'situational' and 'social' approaches. One of the main proponents of 'situational' crime prevention, erstwhile Head of the Home Office Research and Planning Unit, Ron Clarke has suggested that:

> It refers to a pre-emptive approach that relies, not on improving society or its institutions, but simply on reducing opportunities for crime. . . . Situational prevention comprises opportunity-reducing measures that are (1) directed at highly specific forms of crime, (2) that involve the management, design or manipulation of the immediate environment in as specific and permanent way as possible (3) so as to increase the effort and risks of crime and reduce the rewards as perceived by a wide range of offenders.
>
> (Clarke, 1992: 4)

As Clarke himself has pointed out, situational prevention owes a major theoretical debt both to Oscar Newman's theory of defensible space (Newman, 1972) and to the notion of crime prevention through environmental design (Jeffrey, 1971). It was Newman's view that a link could be demonstrated between high-rise public sector housing and increased crime rates. The design of the buildings was such that residents were discouraged from looking after and protecting them. He went on to specify aspects of design, such as unsupervised access points, that contribute to levels of crime. Opportunities for crime could be reduced by correcting such design faults.

Critics of situational prevention tend to view it as a superficial response to what they regard as the more 'fundamental' causes of crime, such as poverty, poor housing, unemployment and inadequate education and parenting. As Weatheritt has put it, 'on this view, it is not the physical environment which needs to be manipulated, but rather the social conditions and psychological dispositions that create offenders in the first place. . . . What is needed, therefore, is programmes of action which will help change people's attitudes to offending, encourage respect for law and reduce the wish to commit crimes' (1986: 57). By contrast, then, 'social' crime prevention can be linked to control theory which focuses on the informal controls that are held to inhibit offending behaviour most of the time. Social crime prevention is a set of programmes for maintaining and reinforcing informal social controls and social bonds – it is 'concerned with affecting social processes' (Crawford, 1998: 17). To the extent that such programmes enable 'communities' to regulate themselves more effectively, they also form part of what is sometimes referred to as 'community-based crime prevention' (Hope and Shaw, 1998), a sub-category of social crime prevention concerned with the conditions within communities which influence offending. Such programmes tend to combine both situational and social measures to promote crime prevention, fear reduction or what has more recently been referred to as 'community safety'. Crawford (1998: 19) offers a general graphic classification of approaches to crime prevention.

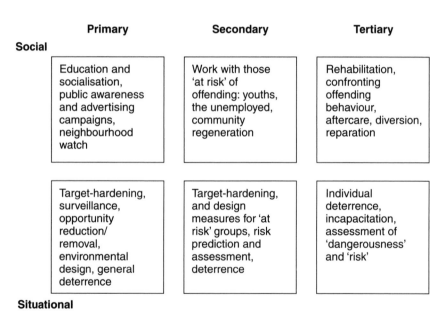

	Primary	Secondary	Tertiary
Social	Education and socialisation, public awareness and advertising campaigns, neighbourhood watch	Work with those 'at risk' of offending: youths, the unemployed, community regeneration	Rehabilitation, confronting offending behaviour, aftercare, diversion, reparation
	Target-hardening, surveillance, opportunity reduction/ removal, environmental design, general deterrence	Target-hardening, and design measures for 'at risk' groups, risk prediction and assessment, deterrence	Individual deterrence, incapacitation, assessment of 'dangerousness' and 'risk'
Situational			

Figure 5.1:   A process/target two-dimensional typology of crime prevention
Source: Crawford (1998:19).

The rebirth of crime prevention

As Gilling (1997) notes, although crime prevention – broadly conceived – has long historical antecedents, for the bulk of the nineteenth and twentieth centuries there was relatively little official interest in harnessing and managing crime prevention activities in the community. On the contrary, for much of that time 'there was a pervasive belief that the new criminal justice institutions would prevent crime alone' (1997: 71). Indeed, as we saw, for example, in relation to police history in the last chapter, promoting such a view was a key element in establishing the legitimacy of criminal justice institutions. It was in large part the increasing visibility of the cracks in such an argument that led to the growing emphasis on crime prevention and, more particularly, on 'appeals to community' (Crawford, 1997) in official criminal justice policy more generally.

The cracks in the criminal justice edifice were numerous. First, the assumption – widely held – that improving social and economic conditions in post-War society would lead to diminishing levels of crime was increasingly hard to sustain by the late 1970s. Second, the belief that the criminal justice system (indeed, the state generally) could be relied upon to control crime if only the right methods and level of resources were provided was also shown to be unfounded. As we have seen in relation to the prison, by this time belief in the rehabilitative qualities of custodial punishment had largely disappeared. The 'optimism of the late-1950s, that the system could be adapted to control crime, initially gave way to crisis management, as measures such as the suspended sentence, parole and community service were designed to take some pressure off our bulging prisons, and latterly melted into a pessimism that "nothing works"' (Gilling, 1997: 75). As Crawford (1998) notes, this pessimism led to a shift within criminology away from a focus on the offender and towards the offence.

It was against this background that what Gilling (1997) refers to as 'unfocused crime prevention' gained ground. This form of 'primary' crime prevention involved a generalised appeal targeted at the general population. This he traces to the late 1950s and campaigns involving both government and the insurance industry encouraging the public to protect their property. It was still some distance, however, from assuming the status of a 'policy'. In 1960, the then Home Secretary, R.A. Butler, established the Cornish Committee on the Prevention and Detection of Crime, and in 1963 the Home Office established the National Crime Prevention Centre at Stafford for training specialist police officers. The Cornish Committee reported in 1965 (Home Office, 1965b) and in its report acknowledged the potential role of the wider community in the prevention of crime. In relation to the formal criminal justice system it recommended the appointment of specialist crime prevention officers – indeed, departments – within police forces, and that a much more professional approach was needed in respect of the publicity material used by the police (see Chapter 3). It also recommended the establishment of crime prevention panels as a means of building relationships between the police and other organisations with a role to play in the prevention of crime. A Circular from the Home Office recommended to forces that such panels should be set up, and almost 60 were in existence by the end of the decade. The panels have no formal status and have generally been chaired by the police. Their primary purpose is to consider crime prevention proposals and to help in the process of publicising campaigns and initiatives aimed at improving security measures. They have tended to focus fairly narrowly on physical security (Gladstone, 1980). The Cornish Committee also recommended the establishment of a Standing Committee on Crime Prevention and such a Committee was set up in 1966, and began publishing the journal *Crime Prevention News* in 1969.

There was, as Gilling observes, an institutional framework for crime prevention by the 1970s 'even if it did not amount to very much' (1997: 79). By the end of the decade, the situation had changed markedly. In part, this was a consequence of the limitations of the crime control capacity of the criminal justice system becoming increasingly evident. Thus, in relation to policing, for example, research had shown that traditional methods of policing – especially beat patrol – were unlikely to lead to successful detection of crime. Moreover, by the early 1980s, research – including the British Crime Survey – was showing how much crime simply went unnoticed by the police and how little crime actually resulted in successful prosecution in court. The logical conclusion from this was that the formal criminal justice system could not control crime, no matter how efficient or well-resourced it might be.

Other research emanating from the Home Office Research and Planning Unit at around this time strongly influenced the trajectory of crime-prevention policy in Britain. Informed by rational choice theory, as was suggested above, 'situational crime prevention' sought to reduce opportunities for crime by analysing the circumstances of particular offences, and then implementing and testing particular approaches. Though situational prevention offered the possibility of a more positive criminal justice policy, a number of barriers remained. Key among these were 'implementation' and 'politics' (Gilling, 1997). Although, in theory, preventative strategies could be identified, getting organisations to work jointly to implement them successfully could not be taken for granted (see Hope and Murphy, 1985). Moreover, persuading politicians and opinion-formers – particularly within the criminal justice establishment – that a new approach to tackling crime was necessary was also far from straightforward. However, a number of factors served to bring situational prevention closer to the core of the criminal justice agenda.

According to officials within the Home Office, the coming of the Conservative government in 1979 made something of a difference to the nature of criminal justice policy-making. Crucially, however, it was suggested that the arrival of a new Permanent Secretary, Sir Brian Cubbon, was key. According to the then Deputy Under-Secretary for the Criminal Department:

> The original emphasis on crime prevention was very much [his] own
> initiative. . . . Originally this was [the] Permanent Secretary looking for and
> finding a new theme to develop in the Office irrespective of the political

administration. It wasn't until quite a bit later on that the political
administration seized on it as an attractive political programme.

(quoted in Jones et al., 1994: 96)

The Head of the Research and Planning Unit at the time, Mary Tuck, confirmed this, suggesting that debate about crime prevention policy had
been going on since at least the mid-1970s. During the 1980s, the focus of
attention began to move, slowly, from purely situational approaches to a
combination of situational and social crime prevention initiatives.
According to Home Office officials, William Whitelaw did not see a major
role for crime prevention, and was only marginally involved in the development of policy, though he did not interfere with it in the main (Jones
et al., 1994; see also Heal, 1991). Whitelaw's successor, Leon Brittan, was
less sceptical about crime prevention, and senior officials began to attempt
to impress upon him the potential attractiveness of new initiatives in this
area. The report of a Home Office Working Group on co-ordinating crime
prevention efforts, published in 1980, outlined a four-stage methodology
for crime prevention which, though amended, has been the dominant
method ever since. The four stages are summarised by Crawford
(1998: 36) as:

- A thorough analysis of the crime problem, 'high crime' area, or situation in which the offence occurs, in order to establish the conditions
  that need to be met for the offence(s) to be committed.
- The identification of measures which would make it more difficult or
  impossible to fulfil these conditions.
- The assessment of the practicability, likely effectiveness, and cost of
  each measure.
- The selection of the most promising measures.

In practice, two further stages have been added:

- An implementation process.
- The subsequent monitoring and evaluation of the initiatives undertaken.

The movement of crime prevention toward the centre of the agenda got
a further boost as a result of a speech given by the Lord Chief Justice in
March 1982, in which he pointed to the potentially important role of
institutions outside the criminal justice system in attempting to stem the
continuing rise in crime rates (Laycock and Heal, 1989). His argument
was taken up by the Home Secretary, who announced the establishment
of an inter-departmental working group on crime reduction, to be
chaired by the permanent secretary Sir Brian Cubbon, and a conference
at the Police Staff College at Bramshill, then under the direction of
Kenneth Newman, both of whom were in sympathy with the philosophy
of crime prevention.

In addition to these factors, the police generally were more sympathetic at this time to the idea of collaboration in crime prevention than they had perhaps previously been. In part, this was the result of spectacular 'failures' such as Swamp 81 in Brixton, but also the more general perceived failure to impact on crime despite the heavy investment in resource terms made by government in the early 1980s. The consequence of this 'failure' saw the imposition of the government's FMI on the police, and with it the threat that further increases in resources would be tied to efficiency. In addition, as we have seen, there were those within the service who were attempting to establish a new, more community-focused model of policing, and individuals like John Alderson espoused a philosophy of policing which, though distinct from some of the crime prevention messages emanating from the Home Office, was not incompatible.

The key difference between the policing philosophy of people like John Alderson, and indeed Kenneth Newman when he moved from Bramshill to the Metropolitan Police, and situational crime prevention, was the differing emphasis each placed on the social and economic causes of crime, and the role of the 'community' in responding to it. As Gilling (1997: 86) notes, 'in the context of the early 1980s, the vision of social crime prevention implicit in much of the community policing rhetoric served less as a block on progress than as an indicator of a contest that lay ahead'.

The profile of crime prevention within the Home Office was reinforced with the establishment of the Crime Prevention Unit and the mutation of the Standing Committee on Crime Prevention into the Standing Conference. Crucially, a Circular on crime prevention addressed to police, probation, education, social services and local authorities was drafted by an inter-departmental group during 1983 and released as 8/84. The Circular was hugely influential and was described some years later by one leading commentator as 'the most comprehensive statement of British policy on crime prevention' (Waller, 1989: 25). The advice contained in the Circular spanned both situational and social approaches to the prevention of crime. Heavily influenced by the approach associated with Ron Clarke, the Circular stated that:

> Whilst there is a need to address the social factors associated with criminal
> behaviour, and policies are continually being devised to tackle this aspect of
> the problem, these are essentially long-term measures. For the short term,
> the best way forward is to reduce through management, design or changes in
> the environment, the opportunities that exist for crime to occur.

The circular emphasised the traditional role of the police in the prevention of crime, and then went on to outline the potential contribution of other agencies: 'since some of the factors affecting crime lie outside the control or direct influence of the police, crime prevention cannot be left to them alone. Every individual citizen and all those agencies whose policies and practices can influence the extent of crime should make their contribution. *Preventing crime is a task for the whole community.*'

Though the Circular further raised the profile of situational prevention, and outlined the importance of inter-agency co-operation between the police and other agencies, it did not increase the resources available to those agencies deemed to have responsibility for such measures. Interestingly, the profile of crime prevention remained relatively low within the Home Office at this time, the first mention of the subject in a Home Office Annual Report only occurring in 1985 (Koch, 1998). Two years after the 1984 Circular, a special seminar on crime prevention was held at 10 Downing Street, chaired by the Prime Minister. The seminar placed a particularly strong emphasis on the need for the business community to support the development of crime prevention measures, and it led directly to the creation of the Ministerial Group on Crime Prevention. Following the 1987 election, the new Home Secretary, Douglas Hurd, decided to make crime prevention a major plank of policy. There had been a manifesto promise to put more resources into crime prevention, and a Minister of State, John Patten, was put in charge of developing a 'total response' to crime, and the Ministerial Group on Crime Prevention (consisting of 13 ministers) attempted to co-ordinate crime prevention initiatives between government departments.

The problem of governance

The next major step was the establishment of what was known as the Five Towns Initiative. Beginning in 1986, the initiative was to run 18 months in the first instance. The areas chosen – Bolton, Croydon, North Tyneside, Swansea and Wellingborough – were intended to represent a wide geographical spread and a range of social conditions. Each area was provided with funding for a 'co-ordinator' whose responsibility was to service a multi-agency committee overseeing crime prevention activity locally. The approach first established by the Five Towns project was extended in the Safer Cities project, which started in 1988 as part of the government's Action for Cities project (and therefore not simply about crime prevention). The Safer Cities programme was also carried out on a much broader scale than Five Towns, involving nine local authority areas in its first year, and with the ultimate aim of including 20 local projects.

It was intended to provide a more coherent approach than the Five Towns projects, focusing on the delivery of public services generally and the wider structure of society in a medium to large-sized local authority area. The primary aims of the Safer Cities programme were to reduce crime, to lessen fear of crime and 'to create safer cities where economic enterprise and community life can flourish'. Home Office funding for

Safer Cities was more substantial than that available for the Five Towns project, covering the cost of a co-ordinator and two other staff, accommodation, running costs and grant funds to support local initiatives. By the end of its first phase, an enormous range of crime prevention activities, totalling over £20 million had been established, with some evidence of a reduction in the risk of burglary in some areas (Ekblom et al., 1997). A second phase of the Safer Cities Programme was announced in 1992, with projects starting in 1994. Responsibility for the Programme was transferred from the Home Office to the Department of the Environment as part of the Single Regeneration Budget (SRB) and covered 32 towns and cities.

The Safer Cities programme was criticised for a number of reasons. First, not being tied into existing local authority structures, particularly structures for ensuring accountability, it was argued that Safer Cities suffered a 'democratic deficit' (Crawford, 1998). Second, it was criticised as a vehicle for the dissemination of government ideology (King, 1991, though see Crawford, 1998). Finally, it was criticised for its short-term orientation (Crawford, 1997). According to Crawford (1997: 33), Safer Cities represented 'a classic "trickle down" process whereby central government has sought to implant a particular model of policy formation and implementation, and to stimulate its spread through "seed-corn" funding. Despite its problematic structure and short-term project orientation it impacted on grass roots projects, as well as voluntary and statutory organisations and business, raising the profile of crime prevention and inter-agency partnerships'.

Without doubt, the best known and most widely adopted crime prevention programme in Britain has been Neighbourhood Watch (NW). NW appeared first in Britain in the early 1980s, and was promoted force-wide by the Metropolitan Police in 1983. Sir Kenneth Newman sold the initiative as something that would involve community, or neighbourhood self-help, supported and advised by the police. Neighbourhood groups would be formed to carry out informal surveillance, thereby deterring thieves through 'opportunity reduction' and providing an early warning system for the police. The spread of NW has been remarkable. Within a decade of its establishment, over five million households were covered by one of over 100,000 schemes in England and Wales (Central Statistical Office, 1994). Despite its increasing ubiquity, subsequent evaluations of NW have indicated that it is of limited impact in its primary objective of reducing crime (Rosenbaum, 1988; Bennett, 1989), and that a significant part of the reason for this lies in 'programme failure': failure by both the police and the public to implement programmes fully. The police have been central to the setting up of NW all around the country, yet generally they are not in a position to deploy sufficient resources to sustain the schemes which, without their input, quickly fall into disuse (McConville and Shepherd, 1992). Moreover, schemes tend to flourish in parts of the country which have relatively low crime rates and, consequently, such police resources as are devoted to crime prevention are diverted away from those areas where they are most needed (Laycock and Heal, 1989).

The main issue affecting, and arguably inhibiting, the development of crime prevention at this time was the unwillingness of government to task any one agency with taking lead responsibility for such measures. Interviews conducted by PSI researchers within the Home Office revealed an ambiguity about leadership (Jones et al., 1994). This was illustrated not only in Circular 8/84, but also in its successor 44/90, although there were some senior officials in the Home Office who argued that this was a deliberate policy:

> In practice we couldn't have given the Safer Cities money to the police because we would have seriously endangered our relationship with local authorities who expect to have some involvement in this area. If we gave the money instead to local authorities, that would endanger our relationship with the police. The policy is to keep all the players in play. It's a balancing act. The Home Office can't decide how it will develop, which agency will play the greatest role. We can only start things off, and act in a Machiavellian way if necessary to keep them going, to keep everyone involved, then wait and see how they develop. We can't directly control it.
>
> (quoted in Jones et al., 1994: 99)

Numerous commentators have suggested that this was merely the Home Office ducking the issue (see Crawford, 1998) with the consequence that responsibility tended to fall to the police. There were clearly also significant ideological inhibitors at play at this time; it was, as we shall see, central government reluctance to invest responsibility or resources in local government that was equally important in maintaining a lack of clarity about leadership in crime prevention. This was increasingly problematic given a certain 'dampening of enthusiasm' (Gilling, 1997: 92) for purely situational prevention and the increasing emphasis that was being placed upon a hybrid of situational and social approaches – increasingly referred to as 'community safety' – a move signalled as early as Home Office Circular 8/84. There are numerous reasons for the shifting emphasis in crime prevention. Gilling suggests that the dampening enthusiasm for situational approaches was especially visible within the research community. In addition, increasing attention was being paid to the problem of crime displacement – the possibility that hardened targets might simply prompt offenders to look for new targets rather than to desist from offending. Nonetheless, it is important not to interpret this as indicating anything more than the fact that a broader perspective on crime prevention was beginning to emerge. In spite of the interesting 'social' crime prevention projects that were running across the United Kingdom, the reality, as Crawford (1997: 34) correctly observes, was that 'the crime prevention juggernaut was being driven almost exclusively by opportunity reduction and situational approaches'.

Heal (1992) argues that the increasingly multi-agency context in which crime prevention activities were located also affected the nature of such activities. Home Office research in the early 1980s had indicated that situational methods often proved too inflexible in practice (Hope and Murphy, 1983) and did not (always) take account of the practical politics of implementation on the ground. As increasing numbers of agencies were drawn in to preventative programmes, so a more corporate approach emphasising partnership and multi-agency collaboration began to emerge. Within the Home Office, the key officials referred to above were again instrumental in moving ministers from a purely situational approach towards the hybrid model. John Patten, then Minister of State in the Home Office, went on an official visit to France and Germany to look at social crime prevention measures and decarceration initiatives. He was reportedly impressed by some of the things he witnessed, and a subsequent Green Paper, it was suggested, included some ideas imported from these visits. In the opinion of senior civil servants he was firmly nudged in the direction that the officials wished him to go. The policy-making model in operation in this case, according to several senior officials, was one in which policy is largely framed by experts and then 'sold' to ministers (Jones et al., 1994).

According to Gilling (1997), the shift towards community-based crime prevention towards the end of the 1980s also served an important ideological function for the Conservative administration. In part, he suggests, crime prevention was adopted straightforwardly for its pragmatic potential. In addition, however, with the growing evidence that the beleaguered criminal justice system did not hold the 'answer', responsibility was increasingly placed on 'the community' to take action against crime. Active citizenship, NW and a publicity campaign under the general rubric 'Crime, Together We'll Crack It' formed a central part of the strategy. 'Consequently, from the end of the 1980s, the community safety phase of crime prevention policy tended to rely upon a dual strategy, which mixed reason and ideology. First there was a concerted effort to pass the responsibility down through the community to the individual citizen, and secondly there was an attempt to locate it within multi-agency structures. The concept of partnership linked the two' (Gilling, 1997: 95).

Another important initiative was the establishment of Crime Concern. Springing from a pledge in the Conservative Party manifesto of 1987 which promised to 'build on the support of the public by establishing a national organisation to promote the best practices in local crime prevention initiatives' (Conservative Central Office, 1987: 58), it was established by the new Conservative administration, and funded initially by the Home Office. A voluntary organisation and a charity, in contrast with some of the other initiatives outlined so far, this was a project driven by senior politicians independently of officials who had taken the lead in other areas of crime-prevention policy. According to the Deputy Under-Secretary in the Home Office at the time:

The Conservative Party had worked up its proposal for a national crime prevention body which featured in the manifesto. That was generated on the political network, and the Home Office didn't have a great deal to do with it, and I'm not sure we entirely understood what was in politician's minds in putting it in the manifesto, but eventually it was given effect as Crime Concern, after quite a lot of discussion . . . about what form this national body might take.

(quoted in Jones et al., 1994: 100)

Crime Concern built on earlier experience with the National Association for the Care and Resettlement of Offenders (NACRO) – a voluntary organisation established without initial government support. By the early 1980s, its interests were broad and covered crime prevention in high-crime urban environments. Its Safe Neighbourhoods Unit launched a number of pioneering schemes, increasingly with support from both the Home Office and the Department of the Environment. Crime Concern's initial task was to attempt to improve the quality of life by stimulating crime prevention. The initial plan was to build on what was already in existence: neighbourhood watch, crime prevention panels and crime reduction programmes such as Safer Cities. Crime Concern received three years' 'pump priming' money from the Home Office, but quickly attempted to engage the co-operation of the private sector in developing good-practice models and communication networks. As one example, it quickly established a consultancy service providing crime audits for businesses and that was followed by a number of initiatives which sought to raise funding from the private sector. Early on, it outlined the areas of work in which the organisation was to concentrate its activities: youth initiatives, crime prevention panels, neighbourhood watch, local crime reduction programmes, and business and crime. Crime Concern did not become financially self-sufficient within the target period of three years, and Home Office funding was extended for a further period.

The issue of lead responsibility for crime prevention was put back on the agenda as a result of the report of the Morgan Committee – an inquiry established by the Standing Conference on Crime Prevention. Home Office Circular 44/90 had been accompanied by a booklet entitled 'Partnership in Crime Prevention', which contained examples of crime-prevention initiatives and some examples of good practice. The booklet led indirectly to establishment of the Morgan Committee, whose terms of reference were to: 'consider and monitor the progress made in the local delivery of crime prevention through the multi-agency or partnership approach, in the light of the guidance in the booklet 'Partnership in Crime Prevention' and to make recommendations for the future. The Morgan Committee's final report (Standing Conference on Crime Prevention, 1991) contained 19 major recommendations, which included:

- The introduction of a statutory responsibility on local authorities (alongside the police) for the 'stimulation of community safety and crime prevention programmes, and for progressing at a local level a multi-agency approach to community safety'.
- The establishment of a local authority co-ordinator, with administrative support wherever possible.
- More specific attention at a local level to involving businesses as a partner 'instead of regarding it solely as a possible source of funds'.
- Ensuring that police and other agencies' information systems are compatible, to aid data exhange.
- Local crime partnership should exploit the 'important resource represented by the voluntary effort'.
- The establishment of an independent standing conference with co-ordinating responsibilities.
- Government should examine how the strong focus needed at the centre could be provided by strengthening existing organisations or creating new ones.

The Morgan Committee declared their preference for the term 'community safety' over 'crime prevention'. The latter, they suggested 'is often narrowly interpreted and this reinforces the view that it is solely the responsibility of the police' whereas the former, 'is open to wider interpretation and could encourage greater participation from all sections of the community in the fight against crime' (1991: 13). The Morgan Committee were critical of what they saw as confusion at a local level, with numerous centrally funded crime prevention schemes running undue risks of overlapping with each other and consequently duplicating efforts: 'What is clearly perceived at a local level is a tendency for government departments to promote *ad hoc* initiatives, often implemented without proper consultation either with other government departments or with the local authorities' (1991: 26).

Although a decade or so earlier there had been little acceptance within local government of responsibility for crime prevention (Crawford, 1997), by the time of the Morgan Report, Community Safety Departments and Officers had become relatively commonplace within local government – at least in metropolitan areas. In 1990, the Association of Metropolitan Authorities (AMA) published a framework document in which they called for a statutory responsibility for crime prevention to be given to local councils (AMA, 1990). The AMA argued that: 'the absence of elected members from crime prevention structures may have the effect of marginalising crime prevention from local political issues. Any meaningful local structure for crime prevention must relate to the local democratic structure' (quoted in Crawford, 1997: 39). This emerging consensus between local authority representatives, much academic opinion and, most importantly, the Morgan Committee, coincided, however, with an exceedingly unsympathetic government. The Conservative government was in the run-up to a General Election, was concerned about too great an emphasis on the socio-economic bases of crime and was heavily engaged in attempting to decrease – not increase – the powers and responsibilities of local authorities.

In the aftermath of the General Election, the National Board for Crime Prevention was established, chaired by a Home Office minister (initially Michael Jack, later Charles Wardle) and including representatives from statutory and voluntary sectors and from business. There was no sign, and no likelihood, of the Morgan Committee's recommendation about the local direction of crime prevention/community safety being acted upon. Government action centred around the release of the 'Partners Against Crime' initiative in late 1994 and the subsequent reassertion of government support for the idea of 'active citizenship'. This involved increased support for neighbourhood watch, the introduction of the idea of 'walking with a purpose' and 'Street Watch', and the avowed aim of increasing by a substantial amount the number of special constables employed by police forces (the hope being to double numbers to 30,000).

In 1995, the National Board for Crime Prevention became the National Crime Prevention Agency, with a smaller and slightly less criminal justice-oriented membership. Again, it was governed by a Board chaired by a Home Office minister (this time, David Maclean). The first director of the agency had previously been Assistant Chief Constable in Sussex Police. Though the Agency sounded something like the independent body envisaged in the Morgan Report, in reality it was nothing of the sort, having neither the co-ordinating powers envisaged in that Report nor 'the agenda-setting powers of comparable national organisations in other European countries such as Sweden, France and the Netherlands' (Crawford, 1998: 41). Indeed, it appears there was some dispute within the Home Office as to appropriateness of applying the term 'agency' to the body at all.

Though accepting that the categories and historical periods are not as neat as they appear schematically, Gilling (1997) suggests that, in general terms, a number of distinct phases in the recent history of crime prevention can be identified. The first, which covered the period from the mid-1950s to the mid-1970s, was dominated by theoretically uninformed, 'unfocused' crime prevention. The situational crime prevention model then rose to prominence and dominated in large part until the mid-1980s, since when a broader, more holistic model, generally identified by the rubric 'community safety', has held sway. He argues that the 'key moment' in the history of crime prevention, was the early 1980s, when it appeared to offer politicians 'a route out of a number of blind alleys and potential crises into which the criminal justice system had been led' (1997: 104). From this point onward, however, it has increasingly been a site of political conflict in which the battle over different crime control

Table 5.1: Key developments in crime prevention in the United Kingdom, 1975–2001

The Effectiveness of Sentencing: A review of the literature	1976
Crime as Opportunity	1976
Designing Out Crime	1980
Co-ordinating Crime Prevention Efforts	1980
'Situational Crime Prevention'	1980
First British Crime Survey Report	1983
Crime Prevention Unit set up	1983
Home Office Standing Conference	1983
Home Office Circular 8/84, *Crime Prevention*	1984
First Crime Prevention Unit Paper	1985
Five Towns Initiative	1986
Gas and suicide	1988
Getting the Best out of Crime Analysis	1988
Safer Cities	1988
Crime Concern 1988	1988
First Kirkholt report, beginning of repeat victimization focus	1988
Crash helmets and motor-bike theft	1989
Home Office Circular 44/90	1990
Morgan Report	1991
Police Research Group established	1992
Single Regeneration Budget	1993
First CCTV challenge	1995
Repeat Victimization Task Force set up	1996
First issue of *International Journal of Risk, Security and Crime Prevention*	1996
National Training Organisation	1998
Home Office Research Study 187	1998
Policing and Reducing Crime Unit established	1998
Crime and Disorder Act 1998, and guidance	1998
Beating Crime	1998
Crime Reduction Programme	1999
Safety in Numbers	1999
Crime Targets Task Force	1999
Foresight Programme	1999
Calling Time on Crime	2000
The Home Office Policing and Crime Reduction Directorate	2000
Appointment of Regional Crime Directors	2000
Preparation and publication of 'toolkits' to deal with specified problems	2001

Source: Tilley (2002: 14)

agendas has been fought. Nick Tilley (2002) provides a useful tabular summary of the key developments in crime prevention since 1975 (see Table 5.1).

As Chapter 2 illustrated in relation to prisons and the use of custodial penalties, the 1990s quickly became a period in which the Home Secretary and his Shadow appeared to be engaged in competition to 'out-tough' each other. The criminal justice agenda once more became dominated by punitive rhetoric and a practical emphasis on crime control (including, *inter alia*, a sharp and sustained increase in the prison population, the introduction of new community penalties and the amendment of the Criminal Justice Act 1991). On the surface, neither the rhetoric nor the practice would appear to be compatible with continuing interest in crime prevention, particularly social or community crime prevention. Nevertheless, crime prevention continued to be a central element within contemporary crime control strategies. In addition to the continued emphasis on NW, on attempts to expand the special constabulary and the establishment of the Crime Prevention Agency, a significant new government initiative concerning closed-circuit television (CCTV) was also launched. The CCTV Challenge Competition, established in 1995, invited bids from local authorities for Home Office funding for the installation of cameras in public places. As Crawford (1997: 42) argues, the post-1993 '"punitive counter-tendency", whilst reflecting an important element within the more enduring policy frame, by no means reflects its totality'.

New Labour and community safety

> The late 1990s have seen crime prevention breaching specialist walls,
> breaking into mainstream politics and practice.
>
> (Tilley, 2002: 21)

In its pre-election publications and pronouncements, the Labour Party made it clear that community safety and crime prevention were to be key elements in its criminal justice strategy once elected. They made a manifesto commitment to implement the major recommendations of the Morgan Committee, and soon after the election published precise details of their plans, first in a consultation document (Home Office, 1997b) and then in the, then, Crime and Disorder Bill.

The degree of difference between the outgoing Conservative government and the new Labour administration in relation to community safety was well illustrated in the first paragraphs of the consultation document, *Getting to Grips with Crime*. The document opened with a discussion of the

Morgan Report and, in particular, the key strategic role of local authorities. The document stated:

> Even though the previous administration chose not to implement the Report, many of Morgan's key findings have in fact been taken on board spontaneously by partnerships all over the country, to their benefit and – most importantly – that of local communities. . . . The years which have elapsed since Morgan have seen a complete acceptance of the partnership concept at all levels of the *police service*. The service now explicitly recognises that it cannot cope with crime and disorder issues on its own. . . . The Government accepts the principle set out in Morgan that the extent, effectiveness and focus of existing local activity would be greatly improved by clear statements in law as to where responsibility for this work lies.
>
> (Home Office, 1997b: 3–5)

What it then went on to say, however, was that in its forthcoming Crime and Disorder Bill it proposed to include provisions to give local authorities *and* the police new duties to develop statutory partnerships to help prevent and reduce crime. This approach neatly side-stepped the issue of a 'lead' agency in crime prevention. The government said that it was not persuaded that the Morgan view that giving local authorities lead responsibility would be workable in practice. Its views, rather, were that the 'principles of partnership' required joint working and collective responsibility. Consequently, they proposed that responsibility should lie jointly with the chief constable and the district or unitary authority (or London borough) or, where two-tier structures still exist, with the county council.

The new structures and requirements are set out in detail in the Crime and Disorder Act which finally completed its tortuous passage through parliament in July 1998. Clauses 6–8 are key. Clause 6 places the statutory duty on chief police officers and local authorities, in co-operation with police authorities, probation committees, health authorities to formulate and implement a 'strategy for the reduction of crime and disorder in the area'. Before formulating the strategy the responsible authorities are required by the Act to:

- carry out a review of the levels and patterns of crime and disorder in the area;
- prepare an analysis of the results of that review;
- publish in the area a report of that analysis; and
- obtain the views on that report of persons or bodies in the area (including police authorities, probation and health and any others prescribed by the Home Secretary) whether by holding public meetings or otherwise.

The Act is also specific about what the strategy should contain. Not surprisingly in these managerialist times, at the top of the list comes 'objectives to be pursued by the responsible authorities' followed by 'long-term and short-term performance targets for measuring the extent to which such objectives are achieved'. Once a strategy has been formulated, it is to be published by the responsible authorities. The publication should include details of: the bodies involved in the strategy; the results of the local audit; and the objectives and performance targets. In this way it parallels in many respects the nature of local policing plans, published annually by local police authorities, as a requirement of the Police and Magistrates' Courts Act 1994 (see Chapter 4). Indeed, how local community safety strategies and local policing plans are to be fitted together locally will be of great interest. The government's consultation document suggested two important links. First, it suggested that police authorities should be one of the key agencies with which the community safety leadership group should formally collaborate in drawing up its community safety strategy (and this is enshrined in the Act). Second, it suggested that given that local policing plans are required by statute not only to take into consideration national objectives but also local needs and circumstances, the crime and disorder audit to be conducted by the leadership group might be one of the key building blocks in the local policing plan.

The emphasis on community safety in the Crime and Disorder Act 1998 is, therefore, firmly local. As yet, the government has not been particularly prescriptive about how responsible authorities should go about their job of reducing crime and disorder locally. This is somewhat in contrast to the Police and Magistrates' Courts Act 1994 in which *centralising* as well as localising tendencies were rather more visible (see Chapter 4 and Jones and Newburn, 1997). The Crime and Disorder Act 1998 places its emphasis on 'local partnerships, local needs and priorities and local audits'. Nonetheless, as has been noted in this and other chapters, one of the dominant themes in criminal justice policy in the past decade has been increased managerialism and, with that, increased oversight and control from the centre. With the setting of targets from the centre, scrutiny by HMIC, the Audit Commission and others, and appointment of Regional Crime Reduction Directors, it is clear that community safety is unlikely to be an exception to encroaching bureaucratisation and managerialism. As Phillips (2002: 179) notes:

> This is a new and fast-moving area of policy and it is impossible to predict what the future holds for the new structures established to tackle local crime reduction/community safety. It does, however, seem likely that the future will see further prescription, major auditing and inspection of local partnerships through a variety of means, including rigorous performance management. This will be complemented by guidance from the centre.

In terms of the early activities of crime and disorder partnerships, perhaps predictably, many of the early signs were mixed. Research undertaken by the Home Office (Phillips, 2002) suggested that whilst crime and disorder partnerships continued to experience many of the difficulties that had previously been identified in multi-agency activity, there were also a number of very positive signs in the working practices of the newly established 376 partnerships. Based on an in-depth study of three partnerships, the study found little evidence, for example, of the conspiratorial model of multi-agency working referred to by previous researchers as the 'police take-over' (Sampson et al., 1988). Rather, partnerships did not appear to be dominated by any one agency. That said, the reverse problem of the absence of certain agencies, and, in particular, the health authorities, has been widely noted (Audit Commission, 1999; HMIC, 2000).

The Home Office research also noted a number of ways in which sources and forms of conflict within multi-agency working were side-stepped or avoided by crime and disorder partnerships. Conflict within the auditing process was avoided in some cases by outsourcing the work to external consultants. In addition, the legislation and accompanying guidance had stressed a 'nothing ruled in, nothing ruled out' approach which also facilitated a relatively open and consensual approach. Phillips (2002: 172–3) concludes: 'there was little indication that conflict – destructive or constructive – was yet part of the landscape of partnership relations. There had been few occasions on which conflictual situations had arisen, and optimism about the partnership approach was still very much in evidence at the time.'

There is one other, final, element of the Crime and Disorder Act 1998 that deserves some attention here. The Act introduces a range of new court orders – the bulk of which are discussed in Chapter 8. One of the new orders is the 'anti-social behaviour order' (ASBO). Prior to the publication of the Bill, this proposed new order was referred to as a 'community safety order' (Home Office, 1997a). Outlining its rationale for the new order, the government said:

> Anti-social behaviour causes distress and misery to innocent, law-abiding
> people – and undermines the communities in which they live. Neighbourhood
> harassment by individuals or groups, often under the influence of alcohol or
> drugs, has often reached unacceptable levels, and revealed a serious gap in the
> ability of the authorities to tackle this social menace.

The solution proposed by the government was a court order which could be applied for by a local authority or the police, which would apply to named individuals aged over ten who had acted 'in an anti-social manner, that is to say, in a manner that caused or was likely to cause harassment, alarm or distress to one or more persons not of the same household as himself'. Originally designed as a response to the perceived problem of 'noisy neighbours', the order involves a combination of civil and criminal proceedings (granted in a magistrates' court, but requiring only the civil burden of proof). The definition of anti-social behaviour has a 'remarkably wide potential coverage' which, according to one group of distinguished commentators, would be 'bad enough if the order were of a genuinely civil nature but doubly disturbing if, as we believe, the order is a criminal disposal in substance' (Gardner et al., 1998: 26).

What is interesting about the order – particularly given its original title – is how uneasily it appears to sit with the rest of the government's policies on community safety, which are more preventative and less punitive in character. Running through the Crime and Disorder Act 1998 there is this amalgam of preventative, ameliorative and punitive elements. As Faulkner (1998: 8) describes it: 'the new government's approach to the problems of crime and justice . . . is based on prevention and support for people in difficulty, combined with the coercion of those who do not comply'. Thus, the Act introduces child curfews and ASBOs, as well as removing the principle of *doli incapax*. Even the more preventative orders, such as the parenting order and the drug treatment and testing orders, are to be enforced by severe penal sanctions in cases where other conditions have not worked. None of this is at all surprising. The mixture of prevention, populism and punishment has characterised many of the new Home Secretary's speeches during the first New Labour administration. This is perhaps best illustrated by the speech Jack Straw gave at the launch of the London Borough of Lewisham Community Safety Strategy in September 1995. This was the speech in which he railed against the 'aggressive begging of winos and addicts' and the 'squeegee merchants who wait at large road junctions to force on reticent motorists their windscreen cleaning service . . . Even where graffiti is not comprehensible or racialist in message'; he went on, 'it is often violent and uncontrolled in its violent image, and correctly gives the impression of a lack of law and order on the streets' (Anderson and Mann, 1997). The speech not only reflected much progressive thinking about community safety and the need for local leadership and partnerships, but also, in the excerpt quoted above, part of the thinking taken from Wilson and Kelling's 'Broken Windows' thesis (Wilson and Kelling, 1982). Though there was some fairly quick backtracking from elements of the speech in the days that followed, the 'populist punitiveness' (Bottoms, 1995) that inspired it was clearly visible in elements of the Crime and Disorder Act 1998.

In November 1999, the Labour government published its Crime Reduction Strategy. The Strategy announcement began by reiterating some of the tough rhetoric so beloved by the Home Secretary and Prime Minister at that time:

> The government is embarked on a crusade against crime. . . . We must, in other words, be tough on crime and tough on the causes of crime. . . . It means tough and consistent prison sentences for serious criminals, far more rigorous enforcement of community sentences and zero tolerance of anti-social behaviour.
>
> (crimereduction.gov.uk/crsdoc1.htm)

The Comprehensive Spending Review provided £400 million for the Crime Reduction Programme. The money was to be spent on a variety of crime reduction initiatives and, crucially, on the evaluation of those initiatives. The government was committed, it announced, to using 'hard evidence' as the basis for the approach to reducing crime. All police authorities and crime and disorder partnerships were required to set five-year targets, and annual milestones, for the reduction of vehicle crime, of burglary and of robbery. From 2000, information has been published not just by police force area, but by Basic Command Units. In some respects, the Crime Reduction Programme was a brave and rather optimistic strategy. Indeed, the promise that crime policy would in future be evidence-based bordered on the naïve. And so it has proved, for as the preceding and following chapters illustrate, short-term, narrowly political bases for policy-making in this arena have been no less visible in the early years of this century than they were in the final years of the last.

Conclusion

Crime prevention has, in some respects, come a long way in what is a relatively short period of time. As stated at the outset, despite the suggestion from its original Commissioners that crime prevention was one of the central functions of the Metropolitan Police, governments have only become explicitly interested in crime prevention in the past 20 years. In that time, fashions have changed and the focus has gradu-ally moved from *primary* preventative activities towards, and sometimes beyond, *secondary* prevention. Indeed, community safety is now for many the preferred term, and the use of the term has spread as fear of crime has increased, and the focus of public concern has moved increasingly towards incivility, anti-social behaviour and disorder in public (and quasi-public) places. The consequence, as Crawford (1998: 27) points out, how-ever, is that 'the institutional growth of crime prevention has served to marginalise certain issues', namely 'offending which takes place in "private spheres", behind peoples' backs, or which involve a less visible and more indirect relationship between offender and victim'.

In a related but slightly different vein, Pease (1997) has suggested that despite the significant successes in primary prevention that have been achieved, there is unlikely to be much more progress unless inducements to improve are set in place. Without such inducements, his fear is that 'primary crime prevention may fall further out of fashion, to be replaced by secondary and tertiary measures whose efficacy is much less impres-sive, and which carry with them the baggage of blame and punishment' (1997: 987). What seems certain in all this is that we are currently at an important juncture in the macro-politics of crime prevention and com-munity safety. Rising crime, increasing fear of crime and the growing appreciation of the 'limits of the sovereign state' (Garland, 1996) are leading to new, and apparently insatiable demands for increased security

(Police Foundation/PSI, 1996). As was suggested in Chapter 4, in relation to policing the consequence is a remoulding of the policing division of labour in response to the fragmentation of social control needs and the increasing diversity of suppliers in the marketplace (see also Jones and Newburn, 1998). Similarly, in relation to crime prevention, 'we are witnessing a redrawing of what constitutes the legitimate responsibilities of individuals, collectivities, and the state' (Crawford, 1997: 296). Central to this redrawing of boundaries and responsibilities are the notions of 'community', 'partnerships' and 'responsibilities', all of which are clearly visible – indeed prioritised – within the Crime and Disorder Act 1998. The terminology and rhetoric used in the Act was already firmly embedded in the language used by professionals and practitioners working in the field, who had been moving in this direction even under a less sympathetic government. This approach will now be reinforced by the new legislation and 'will undoubtedly reinvigorate community safety in Britain and will entrench a partnership approach to the delivery of crime prevention' (Crawford, 1998: 61). Whether sustainable change will be delivered at a local level remains the key question now.

Chapter 6

Probation: from advise, assist and befriend to punishment in the community

The origins of the probation service

The probation service as we know it today has its origins in the Victorian temperance movement and the police court missionaries who began work in the 1870s and 1880s. Although the legal basis for alternatives to imprisonment increased during the course of the nineteenth century, it was not until the first decade of the twentieth century that probation was put on a statutory footing. The nature and scale of the work undertaken by probation officers has changed markedly during the last 90 years, with the pace of change being most marked in the past 25 years.

As far as the nineteenth century is concerned, there are two developments which are central to an understanding of the origins and emergence of the probation service: the changing jurisdiction of the magistrates' courts, and increasing concern about drunkenness and the disorderly behaviour that drinking frequently led to.

In the second half of the nineteenth century, the magistrates' courts moved from, as White describes it: 'administering a partial, private executive justice in minor matters . . . [to being] recognizably courts of justice' (quoted in McWilliams, 1983: 130). A number of significant Acts of Parliament resulted in offences which had previously been dealt with in assizes or quarter sessions, becoming the business of the magistrates' courts. These included the Juvenile Offenders Act 1847 (extended in 1850), which allowed certain larcenies committed by juveniles to be dealt with by magistrates, the Criminal Justice Act 1855, which extended these powers to cover adults faced with similar charges, and further legislation in 1868 which extended the provisions to some cases of embezzlement.

In addition, several pieces of legislation made provision for offenders 'to enter into recognizances' with the court. Beginning with the Juvenile Offenders Act 1847, and following it the Criminal Law Consolidation Act

1861 and the Summary Jurisdiction Act 1879, magistrates' courts were given the power 'where the offences were thought so trifling as to make punishment unnecessary, to discharge the offender on his own recognizance, with or without sureties, to appear for sentence when called upon, to keep the peace and be of good behaviour' (Jarvis, 1972: 10). It was against this background that the idea of supervision of such offenders emerged. However, before considering supervision in more detail there is one other development that needs to be considered.

The second half of the nineteenth century saw a dramatic rise in concern about drunkenness, and in the numbers convicted of and imprisoned for drunkenness and for disorderly behaviour. McWilliams (1983) notes that there were over 88,000 offenders convicted of such offences in 1860, and by 1876 this had risen to over 200,000. In the same period, the numbers imprisoned rose from just under 4,000 to almost 24,000. Indeed, McWilliams suggests that in London arrests for drunk and disorderly, drunkenness, and disorderly prostitutes and disorderly characters represented over half of all recorded crime in the capital. At roughly this time temperance movements and related moral campaigns emerged both in Britain and abroad (on the case of the United States see, for example, Gusfield, 1963).

In the 1860s, the Church of England Total Abstinence Society was established, though relatively quickly it amended its approach in order to incorporate people other than abstainers, and in 1873 changed its name to the Church of England Temperance Society (CETS). Jarvis (1972) quotes its basis as being: 'Union and co-operation on perfectly equal terms between those who use and those who abstain from intoxicating drinks.' He argues that its large membership was its major strength, enabling a nationwide movement to develop within a relatively short space of time, although its focus on temperance and not abstinence was also crucial. The membership of the CETS had reached close on one million by the 1890s. It had three primary goals: the promotion of temperance; the removal of the causes which lead to intemperance; and, crucially for our purposes here, the reformation of the intemperate.

Reforming or 'reclaiming' drunkards through a mission to the police courts was, it is suggested, initially the idea of a printer named Frederick Rainer who, in a letter to the CETS, bemoaned what he saw to be the fate of the drunk facing the courts: 'offence after offence, sentence after sentence appears to be the inevitable lot of him whose foot has once slipped' (quoted in Jarvis, 1972). The first two police court missionaries, George Nelson and William Batchelor, were both ex-Coldstream guardsmen and were appointed in 1876 and 1877. They worked in the Bow, Mansion House, Southwark and Lambeth courts in London. McWilliams (1983: 134) describes their initial efforts in the courts as being 'directed to exhorting offenders to give up drink, distributing uplifting tracts and taking pledges of abstinence'. The work in the courts expanded quickly and came to dominate the activities of the missionaries within the period of a decade. The work was 'unapologetically evangelical', the aim being 'to reclaim the lives and souls of drunks appearing before the courts. They would ask the magistrates to bind individuals over into their care and they would undertake to secure their "restoration and reclamation"' (Mathieson, 1992: 143).

There is one crucial further linking step between the work of the police court missionary and what in the twenty-first century we associate with the probation officer. McWilliams (1985: 253) describes it as follows:

> It is important to recall that in their work in the courts the missionaries were not pleading for mercy for all offenders; such a course would undoubtedly have been self-defeating. Rather their pleas were reserved for those offenders deemed suitable for moral reform and this ensured, at least at the beginning, that in addition to intrinsic worth a missionary's plea also had a sort of novelty value. Even with selective application, however, the strong possibility existed that special pleading would become a routine. . . . The missionaries began to depend upon a form of justification for their pleas and this was that offenders worthy of mercy could reform under kindly guidance; that is to say that the missionaries' pleas in court began to be linked to the notion of *supervision*, and in particular to the idea that some offenders were suitable for reform under supervision.

As supervisors of offenders deemed to be deserving of mercy, the missionaries increasingly played a part in the process of determining which offenders were to be considered 'suitable for moral reform'. This meant undertaking inquiries prior to sentencing and although it is not clear when they first undertook such work for the courts, it is likely that they were doing so by the time that the extension of supervision from 'licence holders and habitual criminals' to first offenders at risk of imprisonment was made by the Probation of First Offenders Act 1887.

The previous year, Howard Vincent MP, had introduced a Bill into the House of Commons which would have extended very significantly the powers to release offenders on recognizance. The dissolution of Parliament brought the end of the Bill, and a much-amended version was passed a year later. Although it was the first point at which the word 'probation' was entered onto the statute book, the Act represented only a moderate extension to the system of supervision that was emerging. Though the Act only applied to first offenders, it covered a broader range of offences than had the 1879 Act, for example, including those convicted of larceny, false pretences and other offences punishable with not more than two years' imprisonment. In addition, the courts 'were required to have regard not simply to the triviality of the offence, but to the 'youth, character and antecedents of the offender, and to any extenuating circumstances' (Jarvis, 1972: 13).

Jarvis notes that by 1907 – the point at which the modern probation service originates – there were 124 male and 19 female missionaries from the CETS working in the courts, together with a small number of missionaries from other bodies. Despite the central role played by the police court missionaries in the nineteenth and early twentieth century, most commentators are agreed that it would be a gross oversimplification to suggest that the probation service grew directly from such work (see, for example, Bochel, 1976). The missionaries provided a model for work with offenders and established the ground on which a welfare organisation could work in the courts, but 'the idea which led directly to the passing of the Probation of Offenders Act in 1907 stemmed from American experience and practice, and was actively supported in this country, not from a concern for adult offenders, but from a profound anxiety over the treatment of children by the courts' (Jarvis, 1972: 9).

The 'American experience' is a reference to an experiment in the State of Massachusetts at the turn of the century. The Howard Association, as it was then called, provided the Home Secretary with an account of the Massachusetts system, together with evidence that it had been collecting about a variety of methods of dealing with juvenile offenders. Bochel (1976) notes that the 'situation was ripe' for a decision to be taken to introduce a system of probation. A Liberal government had just come to power, Herbert Gladstone, who had been Chairman of the Departmental Committee on Prisons, had become Home Secretary and there was quite widespread public concern about the treatment of juveniles (see Chapter 8).

The Probation of Offenders Act 1907

In 1906, the CETS, sensing that change was in the air, had visited the Home Office to offer the services of the police court missionaries as probation officers. The Probation of Offenders Bill was described in its Second Reading in the House as a proposal: 'of a non-controversial character. The government has not heard a whisper of opposition to it from any quarter of the House. Its purpose is to enable the courts of justice to appoint probation officers, to pay them salaries or fees, so that certain offenders whom the court did not think fit to imprison, on account of their age, character or antecedents, might be placed on probation under the supervision of these officers, whose duty it would be to guide, admonish and befriend them' (Jarvis, 1972: 15). The Bill received Royal Assent in August 1907.

Section 2 of the Act is perhaps its most important element. It says that where an offender has been released on condition of their recognizance, they should: 'be under the supervision of such person as may be named in the order during the period specified in the order'. Such an order was in future to be referred to as a probation order. Conditions could be attached prohibiting the offender from frequenting with undesirable persons or in undesirable places and requiring abstention from alcohol. Petty Sessional

Divisions (PSDs) were given the power, but not compelled, to appoint probation officers for their area. The duties of such officers were:

> To visit or receive reports from the person under supervision at such
>   reasonable intervals as the probation officer may think fit;
> To see that he observes the condition of his recognizance;
> To report to the court on his behaviour;
> To *advise, assist and befriend* him and, when necessary, to endeavour to find
>   him suitable employment (emphasis added).

This was the point, then, when a probation service started to emerge. The Act came into operation at the beginning of 1908, by which time it was assumed local authorities would have had time to make appointments and establish pay scales. The Home Secretary remained responsible for the Metropolitan Police court area and, in the event, many of the standards and operations established there became models for practice elsewhere. Crucially, it gave the Home Office direct experience of establishing, maintaining and administering a local service.

Although the legislation was, in Jarvis' words 'a great advance', there were a number of limitations to the new system it introduced. As was suggested above, probation officers were to be appointed by justices on a petty sessional division basis. However, many of the areas were too small to provide enough work for a probation officer. Because the legislation as drafted was permissive and there was no regional or national machinery for co-ordinating work in PSDs, there was little onus upon, or support for local areas in establishing a probation presence in court. The establishment of a more bureaucratic form of organisation did not occur until the 1920s.

With the accommodating position adopted towards the new system of probation by the CETS, and the experience that the police court missionaries had gathered by this point, it is perhaps not surprising that in the vast majority of cases in which a missionary was already working in a particular local area, it was they who were appointed as a probation officer. This was not universally popular, however, and Jarvis (1972: 22) quotes the Howard Association's Annual Report of 1908 as saying: 'large numbers of persons, male and female, have been appointed probation officers, some it is to be feared not possessing the personal qualities that fit them for the delicate and important work. . . . The Committee . . . feel that the wholesale appointment of volunteers, regardless of training and capacity, is likely to bring discredit upon a most useful Act and jeopardise its efficient working and ultimate success.'

A Home Office Departmental Committee which reported in 1909 was the first sign that some form of central oversight of the new probation service was thought to be necessary. The Committee stayed well short of recommending a full-scale central co-ordinating body, but it did nevertheless suggest that there should at least be one official whose function it would be to: furnish 'any information with regard to [probation work] that may be asked for' (quoted in Jarvis, 1972: 24).

The numbers placed on probation at this time remained relatively low. Indeed, the number dropped between 1913 and 1919 from just over 11,000 to 9,655 (though it varied somewhat between these dates). The role of the CETS was undiminished, though the concern expressed by the Howard Association just after the introduction of the Act was becoming increasingly widespread. There was a growing dissonance between the CETS's emphasis upon temperance, and the more secular philosophy held by the court-based social work agency which was slowly but surely emerging.

There was relatively little emphasis on training for probation officers at this point. Some training for the non-missionary probation officers was provided in the University settlements and the Charity Organisation Society, but relatively little training was provided for the missionaries; the schemes which existed were run for parochial workers by a variety of religious bodies (Bochel, 1976). Juvenile crime in particular continued to rise throughout the War years and criticism of the police court missionaries was undiminished.

The emergence of bureaucracy

The position remained unchanged for some while, despite the establishment in 1920 of a Home Office Departmental Committee to: 'enquire into the existing methods of training, appointing and paying probation officers, and to consider whether any, and if so what, alterations are desirable in order to secure at all courts sufficient number of probation officers having suitable training and qualifications, and also to consider whether any changes are required in the present system of remuneration.' The Committee recommended that government should meet half the cost of providing probation officers, and that it should do so via a central government grant. In doing so, it was careful to state that the new system of finance and control should be established 'without direct interference with the organisation along local lines' (quoted in May, 1991: 11). The establishment of local probation committees made up of representatives from the Bench was also recommended.

It was in the mid-1920s that the basis of a national, bureaucratic probation machinery was established. Central were the Criminal Justice Act 1925 and the Criminal Justice Amendment Act 1926. These laid the foundations for an administrative framework for the probation service. PSDs were designated as probation areas and, crucially, for the first time it became mandatory for the PSD to employ one or more probation officers.

The Home Secretary was given powers to combine PSDs into a single probation area in order to overcome the work limitations outlined above. Such combined areas would have a (combined) probation committee. Probation officers were to be appointed by the probation committee, which would also pay them, oversee their activities and receive regular reports from them. The work was to be financed by the local authority and by central government. Finally, it would be the duty of probation officers to supervise offenders placed on probation by assize courts and quarter sessions as well as courts of summary jurisdiction.

The next step was the issuing by the Home Office of the 1926 Probation Rules which introduced the distinction between principal probation officers and others, and enabled probation committees to appoint such officers at a higher salary than other probation staff. Later on, posts such as senior probation officer, and deputy and assistant principal (subsequently chief) probation officer were introduced, but none of this happened quickly (McWilliams, 1981). It was thus the introduction of more formalised methods of financing, regulating, and organising the probation service, beginning in earnest in the 1920s, which really began to transform it into something akin to the service we recognise today.

The rise of the 'diagnostician'

In a series of articles, McWilliams (McWilliams, 1981, 1983, 1985, 1986, 1987) charts the changes in the philosophical basis of 'probation practice' from the earliest days of the police court missionaries onwards. At about the period under discussion here, he suggests that a gradual movement began away from the 'missionary ideal' towards what he and others have referred to as a more therapeutic or diagnostic approach to work with offenders (see also May, 1991). Crudely stated, the argument advanced by such authors is that in selecting those offenders deserving of mercy, the missionaries employed the 'doctrine of the stumbling block', this being the impediments (such as drink) to the offender's understanding of the gospel. The offender could either work towards or be coerced into removing such stumbling blocks. Once these impediments became *the reason* why individuals behaved in the way they did, then there was little philosophical difference between such a view and the views held by the growing band of diagnosticians with a more scientifically informed medical model of individual failings. The change – and this, of course, was very gradual – was from a system dominated by missionaries whose task it was to reform the wicked, to one run by professionals who wanted to 'heal the sick' (May, 1994).

Two documents published in the 1930s are quite central in understanding the rise to prominence of the diagnostician. The first of these is *A Handbook of Probation and Social Work of the Courts* (Le Mesurier, 1935) which was produced by the National Association of Probation Officers (NAPO) in the year prior to the publication of the second document, the *Report of the Departmental Committee on the Social Services in the Courts of Summary Jurisdiction* (Home Office, 1936). Both dealt with court work and social enquiry reports at some length, though the emphasis in each is somewhat different (McWilliams, 1985). The NAPO Handbook attempted to establish the link between scientific diagnosis and professional practice, whereas the Departmental Committee went little further than outlining the importance of the provision of information before the courts. It said in its report, however: 'There are no doubt some defects in the provisions of the law, but the neglect of so many courts to carry out the intentions of the legislature either in the letter or the spirit has contributed to the failure of the probation service to meet adequately the increasing responsibilities placed upon it at the present day' (quoted in Jarvis, 1972: 51). Its recommendations were, in the long term, influential. They included the proposal that, despite the enormous contribution of the police court missionaries, probation should become a wholly public service. Crucial in this was the very strong view held by NAPO, including its missionary members (who made up about half those employed), that it should no longer be a part of the Mission:

> . . . whilst both the Handbook and the Departmental Committee moved
> decisively away from the concept of a service founded on vocation and
> missionary spirit and towards a basis in science, diagnosis and treatment,
> both texts made considerable efforts not to lose the missionary element. . . .
> The foregoing may appear contradictory, but that is not actually the case; we
> must remember that the issue was clearly seen as administrative rather
> than ideological; it was the *Mission* which was to be rejected, *not* the
> missionary zeal.
>
> (McWilliams, 1985: 271)

The Committee also recommended an increase in the central control of the probation service and the creation of a separate probation branch in the Home Office. Of the Committee's recommendations that could be acted upon without the need for new legislation, many were set in train without much delay. Others were incorporated in a Criminal Justice Bill, but the outbreak of the Second World War prevented its passage, and it was some ten years before a new Act was passed. The emergence of a fully fledged public service was not far off, however, and in 1937 Sir Samuel Hoare, the then Home Secretary, said that 'the system under which candidates for the Probation Service are nominated so far as the adult courts are concerned, by the London Police Court Mission, can no longer be defended, and . . . there is a need to bring the whole of the probation staff under unified public control' (quoted in Jarvis, 1972: 56).

From its somewhat precarious beginnings, probation had by this stage become quite firmly established. As has already been noted, there were under 10,000 people placed on probation in 1919. This rose to 25,000 in 1936, and 35,000 by 1943 (with 50,000 in total under supervision). In 1945, the 1936 proposal to create a division in the Home Office with responsibility for probation was put into practice, though administratively the division was still located within the Childrens' Branch.

A new era was signalled by the passage of the Criminal Justice Act 1948, which repealed the 1907 Act and all other legislation dealing with probation. It established a new administrative structure for the service, provided for an increase in the central government grant to a maximum of 50 per cent, set out in full the powers of the courts as far as probation was concerned, and extended the responsibilities of probation officers to include after-care. Three years later, NAPO was arguing for an extension of the after-care responsibilities of its members on the basis that officers were 'specialists in casework with offenders in the community' (quoted in McWilliams, 1981: 102). As we shall see below, the Advisory Council, to whom NAPO had been giving evidence, rejected the idea of a separate after-care service and plumped for 'an enlarged probation and after-care service' on the grounds that there was 'clearly a strong case for concentrating in a single service social work in the community with delinquents, whether they are probationers or offenders released from correctional establishments' (McWilliams, 1981).

A further review of the service was established in May 1959 under the chairmanship of Ronald Morison QC. His Committee's terms of reference were to inquire into 'all aspects of probation in England and Wales and Scotland and the approved probation hostel system'. It took three years to report, and was not particularly radical in the vision it offered. It concluded that: 'The present functions are, with a few minor exceptions which we have specified, appropriately and desirably performed by the service. Almost all types of work are increasing or likely to increase and ... the service must be organised, recruited and trained to meet this situation' (Home Office, 1962, para. 157).

Writing in 1978, Haxby said that 'the service today looks very different from the service which was reviewed and discussed in the Report of the Morison Committee in March 1962 (Haxby, 1978: 15). Many of the changes in probation policy and practice stem from the work of two further committees that reported in the early 1960s. The first of these was the Streatfield Committee, which reported in 1961, the second the Advisory Committee on the Treatment of Offenders, which reported in 1963.

The Streatfield Committee, in attempting to clarify the role of the probation officer in court, said that 'whatever the circumstances in which the probation officer gives evidence he [sic] appears as a witness of the court and not as a witness for the defence or prosecution. He provides the court with relevant background information which is not necessarily for the defence or against it' (Home Office, 1961b, para. 367). The primary consequence of the Streatfield Committee's report was to strengthen the emphasis placed upon national rather than local policies, and to move the focus from particular offenders to particular classes of offender. As McWilliams (1987: 104) notes: 'This was a profound change, but one which was apparently unnoticed in these terms at that time.'

As has already been briefly mentioned, in 1963 a report of the Advisory Council on the Treatment of Offenders (ACTO), *The Organisation of After-Care* (Home Office, 1963), reviewed the arrangements for the organisation of statutory and voluntary after-care. In short, what it recommended was an expansion and reorganisation of the probation and after-care service. Those organisations which were at that time involved in after-care – whether compulsory or voluntary – were to be wound down and replaced by a common service, and all after-care in the community should henceforward become the responsibility of the new expanded and reorganised probation and after-care service. As a result, a new probation and after-care department was created in the Home Office. The Report framed its conclusions in the following manner:

> An expansion of the probation service in England and Wales to deal with after-care on the lines we have recommended must be accompanied by a reorganisation of that service. The probation service would . . . extend beyond its hitherto accepted role of a social service of the courts, that part of its work concerned with after-care would be carried out, not upon the court's directions, but as a continuation in the community of the treatment begun in custody.

ACTO thus emphasised the development of welfare work within prisons, and initially suggested that such work should be undertaken by people with the same professional standing as probation officers. Eventually, it was decided that the work should be undertaken by probation officers on secondment, and by 1966 the expanded probation and after-care service assumed responsibility for this work from the Discharged Prisoners' Aid Societies. As May (1991: 17) puts it: 'Administratively at least this changed the "long-standing antipathy" probation officers had towards prisons.'

Similarly, probation officers were also given responsibility for the after-care of detention centre trainees in 1964, though for the first time the new arrangements were announced in a Home Office Circular. This pattern was repeated when responsibilities for borstal trainees and young prisoners were introduced in 1967, and for those sentenced to life imprisonment from 1968. By the same process that had occurred in prisons, social workers in borstals, remand and detention centres also became probation officers on secondment.

The changes brought about in the 1950s and 1960s were, not surprisingly, reflected quite starkly in the work undertaken by probation officers. McWilliams (1987) shows that in the 1950s the (criminal) supervisory caseload increased by over 35,000 cases, though the categories of work remained largely unchanged. During the decade from 1961, that caseload increased again, but there was a major redistribution of work with the proportion of probation cases declining, whilst the proportion of after-care cases rose. These changes are summarised in Table 6.1.

Table 6.1: Offenders supervised by the probation service (England and Wales) by type of supervision, 1951–81

Type of supervision	Percentage of offenders			
	1951	1961	1971	1981
Probation	82.4	75.5	56.5	31.9
C&YP Acts 1933–69	5.8	7.1	11.4	10.9
Money payment supervision	2.0	3.8	5.7	5.0
After-care	9.9	13.5	26.4	37.6
Susp. sentence supervision	–	–	–	1.9
Community service	–	–	–	12.8
Number	55,425	90,459	120,613	157,350

Source: McWilliams, 1987

Haxby (1978: 17) summarises these sweeping changes by suggesting that taken together they: 'represented a major shift in the focus of the service. In the future many probation officers could expect to spend some part of their career working in a penal institution, and a large part of the field officer's work would not in future derive directly from the decisions of judges and magistrates.'

It was not necessary to introduce legislation to bring in such changes, though it was novel for the executive – in the shape of the Home Office – to take such a directive role. Nevertheless, there was new legislation soon after: the Criminal Justice Act 1967 formalising the status of probation and after-care 'areas' and 'committees'. It further cemented the role of the probation officer in prison through the introduction of parole and, perhaps most notably, it introduced the first 'totally new sentencing option for the adult offender since the statutory creation of probation sixty years earlier': the suspended sentence of imprisonment (Bottoms, 1980). Although the government initially argued that the suspended sentence and probation ought to be kept separate, suspended sentence supervision orders were introduced following a recommendation by the Advisory Council on the Penal System in 1970.

The Children and Young Persons Act 1969 (which is dealt with in greater detail in Chaper 8) ended the use of probation for juveniles, the responsibility for supervising such offenders passing in many cases to social workers. Nevertheless, two pieces of legislation in the early 1970s further extended the functions of the probation service. The Criminal Justice Act 1972, later amended by the Powers of Criminal Courts Act 1973, empowered probation committees 'to provide and carry on day training centres, bail hostels, probation hostels, probation homes and other establishments for use in connection with the rehabilitation of offenders'. It attempted to discourage the courts from using custodial sentences by requiring them to consider a Social Inquiry Report (SIR) before imposing a custodial sentence on an offender under the age of 21, and on those over 21 who had not previously served a term of imprisonment. In addition, it introduced community service orders (CSOs), allowing courts to order offenders to undertake up to 240 hours of unpaid work as an alternative to a short custodial sentence, and this was to be run by the probation service. Similarly, day training centres (as opposed to Day Centres which were introduced by the Criminal Justice Act 1982) – which offenders could be required to attend for up to a maximum of 60 days for full-time, non-residential training – were also to be run by the service.

Community Service has become a central part of the work of the probation service since this point, and it is worth looking at its introduction in somewhat more detail. The Advisory Council on the Penal System, chaired by Baroness Wootton, had been set the task not only of expanding the range of non-custodial disposals, but also devising new alternatives to imprisonment. Its 1970 report examined the possibility of introducing some form of community service which would require adult offenders to undertake unpaid work for the community. It was introduced in six experimental areas in 1973, and CSOs could be imposed on offenders convicted of offences punishable by imprisonment, though offenders had to consent to the order being made. The experiment was evaluated by the Home Office which concluded: 'that the scheme is viable; orders are being made and completed, sometimes evidently to the benefit of the offenders concerned. However, the effect on the offenders as a whole is not known; the penal theory underlying the scheme is thought by some to be uncertain; it has not made much of an impact on the prison population' (Pease et al., 1977, quoted in McIvor, 1992). Nevertheless, in 1974 the government announced that community service would be extended to the rest of England and Wales and the extent to which it was used grew throughout the decade.

From 'alternatives to custody' to 'punishment in the community'

If the 1960s witnessed a number of quite far-reaching changes to the nature and operation of the probation (and after-care) service, the backdrop was one of a continuing emphasis on scientific treatment and diagnosis. The rate of change in the 1970s was no less rapid than that in the 1960s, but it was qualitatively different in that the philosophical basis of probation practice began to face a series of challenges. Harris (1994) identifies three sources of attack on the established systems and values.

The first change, as should already be clear, was that the government began to identify the probation service as a vehicle for the management of more serious offenders in the community, including increasing numbers on post-custodial and parole licence. Although increased resources were part of the package, one of the consequences, he suggests, was a diminished degree of officer autonomy. In other words, a further move away from judicial power towards that of the executive was underway. Crucially, initiatives had been introduced by government which, some believed, compromised the traditional welfare philosophy of probation. Thus, for example, whilst parole 'was intended not only to reduce the prison population, but to assist in the process of resettlement of the offenders in the community . . . it also incorporated elements of "public protection" in the community, through the monitoring of the parolee's progress by a probation officer' (May, 1994: 864). Day training centres and bail hostels were also introduced with the intention of stiffening up the public image of community-based sanctions by adding conditions to probation orders. There was, in short, declining confidence in the potential of the standard probation order.

Second, at around this time there emerged the 'new criminology': at its heart a sociology of deviance that questioned the functions of the criminal justice system, including the 'nature' of probation. Could it be, as Harris puts it, 'that the service, far from acting in a humane manner, was a repressive arm of the state' (1994: 935–6). Insights derived from such a sociology of deviance led to a questioning of the role of the 'neutral' professional and, as one consequence, to the development of radical social work practices and groupings. The third challenge was to the very idea that intervention by probation officers might have some effect on the individual's propensity to offend. An increasing body of research at this time cast doubt on the effectiveness of a variety of approaches. The dominant position occupied by the 'rehabilitative ideal' which had formed the basis for the introduction of many non-custodial initiatives, was no more, and a form of penal pessimism developed. As Bottoms and McWilliams (1979: 159) put it:

> The reformation of the criminal . . . has been central to the English approach to criminal justice since the end of the nineteenth century. . . . But penological research carried out in the course of the last twenty years or so suggests that penal 'treatments', as we significantly describe them, do not have any reformative effect, whatever other effects they may have. The dilemma is that a considerable investment has been made in various measures and services, of which the most obvious examples are custodial institutions for young adult offenders and probation and after-care services in the community. *Are these services simply to be abandoned on the basis of the accumulated research evidence?* Put thus starkly, this is an unlikely proposition but one which, by being posed at all, has implications for the rehabilitative services concerned. *Will this challenge evoke a response by . . . probation officers* by the invention of new approaches and methods?

Part of the answer to this was that a significant proportion of the energies of the probation service had gone into adapting to the increasing responsibilities and changing circumstances in which it has been operating in the

20 years since Bottoms and McWilliams' observation. If anything, the pace of change increased during this period and the service itself had less and less control over its working environment as central government progressively intervened. As one indication of its seriousness, the government grant for the administration of local services was increased from 50 to 80 per cent in 1971. It is the consequences of the decline in confidence in the treatment model that had the most profound effect on the probation service in the 1970s and, indeed, thereafter. The service no longer felt itself to have a coherent sense of mission and purpose. The traditional function as set out in the 1907 Act, 'to advise, assist and befriend', was increasingly being challenged by the requirement on probation officers that they administer what they perceived to be ever more punitive community-based sanctions, thus turning them into 'screws on wheels' (Haxby, 1978: 162). Toughening-up the form and the content of community sanctions has been perhaps the major characteristic of policy in this area since the early to mid-1970s.

This change of emphasis has stimulated an extensive and sometimes heated debate within the service itself and, as early as 1969, Murch argued that it had a choice; either it could become 'some form of correctional service linked to the penal system (a crime treatment service) or a less symptom specific, more general social work agency linked to the courts (a court social work service)'. He went on to argue that if the treatment of offenders was identified as the primary function of probation, then other more general social work activities would increasingly be seen as being of secondary importance.

Table 6.1 summarised the changes in the service's caseload between 1951 and 1981. Expansion and diversification is primarily what happened in the 1970s (McWilliams, 1987). The criminal caseload grew markedly, though the level of probation orders fell to an all-time low by 1977. The expansion came via continuing increases in after-care, together with the introduction of CSOs and, though less marked, Suspended Sentence Supervision Orders (SSSOs).

In parallel with the development of policy in relation to policing (Chapter 4), the key element of the probation narrative for the past 20 to 25 years has been the increasing involvement of and direction from the Home Office. The election of a new government on a 'law and order' ticket in 1979 ('We will spend more on fighting crime, whilst we economize elsewhere') is widely associated with a sea-change in criminal justice policy. The 1980s witnessed massively increased expenditure on criminal justice (Fowles, 1990; NACRO, 1992) and, after a slight delay, significantly increased emphasis on 'value for money'. At the heart of government policy was an avowed determination to 'crack down', to be 'tough on crime'. Such a project, however, was not without its contradictions, for as Brake and Hale (1992: 11) point out: 'on the one hand [the government] favoured a firm hand concerning law and order, but on the other this was limited by the overcrowding of the prisons, forcing it to rethink and disguise "soft options" as *punishment in the community*' (emphasis added).

As we have already seen, however, moves to stiffen community sanctions and to present them as a tough alternative predate the 1979 election by some years. Thus, although it had a somewhat different meaning from the Intensive Probation initiative launched in 1990, experiments in intensive counselling – involving significant increases in the amount of contact between client and counsellor – were taking place in the early 1970s (for details of the IMPACT experiment (Intensive Matched Probation and After-Care Treatment) see Folkard et al., 1974 and 1976).

In a semantic affirmation of the spirit of the times, the Criminal Justice Act 1982 removed 'After-Care' from the Probation Service's title. It introduced day centres and also included a provision that would allow courts to add requirements to probation orders: either requiring offenders to engage in or refrain from certain activities for a maximum of 60 days, thus increasing the surveillance and social control aspects of supervision.

Statement of National Objectives and Priorities

Rather than 1979, it is most clearly 1984 that represents one watershed in the recent history of the probation service (McLaughlin and Muncie, 1994; Mair, 1995). It was the year in which the Home Office published its *Statement of National Objectives and Priorities* (SNOP) for the probation service (Home Office, 1984c). When it was published as a draft document, it had the rather less fearsome title of 'The Future Direction of the Probation Service'. The published version, however, 'represented the most penetrating government intervention ever in the affairs of the probation service and required each probation area to respond with its own local statement, to be measured against the Home Office's national statement. The process of tighter control had begun' (Mathieson, 1992). The National Audit Office (NAO, 1989: 2), in describing this process, said very simply 'the Home Office are taking more direct and positive action to secure improvements in local management and performance'.

SNOP outlined how the resources available to the service might be 'effectively and efficiently' used, and suggested that this was the responsibility of both the local probation committee and the Chief Probation Officer (CPO). Indeed, as the degree of Home Office direction increased during the course of the decade, so CPOs were progressively targeted as the focus for official 'advice'. Given that local probation committees are autonomous this is perhaps not surprising, but it puts CPOs in the difficult position of ensuring that the local service meets national guidelines whilst simultaneously being responsible to the local committee for the efficient use of local resources. The balance in this emergent tripartite structure is different from that which governs local constabularies, but some of the tensions are very similar.

SNOP was the first visible outcome of the application of the government's Financial Management Initiative (FMI) to the probation service. A similar process was taking place in relation to local policing budgets in the early 1980s, despite the 'spend, spend, spend' policy that had been announced prior to the 1979 General Election. SNOP was an agenda-setting document. May (1994: 873) summarises its approach as follows:

> Along with statutory changes in the Criminal Justice Act 1982, it was intended as a means for achieving the government's aims. SNOP prioritized the work of the probation service in both the provision of alternatives to custody and the preparation of social inquiry reports, the theme being to target offenders who were 'at risk' of imprisonment. This clearly represented a change of focus away from the traditional probation client, who was 'in need' of a social work service, towards those thought to represent such 'a threat' to society that a period of incarceration would be a justified response on the part of the courts. As such, SNOP stipulated that the probation service prioritize these ends in areas of its activity, even if this meant diverting resources from other areas of probation work such as prisoner through-care and divorce court welfare work.

One of the intentions behind SNOP then was to encourage a degree of uniformity and consistency between individual probation services. Although this in itself was not uncontentious – hitherto diversity had generally been celebrated in the service (Mair, 1995) – it was the prioritising of work that caused the greatest furore. SNOP elevated the provision of alternatives to custody above all other aspects of probation work, followed by the preparation of SIRs. In relation to through-care, it required no more of local services than the commitment of sufficient resources to ensure that the statutory minimum was undertaken. Even lower priority was accorded to community work and to civil work.

Individual probation services responded with Statements of Local Objectives and Priorities (SLOP) and one review of these documents (Lloyd, 1986) found great diversity in the responses. Crucially, Lloyd suggested that it was differences in philosophy which underpinned this diversity. During 1986 and 1987 the Home Office, through Her Majesty's Probation Inspectorate (HMIP), also monitored the implementation of SNOP. It too noted considerable variation in responses, with only a minority of areas identifying improvements in management practice as a result of implementation. Some areas continued to refuse to prioritise their activities (National Audit Office, 1989). Perhaps the significance of SNOP is that it was part of a raft of initiatives which increased central oversight and control of local service provision, in particular through the increasing amount of information that was required from, and was kept on, individual services.

The Probation Information System (PROBIS), which was developed within the Home Office, standardised the information kept by probation services. Information gathering, the development of performance indicators, questions of measurement and financial administration and management – the development, for example, of resource management information systems – have come to dominate much official thinking about probation. The provision of better information for the courts was the subject of Home Office Circular 92/1986, *Social Inquiry Reports*, which examined the purpose and content of such reports. This followed on from two Circulars published in 1983 (83/17 and 83/18) and emphasised the point that the SIR should contain impartial professional judgement and not special pleading; that it should be concise and not contain jargon; that it should, wherever possible, contain supporting evidence for the information provided; and that reports should be costed carefully and should be targeted where there was either risk of custody or the likelihood of a probation order. This led Harris (1992: 147) to conclude that the 'Home Office approach to the social inquiry report is a microcosm of its approach to criminal justice more generally: the articulation of broad brush policies involving prioritisation, economy of content and relevance to major sentencing concerns, but with policy implementation left to local negotiations'.

A further Home Office report (the Grimsey Report) on the Probation Inspectorate recommended 'efficiency and effectiveness' inspections (Home Office, 1987), and in 1989 the Audit Commission issued a report entitled *The Probation Service: Promoting Value for Money*. This is discussed in greater detail below in connection with government policy as set out in the 1989 Green Paper.

In 1987, a joint publication from ACOP, CCPC and NAPO, entitled *Probation: the next five years*, attempted to provide some sort of unified approach in the face of rapid change. The document affirmed the service's commitment to civil work and to through-care, both of which had been accorded a low priority by the Home Office in SNOP. It also, as the majority of subsequent documents in this area were to do, made the point that community sanctions were significantly cheaper than custody and therefore could be supported on 'efficiency' grounds as well as in terms of their 'effectiveness'. The debate within the probation service rumbled on, however, and within a year ACOP had published its own document which reflected, in both its title and its approach, the increasing punitiveness of the times. The document, *More Demanding Than Prison* (ACOP, 1988), suggested that the service concentrate its attentions on those most at risk of custody. In addition to outlining the demanding nature of the community sanctions being proposed, it also followed the growing trend and emphasised the relative economy of using such an approach.

The line taken by ACOP was not greatly dissimilar from that espoused for the service by the Home Office when it published the *National Standards for Community Service Orders* (Home Office, 1988a). The National Standards made great play of the need to ensure that community penalties such as the CSO are viewed with confidence by sentencers, and that this was to be achieved by 'ensuring that CS makes uniformly stiff demands on offenders' (quoted in May, 1991: 47). The culmination of all the government's initiatives in relation to the probation service and community sanctions throughout the decade was its 1988 Green Paper: *Punishment, Custody and the Community* (Home Office, 1988b). As one commentator put it: 'the implications of this document are particularly profound, although its ideas and proposals do not represent any sudden change with regard to probation' (Mair, 1989: 35).

Punishment, custody and the community

The government's thinking was summed up in this document. The approach adopted in it can be crudely summarised as one in which it is acknowledged that custody is not the most appropriate penalty for the majority of offences and that it should be reserved for the most serious offences. The majority of offenders would, by contrast, be dealt with in the community. This approach has been described as one of 'bifurcation' (Bottoms, 1980) or even, given the increased emphasis on stiff punishments in the community, as 'punitive bifurcation' (Cavadino and Dignan, 1992).

The Green Paper was direct in its views on imprisonment. It pointed out that in 1987 over 69,000 offenders were sentenced to custody and it questioned whether this was the most effective sanction for all those offenders. It suggested that custody was most likely the right punishment for the majority of violent offenders, but pointed out that 95 per cent of recorded crime was non-violent. For less serious offenders, custody might not be the right option:

> Imprisonment restricts offenders' liberty, but it also reduces their responsibility; they are not required to face up to what they have done and to the effect on their victim or to make any recompense to the victim or the public. If offenders are not imprisoned, they are more likely to able to pay compensation to their victims and to make some reparation to the community through useful work. Their liberty can be restricted without putting them behind prison walls. Moreover, if they are removed in prison from the responsibilities, problems and temptations of everyday life, they are less likely to acquire the self-discipline and self-reliance which will prevent reoffending in future. *Punishment in the community would encourage offenders to grow out of crime and to develop into responsible and law abiding citizens.*
>
> (para. 1.1, emphasis added)

Community-based sanctions were to be thought of as punishments which restricted liberty, but which enabled offenders to face up to the effects of their crimes, thus potentially being of benefit to the victim, and economical for the tax-payer.

The Green Paper made a variety of recommendations not only for the introduction of new measures, but also for changes that were felt might improve existing arrangements. It referred to the fact that national standards for CSOs were already being introduced, and that the intention was that these standards should ensure that the orders were 'more rigorous and demanding'. It pointed to the Criminal Justice Bill, which was then before Parliament, which contained a provision which, it was argued, would make it more likely that compensation would be paid to victims (see Chapter 9 for details).

In relation to probation orders, it suggested that written statements of an agreed programme of activities, including the courts' requirements, should be available to the courts, the supervising officer and the offender. It reinforced the importance of targeting the work of the probation service on those most at risk of custody (possibly using risk prediction scales) and, in particular, on young adult offenders (then 17–20-year-olds). Young adults not only had high rates offending, but also accounted for about one-fifth of the custodial population and it was hoped that some of the impact that had been visible in relation to the juvenile custodial population (see Chapter 8) could be transferred to young adults.

As far as proposals for the future were concerned, the Green Paper began by setting out the three principles underpinning alternatives to custody where a fine alone, given the seriousness of the offence, would be inadequate. First, that it should restrict freedom of action – as a punishment; second, that it should involve action to reduce the risk of further reoffending; and third, that it should involve 'reparation to the community and, where possible, compensation to the victim'.

The Green Paper set out a number of possibilities in relation to restricting the liberty of offenders. These included: introducing curfew powers for the courts to require offenders to stay at home at specified times; extending and formalising the existing experiments in 'tracking' – where ancillary probation staff are used to maintain frequent contact with the offender; and the introduction of electronic monitoring – which could be used as a method of enforcing curfews or supplementing the process of tracking – though the Green Paper suggested that it could most appropriately be used to keep offenders out of custody.

The economics of punishment and the fiscal imperative behind the Green Paper was spelt out very clearly:

> It costs about £1,000 to keep an offender in prison for four weeks. The cost of punishment in the community should not exceed the cost of imprisonment, which is a more severe sentence. If the courts are to have a wide discretion with powers to place a range of requirements on offenders, they should take account of the costs to the taxpayers of carrying out the requirements. The courts will therefore need regular and up-to-date information about the cost of imprisonment and that of the individual components of the new order, e.g. the cost of a day's attendance at a day centre (now about £30), the cost of 10 hours' community service (about £35), the cost of tracking an offender

(about £15 a day). While the suitability of a penalty cannot be measured solely in terms of cost, the total cost of the requirements for an individual offender could be a useful check on whether the penalty is proportionate to the offence.

(para. 3.37)

The proposals were presented as being a great opportunity for the probation service, though given what has been said above about the history and philosophy of the service, a less than entirely positive reaction was undoubtedly anticipated. The Green Paper therefore concludes by exploring whether there are other agencies which might become involved in providing 'punishment in the community'. The police – with the exception of those officers working in attendance centres in their spare time – have no role in punishment or supervision of offenders; the prison service, it suggested, is not geared up to providing supervision in the community; and the private sector, though it might play some part in monitoring curfews, would find it difficult to take on wider ranging responsibilities. The Green Paper therefore suggests the possibility that the probation service might contract with one or more of these other agencies, including the voluntary sector, to organise punishment in the community, but that it would continue to supervise the order.

Just in case the probation service did not like this new role being shaped for it, the Green Paper went on to say: 'Another possibility would be to set up a new organisation. . . . It would not itself supervise offenders or provide facilities directly, but would contract with other services and organisations to do so. . . . The new organisation could contract for services from the probation service, the private or voluntary sector and perhaps for some purposes from the police or the prison service. . . . A new organisation would be able to set national standards and to enforce them, because they would be written into contracts' (para. 4.4).

Enter the auditors

When we come to look back from the perspective of the early twenty-first century on the changes that have taken place in the outlook of the probation service, it is as well to remember the far-reaching structural reforms that a radical government with a broad policy of privatisation was willing to consider in the mid to late-1980s. There was no let up for the probation service after the publication of *Punishment, Custody and the Community*. The previously mentioned inquiries by the Audit Commission and the National Audit Office were also underway, and the former used the Green Paper as its yardstick for evaluating the role and performance of the probation service.

The Audit Commission's press release of 1989 provides an interesting summary of their diagnosis of the situation facing the probation service in that year. Under the heading: 'The probation service needs to retarget its activities and develop new skills', the release read:

> Britain's prisons are grossly overcrowded and courts are under pressure with record numbers of people remanded in custody. The probation service needs to re-target its activities and develop new skills if, as the Government intends, it is to play a greater role in solving the problem.
>
> The 'market share' of the Probation Service has already grown from 9% of all sentences in 1977 to 16% in 1987. But that growth has not been matched with a reduction in the proportion of offenders going to prison, rather with a reduction in the number fined. It seems that many magistrates and judges lack confidence in probation and community service orders as alternatives to custody. It is in changing their perception that the Probation Service faces its single most important challenge.
>
> Indeed, there is evidence to suggest that more effort by local probation services (e.g. more social inquiry reports) now results directly in offenders being given more serious sentences – probation rather than a fine – which makes them more likely to end up in prison if they reoffend. There is also little evidence that probation reduces the propensity to reoffend.
>
> All this means that unless changes are made, increased emphasis on probation could have the opposite effect of that intended.

As a consequence, the Audit Commission recommended that the probation service should focus its activities by targeting more serious offenders; should evaluate the impact of that supervision; should work more closely with other agencies, particularly sentencers; and should establish more robust management procedures. It therefore downplayed casework skills – the bedrock of probation practice for the previous 40 or 50 years – and emphasised the centrality of intensive supervision and management of the offender. Predictably, the response in the service was critical with NAPO, for example, rejecting outright the Commission's proposals.

A parallel study was conducted by the National Audit Office (NAO), looking at the Home Office's control and management of the probation service. The NAO affirmed the general process that was taking place saying that although the primary responsibility for the management and delivery of probation work had hitherto lain primarily with local probation committees and probation officers, 'increasing demands, finite resources, and *the need to harness probation work more closely to central policy objectives* mean that Home Office oversight and monitoring will inevitably assume greater prominence' (NAO, 1989: 6, emphasis added). It recommended improved information gathering and provision in relation to probation service work generally, about the use of resources and the costs and benefits of different interventions, and greater exchange of information with other criminal justice agencies.

Crime, justice and protecting the public

Following on some time after the Green Paper, a White Paper containing the government's proposals for legislation was published in 1990 (Home Office, 1990c). It was a provocative document, and an editorial in the *Criminal Law Review* noted that: 'the proposals may be said to go further than any statement by a modern British Government in setting out aims of sentencing and in foreshadowing legislation which is designed to structure the sentencing discretion of the courts. The White Paper also contains declarations of intention on a range of other penal issues. The Home Office requests comments [within three months], but the proposals are so far-reaching that the debate will inevitably continue well beyond' (*Criminal Law Review*, 1990: 217).

One of the most interesting aspects of the White Paper is that it set out the grounds of the government's interest in sentencing policy. Though reaffirming the independence of the judiciary – 'no government should try to influence the decisions of the courts in individual cases' – it nevertheless declared that 'sentencing principles and sentencing practice are matters of legitimate concern to Government' (para. 2.1)

Underpinning the White Paper was the principle of 'proportionality' or 'just deserts'. Wasik has described the desert approach to sentencing as one which 'emphasises the moral requirement of maintaining a proper proportion between offence and punishment' (1992: 124). The sentence should therefore be commensurate with the harm caused by the offender and the degree of culpability involved. The emphasis that was therefore placed on deterrence was considerably diminished. The White Paper outlined a whole set of sentencing reforms and early release arrangements with the aim of creating 'a coherent framework for the use of financial, community and custodial punishments'. The White Paper was, with an important exception described below, quite clear about the priority of desert over deterrence:

> Deterrence is a principle with much immediate appeal. . . But much crime is committed on impulse, given the opportunity presented by an open window or unlocked door, and it is committed by offenders who live from moment to moment; their crimes are as impulsive as the rest of their feckless, sad or pathetic lives. It is unrealistic to construct sentencing arrangements on the assumption that most offenders will weigh up the possibilities in advance and base their conduct on rational calculation. Often they do not.
>
> (para. 208)

As was suggested above, the White Paper made one exception to its advocacy of just deserts. It advocated a 'twin-track' policy of sentencing (Ashworth, 1994b) and separated out the sentencing of offenders convicted of a violent or a sexual offence from all others. In essence, the the White Paper argued that there was an overriding need for public protection which meant that desert principles had to be suspended in such cases, with the consequence that the sentence passed could be significantly longer than that justified on the basis of just deserts.

The White Paper reiterated the disadvantages of imprisonment that had been outlined in the Green Paper (that it encourages dependence; may encourage criminal tendencies; and is expensive) and made a number of recommendations in relation to community penalties, including the proposal that the probation order become a sentence in its own right, together with a 'combined order' of community service and probation. These proposals for further stiffening of community sanctions were accompanied by another Green Paper, *Supervision and Punishment in the Community: A Framework for Action* (Home Office, 1990a), which outlined recommendations for standards of probation practice. This signalled to the probation service that the national standards that had been introduced for CSOs in 1989 were to be extended to report-writing, probation orders, supervision orders – and any new orders – the management of hostels and supervision before and after release from custody.

The legislative outcome of *Punishment, Custody and the Community* and *Crime, Justice and Protecting the Public* was, of course, the Criminal Justice Act 1991. It was the product of a decade of consultation, proposal and counter-proposal and, seen from today's perspective, was unusual, though laudable, for this very reason. One set of commentators who were closely involved in the process said that: 'these policy initiatives by the Home Office were accompanied by extensive consultations, training exercises and "special conferences" across the criminal justice process. Unprecedented efforts were made closely to consult senior members of the judiciary, although officials later appeared to regret that more could not be done during the actual drafting stage' (Gibson et al., 1994: 81).

The Criminal Justice Act 1991

> The key underlying principle of the sentencing provisions is that: 'The court should try to arrive at a sentence which is commensurate with the seriousness of the offence, taking account of aggravating and mitigating circumstances'. The so-called theory of 'proportionality' – the punishment fitting the crime – or 'just deserts'.
> (John Halliday, Deputy Under Secretary of State, Home Office, quoted in Gibson et al., 1994: 33)

Following the general thrust of the White Paper, the Act encouraged greater use of community sanctions within a sentencing framework informed by just deserts, but not completely constrained by it. In its original form, the Act sought to restrict the courts' powers to sentence 'on record', reduce the power of the executive in relation to discharge from prison, and to introduce 'unit fines' which, it was argued, would ensure greater equality through being related to offenders' disposable income. It also included provision for curfew orders and for electronic monitoring or 'tagging'.

Prior to the 1991 Act, the probation order was made instead of sentencing the offender. From this point onwards, the probation order became a sentence of the court, a change of significant symbolic importance for the service. Perhaps most far-reaching for the probation service was the introduction of what now became known as the 'combination order': the power of the court to sentence an offender to probation (with requirements if considered appropriate) and community service for the same offence. The intention clearly was to give the courts confidence that there were sentences at their disposal which were appropriate for use in relation to offenders who might otherwise have been incarcerated, i.e. that were sufficiently punitive. Specifically, it combined the probation order 'with its emphasis on the rehabilitation of offenders, with community service with its emphasis on punishment' (May, 1994: 876). This is a combination that ten years previously might have split the probation service in two. Such had been the success of the process of consultation, (or the long, slow process of culture change), however, combined with the very real threat contained in the 1988 Green Paper, that relatively little fallout from the Act was visible.

The just deserts approach of the Act was intended to have a profound effect on the probation service, indeed to put it 'centre-stage'. One of the keys to this was the intended role of the service in helping the courts determine the seriousness of the offence prior to sentencing. This meant a somewhat new role for the SIR – now renamed the 'pre-sentence report or PSR. Following the Act, PSRs were to be one, if not the key source of information for assessing not only seriousness but also suitability – whereby a community order must be the one that is most suitable for the particular offender. It became mandatory for courts to obtain a PSR before the vast majority of custodial or community penalties could be passed.

Section 12 of the 1991 Act created a new order, the curfew order. These orders, which were to be available for offenders aged 16 or over, require the offender to be at a place specified in the order for the period specified in the order – usually the offender's home. The curfew could operate from a minimum of two hours to a maximum of 12 hours per day for up to a total of six months. In addition – and a particular difficulty for many probation officers – such orders could henceforward be monitored using electronic 'tags'. As far back as 1987, the House of Commons Home Affairs Committee in a report on the *State and Use of Prisons*, had suggested that the Home Office should be examining the use that was being made of electronic tags in the United States. The possibility of such tags being used in the United Kingdom was raised in the 1988 Green Paper, and later that year the Home Office had set in train plans for experiments in this area. The conclusions from this experiment were, to say the least, mixed. The rate of time violations recorded was quite high, as was the level of equipment failure. Sentencers reported little confidence in tagging as an alternative to remands in custody, and, overall, most of those involved in the trials were sceptical of electronic monitoring and thought that if it had a place in the future of criminal justice in the United Kingdom, then it was probably a relatively small place (Mair and Nee, 1990: 68).

The final major change brought about by the 1991 Act – though this is dealt with in greater detail in Chapter 8 – is the introduction of the youth court. This replaced the juvenile court and deals with offenders aged 10–17, as opposed to 10–16 as was the case in the juvenile court. Consequently, this brought together elements of the juvenile and adult court systems which previously had had separate practices and procedures. A joint Home Office/Department of Health Circular issued in 1992 said that the new provisions would 'need to be carefully planned locally, in order to make the best use of opportunities and resources for constructive work with offenders in this age group and to avoid conflicts in objectives and working methods, duplication of effort, or failure to provide the necessary support'. In practice, this meant close co-operation between the probation service and social services, with an assumption that the two organisations would produce local action plans for dealing with 16 and 17-year-olds.

Partnership has, in fact, become somewhat of a buzz-word in recent years. As one example from a different area, as it has become progressively clear that the police cannot be held responsible for the overall level of crime in society, or indeed in a local community, so more and more emphasis has been placed on the role of other agencies, organisations and individuals in the prevention and detection of crime. 'Community policing' is one initiative that has developed as a result (Rosenbaum, 1994) and as an element of this, the notion of 'partnership' has become one of the most frequently used ideas in relation to modern policing. In a by no means dissimilar manner, the links between the probation service and other agencies working with offenders have increased markedly in recent years.

This has been supported by government and, according to the decision paper *Partnership in Dealing with Offenders in the Community* (Home Office, 1993b) approximately five per cent of each probation service's budget should be allocated to partnership work (Mair, 1995). This in many ways merely reflects the government's continuing commitment to a mixed economy in criminal justice. This has sometimes been presented as a policy of privatisation and, when certain developments are focused on narrowly, this is how it can appear. However, in almost all the areas of criminal justice in which the private sector has gained ground, the public sector and the voluntary sector have also been involved. Thus, for example, the above-mentioned decision document not only signalled the possibility of putting the running of bail hostels out to tender, i.e. potentially privatising them, but also encouraged greater involvement on the part of the voluntary sector in bail accommodation, prisoner welfare work, skills training and so on (McLaughlin and Muncie, 1994). Of course, underlying all this is the continuing concern with economy, efficiency and effectiveness. The core task and method of the service, at least as far as the government is concerned, is no longer the application of social work skills with offenders in the community, it is the strategic management and administration of punishments in the community.

The emphasis on information, measurement, management and administration can perhaps be seen at its clearest in the national standards which were first issued in relation to CSOs in the late 1980s, and then in relation to the rest of the work of the probation service not long after the Criminal Justice Act 1991, which came into force in October 1992. Covering five main areas of activity – pre-sentence reports, probation orders, combination orders, hostel management and pre- and post-release supervision of prisoners – central oversight of the service is at unprecedented levels. The centre has, however, more recently changed its mind, not only in relation to the role and centrality of the probation service, but on criminal justice policy generally.

It has long been known that a change of minister, or ministers, in a government department may have quite a profound impact on the direction and thrust of policy (Bottoms and Stevenson, 1992; Downes and Morgan, 1994), but it is probably fair to say that the extent, the speed and the manner of the reversal of criminal justice policy after the passage of the 1991 Act took virtually everybody by surprise. The appointment of Kenneth Baker brought the first signs that a more prison-oriented approach might be on the horizon, a view that his successor Kenneth Clarke was all too happy to confirm. The details of the reversal of policy are discussed in more detail in the next chapter, but the key elements allowing sentencers once again to look at all the offences before it (and not simply one offence and one associated offence as specified in the 1991 Act), and to take into account previous convictions have forced the probation service to change certain practices. More importantly, the renewed emphasis on prison, and the consequent demotion of community penalties means, at least in theory, that far less emphasis is placed on the work of the service. Furthermore, as part of the process of increasing central managerial control, in 1992 probation budgets became cash-limited. Whilst the probation service was centre-stage with increased resources promised, cash-limiting was not a major problem, but now as probation drops down the list of government priorities, the means are in place to impose significant cuts in probation budgets and, indeed, such cuts are promised.

The emergence of a more punitive approach to criminal justice policy-making in the 1990s has been noted in several of the previous chapters. Needless to say, the probation service was affected quite significantly by this change of climate. Initially, this was most visible in relation to the training of probation officers. From the early 1970s, probation training had been governed by the Central Council for Education and Training in Social Work (CCETSW). However, by 1990 the government were making it clear, via the Green Paper, *Supervision and Custody in the Community*, that social work principles were no longer necessarily to be considered the key principles in probation training. In particular, and there was little surprise in this given the Audit Commission's assessment of probation, that management skills should be given greater emphasis in future. Competence-based training was to become the order of the day. The Home Office undertook an internal review of probation training during 1994, and issued a consultation document in 1995 in which it suggested ending the higher education monopoly on training. The Home Secretary made it clear that he did not consider social work with offenders to be as important as the administration of punishment in the community, that the holding of a social work diploma was not vital to successful practice as a probation officer, and he expressed the hope that people with a military background might be recruited to the service. Though New Labour shared much of the punitive rhetoric of the outgoing Conservative administration, the new Home Secretary's view of probation training was not at one with his predecessor's. During 1997, he announced the intention to establish a Diploma in Probation Studies, which would be a mixture of higher education-based courses and work-based assessment. Though this is discernibly different from the approach of the previous administration, it nonetheless shares its overriding concern with management and administration over welfare.

The other fairly immediate consequence of the return to 'populist punitiveness' was that punishment became the most emphasised element in community penalties. In early 1995 another Green Paper was issued, the title of which – *Strengthening Punishment in the Community* – made clear its intentions (Home Office, 1995b). In it, the government made clear its intention to tackle the fact that too often probation 'supervision is still widely regarded as a soft option'. Two years previously, the Chief Inspector of Probation had noted that 'unfortunately too many users of probation services and the public appear unconvinced that current forms of supervision are either sufficiently rigorous to constitute adequate punishment or sufficiently effective to reduce criminal behaviour' (Home Office, 1993c). The approach taken in the Green Paper reflected the government's scepticism about the value and appropriateness of social work training, and a single integrated community penalty was mooted. Brownlee (1998: 28) suggests that it was abundantly clear that the 'principal aim of the proposed changes was to secure a further shift in responsibility for the implementation of community sentences towards the courts' and away from probation officers and other 'caring professionals'. The proposal for an integrated sentence was widely criticised, but the general anti-social work thrust of the Paper was, as we have seen, pursued with vigour.

Following the consultation process a White Paper was published in 1996. Entitled, *Protecting the Public* (Home Office, 1996a), it affirmed the government's support for prison, underlined its view that community penalties were currently insufficiently tough and, more particularly, articulated the view that what such penalties should be focusing upon was inculcating a sense of personal responsibility among offenders. There was widespread criticism of the White Paper, in particular, from the Lord Chief Justice, the Archbishop of Canterbury and several ex-Home Secretaries. Absent, however, among the distinguished critics of the proposed changes were Her Majesty's Opposition. Indeed, even in government, the Labour Party continued largely to sing from the 'Tough on Crime' half of its famous hymn-sheet. The approach to community penalties was to continue to emphasise 'toughness'. Whilst it might be, indeed has been, argued, that the intention was to encourage sentencers to use community penalties more frequently, the reality is that despite this the prison population continued to rise at what most commentators appear to believe is an alarming rate. In Brownlee's (1998: 192) view, the then 'Home Secretary's policy, which seems to be one of "tough and tougher" and which aims to rebuild the liberal balance implicit in the bifurcatory 1991 arrangements upon the punitive rhetoric of the 1993 counter-reforms, appears self contradictory and may, therefore, prove self-defeating in the longer run'. Nonetheless, according to one Home Office insider, there was a noticeable difference in attitude to probation:

> When the new Labour Government came to office in 1997, Ministers were prepared to look more favourably upon the probation service. They did not have the same attitude that 'prison works', and the implied corollary that community punishment does not.
>
> (Hopley, 2002: 299)

Though no reference was made to reform of probation in the Labour Party's 1997 election manifesto, the first 18 months of the new Labour government saw a series of leaks outlining potential shake-ups of the service. These included merging it with the Prison Service to create a national 'corrections service' and changing the name of the probation service to reflect the changed climate within which it was working. A number of options were floated, including the Public Protection Service, the Offender Risk Management Service or the Community Justice Enforcement Agency. These were floated in a consultation document released by the Home Office in August 1998, which once again suggested that the terms traditionally associated with community penalties were too often perceived to be 'soft'. Though criticisms of the proposals were voiced – and certainly there appeared to be scepticism of the proposal to change the name of the service – the idea of creating a national service appeared even at the time to be accepted as a *fait accompli* by the Association of Chief Probation Officers. Indeed, its chairman said that 'the advantages of a national service will be in giving community sentences greater consistency, a national identity and the possibility of more resources'. It would also provide for the possibility, he said of 'a more direct relationship with the Home Secretary' (*Guardian*, 7 August 1998).

The probation service and 'What Works'

At the heart of the New Labour modernisation agenda there has been an emphasis on 'what works' and 'cost effectiveness'. The what works paradigm has led to apparent government desire to prioritise evidence-based policy and practice, to invest massively in research and evaluation and to promote accreditation programmes. Not only is there an inherent centralising momentum in the what works paradigm, however, but there is also a tension between what one might characterise as *effective* interventions ('What Works') and *efficient* justice (what it costs and how long it takes). Across government, the Treasury has become increasingly important. Just as the comprehensive spending review gave impetus to the adoption of the what works paradigm so, via Treasury-led emphasis on cost-effectiveness, the linking of costs to outcomes and the measurement of the financial impact of interventions has determined much of the shape of the government's crime-control agenda. Nowhere has this been more visible than in relation to the community penalties and the probation service.

Part of the attraction of the 'third way' in criminal justice was the promise it held in steering a course between Old Labour welfarism and New Labour punitiveness. At the heart of this programme was the explicit distancing of government from old-fashioned 'nothing works' pessimism and the rise of the 'What Works' agenda. This has had its most profound effect on the probation service and the system of community penalties in England and Wales. Influenced in particular by cognitive-behavioural approaches developed in Canada and by research, especially meta-analytical research (Andrews et al., 1990; Lipsey, 1992), which claimed to show significant impacts with some offenders under some circumstances, the 'what works' agenda revived, albeit in a more limited fashion, faith in the idea of rehabilitation (Raynor and Vanstone, 2002). In 1999, the Home Office issued its Correctional Policy Framework (which forms the basis of its 'What Works' approach):

> Correctional policy is driven by What Works principles. This means that offending behaviour programmes should involve planned interventions over a specified period of time, which can be shown to change positively attitudes, beliefs, behaviour and social circumstances. Usually, they will be characterized by a sequence of activities designed to achieve clearly defined objectives based on a theoretical model or empirical evidence. There should also be a capacity to replicate the programme with different offenders to achieve the same results.
>
> (Home Office, 1999)

In 1999, a Joint Prisons and Probation Accreditation Panel (JPPAP) was established. Like the Youth Justice Board (YJB), the JPPAP was a non-departmental public body. Chaired by Sir Duncan Nichol, and comprising a range of academics and criminal justice professionals, the Panel's central function is to accredit programmes that, on the basis of rigorous research, are believed to reduce re-offending. According to the Panel (JPPAP, 2000), the principles associated with effective interventions include:

- Effective risk management.
- Targeting offending behaviour.
- Addressing the specific factors linked with offenders' offending.
- Relevance to offenders' learning style.
- Promoting community reintegration.
- Maintaining quality and integrity of programme delivery.

Progress has been significant according to Raynor (2002: 1189–90), himself a member of the Panel: 'From being unable in 1997 to point to more than a handful of evaluated effective initiatives, the Probation Service had been transformed within a few years into an organization able to offer quality-controlled programmes throughout England and Wales, in what is believed to be the largest initiative in evidence-based corrections to be undertaken anywhere in the world.' Moreover, '"What Works" is no longer a minority interest struggling for influence in penal policy, but an orthodoxy and a basis for policy, with all the benefits and costs which that implies' (Raynor, 2002: 167). The 'What Works' approach has been by no means without its critics. Indeed, Raynor himself has noted more recently that whilst 'it is true that the evidence base in Britain is still fairly small, and although existing research projects will enable it to grow rapidly, not all of it will necessarily support the management decisions which have already been taken. Some of these may have to be changed if the commitment to evidence-based policy is to be maintained' (Raynor and Vanstone, 2002: 105). The probation service, in the form of its main union, NAPO, has been critical of the impact of the approach on the ability of its members to use their own skills and judgement when working with offenders. Others have been sceptical about the research evidence itself, querying whether the evidence for some programmes was as firm as it was being presented as being (Merrington and Stanley, 2000) or questioning the apparent adherence to a narrow cognitive-behavioural dominated model of working with offenders (Mair, 2000).

In a classic piece of New Labour managerialism, an entirely new vehicle was created for the implementation of a what works-led agenda in relation to non-custodial penalties. With relatively little public discussion, and no visible professional dissent, after almost a century, the 54 local probation services in England and Wales were disbanded and replaced by the National Probation Service for England and Wales in April 2001. The aim was that this new Service would be more effectively controlled from the centre and that the raft of new programmes, influenced by the What-Works agenda, could be rolled out quickly and as uniformly as possible. In fact, it had originally been mooted that the prison and probation services be merged into a single corrections service (Home Office, 1998a). In the event, this did not take place, although it remains very much on the New Labour agenda at the time of writing.

The Criminal Justice and Court Services Act 2000 – given Royal Assent at the end of November 2000 – created the new National Probation Service for England and Wales, thereby radically restructuring a service that had been in existence for almost a century. The new structure comprises 42 local areas, each contiguous with local police force boundaries, each of which has a local probation board. The latter replace the previously existing 54 Probation Committees. From 1 April 2001, the new national service has been directly accountable to the Home Secretary. Where previously funding had come jointly from the Home Office and local authorities (though in a ratio of approximately 80/20), the new service is directly and, in effect, completely funded by the Home Office. In addition, the Act removed responsibility for Family Court work from the probation service and gave it to a new Family Court Advisory and Support Service (CAFCASS).

The Act defines the purpose of the service as 'assisting courts in sentencing decisions and providing for the supervision and rehabilitation of persons charged with, or convicted of, offences' (Probation Circular 25/2001). The aims of the service are:

1. to protect the public;
2. to reduce offending;
3. to provide for the proper punishment of offenders;
4. to ensure that offenders are aware of the effects of their crimes on their victims and on the public; and
5. to rehabilitate offenders.

The role of local probation boards includes employing staff, contracting for provision of services, providing hostel accommodation and contributing to the development and implementation of the local crime reduction strategy. More generally, the Act allows for 'national priorities to be interpreted in the light of local circumstances and local needs' (Probation Circular 52/2001) and it is this provision that provides the space within which the nature of the emergent 'tripartite relationship' between the service, probation boards and the Home Secretary can develop. Nonetheless, when compared even with the reformed police authorities, the new system of governance for the probation service is highly centralised.

One of the more controversial aspects of the new legislation concerned the changes made to the nomenclature of community penalties.

The tough on crime rhetoric and practice of successive administrations had seen the probation service under considerable pressure – indeed sometimes hostile attack. As was noted above, during the 1990s, it was mooted on more than one occasion that the Probation Service should be renamed and/or merged with the Prison Service. Under New Labour, both of these suggestions received new impetus. Though the Probation and Prison Services have not as yet been merged, there is a clear indication in the White Paper, *Justice For All* (Home Office, 2002a), that the idea has not been dropped altogether. For a time, it appeared that the Home Secretary was keen on renaming the Service, and 'Community Rehabilitation and Punishment Service' was seriously debated for a time. In the event, and not simply because of the unfortunate acronym that would have resulted, the idea was dropped. However, the desire to toughen the appearance of community punishment was acted upon, with the major and long-standing orders all being renamed. The 2000 Act renamed the probation order the 'community rehabilitation order', the community service order became the 'community punishment order' and the combination order became the 'community punishment and rehabilitation order'. These largely symbolic[1] changes, removing recognisable terms from statute in order to serve shorter-term political ends, have been quietly resisted. It appears, to date at least, that the probation order and the CSO retain currency among probation officers and journalists – and, indeed, occasionally, civil servants and even ministers – and are some way from having disappeared from the criminal justice lexicon.

Concluding comments

No better example can be found in the Parliament elected in 1997 of the interaction between the Government's promotional and managerial imperatives than its policies towards community penalties.

(Windlesham, 2001: 233)

A number of themes can be identified in the recent history of probation – most by no means confined to this area of criminal justice policy. The first theme of *managerialism* could actually be described in a number of ways, but it includes bureaucratisation, performance measurement and administrative control. The role of the probation service 'is now no longer welfare inspired but driven by court advocacy and the coordination of voluntary and private agencies' (McLaughlin and Muncie, 1994: 124).

There is more to it, however, than merely the subjugation of professional skills to management ideals and the primacy of value for money. The second major theme is *centralisation*. Though the trajectory has not been entirely consistent, or the pace uniform, perhaps the overriding

feature of change in this area has been the increasing power and control
exercised by the centre. Initially, the increasing frequency of criminal
justice legislation in relation to probation in the 1980s and 1990s, not
to mention Home Office Circulars, Green Papers, White Papers, consultation documents, decision documents, national objectives and priorities
followed by national standards, computerisation and the resource
management information system illustrated that in the tripartite structure of probation governance, it is the Home Office rather than the Chief
Probation Officer or the local probation committee which drove probation policy. To that extent, the more recent reforms are in many respects
of a piece with what preceded them. Thus, even before the radical
reforms of the past few years, it was clear that managerialism and
centralisation had had a profound impact on the underlying philosophy
of the probation service. As one informed commentator put it almost
a decade ago, the probation service has, during its relatively short history,
'moved from a theologically to a psychiatrically driven discourse and then
to what has been termed a post-psychiatric paradigm based less on therapy than on system involvement and offender management' (Harris,
1994: 34).

A highly centrally controlled, national service has been created. The
climate into which this new service emerged was a considerably 'tough-
ened' one in which the language of punishment replaced the original
mission of to 'advise, assist and befriend' (that duty was repealed by the
Criminal Justice and Court Services Act 2000). As with so much of the
New Labour penal landscape, however, the combination of 'tough on
crime' and 'tough on the causes of crime' messages meant that philosophical clarity was by no means always present. Two descriptions of the
aims of the new national probation service serve to illustrate this. First, in
his speech to launch the new National Probation Service in July 2001, the
Home Secretary, David Blunkett, said:

> I am not going soft. I've not abandoned my roots. I represent a deeply
> deprived inner-city community who have had their bellyful of people
> apologising for those who destroy lives. Undoubtedly, people learn more
> about crime in prison than they will learn anywhere else in their lives. The
> object is not to increase the prison population, but to prevent people going
> into prison in the first place. Rehabilitation is the highest possible priority
> for those who enter the criminal justice system.[2]

By contrast, in his foreword to the 2000 National Standards, the then
junior Minister, Paul Boateng, said:

> We are a law enforcement agency. That is what we are. That is what we do.
> (Home Office, 2000b)

For all that rehabilitation, via 'What Works', may remain on the agenda,
it is clear that Boateng's description gets closest to the heart of the

modern probation service. The new managerialism that has been applied to probation goes much further than simply attempting to measure whether the service is efficiently and economically run and, instead, seeks to measure whether it is 'effective'. That is, from now on, the probation service is to be judged by 'outcomes' rather than 'outputs' – or at least that is the avowed intention. To what extent the evidence-base exists to make such aims realistic is at best questionable. Nonetheless, as Boateng's description implies, a continuing role for the probation service in the management of offenders – both on community penalties and the increasing numbers released from custody – should be secure for some time to come.

Notes

1. Lord Hurd of Westwell noted in Parliament that little 'good is done in the real world by altering the labels on people's official notepaper and on their office doors' (quoted in Windlesham, 2001: 240).
2. Home Office press release 'Put the sense back into sentencing', 5 July 2001.

Chapter 7

Sentencing and non-custodial penalties

It is often suggested that one of the basic conventions in British criminal justice is that there exists a separation between penal policy and sentencing policy. Thus, and crudely, it is sometimes argued that penal policy is a matter for the government, whereas sentencing policy is a matter for the judiciary. Furthermore, in an attempt to sustain such a separation, the principle of judicial independence is sometimes invoked. Such an interpretation of the idea of judicial independence has, however, been widely criticised. Commentators such as Ashworth (1992) challenge the idea that the principle of judicial independence can be so broadly defined, and he suggests that the separation of penal policy and sentencing policy, rather than being a constitutional principle, is in fact merely a policy preference. Nevertheless, as has been suggested, the idea that such a separation actually exists in principle has a certain currency, a currency it acquired 'largely as a result of parliamentary abstention which had its origins in the late nineteenth century and reached its zenith in the third quarter of this century' (Ashworth, 1992: 41).

As a number of writers have pointed out, irrespective of whether or not the principle of judicial independence should imply a distinction between penal policy and sentencing policy, there is some evidence that the separation has been challenged in recent years: 'government ministers have with increasing frequency addressed remarks to sentencers, and the judges have declared that they are taking account of the gross overcrowding in the prisons' (Ashworth, 1983: 98). Not only is it being challenged, but Ashworth (1983), among others, has argued that it is right that it should be challenged, for those responsible for the formulation of penal policy have, he believes, tended to have too little regard to sentencing, and that what is required is some means of improving co-ordination of policy in the criminal justice system.

As will by now be clear, if one concern has dominated penal policy over the past 25 years, it has been the aim of reducing the prison population (see Chapters 2 and 6), though this aim has apparently ceased to be a concern for Home Secretaries in the past decade. Equally, it has been the overriding concern with prison numbers which has led to gradual breaking down of the previously existing convention that sentencing policy was not a matter for the executive. In seeking to limit custody, the key method that has been utilised during the last two to three decades has been the introduction and use of an increasing array of alternatives to immediate custodial sentences. The assumption has been that such alternatives would help 'exert some influence over the number of occasions on which courts resort to immediate custody' (Ashworth, 1983: 116).

The focus of this chapter is upon the introduction and use of alternatives to custody, and the impact of such changes on the size of the custodial population. As we move on to look at the recent trends in the use of non-custodial penalties by the courts, the reason for beginning this chapter with a brief discussion of the ideas of sentencing policy and judicial independence will become clear. The reason, in short, is that the ever-increasing range of alternatives – what Ashworth (1992: 242) calls the *policy of proliferation* – has not been a success. There has been no marked fall during the past 25 years in the use of custodial sentences – indeed, quite the reverse. What are the reasons for this failure? The first reason, according to Stern (1989), is that already alluded to: there is a 'taboo' which until recently inhibited discussion of sentencing policy. The taboo acted to prevent or limit the extent to which politicians felt able to recommend changes in sentencing policy. Indeed, 'the whole idea of sentencers being influenced by Home Secretaries is highly contentious' (Stern, 1989: 41). Second, the practice of sentencing is highly individualistic and subject to wide geographical variation. Given the absence of consistency in sentencing 'it is no wonder that . . . the intentions of the policy-makers, even if they were accepted as legitimate, are thwarted' (Stern, 1989: 42). Finally, even if recommendations are made, there has only very recently emerged a formal mechanism for translating them into practice. Sentencers are not government officials, they use their personal judgement in applying the law in each case they are faced with. In beginning to unpick what has happened since the late 1960s, it is worth beginning by looking at the use and impact of some of the major non-custodial sentences in turn.

The probation order

The probation order was dealt with in detail in the last chapter and it will be sufficient here merely to review the changing pattern in its use over the past three decades or so. From the mid-1960s, and through the 1970s, there was an almost continual decline in the use of the probation order (see Table 7.1). Whilst there is no simple explanation for this decline, the introduction of the suspended sentence of imprisonment and of community service orders clearly played a part. Bottomley and Pease (1986) have also suggested that some of the decline in the 1970s may have been due to a tendency on the part of sentencers to fine rather than use probation, a tendency which itself declined in the 1980s as unemployment rose and financial penalties became an apparently less appropriate option in many cases. The low point for the probation order came in 1978, when only five per cent of people aged 21 and over sentenced for indictable offences received probation. This had risen back to eight per cent by 1989 (the figure had been 15 per cent in 1938).

The six-month probation order was introduced in 1978 and it proved popular, as did shorter orders more generally. Approximately one-quarter of probation orders in the early 1970s were of three years in length, but the proportion had declined to under one in 20 by the mid-1980s. By contrast, the proportion of one-year orders increased from one in ten to one in three during the same period. The trend in the period immediately before the Criminal Justice Act 1991 was towards greater use of probation, and the Act sought to reinforce this process. However, the whole nature of the probation order has now, of course, changed. Prior to the Criminal Justice Act 1991, a probation order was made 'instead of sentencing' the offender. Since the passage of the Act, probation has become a sentence of the court, i.e. a *punishment*. The Act states that the court may not impose a community sentence, for example, probation, unless the offence 'was serious enough to warrant such a sentence'. Consequently, therefore, the court must be satisfied that the offence was too serious to warrant, say, a fine or a discharge. The 1991 Act also consolidated powers first introduced under the Powers of Criminal Courts Act 1973 to attach conditions to a probation order. The conditions may include requirements to reside in a probation hostel or another approved place, to take part in or refrain from certain activities, to attend a non-residential probation centre and/or to undertake treatment for medical or psychiatric conditions or alcohol or drug dependency. This consolidation was part of the general 'strengthening' of probation orders that occurred during the 1990s. 'Intensive probation' was intended to operate towards the top of the tariff with offenders very much at risk of custody. Despite this, the increase in the relative use of probation orders has been only slight, and there is little evidence that 'up-tariffing' has occurred, though the proportion of probationers who have previously served a custodial sentence has increased over the past decade (Brownlee, 1998). The probation order was renamed the Community Rehabilitation Order under the Criminal Justice and Court Services Act 2000.

Community service orders

Community service orders (CSOs) were introduced by the Criminal Justice Act 1972, but were not in operation nationwide until the mid-1970s. CSOs were, in part, the product of the deliberations of the

Advisory Committee on the Penal System. The ACPS had produced a report in 1970 on *Non-Custodial and Semi-Custodial Penalties* (known as the Wootton Report) which recommended the introduction of CSOs as an alternative to custody, though it suggested that it also had the potential attraction of being different things to different people:

> To some, it would be simply a more constructive and cheaper alternative to short sentences of imprisonment; by others it would be seen as introducing into the penal system a new dimension with an emphasis on reparation to the community; others again would regard it as a means of giving effect to the old adage that the punishment should fit the crime; while still others would stress the value of bringing offenders into close touch with those members of the community who are most in need of help and support.
> (ACPS, 1970, quoted in Ashworth, 1992: 267)

However, as Ashworth points out, no attempt was made either by the ACPS or by the government to locate CSOs within courts' broader sentencing practices. Indeed, Ashworth (1983) describes community service as a good idea, but in many ways a vague idea: 'It stands as a prime example of the failure of those concerned with penal policy-making to pay sufficient attention to the sentencing implications of what they do' (1983: 118). Crucially, although the CSO was introduced essentially as an alternative to custody, this was not made clear in the Criminal Justice Act 1972, which simply restricted their use to imprisonable offences.

Under a CSO, an offender was required by a court, assuming that the offender consented, to undertake between 40 and 240 hours of unpaid work. The work was organised and supervised by the probation service. The CSO became an established sentence fairly rapidly, accounting for four per cent of sentences received by persons aged 21 and over convicted of an indictable offence in 1980, rising to seven per cent in 1987 and nine per cent in 1993. Approximately one in six young adult offenders are dealt with in this way, and it has always been a sentence that is used disproportionately on this age group. As to its impact as an 'alternative to custody', research by Pease (1980; 1985) suggested that only something in the region of half of those receiving CSOs would otherwise have been sentenced to custody. In a similar fashion, Young (1979: 140) concluded: 'the hope that the community service order would divert a substantial number of offenders from custodial sentences may have been unduly optimistic. . . . It might have been hoped that, in the courts which made greater use of imprisonment there would have been more scope for the use of the community service order as an alternative to it; in fact, in general the reverse was true.'

The increasing 'punitiveness' affecting criminal justice generally in the mid-1990s also impacted on community service. Consent to the order was generally considered to be one of the key prerequisites for the making of an order, in order to avoid the charge of 'forced labour'.

The Conservative administration, however, took the view that this should be unnecessary, given the number of safeguards covering the conditions under which community service was undertaken. Willingness to comply with the order was, they suggested, the most important factor and that courts should be free to impose a CSO irrespective of the views of the offender. The removal of the requirement that the offender consented to the making of an order was included within the Crime (Sentences) Act 1997 – legislation largely supported by the New Labour government. Again, the order was renamed by the Criminal Justice and Court Services Act 2000 and is now known as the Community Punishment Order. The Combination Order – community service and probation combined (see below) – is renamed the Community Punishment and Rehabilitation Order.

The fine

The most long-standing of the non-custodial penalties which currently exist is the fine. Initially, courts required that fines be paid in full and it was not until 1914 that paying by instalments became possible. One consequence of this was a very sharp reduction in the number of offenders imprisoned for non-payment of fines. The major increase in the use of fines took place after the Second World War, when the range of indictable offences that could be punished in this way was considerably broadened. By the 1970s, over half of adult offenders convicted of indictable offences were fined, and it is incontrovertibly the most successful community penalty at displacing custody. Part of the success of the fine has been at the expense of probation (Bottomley and Pease, 1986; Cavadino and Dignan, 1992) and the conditional discharge. As was suggested above, the increasing popularity of the fine seemed to tail off in the 1980s, a time when the use of other non-custodial penalties and, indeed, custody itself was rising quite dramatically. Undoubtedly, unemployment and the consequent inability of many offenders to pay substantial financial penalties were significant factors in this transformation.

Varying ability to pay, and how this ability should be assessed and the level of fines set, has been an ever-present difficulty with this penalty. Many European countries have sought to solve such difficulties by using a system known as the 'day fine', where the level of the fine is linked to a fixed proportion of the offender's income. Such a system – known as 'unit fines' – was introduced by the Criminal Justice Act 1991 and subsequently withdrawn by the Criminal Justice Act 1993. Ostensibly, the introduction of the unit fine system was an object lesson in 'good government'. Possible changes were widely canvassed, significant consultation took place with the majority of interested parties, a rigorous evaluation of an experimental system in four Crown Courts was undertaken and published, and yet the new system was barely in operation before it was dismantled. We will return to this remarkable penal *volte face* below when the Criminal Justice Act 1991 is discussed in greater detail.

The suspended sentence of imprisonment

The suspended sentence of imprisonment was introduced at the same time as parole, by the Criminal Justice Act 1967. As was suggested in Chapter 2, it had been considered and rejected twice in the 1950s by the Advisory Council on the Treatment of Offenders, and interest in the measure was reawakened in the 1960s – indeed, as with many criminal justice measures at the time, it received cross-party support. Ashworth (1983: 116) argues that: 'the popularity of the suspended sentence with the government of the time was strongly connected with their desire "to find ways of emptying the prisons".' In addition, however, it was also believed that it would prove to be a useful extra non-custodial penalty.

Up until 1972, courts were required to suspend the majority of prison sentences of under six months. The situation now is that courts are empowered to suspend prison sentences of two years or less, for a period of between one and two years. If during the period of the suspension the offender is convicted of committing a further offence, the court is obliged to send the offender to prison.

The problem with the suspended sentence as a method of controlling the use of custody is that it seems clear that its use has by no means been confined to those cases in which immediate custody would otherwise have been ordered. Though estimates vary, it is suggested that up to half of those given suspended sentences would not have been sentenced to immediate custody had the suspended sentence not existed. Research by Bottoms (1981) points to a number of reasons for this state of affairs. First, in addition to the aim of avoiding imprisonment, it appears that there was a more generalised 'special deterrent' theory associated with the suspended sentence which encouraged courts to use it in place of certain non-custodial sentences in some circumstances (Bottomley and Pease, 1986) despite legal rules to the contrary. Second, some courts have tended to impose longer sentences when the sentence was suspended than they would have done when ordering immediate imprisonment (Bottoms, 1981: 6). Bottomley and Pease (1986: 91) sum up the limited impact of the suspended sentence on the prison population in the following way:

> Three in ten of all offenders given suspended sentences are reconvicted of a new offence before the period of suspension has expired. Judicial instructions specify that under these circumstances the suspended sentence is usually activated (i.e. you go directly to jail). They further specify that any

prison sentence in respect of the new offence be served consecutive to, and not concurrent with, the activated suspended sentence. In consequence, many of those reconvicted after a suspended sentence eventually go to prison for longer than they would if the original sentence had not been suspended. When it is also remembered that no more than half of those given suspended sentences would previously have been given a custodial sentence, it is clear that any contribution made by the suspended sentence to the reduction of the prison population can only be marginal. More importantly, the operation is unfair.

The general trends in the use of the major custodial and non-custodial penalties over the past 40 years are contained in Table 7.1 below.

Recent history in sentencing practice can be divided into a number of periods. Ashworth (1983) distinguishes between the periods 1967–72 and 1973–81, and to this may be added the period up to and just beyond the Criminal Justice Act 1991 and, finally, the period since 1992. Ashworth has argued that the main characteristic of penal change between 1967 and 1972 was the introduction of a series of new penalties for the courts to use in the sentencing of offenders. In the period following this up until the early 1980s, it 'was the orchestration of changes in the sentencing practices of the courts' (1983: 132). As we have seen above, there had been significant statutory change in the late 1960s and early 1970s, and even though there was very little legislative change between 1973 and 1981, there was nevertheless quite considerable change in sentencing practice (see Table 7.1). Thus, in the mid-1970s, the use of immediate and suspended imprisonment were at their lowest proportionate level and the fine was at its highest. From that point onwards, the fine and probation have taken a smaller share, whereas the use of immediate

Table 7.1: Percentage of offenders sentenced for indictable offences, by selected sentences (all courts), 1963–2001

	Probation Order*	CSO**	Combination Order***	Fine	Imprisonment Suspended	Imprisonment Immediate
1963	20			40		14
1968	15			44	9	9
1973	7			51	6	8
1978	5	3		51	7	9
1983	7	7		43	7	9
1988	9	8		39	8	11
1993	10	11		34	1	11
2001	12	9	3	24	1	19

Source: Criminal Statistics England and Wales.
* *Now the Community Rehabilitation Order*
** *Now the Community Punishment Order*
*** *Now the Community Punishment and Rehabilitation Order*

imprisonment and community service has increased. As we saw in Chapter 2, with the decline of the rehabilitative ideal the principal justifications for imprisonment changed during this period.

In addition to changes in penal policy and sentencing practice, Ashworth (1983: 132) also suggests that the way in which penal policy was made and promulgated also changed. Indeed, he distinguishes between two periods, 1973–78, and the period 1979–81. In the first of these the Advisory Council on the Penal System 'assumed a much more assertive role than it had hitherto thought appropriate. . . . The use of the ACPS as a vehicle for formulating and promulgating policy passed away in 1979 with the demise of that body. In its place rose government ministers and the Lord Chief Justice, a combination peculiarly appropriate to the kinds of change which were thought necessary – changes in sentencing practice rather than legislative structure'. What were these changes in sentencing practice that the government wished to encourage?

The policy advocated by government ministers was one of 'bifurcation': wherein long custodial sentences would be reserved for the violent, the dangerous and those from whom the public need protection; and shorter sentences or non-custodial sentences would be increasingly used for the more run of the mill offenders. Indeed, in considering penal policy in detail in this period, Hudson (1993) suggests that three themes or trends, each of which can be considered as a dichotomy, can be identified. Thus the first of these, bifurcation, is set against 'continuum', the other two trends being informalism/formalism and corporatism/individualism. It is worth considering each of these briefly in turn, before moving on to consider penal policy in the 1990s.

The first trend – continuum/bifurcation – is based partly around the proliferation of sentencing options that developed in the 1970s and 1980s. Continuum refers to the idea that there should be some consistency in the nature of punishments. Hudson refers to an influential book by the American criminologist, James Q. Wilson, in which he suggests that the deprivation of liberty should be the common feature of all punishments for criminal acts. The continuum would range from those disposals which had only a marginal effect on the offender's liberty on the one hand to imprisonment on the other. 'The continuum principle can be seen at work in many of the innovations of the 1970s and 1980s: weekend or part-time prison in continental European countries; the more rigorous day centre requirements in England, as well as residential blocks in intermediate treatment programmes for juveniles' (Hudson, 1993: 33). The opposite trend to this is the aforementioned 'bifurcation', which can be seen in the increasing sentence lengths for certain serious offences – and consequent increasing custodial population despite the declining proportionate use of imprisonment – during this period.

The second dichotomy is that of informalism/formalism. One of the responses to the feeling that the increasing expenditure on criminal justice and the increasing array of sanctions available to the courts was having precious little effect on levels of crime was to move away from formal processes for dealing with offenders. Particularly in relation to juvenile justice policy (see Chapter 8), a policy of 'diversion' was increasingly advocated. By this was meant, at its most minimal, diversion from custody and, at its most far-reaching, diversion from formal criminal justice processes. This might mean amongst other things the *de facto* decriminalisation of certain offences; informal cautioning rather than charging, or referral to mediation schemes rather than charging and prosecuting. During the 1980s, however, there developed a fairly full-blown critique of the proliferation of diversion schemes and alternative forms of dispute resolution. The majority of the arguments gelled around Cohen's (1979) 'dispersal of discipline' thesis. Crudely summarised, Cohen's argument was that there has been a dispersal of discipline and social control via the increasing use of community-based penalties and the policy of diversion. One of the unintended consequences of informalism was to draw into the criminal justice system people who would not otherwise have been dealt with under formal procedures. In addition, 'diversion schemes also formalised the informal by giving quasi-official powers to new people – parents, social workers, colleagues became parties to contracts, treatment, reporting' (Hudson, 1993: 40). In his critique of Cohen, Bottoms (1983) suggests that an analysis of the period since the War shows that both imprisonment and probation declined as a proportion of all offences and that, in fact, it was the penalties not involving supervision – such as the fine and the suspended sentence – which flourished. This, as we have seen, was reversed in the 1980s, with a significant decline in the proportionate use of the fine, and a commensurate increase in the use of probation, community service and imprisonment.

One of the consequences of the critique of informalism was the development of the contradictory trend towards formalism. Formalism involved a desire to return to type of classical or formal justice model. The most influential of these were based on the 'just deserts' principle which would link sentencing to the seriousness or gravity of the offence under consideration. At its core, however, Hudson (1993) suggests that this model contained a desire to curb professional discretion through sentencing guidelines (generally via the Court of Appeal). In addition, the Criminal Justice Act 1982 imposed limiting criteria for imposing custodial sentences on offenders under the age of 21 and on any offenders not previously sentenced to custody. Hudson (1993: 45–6) concludes that: 'The innovations of informalism have been maintained, but have been incorporated in the formal justice system. They have been subjected to more and more control by the state, to more formal procedures and criteria, so that the combined effect of the seemingly contradictory impulses to formalism and informalism has been aggregative rather than counter-balancing.'

The final trend Hudson identifies is that of corporatism/individualism. She suggests that there was an increasing trend throughout the 1980s to individualise penalties, particularly non-custodial penalties, by specifying programmes tailored to the needs of the individual offender. However, 'this greater differentiation and individualisation which can be demonstrated in criminal justice policy and practice is largely, however, a tactic in a strategy which is anything but individualistic' (Hudson, 1993: 47). The 'corporatist' approach within which this individualisation has occurred has, for example, refocused attention on crime rates rather than individual offenders, and on prison numbers and overcrowding rather than the effects of punishment on the individual.

Much of what happened in the 1980s appears to have occurred despite the absence of a well-developed or articulated penal policy. Nevertheless, the primary driving force remained the crisis in the prison estate. Despite the proliferation of alternatives to custody in the 1960s and 1970s, the policies of bifurcation and informalism and, crucially, increasing attempts to limit judicial discretion throughout the 1980s, the prison population continued to rise (see Chapter 2). This, together with the collapse of faith in reductivist goals and increasing recognition of the sentencing disparities which existed in different parts of the country (see Ashworth, 1984), led to pressure for reform of sentencing policy. As Wasik (1992: 127) argues: 'the apparent ineffectiveness of the Court of Appeal in persuading sentencers to send fewer offenders to custody, and for shorter periods of time . . . persuaded the legislature that this objective ha[d] to be achieved by legislative reform to fetter the discretion of sentencers.' The result was the Criminal Justice Act 1991.

The Criminal Justice Act 1991

Out of the variety of competing sentencing principles still around during the 1970s and 1980s, it was desert theory that by the end of the decade had won the day. The desert approach to sentencing puts the emphasis upon the moral requirement to maintain some proportion between offence and punishment. The primary assumption behind the punishment is that it should be what is deserved for the offence, having regard to the seriousness of the harm caused or risked by the offender and their degree of culpability. Desert theory treats the sentencing of offenders as something that is quite distinct from either tackling the causes of offending or attempting to do something about overall crime levels in society.

It would be wrong, however, to present the ascendancy of just deserts at this time as if were merely the triumph of one principle over another. Whilst there was certainly waning confidence in the reductivist strategy which placed so much emphasis on deterrence, the placing of faith in just deserts and subsequent Criminal Justice Act's barriers to the use of custody 'owed just as much to pragmatic considerations about the costs and benefits of punishment in prison as to any weakening of resolve to be "tough on crime"' (Raine and Willson, 1993: 39). Perhaps the clearest indication that desert principles were in the ascendancy was in the publication of the 1990 White Paper, *Crime, Justice and Protecting the Public*. It was very clear about the limitations of deterrence as a basis for penal policy:

> Deterrence is a principle with much immediate appeal. . . . But much crime is committed on impulse, given the opportunity presented by an open window or unlocked door, and it is committed by offenders who live from moment to moment; their crimes are as impulsive as the rest of their feckless, sad or pathetic lives. It is unrealistic to construct sentencing arrangements on the assumption that most offenders will weigh up the possibilities in advance and base their conduct on rational calculation. Often they do not.
>
> (Home Office, 1990c, para. 2.8)

The White Paper proposed reforms both to sentencing and early release arrangements, with the aim of creating 'a coherent framework for the use of financial community and custodial punishments'. In doing so, it proposed that proportionality should be the basis upon which decisions about the severity of sentences should be made (Wasik and von Hirsch, 1990). Thus, under the new structure the courts would continue to decide both upon sentence severity in relation to individual offences and on the weight given to any aggravating or mitigating circumstances. The major recommendations in the White Paper were incorporated in to the Criminal Justice Act 1991.

Wasik (1992: 131) suggests that the best way to understand the Act is:

> as laying down a set of general guidelines for sentencing. There is no American style sentencing grid, so that guidance is by general principles expressed in words rather than by numbers. The Act deals with custodial sentences, community sentences, fines and discharges which can be seen as occupying four distinct levels in a pyramid, with custodial sentencing at the top and discharges at the base [see Figure 7.1]. Selection of the appropriate level for sentencing in this hierarchy is crucially dependent upon the seriousness of the offence of conviction. Offence seriousness determines into which sentencing 'box' the sentence will fit, and also at what level within that particular 'box'. Of course, offence seriousness has always been an important element in sentence decision making but . . . other factors have been used by sentencers to override it. The importance of the Act lies in its conceptual framework, and its emphasis upon the proportionality between offence seriousness and penalty severity.

Although in establishing a framework the Act prevented the use of custody unless the court was satisfied that the offence was 'so serious that only a custodial sentence could be justified', it did allow for an exception to this framework. Thus, in cases of violent or sexual offences, courts could impose a prison sentence if it was believed that only such a

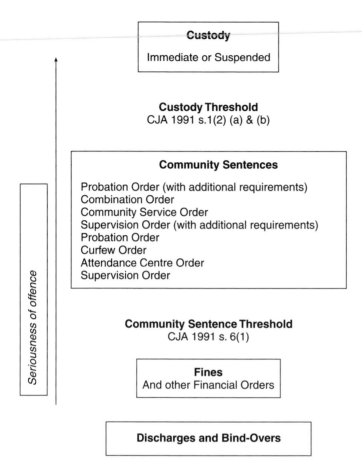

Figure 7.1:   The sentencing framework in the Criminal Justice Act 1991
Source: Brownlee (1998)

sentence would be sufficient to protect the public from serious harm from the offender. Such a sentence could also be longer than would be proportionate to the seriousness of the offence that had been committed. It is in relation to the application of 'just deserts' to community penalties that Wasik (1992) suggests that the Act is perhaps most innovative, for up until this point such principles had rarely been applied to non-custodial penalties. The Act states that a court shall not pass a community sentence 'unless it is of the opinion that the offence, or the combination of the offence and one other offence associated with it, was serious enough to warrant such a sentence'. Thus, the only justification for imposing a community sentence under the Act is offence seriousness and, crucially therefore, community sentences are not to be considered to be 'alternatives to custody', but as distinctive penalties in their own right. Indeed, it was at this point that the probation order became a sentence in its own right rather than an order made in place of a sentence. The Act then represented a significant departure not only from previous legislation, but from the previous style of policy-making. As one senior Home Office official commented:

> The Act can be seen as a first attempt to construct a truly comprehensive piece of legislation governing sentencing. It covers the whole process: virtually the whole range of disposals available; the reasoning to be applied when reaching decisions; the methods by which sentences can be calculated and implemented; and, in the case of custody, the whole process from reception, right through to the expiry of the the term imposed. The sheer scale of the attempt, taken as a whole, is probably unprecedented. Previous reforms have been more piecemeal. . . . The Act breaks new ground in another way. This Act – as distinct from any others on the subject – seeks to incorporate a clearly stated set of principles about sentencing – a sentencing philosophy if you like. . . . Governments habitually explain their policies in White Papers – in this case, the White Paper 'Crime, Justice and Protecting the Public'. If this is the case, the Act seeks to incorporate the policies in statutory form.
>
> (quoted in Gibson et al., 1994: 33)

In what ways, then, did the Criminal Justice Act 1991 alter the range of non-custodial penalties outlined at the beginning of this chapter? One of the primary aims of the 1991 Act was to promote community penalties as tough and demanding, and as realistic options for courts, who were to be discouraged from overuse of custodial sentences. As the Green Paper published in 1988 put it: 'Imprisonment is not the most effective punishment for most crime. Custody should be reserved as punishment for very serious offences, especially when the offender is violent and a continuing risk to the public. But not every sentencer or member of the public has full confidence in the present orders which leave offenders in the community. [Hence] . . . the Government's proposals, which aim to increase the courts' and the public's confidence in keeping offenders in the community' (Home Office, 1988b: 1–2).

One consequence of the proportionate approach to sentencing is, as suggested above, that community penalties can no longer be considered to be 'alternatives to custody'. No longer was it the case that a court might consider a custodial sentence to be the appropriate one, but then decide that an alternative strategy might be pursued in relation to a particular offender. The idea in the new scheme was that community punishments should themselves be sufficiently demanding so that they could be used in all but the most serious of cases.

One of the key changes introduced by the 1991 Act was the amendment of the system of fines. Largely in response to perceived difficulties and inequities in the operation of the system of financial penalties, the 1991 Act contained provision for the introduction of what has been called the 'unit fine'. In essence, and using a set of guidelines, offences before the court were to be assessed in terms of their number of units of 'seriousness'. This could range from 1–50 units. Once the seriousness of the offence had been determined in this manner, the offender would be required to complete a means form which would assess their weekly disposable income. This would determine the amount to be paid per individual unit, subject to the statutory minima and maxima of £4 and £100. In principle, the intention was that fines should be equalised in terms of their impact upon offenders committing similar offences but who were of vastly differing means. A lot of effort went into piloting the new system. In the four Crown Court centres in which the research was conducted, fines were paid more quickly, there were fewer committals to prison for default, the poorest defendants were fined the least and there was no extension in the use of fines (Moxon et al., 1990). However, unit fines once formally introduced were widely criticised almost from the outset. Raine and Willson (1993: 38) suggest that 'the "professionals" were wary about their discretion being eroded and many were opposed to the scheme, especially when a serious offence by a low income defendant attracted a smaller fine than a minor one by a comparatively wealthy defendant'. We will return to unit fines below.

One of the consequences of the Act was to end the status of the probation order as a conditional release granted instead of a punishment, and to make it a sentence in its own right. It became one of several 'punishments in the community'. In addition, the minimum age at which an offender could be placed on probation was lowered from 17 to 16 years, and the criteria for the making of a probation order were clarified. As has been suggested, the policy of bifurcation which underpinned the White Paper and the 1991 Act consisted in part of an attempt to persuade sentencers to increase their use of community sanctions. In doing so, the Act introduced a new, tough community penalty: the 'combination order'. This was probation and community service combined; the minimum period of supervision being 12 months, the maximum three years. Section 12 of the 1991 Act created a new order, the curfew order. In addition, there was also provision for electronic monitoring to take place, although a curfew order could be made with such 'tagging'. These orders could be made on anyone over the age of 16 and they required the offender to be in a specified place at a specified time.

What of the suspended sentence of imprisonment? How did this penalty fit into the new system? As Cavadino and Dignan (1992) argue, the suspended sentence does not fit easily into the just deserts framework established by the 1991 Act. Most importantly, the problem centres around the fact that it is in theory the most severe penalty short of immediate custody, yet many sentencers clearly perceive it to be somewhat less punitive in practice. This was clearly articulated in *Custody, Justice and Protecting the Public* (Home Office, 1990c): 'In practice, however, many offenders see a suspended sentence as being "let off", since it places no restrictions other than the obligation not to offend again. If they complete the sentence satisfactorily, all they have felt is the denunciation of the conviction and sentence, any consequent publicity and, of course, the impact of acquiring a criminal record. The suspended sentence does not fit easily into the proposed new sentencing arrangements'. The 1991 Act abolished the partly suspended sentence and in relation to the fully suspended sentence provided that courts could not impose such a sentence unless, first, the case was one in which immediate custody would have been justified and, second, that the suspension of the sentence could 'be justified by the exceptional circumstances of the case'. The result, Ashworth (1992: 277) suggests 'is confusion perpetuated and confounded'.

Overall, however, the Criminal Justice Act 1991 was greeted very favourably by penologists, criminologists and many criminal justice pressure groups. Paul Cavadino of NACRO, writing in 1992, said: 'Taken overall, the Criminal Justice Act 1991 has the potential to bring about a more rational and coherent sentencing framework which uses custody more sparingly and community sentences more appropriately. Whether it fulfils this potential in practice will depend on the joint efforts of all agencies working in the criminal justice system to make the best use of the Act's many positive features'. In terms of sentencing trends after the Criminal Justice Act 1991 there appear to be two distinct phases (Gibson et al., 1994). There was, first of all, a short period in which the use of custody fell, followed by a longer period in which the trend was reversed. As a consequence of the first phase, the number of prisoners held in police cells was substantially reduced and was halted, temporarily, in February 1993. During this first phase it appears that the use of community service orders increased fairly substantially, though the number of probation orders fell. In addition, of course, there was the use of the completely new community penalty: the combination order. Finally, there was some evidence that in the wake of the introduction of the unit fine system that the overall use of the fine for indictable offences was increasing (Home Office Statistical Bulletin 25/93).

Retreat from the 1991 Act

Despite the extensive process of consultation that had preceded the White Paper, the broad degree of support for the intentions behind the legislation that there appeared to be amongst criminal justice professionals and practitioners, and some of the early positive signs visible in sentencing, it was not long before a governmental retreat from the 1991 Act began. It started with the arrival of Kenneth Baker as Home Secretary and the reintroduction of penal populism in the form of campaigns against 'bail bandits' and 'joyriding' – the latter ending with the hasty passage of new legislation: the Aggravated Vehicle Taking Act 1991. It was, however, the appointment of Kenneth Clarke as Home Secretary that signalled a more radical change in the criminal justice policy agenda (his impact on policing policy has already been noted in Chapter 3). One of his first moves was to initiate, with the support of the police and the press, a campaign against so-called 'persistent young offenders' (Hagell and Newburn, 1994) and, more specifically, to recommend the possible introduction of new (custodial) measures to deal with the perceived problem caused by such offenders. This is discussed in greater detail in the next chapter.

Kenneth Clarke, whilst Home Secretary, avoided becoming personally associated with the implementation of the 1991 Act and gave every impression of being generally unhappy with it. The new Lord Chief Justice, Lord Taylor of Gosforth, entered the debate, criticising the new framework introduced by the Act:

> However forward-thinking the penologists, criminologists and bureaucrats in government departments may be, their views should not be allowed to prevail so as to impose a sentencing regime which is incomprehensible or unacceptable to right-thinking people generally. If this happens, there could be a real risk of aggrieved parties taking the law into their own hands. . . . I believe the fundamental error underlying the Act is a misconceived notion that sentencing should be programmed so as to restrict the discretion of the sentencing judge. . . . The laudable desire to reduce and confine custodial sentencing to cases where it is really necessary has led to restrictive provisions forcing the judges into an ill-fitting strait-jacket.
>
> (quoted in Raine and Willson, 1993: 90)

He was followed into the fray by the Magistrates' Association, which was publicly critical of s. 29 of the Act (which dealt with the admissability of previous convictions) and of unit fines, which were held to be causing sentencers significant difficulties. Among these, two were key. First, as Brownlee (1998: 145) notes, 'there was a sense among magistrates that the rubric in which unit fines were handed out diminished the denunciatory effect of the sentence'. That is, the direct link between the size of the fine and the seriousness of the offence was perceived to have been largely removed from court. Second, the increase in the maximum permissible fines had the effect of not only leading to higher fines, but also greater differentials. Concern among the bench and scepticism among the public were fanned by highly critical reporting in the press (there was a major furore, for example, over a case in which someone was fined £1,000 for dropping a crisp packet in the street).

Kenneth Clarke's response was to appear to be sympathetic to the criticisms and to promise an inquiry into the alleged shortcomings of the legislation. Whilst the subsequent relocation of Mr Clarke to the Treasury might have been expected to have resulted in a return to normal business in the Home Office, his replacement, Michael Howard, soon signalled that he desired to be seen to be just as 'radical' as his predecessor. In addition to contradicting the bulk of the advice and evidence he was given on the limitations of imprisonment as a criminal justice strategy, he embarked on what appeared to be a one-man crusade to reintroduce the type of hard-line policies of 20 years previously. These included restricting cautioning, toughening bail decision-making, restricting juvenile justice agencies' work with young offenders and restricting prisoners' rights. In the country at large, public worries about crime were heightened by the brutal and shocking murder of two-year-old James Bulger in February 1993, and the very high profile trial of the two ten-year-old defendants later in the year. At the 1993 Conservative Party conference, the Home Secretary in outlining his criminal justice policy – a policy which he recognised would lead to an increase in the use of custodial sentences – said: 'I do not flinch from that. We shall no longer judge the success of our system of justice by a fall in our prison population. . . . Let us be clear. Prison works'. This reassertion of Thatcherite 'law and order' values culminated in the passage of legislation to amend the 1991 Act, an Act which after years of consultation had only been in force a matter of months.

The Criminal Justice Act 1993 reversed some of the key elements of the earlier legislation, in particular, the criteria justifying the use of custodial sentences; the role of an offender's previous record in sentencing; and the unit fine system. Whereas the 1991 Act restricted the courts to no more than two current offences when deciding whether custody was justified, the Criminal Justice Act 1993 amended this so that courts could in future consider the combined seriousness of any number of offences. Second, whereas the 1991 Act stated that an offence should not be regarded as more serious by reason of any previous convictions or any failure to respond to previous sentences, the 1993 Act states: 'In considering the seriousness of any offence, the court may take into account *any* previous convictions of the offender or any failure of his to respond to previous sentences' (emphasis added). Finally, the 1993 Act removed the system of unit fines and replaced it with a system in which fines are 'a flexible product of seriousness and financial circumstances . . . [though] what weight is given to particular factors in a given case are left to the court' (Gibson et al., 1994: 156).

Reflecting upon these changes, one former senior Home Office administrator said: 'The Government's change of direction in its policies on crime and criminal justice is probably the most sudden and the most radical which has ever taken place in this area of public policy' (quoted in Gibson et al., 1994: 84). From early 1993 onwards, and perhaps not surprisingly given the nature of the most recent criminal justice legislation, sentencing trends began to change. First of all, there was a very sharp increase in the prison population, though this was partly a consequence of an increase in the number of prisoners on remand. There was some indication that commencements of both probation orders and community service orders rose, though there also appeared to be a trend towards longer orders (Association of Chief Officers of probation (ACOP), 1994). During the early 1990s these trends continued. Thus, although there was some levelling-off of the proportionate use of community sentences for indictable offences in the Crown Court, the proportionate use of custody rose by four per cent and 12 cent respectively in the magistrates' courts and the Crown Court during 1993 (Home Office, 1994a). Finally, the proportionate use of the fine for indictable offences at magistrates' courts, having risen after the 1991 Act, fell from 45 per cent of sentences at the end of 1992 to around 38 per cent at the end of 1993.

Despite the breadth and the speed of change in penal policy, the legislative programme was, however, still not complete. In addition to reaffirming his belief in the efficacy of imprisonment, Michael Howard announced at the 1993 Conservative Party conference a 27-point package of 'emergency action to tackle the crime wave'. This included restricting the right to silence, reducing the use of cautioning and tightening bail provisions, and the introduction of secure training centres for persistent juvenile offenders. Later in the year, the Criminal Justice and Public Order Bill was introduced, and it included, in some form, all the above-mentioned measures, together with a good deal more. The Bill had a fairly stormy passage in Parliament, but became law in 1994. The Act included, amongst others, provisions for secure training orders for 12–14 year olds (see Chapter 8); increased the grounds for refusing bail; allowed inferences to be drawn from the use of the right of silence; and introduced a new offence of aggravated trespass. Although as a piece of legislation it had little coherence and was, in many ways, merely a mishmash of largely unconnected provisions, it clearly belonged within the Thatcherite 'law and order' crime control tradition. It is in many ways hard to believe that less than half a decade had passed since the desert-based Criminal Justice Bill was first published. It was a piece of legislation that took many years to construct, and yet it was undermined in a matter of months, largely because of political ideology. Despite its detractors, and the apparent ease with which it was dismantled, the Criminal Justice Act 1991 had a great many supporters. Indeed, it was the view of one former Home Office minister that that particular piece of legislation:

> held out greater promise than any of its predecessors in the cycle of criminal justice legislation since 1948. For the first time, after a long and painstaking period of gestation, Parliament was presented with what was intended to be a coherent statutory framwork for sentencing. . . . Both the judicial and political omens were favourable. Despite some reservations about the way the sentencing provisions were expressed, there was no attempt by the higher judiciary to oppose or reject them on the grounds that their independence or prerogatives were being encroached. The discreet consultation with the judges, dating back to the first tentative approach by Whitelaw a decade earlier, paid the hoped for dividend. Politically, the Opposition parties, and the criminologists and the penal practitioners to whom they looked for specialist advice, were generally well disposed.
>
> (Windlesham, 1993: 404–5)

Sentencing reform

According to Cheney et al. (2001: 156) 'sentencing policy during the last 15 years has been characterised by a piecemeal approach and the distinct lack of a coherent rationale'. Related to this, and perhaps its primary cause, is the increasingly politicised nature of this territory. Pretty much every Home Secretary since Kenneth Clarke has expressed some form of dissatisfaction with sentencing policy and, in particular, with sentencing practice. The backlash against the 1991 Act was sudden and dramatic. It also heralded the emergence of a period in which sentencing reform was rarely far from the top of the political agenda. Clarke was architect of the 1993 Act. His successor, Michael Howard, an avowed Americanophile, quickly located himself under the 'prison works' banner. At the 1995 Conservative Party conference, he promoted three sets of changes based in part on United States policy: increased honesty in sentencing ('no more half-sentences for full-time crimes'); mandatory minimum sentences ('if you don't want to do the time, don't do the crime'); and a variant on three strikes ('anyone convicted for a second time of a serious violent or sexual offence should receive an automatic sentence of life imprisonment').

The subsequent White Paper (Home Office, 1996a), *Protecting the Public*, included proposals for automatic life sentences for serious violent and sex offenders and mandatory minimum prison sentences for drug dealers and for burglars. The then Lord Chief Justice, Lord Taylor, attacked the proposals, arguing that:

> There is no evidence that Mr. Howard's proposals will achieve his aims. On the contrary, those who actually work in the system – lawyers, judges, probation and prison officers – are clear that they will not. There is no merit in adopting a macho attitude regardless of its efficacy. The experience of minimum and mandatory sentences in America has been that they clog up the courts and prisons while actually reducing the chances of convicting professional criminals by drastically reducing the number of guilty pleas.
>
> (*The Times*, 23 May 1996)

In the increasingly febrile political atmosphere of the time, with politicians concerned to display their 'toughness' through advocacy of deterrent and incapacitative measures, there seemed little doubt that Howard's proposals would become law. In fact, the opposition in the House of Commons was relatively muted, and as Windlesham notes, 'for close observers the main interest lay not so much in the ritual party political exchanges between Howard and Straw in their opening speeches, but in the signals of dissent on the government's own benches' (2001: 25). Indeed, the most vocal political opposition came from the House of Lords, including several ex-Home Office junior ministers and more than one ex-Home Secretary. Lord Carlisle, a Tory former Minister of State in the Home Office, said:

I am sorry to have to say that I consider that the sentencing proposals are unjustified, illogical and ill-thought through. I believe that in practice they will lead to injustice in individual cases and a far greater increase in the prison population than you [the Home Secretary] anticipate.

(Letter to Michael Howard, quoted in Windlesham, 2001: 23)

Although the sentences proposed were mandatory, the Crime (Sentences) Bill included an 'escape clause' for the life sentence provision which would allow for 'exceptional circumstances' under which the sentence would not be imposed. Perceptively as ever, Lord Chief Justice Taylor commented:

If the escape clause is construed restrictively it will have little effect. . . . If, on the other hand, the escape clause is construed more broadly, it will be said that the judiciary is *driving a coach and horses through the provisions* of the Act and thwarting Parliament. More fundamentally, the proposal subverts the function of the court, which is to sentence according to the justice of each individual case, not to see whether it can be accommodated within a narrow exception and otherwise to take a sentence of the shelf.

(Hansard, 23 May 1996, col. 1026).

In the Lords, an amendment sponsored by Lord Carlisle, together with the Labour and Liberal Democrat front benches, was put forward which extended the escape clause to any of the offences and allowed judges to have regard to specific circumstances relating to the offence or the offender. Predictably, the Home Secretary was most reluctant to accept such an amendment, but with parliamentary time running out, the 1997 General Election having been called, his hand was forced. A clearly unhappy Michael Howard said that he accepted:

. . . that there may be exceptional cases for which a mandatory penalty would be unjust or inappropriate, and that the court needs to have discretion to set aside the mandatory penalty in such cases. At the same time, the whole purpose and point of mandatory minimum sentences is to ensure that persistent burglars and drug dealers know that they can expect a stiff minimum penalty if they continue to offend. Mandatory penalties would have the salutary effect that we expect and intend them to have only if offenders knew that they would be imposed as a matter of course in the generality of cases. This will not now happen. The Lords amendments drive a coach and horses through the provisions of the Bill that deal with burglars and drug dealers.

(*Hansard* HC Deb, vol. 292, col. 982, 19 March 1997)

The Crime (Sentences) Act 1997 therefore introduced three sets of 'three strikes' mandatory sentences. It provided for an automatic life sentence for a second serious sexual or violent offence, a minimum seven year prison sentence for third-time 'trafficking' in class A drugs and a minimum three-year sentence for third-time domestic burglary. During the passage of the Bill, the then Shadow Home Secretary had been careful not to appear to be especially hostile to the Bill. Nevertheless, in some circles it was anticipated that once in power Straw would not implement the three-strikes provisions. Any such hopes were quickly dashed. In an early statement as Home Secretary in July 1997, he committed the government to implementing the automatic life sentences without delay. He then, claiming that the other mandatory minimum provisions had been 'significantly improved by Labour amendments' (*Hansard*, HC Deb, vol. 299, col. 242, 30 July 1997) and that the seven-year sentence for third-time drug traffickers would be implemented later in the year. Ashworth (2000a: 178) describes this 'three strikes' provision for class A drugs offences as 'symbolic' on the basis that under existing practice it would be normal for such an offender to receive a sentence longer than the seven years prescribed in the Act. Indeed, he suggests that as a result of the insertion of the 'escape clause', 'these provisions are relatively toothless' (2000a: 179) and concludes:

> The creation of these prescribed or minimum sentences, together with the automatic life sentence, was a form of political symbolism designed to create resentment of certain types of offender and at the same time to bolster the political fortunes of the Government.
>
> (2000a: 180)

The provision that was anticipated to have the greatest potential to affect the prison population, and the one it was felt Jack Straw was most likely to leave alone, was the three-year minimum for domestic burglars. Of this, Straw simply said in 1997 that it would be considered in future in the light of the prison capacity. As Dunbar and Langdon (1998: 155) rightly therefore argue, the Home Secretary effectively admitted that any reluctance on his part to implement the three strikes burglary provision was not based on any principled objection to the power but 'was founded simply and solely on the likelihood (or, rather, unlikelihood) of adequate resources being available'. Eventually, the measure proved irresistible and, in early 1999, the Home Secretary announced plans to implement the final 'three strikes' provision in the Act.

Considerable attention during the 1990s was paid to the aim of ensuring greater consistency in sentencing. In their election manifesto, the Labour Party 1997 proposed to:

> . . . implement an effective sentencing system for all the main offences to ensure greater consistency and stricter punishment for serious repeat offenders. The courts will have to spell out what each sentence really means in practice. The Court of Appeal will have a duty to lay down sentencing guidelines for all the main offences. The attorney general's power to appeal unduly lenient sentences will be extended.

The 1991 Act had sought to impose new restrictions and politicians had for much of the rest of the decade attempted to limit judicial discretion. For this and other reasons, the 1991 Act is rightly considered to constitute 'a landmark in the development of English sentencing law' (Ashworth, 2000a: 357). However, what the Act did not do, Ashworth argues, is make any substantial changes to the 'transmission mechanism' whereby general rules and principles contained in statute are translated into, hopefully consistent and coherent, practice in court. In many areas there remains a substantial gap between sentencing policy and sentencing practice. This may simply be because of the vagueness of statutory or appellate guidance and the fact that sometimes, of course, such guidance is simply ignored. There is now, as Leng et al. (1998: 130) put it, 'a substantial tradition of the Court of Appeal, under the guidance of the Lord Chief Justice, of issuing sentencing guidelines for various offence categories for the assistance of the Crown Court and, to a lesser extent, magistrates' courts'. In the main, guidance has traditionally focused upon the more serious offences and on the use of custody. There has been comparatively little appellate guidance on community penalties and 'it is perhaps not unfair to say that the Court of Appeal's guidance on the community sentence and custodial sentence thresholds established by the Criminal Justice Act 1991 has been very disappointing' (Leng et al., 1998: 130). Thus, perhaps the most important factor has been, as Ashworth (2000a: 358) notes, the fact that 'in many spheres of sentencing . . . [statute or appellate judgments] are either incoherent or non-existent'.

In response to this diagnosis, Ashworth recommended the introduction of a 'Sentencing Council' as early as 1983. The idea was taken up by the Labour Party later in the 1980s (Windlesham, 1993) but not by the government, whose 1990 White Paper (Home Office, 1990c) focused instead on the idea of partnership between legislature and the courts. The idea was promoted again by Ashworth during the 1990s and was taken up by Labour in opposition and then in government after their election victory in 1997. The Crime and Disorder Act 1998 both introduced a Sentencing Advisory Panel and also placed the provision of guideline judgments by the Court of Appeal on a statutory footing. The Sentencing Advisory Panel has been in operation since July 1999. Its role is to encourage consistency in sentencing and the Court of Appeal must attend to the advice of the Panel before issuing new sentencing guidelines for groups of offences. The Panel itself has the autonomy to propose that the court should issue or revise guidelines.

As Ashworth, himself a member of the Panel, notes in a somewhat understated way, 'the form, membership and powers of the Panel are in some respects significantly different from the detailed proposals' he had made earlier in the decade (2000a: 359). More particularly, the panel is arguably more 'advisory' and less 'directive' than Ashworth's original (1995: 343) proposals that such a body should have the 'task of developing and keeping under review a corpus of coherent sentencing guidance for the Crown Courts and magistrates' courts'. It is still perhaps too early to judge with any certainty how successful the Panel has been and whether its current remit is the appropriate one. In Ashworth's (2000a) view, at the very least the next step should be to consider whether stronger links can be built between the Panel's role in providing advice on consistency in sentencing and broader questions of prosecutorial guidance and criminal justice policy.

The aim of developing a more consistent and coherent sentencing system is also to be seen in the Powers of Criminal Courts (Sentencing) Act 2000 – which consolidates previous sentencing legislation and seeks, if not to codify, then at least to clarify it – and the Criminal Justice and Court Services Act 2000 which, though primarily concerned with the reform of the probation service (see Chapter 6), states its initial purpose as providing for 'courts to be given assistance in determining the appropriate sentences to pass, and making other decisions, in respect of persons charged with or convicted of offences'. One of the potentially most significant changes to sentencing policy and practice in the United Kingdom in recent years was the 'incorporation' into law of the European Convention on Human Rights via the Human Rights Act 1998. In fact, in a strict sense, the Act does not incorporate the Convention, or the rights secured by its Articles (Cheney et al., 2001). Rather, it declares that certain Articles are 'to have effect for the purposes of the Act', with the result that primary and subordinate legislation should be compatible with those Articles so far as possible, and that public authorities must not act in a way which is incompatible with a Convention right. Consequently, and in order to protect parliamentary sovereignty, the Judiciary has no power to strike down or amend primary legislation. However, a 'declaration of accountability' would be expected to 'trigger a very speedy amendment of the primary legislation by statutory instrument' (Cheney et al., 2001: 16).

There is, as yet, no firm indication of just how far reaching the Human Rights Act 1998 is going to be on sentencing policy and practice. In one interesting judgment, however, the automatic life sentence provision in the Crime (Sentences) Act 1997 was, in effect, undermined. A hearing at the Court of Appeal, headed by Lord Woolf, the Lord Chief Justice in November 2000, ruled that, taking into account the European Convention on Human Rights, the 'exceptional circumstances' to be considered by judges could take into account whether the offender was a danger to the public.[1] If not, a lesser sentence could be passed. In effect, the ruling was that the legislation would not contravene Convention rights if courts applied the provision so that it did not result in offenders being sentenced to life imprisonment when they did not constitute a significant risk to the public – effectively returning the law to the position it occupied prior to the 1997 Act.

New Labour Home Secretaries have been operating within difficult territory so far as sentencing and the courts are concerned. The modernising agenda has led in the direction of significant reform of both the organisation of the courts and the framework of sentencing. Populist pressures meant any reform seemingly has to be located, at least in part, within a punitive rhetoric. However, both because of the crippling costs and a continuing, if usually hidden, scepticism about the extent to which prison really did work, both Straw and Blunkett have on occasion appeared loath to continue to drive up the prison population.[2] In order to stimulate fresh thinking, and possibly to distance himself from politically difficult ideas, Straw set up two reviews: the Review of Criminal Courts in England and Wales under Lord Justice Auld (Auld, 2001); and the Review of the Sentencing Framework under John Halliday (Home Office, 2001). The terms of reference of the Auld Review were to inquire into:

> the practices and procedures of, and the rules of evidence applied by, the criminal courts at every level, with a view to ensuring that they deliver justice fairly, by streamlining all their processes, increasing their efficiency and strengthening the effectiveness of their relationships with others across the whole of the criminal justice system, and having regard to the interests of all parties including victims and witnesses, thereby promoting public confidence in the rule of law.

The Review was very clearly located within New Labour's modernising agenda. In announcing the appointment of the Review, the government outlined that its aim was to provide criminal courts that are, and are seen to be: 'modern and in touch with the communities they serve; efficient; fair and responsive to the needs of all their users; co-operative in their relations with other criminal justice agencies; and with modern and effective case management to remove unnecessary delays from the system'. The major recommendations of the Review included:

- The establishment of a national Criminal Justice Board to replace bodies like the Trial Issues Group, as well as local Criminal Justice Boards for giving effect to the national body's directions.
- A unified criminal court which would replace the Crown Court and the magistrates' courts with three divisions:
  - the Crown division, like the Crown Court, with jurisdiction over all indictable-only offences and the more serious either-way offences;
  - the District division, constituted by a judge or Recorder and at least two magistrates, to exercise jurisdiction over a 'mid-range' of either-way cases (that is, those most likely to incur penalties of more than six months' and no more than two years' imprisonment); and
  - the Magistrates' division, like the magistrates' courts, with jurisdiction over all summary cases and the less serious either-way cases.
- The encouragement of greater participation in the jury system through the removal of the right to ineligibility or excusability.

In terms of lasting influence, however, it appears that 'for the next few years the starting point for consideration of changes to English sentencing and sanctions will be the [Halliday Report]' (Tonry and Rex, 2002: 2).

However, they go on to argue (one of them, Michael Tonry, being a member of the Review Team) that the Halliday Review was misconceived (Tonry and Rex, 2002: 2), being insufficiently independent from Home Office politics: 'In particular, the need to accommodate Jack Straw's policy preferences for "seamless sentencing", close community supervision, "custody plus" sentences and punishment increments for successive offences, and to avoid Straw's forbidden ground of the reconsideration of mandatory minimum penalties, distorted the proposals that were made' (Tonry and Rex, 2002: 2–3). The announcement of the Halliday Review made clear the reasons for its establishment:

> Public confidence in our system of justice is too low. There is a feeling that our sentencing framework does not work as well as it should and that it pays insufficient weight to the needs of victims. . . . There is insufficient consistency or progression in sentencing and sentencers receive insufficient information about whether their sentencing decisions have worked.

The Report's recommendations were extensive and added up, if implemented, to a fairly radical overhaul of the existing system. The Report examines the apparent problems with the extant system, outlines its vision of the appropriate philosophical basis for the sentencing system, recommends a number of reforms to the system, covering sentence design, the prison estate, sentencing decision-making and enforcement and the governance of discretion. The Report's criticisms of the existing system were themselves far-reaching, including the alleged failure of the current system to focus on crime reduction and reparation, its failure to deal satisfactorily with previous convictions, its ineffective use of short prison sentences and, indeed, elements of longer sentences, together with the system's general absence of consistency, transparency and clarity.

Philosophically, the Report offers a modification of the 'just deserts' approach, or what is referred to as 'limited retributivism'. The modification of just deserts is undertaken primarily in order to take account of the fact that 'sentence severity should increase as a consequence of sufficiently recent and relevant previous convictions' (Home Office, 2001: para. 2.7). The result would be a 'punitive envelope' indicating the possible range of sentence. The primary influence on the content of the envelope would be utilitarian – selecting the option that would best serve the purposes of crime reduction and reparation. Baker and Clarkson (2002), in their evaluation of the Report's recommendations, argue that such proposals could lead to substantial disparities in the sentences received by offenders who commit similar crimes and have similar records. Indeed, they conclude that despite 'the Report's proposed codified guidelines and the limitation that the actual sentence imposed be within the bands set by the punitive envelope, the reality is the abandonment of the proportionality principle and a return to the "bad old days"' (2002: 93).

The Report made great play of the need for 'seamlessness' both of the management of offenders in custody and the community, and in terms of the relationship between the courts, partner agencies and the public. As intimated earlier, the impression that public confidence in the justice system was low was a primary driving force behind the review, and restoring and maintaining public confidence is effectively presented by the Report as a goal of sentencing policy. Thus, in discussing the body responsible for issuing sentencing guidelines the report recommends that is should 'also be responsible for monitoring their application, keeping them up to date and otherwise revising them as necessary. It should also have regard to the need to promote consistency and public confidence' (Home Office, 2001: ix). Baker and Clarkson's observations are worth quoting at length:

> The corollary of moving towards a mode of working that is more akin to collaborative partnership, and of injecting components of popular participation into the sentencing process, will be to diffuse governance over sentencing beyond the formal institutions of the State. While the former will mean that sentencing discretion is structured according to criteria that go beyond the mere matter of power relations between the arms of government, the latter introduces a democratic element into sentencing in a manner that has not previously been seen.
>
> (2002: 97)

The eventual outcome of both reviews was a White Paper, *Justice For All* (Home Office, 2002a), which recommended a broad range of reform measures, again using the language of modernisation. Most notably, these included the scrapping of the double jeopardy rule (recommended by the Stephen Lawrence Inquiry), unifying the administration of the magistrates' and Crown Court, increasing magistrates' sentencing powers from six to 12 months, creating 'intermittent' prison sentences, 'custody plus' (in which offenders serve a short prison sentence of between two weeks and three months followed by at least six months' community work) and 'custody minus' (a new suspended sentence). Extra expenditure is to be provided to 'modernise' prisons and to improve information technology, all aimed at 'joining up' the criminal justice system, together with the creation of a National Criminal Justice Board and a new Cabinet committee to oversee reform. The overall aim of the reform process is to 'rebalance' the criminal justice system in favour of victims and witnesses at the expense of defendants. Its approach, thereafter, is pragmatic rather than philosophical, attempting to reduce delays, increase detection rates and increase conviction rates. With its emphasis on systems, on efficiency, and on the greater involvement of victims and witnesses, the White Paper is a quintessentially New Labour modernising document.

Conclusion

> The impression is sometimes given by ministers and judges that the prison population is in some sense a product of forces of nature beyond political or judicial control. Like the weather moving in from the Atlantic we can at best track its course and make reasonable preparations for its coming. The analogy is entirely false. It is true that the level of crime is not readily amenable to control by government. But there is no mechanical relationship between the level of crime and the size of the prison population. There is no objective formula for deciding what tariff of punishment should be attached to a particular offence. Nor, to put the issue the other way round, is the safety of the public greatly affected by the number of offenders in prison. No force beyond government control is involved. The size of the prison population is politically determined, *whether by government action or inaction.* It follows that the prisons debate is not just about prisons. It concerns criminal justice policy generally.
>
> (Morgan, 1992b: 13–14)

Chapter 6 outlined the origins and history of the probation service and the 'probation order' (amongst other disposals). This chapter has considered the more recent history of non-custodial penalties and trends in sentencing. The period from the turn of the century to the Second World War saw, in many ways, the high point of probation. It saw the establishment of a professional service and the increasing use of a community-based disposal which, it was believed, would lead to the reform of a significant proportion of those sentenced to such supervision. However, the decline of the rehabilitative ideal, and the ever-increasing size of the prison population in the 1960s and 1970s led to the introduction of a bewildering array of non-custodial penalties, the intention being that they should in many cases be thought of and used as *alternatives to custody* with the aim of reducing the prison population.

The policy of proliferation was, however, generally a failure. As Bottoms (1987: 198) put it: 'Some of the measures seem in certain respects to have had some modest success, yet almost all of them can also be shown to have run into severe difficulties of one kind or another.' The reasons for the failure are highly complex but failure, at least in part, was a consequence of a perception widely held amongst many sentencers that the alternatives to custody were actually 'soft-options' and not alternatives at all. As a consequence of the process of attempting to persuade sentencers of the efficacy of these penalties there was a drift towards a more punitive period in community sentencing in the 1970s and 1980s (May, 1994). Punishment in the community, and the management rather than the treatment of offenders became the order of the day. Still, however, the prison numbers crisis steadfastly remained.

The solution attempted was a radical one, and involved the introduction of a statutory framework which would constrain the use of custody and encourage increased use of community penalties. After an extended process of consultation and deliberation, a desert-based framework was introduced and hopes were high that prison overcrowding, the use of police cells as overspill, and the serious rioting in prisons which accompanied overcrowding, poor conditions and loss of control, would become a thing of the past. For a short time, prison numbers declined and the use of community penalties increased. But it was not to last. The rediscovery of 'authoritarian populism' (Hall, 1979), first by Kenneth Clarke and then by Michael Howard, resulted in the quickest and most complete U-turn in criminal justice policy this century. Just deserts as an explicit sentencing rationale was abandoned in favour of a renewed faith in the deterrent and incapacitative qualities of the prison. As a consequence, there was a 20 per cent increase in the prison population in the two years 1993–94, at the same time as the most punitive elements of community penalties were emphasised. Writing at the time, and lamenting a process that seemed set to continue for some time, Gibson et al. (1994: foreword) wrote: 'Forward looking and considered policies – made following wide consultation and leading to the Criminal Justice Act 1991 – have been eroded without proper scrutiny. Every government has the right to legislate, but criminal justice issues are too important to be rushed through Parliament in the way that they are being at present, propelled by power politics.'

With almost a further decade of penal politics to look back on, it is clear that the trends that were emerging in the early 1990s remain with us. As was outlined in Chapter 2, the prison population is higher than it has ever been – over three–fifths higher than when the first edition of this book was written – and the growth is accelerating. Moreover, though there are periodic expressions of concern about the penal population, rarely is this much more than administrators concerned about 'space'. Penal populism has affected sentencing policy in all areas of penal and criminal justice policy. There have been positive developments. Great effort has gone in to attempting to increase consistency in sentencing. The Human Rights Act 1998, and the incorporation of the European Convention on Human Rights, has considerable humanitarian potential. Nonetheless, the highly politicised nature of the terrain, the desire of politicians to appear 'tough', and the lack of trust in the criminal justice system displayed partly by the public, but particularly by our political leaders, leads to what at best looks like endless tinkering with the system of sentencing and, at worst, is the continuous ratcheting up of the system of penalties available to the courts. In his last public address before his death in 1996, the then Lord Chief Justice, Lord Taylor, concluded with the words: 'I believe our system would now benefit from a period of peace and some careful reflection before embarking on more reform' (Taylor, 1996). With even more change having taken place in the years since, his words are perhaps more apposite than ever.

Notes

1. R *v* Offten and others [2001] 2 Cr. App. R. (S.) 44. Appeals subsequent to the ruling include: Kelly (No. 2) [2001] Crim. L. R. 836 and Close [2002] 1 Cr. App. R. (S.) 55.
2. In a speech on 19 June 2002 at a conference on Modernising Criminal Justice, for example, Blunkett said, 'In the past eight years the prison population has risen from just over 40,000 to just over 70,000 and a fat lot of good it's done us in crime control terms'. See also Blunkett's speech to the National Association of Probation Officers on 5 July 2001, at society.guardian.co.uk/crimeand-punishment/story/0,8150,517211,00.html.

Chapter 8

Youth crime and youth justice

Introduction

It is not unusual for young people to get into trouble with the police. The majority of those that do will only have informal or transient contact, but a significant minority will go on to acquire a criminal record at some point in their adolescence. It is well established that approximately a third of male adults will have been convicted of at least one standard list offence by their 30s (Home Office Statistical Department, 1985), and most of these will have been as a result of offences committed when they were juveniles (Farrington, 1986).

Public discussion of crime, especially where young offenders are concerned, tends to be extremely emotive and characterised by more than its fair share of historical myopia (Pearson, 1983). Before moving on to consider the workings of the modern youth justice system it is worth looking further back at the history of criminal justice policy in relation to young offenders and, briefly, at juvenile crime itself.

Juvenile crime

One cannot know for certain how much crime is committed by young people. As the British Crime Survey (BSC) shows (*inter alia*, Mayhew et al., 1989), a high proportion of crime is not reported to the police. In addition, only a minority of those crimes which do figure in the official statistics are cleared up, with the result that the age of the offender is known. The best indicator we have of 'youth crime' is the number of young people known to have offended, that is, those who have been cautioned for or convicted of a crime. It has now become almost commonplace to argue that compared with times such as the early nineteenth century, current levels of crime are far from unusual (Pearson, 1975, 1983; Gurr, 1976). However, taking a shorter time-frame – the period since the Second World War, for instance – there does seem to be some cause for concern. There was, for example, an almost 150 per cent increase in the number of 14–17-year-old male offenders in the population between 1959 and 1977. However, since that time the pattern of recorded juvenile crime has been rather different. In the period from 1980–90, the number of juveniles cautioned for or convicted of indictable offences fell by 37 per cent, a dramatic turn-around which is discussed in greater detail below.

Nevertheless, it is important to bear in mind that a high proportion of all offences are committed by young people. Indeed, the relationship between age and offending has been the subject of considerable criminological scrutiny. The prevalence of offending peaks in the mid-to-late teens and decreases steadily thereafter (Farrington, 1990). So stable has this relationship been found to be over time and place that it has even been described as invariant (Hirschi and Gottfredson, 1983; Gottfredson and Hirschi, 1990). While such a view has not gone unchallenged (Farrington, 1986), the age-crime curve remains one of the most basic facts of criminology. In addition to age, offending is also closely associated with sex (Newburn and Stanko, 1994). The analysis conducted by the Home Office of the criminal careers of people born in 1953 which found that almost a third of males had been convicted of standard list offences by the time of their thirty-first birthday, also showed by contrast that this was the case for only seven per cent of females (Home Office Statistical Department, 1985). Although numerous, the majority of juvenile crimes are, however, non-violent in character. Finally, offending is for the majority of young people a transient phenomenon. A number of researchers have suggested that most young people commit some offences, which in the main do not lead to significant contact with the police or courts (Belson, 1975; West, 1982), and that the majority of those who are regularly arrested and prosecuted will nevertheless eventually desist. There remain, however, little rigorous data on the reasons that lie behind this desistance.

The history of juvenile justice

The last hundred years of juvenile justice have been characterised by dual tendencies best described as 'punishment' and 'welfare'. However, one need look back no further than, say, 150 years, to find a time when children were not only punished with imprisonment, but were also subjected to transportation and even the death penalty. Although there is some dispute about the extent to which adults and children were treated differently by the criminal justice system, it seems clear that during the latter half of the nineteenth century, alongside the development of the modern construction of childhood (Aries, 1962; Thane, 1981) came increasing concern about the welfare of children, parallelled by the development of the new professions of paediatrics and child psychiatry, and the emergence of the notion of 'delinquency'.

A variety of social reformers campaigned to protect children from danger and exploitation. One of their key demands was that children should be removed from the 'adult' prison system and placed in privately managed, state-funded institutions. In addition, such institutions would also be a source of succour for the orphaned and the destitute. One of the most vocal social reformers was Mary Carpenter, who argued that three types of institution were required, *free schools* for the deprived, *industrial schools* for young vagrants and beggars, and *reformatories* for convicted youngsters (Rutherford, 1986a).

Statutory provision for reformatories began in 1854 as a result of the Youthful Offenders Act of that year. Children under 16 could be sent there after serving a prison sentence for a period of between two and five years. The schools were inspected by the prison inspectors. Legislation in 1857 established the industrial schools, though for a few years these were part of the educational system rather than the penal system. They came under Home Office control after 1860. The initial arrangement was that children aged between seven and 14 who had been convicted of vagrancy could be committed to an industrial school until the age of 15.

One commentator has suggested that the 'acceptance of Mary Carpenter's belief that children should not be dealt with as men, but as children, was a seminal point in the evolution of the modern child' (May, 1973). However, one of the unintended consequences of the introduction of the reformatories and industrial schools was the rapid increase in the number of young people in institutions. According to Rutherford (1986a), 'by 1858 only four years after the enabling legislation there were 45 reformatories holding 2,000 young people. Twelve years later there were 65 reformatories holding 7,000 young people'. Much of the later history of juvenile justice in England and Wales follows a broadly similar pattern of attempts at reform – often dominated by welfarist concerns – followed by an increase in the size of the incarcerated juvenile population.

It was not until almost the turn of the century that the period of imprisonment prior to reformatory school was abolished and, as Harding et al. (1985: 242) note, 'the general trend, in so far as it can be identified, was to a less regimented school environment, emphasising the role of education rather than discipline'. By the 1880s, the number of industrial schools exceeded that of reformatories, reaching a high point in 1915 and falling away thereafter.

Most histories of juvenile justice begin near the turn of the century with the development of the juvenile court (see, for example, Platt, 1969). In the mid-1890s, Asquith, the Home Secretary, set up two departmental committees to examine the penal system. The first, the Gladstone Committee, examined the prison system (see Chapter 1), and the second, chaired by Sir Godfrey Lushington, reformatories and industrial schools. The split between 'punishment' and 'welfare' was evident in the products of these two committees, with the Gladstone Report advocating 'treatment' alongside punishment in prisons, particularly in the case of young prisoners, and the Lushington Committee, by contrast, advocating alternatives to imprisonment, looking in particular to education as one of the remedies for juvenile crime.

By the turn of the century, a number of towns were operating separate juvenile courts, and the election in 1906 of a reformist Liberal government ensured that they were put on a statutory footing, at approximately the same time as the statutory creation of probation, of preventive detention and provision for 'borstal training'. The Probation of Offenders Act was enacted in 1907 (see Chapter 4), followed by the Children Act 1908 (the 'Children's Charter') and the Prevention of Crime Act of the same year. The Children Act 1908 barred under-14s from prison and provided that 14–15-year-olds could only go to prison if the court issued an 'unruly' certificate. It included sections dealing with the prevention of cruelty to children, referred to begging and prostitution, but is best known for establishing juvenile courts. These courts were empowered to act not only in criminal cases, but also in cases of begging and vagrancy. They remained, in essence though, criminal courts.

The Prevention of Crime Act 1908 included provision for 'borstal' institutions. These were intended to cater for the type of person (16–21-year-olds – the 'juvenile-adult category') who 'by reason of his criminal habits and tendencies or associations with persons of such character, it is expedient that he should be subject to detention for such a term and such instruction and discipline as appears most conducive to his reformation and the repression of crime' (quoted in Garland, 1985). It was some time however before any distinctive borstal regime developed. Borstal training involved a semi-determinate custodial sentence (the date of release was determined by Prison Commissioners) of one to three years and release was followed by a period of supervision for a minimum of six months. The aims of the borstal institutions were defined as 'reformation' and training', and these were achieved through 'physical exercise, moral instruction, [and] industrial or agricultural training' (Garland, 1985). As Humphries (1981: 212) notes:

> Although it has often been assumed that penal reform was motivated by a humanitarian concern for the rights and protection of deprived children, in fact the issue that dominated public debates and government reports was that of the control and reformation of rebellious working-class youth. . . . From the turn of the century onwards reformatories were controlled by a professional body of penal administrators who attempted to infuse the system with the public school ethos of Christian manliness and patriotic duty.

Just as juvenile courts had grown informally prior to the passage of legislation so, similarly as we have seen, arrangements for the supervision of offenders within the community also existed before the Probation of Offenders Act 1908. Young people formed by far the majority of probationers, and by 1920, 80 per cent of the 10,000 people under probation supervision were under 21 (Rutherford, 1986a). Although the First World War shifted attention away from penal policy there was, within a few years of the outbreak of war, a significant increase in recorded juvenile crime – from approximately 37,000 juveniles charged in 1913 to over 50,000 in 1917 – and some consequent congestion in the reformatories and industrial schools (Bailey, 1987).

By the early 1920s, there was also some public disquiet following media allegations of brutality in a number of the borstal institutions (Humphries, 1981). In January 1925, a Home Office Departmental Committee on the Treatment of Young Offenders (the Molony Committee) was set up. The terms of reference of the Committee were wide, being to look into the treatment of young offenders under 21 and those who as a result of poor surroundings were in need of 'protection and training'. The Committee favoured the retention of the juvenile court and recommended that magistrates should be given the fullest possible information about those who appeared before them, including their home circumstances and their educational and medical histories (Morris and Giller, 1987). The focus at this time, then, was firmly upon the 'welfare' of young offenders and the 'treatment' necessary to reclaim or reform them.

The principle that young people were not only to be dealt with separately from adults but in a way that promoted their welfare was also to be found in the Children and Young Persons Act 1933. The 1933 Act incorporated much of what the Molony Committee had to say concerning those up to the age of 17 (in fact, the Committee's proposals were given statutory force by the Children and Young Person's Act 1932, which was consolidated by the 1933 Act), though it did not bar 16-year-olds from borstal as the Committee had recommended. It did, however, give legislative effect to what had become administrative practice by prohibiting capital punishment for those under the age of 18. The reformatory and industrial schools were reorganised following the 1933 Act, thereafter being designated 'Schools approved by the Secretary of State', and they continued in this form through to the end of the 1960s.

In 1936, the maximum age for a borstal sentence was raised from 20 to 22, and these institutions constituted the only expanding part of the prison system in the inter-War years. There had been a sea-change during this period: prison numbers had declined, institutions closed, probation thrived and, as one later report claimed 'in a variety of ways . . . Britain became the centre of the prison reform movement' (Home Office, 1979, quoted in Windlesham, 1993). The borstal system was at its high point at this time. The regime that had developed 'was very much that of the boy scout ethos: outdoor pursuits and summer camps and a physically invigorating environment, away from the criminal contamination in urban cities, which would inculcate self-respect and self-reliance' (Harding et al., 1985: 247). The system's reputation dwindled quickly after the Second World War, however, as did its success rates (Mannheim and Wilkins, 1955).

Between 1938 and 1945, recorded indictable offences rose by 69 per cent, and before long the prison population began to swell, and the increase in juvenile crime exposed the difficulties inherent in a system dependant on accommodation provided by charities and local authorities. In 1942, the Home Secretary, Herbert Morrison, began to push for the establishment of a committee on penal reform. Eventually, in 1944 an Advisory Council on the Treatment of Offenders under the Chairmanship of Mr Justice Birkett was set up. The post-War Labour government embarked on an extensive programme of legislation and a Criminal Justice Bill was introduced in 1947. It was heavily based on recommendations made before the War[1] which 'strongly emphasised the unwisdom of sending young persons to prison' (quoted in Bailey, 1987) and, indeed, the 1948 Act did place a number of restrictions on the use of imprisonment. It also introduced remand centres, attendance centres, support for probation hostels and abolished corporal punishment. However, the Magistrates' Association had renewed their demands for a new short-term custodial sentence and this was eventually accepted by the Labour government. The Home secretary, Chuter Ede, told the House of Commons: 'there is a type of offender to whom it is necessary to give a short, but sharp reminder that he is getting into ways that will inevitably lead him into disaster . . . their regime will consist of brisk discipline and hard work' (quoted in Rutherford, 1986a). The detention centre order introduced by the Act was intended to be a short unpleasant sentence which would combine hard work with the minimum of amusement – a sentence not unlike the 'short, sharp, shock' experiment of the 1970s.

Although there was considerable continuity between the Criminal Justice Bill of 1938 and the 1948 Act, there were also significant differences. Thus, although in 1938 a Conservative Home Secretary rejected the idea of Detention Centres, a decade later his Labour successor accepted the idea. Indeed, the provision passed through Parliament with the minimum of debate, as most eyes were directed towards proposals to abolish capital and corporal punishment (Dunlop and McCabe, 1965; Windlesham, 1993). As will be clear from this discussion, the 1948 Act was far from being an entirely punitive piece of legislation, and the continuing concern about the 'welfare' of juveniles also found expression in the Children Act passed in the same year. Influenced by a report from the Care of Children Committee, the Children Act sought to end the placement of neglected children in approved schools alongside offenders, and to that end set up local authority children's departments with their own resources for residential care and trained staff to oversee fostering and adoption, thereby creating 'the first professional social work service exclusively for children' (Harris and Webb, 1987).

The post-War period was characterised by a continued rise in recorded juvenile crime, and it was increasingly suggested that the approved school system was unable to cope with some of the hardened juvenile offenders that were coming before the courts (although provision for detention centres was included in the Criminal Justice Act 1948, the first of these institutions was not opened until 1952[2]). As Windlesham (1993) has argued, from this point on 'the twin claws of the pincer that was to hold the development of penal policy fast in its grip were the remorseless increase in the incidence of crime, and the overcrowding in the prisons'.

The 1950s closed with the Ingleby committee which was set up in 1956 to inquire into the operation of the juvenile court. In its report of 1960, the committee endorsed the structure of the juvenile court, and it rejected any merger of approved schools with other residential accommodation or the removal of responsibility for these institutions from the Home Office. At least one commentator has suggested that a close reading of the report suggests that the committee favoured the development of a local authority-based system of social service based on the Children's Departments established in 1948 as a method of decriminalising juvenile justice (Stevenson, 1989). The major focus of the committee's deliberations centred around the conflict that it felt existed between the *judicial* and *welfare* functions of the juvenile court. This, it suggested, resulted in:

> a child being charged with a petty theft or other wrongful act for which most people would say that no great penalty should be imposed, and the case apparently ending in a disproportionate sentence. For when the court causes enquiries to be made . . . the court may determine that the welfare of the child requires some very substantial interference which may amount to taking the child away from his home for a prolonged period.

The solution proposed by the Committee was to immediately raise the age of criminal responsibility from eight to 12 'with the possibility of it becoming 13 or 14' (Morris and Giller, 1987), and below that age only welfare proceedings could be brought. The major proposals did not become law – the Children and Young Persons Act 1963, by way of compromise, raised the age of criminal responsibility to ten – although one author in particular has argued that they were of considerable symbolic importance to later events (Bottoms, 1974).

The Ingleby Report polarised the two main political parties over the issue of juvenile justice; the Labour Party welcomed its proposal with regard to the age of criminal responsibility, but was critical of what it took to be the Committee's timidity, and in response set up its own inquiry under the chairmanship of Lord Longford. This recommended the total abolition of the juvenile courts on the basis that 'no child in early adolescence should have to face criminal proceedings: these children should receive the kind of treatment they need without any stigma' (quoted in Bottoms, 1974). The alternative was to non-judicial consultation between the child, the child's parents and a newly formed 'Family Service'. The Longford Report was followed by a White Paper, *The Child, The Family and the Young Offender*, which reproduced much of Longford, including proposals to establish family councils and family courts, and to abolish the juvenile courts. On this occasion, with legislation a significant possibility, the proposals were vehemently attacked by lawyers, magistrates and probation officers (Bottoms, 1974). With its small parliamentary majority to protect, the Labour government withdrew the proposals (Clarke, 1980).

Three years later a second White Paper, *Children in Trouble*, was published and this, after some relatively minor amendments, found legislative embodiment in the Children and Young Persons Act 1969. The system of approved schools, and that of remand homes or remand centres for juveniles which existed alongside them, was abolished by the 1969 Act, and they were replaced with community homes with residential and educational facilities (CHEs), though their subsequent history was far from happy. The juvenile court was retained under the Children and Young Persons Act 1969 (the proposal for a family court did not reappear), but the intention signalled by the White Paper was to increase the age of criminal responsibility to 14. Care was preferred over criminal proceedings; the circumstances under which court proceedings were possible were to be narrowed. Thus, 'care and protection' proceedings could be instituted for children between ten and 14, but only when it could 'be established that the child was not receiving such care, protection and guidance as a good parent might reasonably be expected to give' (Morris and Giller, 1987). Juveniles between 14 and 17 could be subject to criminal proceedings, but it was to be necessary in future for the police to consult with the local authority children's department before making an application to a magistrate. The intention was that the juvenile court should become a welfare-providing agency but also 'an agency of last resort' (Rutter and Giller, 1983), referral should only happen in those cases in which informal and voluntary agreement had not been reached between the local authority, the juvenile and the juvenile's parents (Morris and McIsaac, 1978).

It was also intended that detention centres and borstals for juveniles would be phased out and replaced by a new form of intervention – intermediate treatment. 'This (though) was less a policy of decarceration than a reiteration of the traditional welfare abhorrence of the prison system' (Rutherford, 1986b). Indeed, the 1969 Act was itself made up of a series of compromises:

> First, in design, it promoted both diversion *from* courts and the provision of welfare *in* courts. And second, by design, it . . . perpetuated competing conceptions of juvenile offenders and of how best to deal with them. . . . The

full machinery of courtroom adjudication was retained for those who saw juvenile offenders as responsible and who believed in the symbolic and deterrent value of such appearances. At the same time, an emphasis on social welfare . . . was retained for those who saw juvenile offenders as the product of social circumstances [emphasis in original].

(Gelsthorpe and Morris, 1994: 965)

Between the passage of the Act and the putative date for its implementation there was, once again, a change of government, and the new Conservative administration announced that it would not be implementing significant sections of the legislation. The consequence was that juvenile courts continued to function pretty much as they had before – criminal proceedings for 10–14s continued, powers in relation to 14–16-year-olds were not restricted, and the minimum age for qualification for a Borstal sentence was not increased. Perhaps most significantly, although care proceedings on the commission of an offence were made possible, such powers were used exceedingly sparingly, and the more traditional 'punitive' disposals were used increasingly by the juvenile courts during the 1970s – the number of custodial sentences, for example, rising from 3,000 in 1970 to over 7,000 in 1978 (Rutter and Giller, 1983; Cavadino and Dignan, 1992). Indeed, this general trend led an influential group of commentators from Lancaster University[3] to comment that:

The tragedy that has occurred since [the passage of the 1969 Act] can be best described as a situation in which the worst of all possible worlds came into existence – people have been persistently led to believe that the juvenile criminal justice system has become softer and softer, while the reality has been that it has become harder and harder.

(Thorpe et al., 1980, quoted in Muncie, 1984)

Despite the fact that it was only partly implemented, the Children and Young Persons Act 1969 became the scapegoat for all the perceived ills of juvenile crime and juvenile justice in the 1970s, and Rutherford (1986a) has cast doubt on the extent to which practice actually changed. He has suggested that it was 'the ideas and attitudes . . . culminating in the 1969 Act . . . on which the campaign for counter-reform was mounted'. The Act was attacked from all sides, not just those critical of its 'welfare' elements, and within three years of its implementation a sub-committee of the House of Commons Expenditure Committee had been set up to make recommendations for change. The omens were not good, however, for:

the inquiry was based on the assumption that the Act was not working although no evidence was quoted in favour of this. The membership of the Committee included at least two former magistrates and one former manager of an approved school, but nobody with close working or personal connections with the social work profession or social services departments.

(Farrington, 1984)

Although treatment and welfare had been heralded as the basis for progress from the late 1960s onwards, the legislative platform on which such a programme might have been built was never properly constructed. The Expenditure Committee, while accepting that there was a class of juvenile that required care and support rather than punishment, nevertheless was much influenced by the view that there was also, as the Magistrates' Association put it in their evidence: 'a minority of tough sophisticated young criminals . . . [who] . . . prey on the community, at will, even after the courts have placed them in care. They deride the powerlessness of the courts to do anything effective' (quoted in Rutherford, 1986a).[4] This statement, it is worth noting, bears more than a passing resemblance to much of what was said in the early 1990s in relation to so-called 'persistent juvenile offenders'.

As a consequence, the Committee argued that it was important to 'hasten the process in the case of certain offenders to deter others from embarking on criminal activities, to contain a hard core of persistent offenders, and to punish some offenders' (House of Commons Expenditure Committee, 1975, quoted in Morris and Giller, 1987). The aim of the Committee was, then, to make some form of distinction between children who need care and those who, in their words, require 'strict control and an element of punishment', and was critical of the 1969 Act for not doing so, even though the Act deliberately attempted to obscure such boundaries.

In response the government issued a White Paper (Home Office and others, 1976) which was ambivalent in its views of juvenile justice, both recommending a shift away from residential care and towards supervision and fostering, whilst also sharing 'the widespread anxiety that is felt . . . about the continuing problem of how to cope with a small minority, among delinquent children, of serious and persistent offenders. It is in this area . . . that the present measures under the Act are felt to be falling short' (Home Office and others, 1976, para. 3). Though it did not attempt to define how this hard core of persistent juvenile offenders might be distinguished from the majority, it nevertheless signalled the intention to establish different strategies and systems for dealing with each.

It is hard not to agree with Morris and Giller's (1987) conclusion that juvenile justice policy at the end of the 1970s 'bore little resemblance to that proposed in the 1969 Act'. In particular, they suggest, the police and the Magistrates' Association had been successful in establishing their model of 'juvenile delinquency' as the dominant one in operation in the juvenile justice system. Responsibility for the 'persistent juvenile offenders' that they identified as the core of the problem was increasingly placed in the hands of local authority social services departments. A joint working party on persistent juvenile offending that included representatives of the magistracy and local authorities reported in 1978, but failed to agree on how the problem should be tackled, the Magistrates'

Association continuing to press for short detention centre orders, a demand that was being echoed by William Whitelaw, the Shadow Home Secretary, who by this stage was calling for the introduction of 'short, sharp, shock' treatment (Harwin, 1982).

The Conservative manifesto of 1979 had promised to strengthen sentencing powers with respect to juveniles and young adults, and the 1980 White Paper, *Young Offenders*, included proposals for the reintroduction of a limited number of detention centres with 'tougher' regimes, and this 'experiment' began in two centres – Send and New Hall – in 1980. The subsequent Criminal Justice Act 1982 shortened the detention centre sentence: its minimum and maximum lengths were reduced from three and six months to 21 days and four months (Cavadino and Dignan, 1992). Imprisonment for under-21s was abolished and the end of the road for borstals was signalled with the new order for 'Youth Custody' (the institutions becoming known as Youth Custody Centres). The Youth Custody Order was a determinate sentence whose length was fixed by the sentencing court (though with the possibility of remission and parole). The minimum Youth Custody sentence was four months one day, and magistrates and juvenile courts could impose sentences between the minimum and six months, and the government's intention was that the shorter (though 'sharper') sentence, together with a requirement that sentencers should only impose a custodial sentence if they were satisfied that no other alternative was possible,[5] would reduce the number of juveniles held in custody (discussed in *Young Offenders*, 1980, para. 46). There was considerable scepticism in some quarters, however, at the extent to which the government really was committed to the use of community-based alternatives to imprisonment, and there were fears that custodial institutions would become ever more central in juvenile justice (Allen, 1991).

Taken together, the White Paper and the 1982 Act represent a fairly fundamental attack on the welfarist principles that underpinned the Children and Young Persons Act 1969. Gelsthorpe and Morris (1994: 972) have argued that they: 'represented a move away from treatment and lack of personal responsibility to notions of punishment and individual and parental responsibility. They also represented a move away from executive (social workers) to judicial decision-making, and from the "child in need" to the juvenile criminal – what Tutt [1981] called the "rediscovery of the delinquent".'

Unlikely as it may seem against this background, a significant and sustained decline in the use of custody for juveniles is exactly what happened during the 1980s (see Figure 8.1). As Rutherford (1986a) commented, the paradox is that 'the decade of "law and order" was also the decade of what has been called "the successful revolution" in juvenile justice'. One former Home Office minister has described this transformation as 'one of the most remarkable post-war achievements of deliberate legislative enactment' (Windlesham, 1993), and seen against the backdrop of

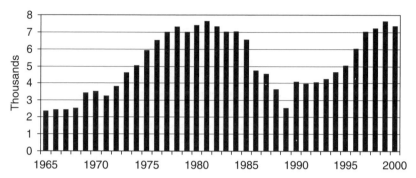

Figure 8.1: Young offenders sentenced to immediate custody, 1965–2000
Source: Criminal Statistics England and Wales.

'evolution, revolution and counter-revolution' in juvenile justice (Morris and Giller, 1987) described above, it is impossible to deny that it is indeed a remarkable achievement. The extent to which it may be attributed to deliberate legislative enactment is, however, somewhat more debatable.

In the first instance, although it cannot explain the full extent of the fall in numbers, there were significant demographic changes during this period which must be taken into account. There was, for example, a 17 per cent decline in the number of males in the 14–16 age group between 1981 and 1988. Furthermore, in the same period the number of young people sentenced also decreased by about 38 per cent. The success of the general policy of 'diverting' juveniles from prosecution meant that there were far fewer candidates for custodial sentences. This policy arose partly as a result of the insight from labelling theory that involvement in the criminal justice process may, on occasion, reinforce rather than deter further offending (Taylor, et al., 1973).

One of the keys to diversion has been the increased use of cautioning by the police. The 1980 White Paper had accepted that 'juvenile offenders who can be diverted from the criminal justice system at an early stage in their offending are less likely to reoffend than those who become involved in judicial proceedings' (para. 3.8). The police clearly have great discretion in dealing with offenders, particularly so with juvenile offenders and, indeed, successive research studies have shown that there are marked variations in the use of cautioning between police forces (Tutt and Giller, 1983; Laycock and Tarling, 1985; Evans and Wilkinson, 1990). A series of Home Office Circulars (in 1978, 1985 and 1990) encouraged the police to use their power to caution. The 14/1985 Circular issued to chief constables included criteria to be applied by the police with the aim of increasing the likelihood of diversion from prosecution and the 1990 Circular included national standards and also, though it suggested they should be used sparingly, recognised the possible use of 'multiple cautions': it countenanced 'offenders being cautioned more than once, provided the nature and circumstances of the most recent offence warrant it'.

Alongside the increase in the use of cautioning there were also changes in the use of non-custodial penalties – diversion once again, this time from custody rather than prosecution.[6] The 1982 Act introduced new requirements that could be attached to supervision orders (Graham and Moxon, 1986). The following year, the DHSS issued a Circular, LAC 83(3), in which it announced that £15 million was to be provided to support intensive Intermediate Treatment (IT) programmes as an alternative to custody. Monitoring of the subsequent development of schemes by NACRO suggests that this initiative may have had a significant impact on the custodial sentencing of juveniles (NACRO, 1987).

In addition to announcing the funding, LAC 83(3) also recommended that work with serious and persistent juvenile offenders should be co-ordinated by inter-agency committees. Subsequently, such committees or panels have been formed, often involving sentencers as well as representatives of other relevant agencies. One of the consequences of this, it has been argued (NACRO, 1989), has been to provide a first step towards a more integrated system of juvenile justice (Allen, 1991). Pitts (1992: 182) has even suggested that 'the IT initiative appears to have been the most successful innovation in the criminal justice system in the post-war period'.

In addition to the decline in the numbers of juveniles sentenced to custody during the latter part of the 1980s, there was also a shift in the use of detention centre and borstal sentences. In the aftermath of the 1982 Act, magistrates took the opportunity to use their new powers to send juveniles to borstal and were much less attracted to the new 'short, sharp, shock' detention centre regimes. In fact the experiment was, largely, a failure; evaluation by the Home Office's Young Offender Psychology Unit concluded that the new regimes seemed to be no more effective than the previous ones. More than half of those sent to detention centres had been reconvicted within a year, irrespective of the type of regime in the centre they served their sentence at (Home Office, 1984d). Despite this, the experiment was, briefly, extended to all detention centres, though aspects of the regime were modified. 'The political damage was limited', suggests Windlesham (1993), 'but it is hard to avoid the verdict that sound penal administration was made to serve the needs of a defective icon of political ideology.'

In the longer term, the government decided to abolish the separate detention centre sentence. The Criminal Justice Act 1988 included a new sentence of 'detention in a young offender institution', and separate detention centres ceased to exist, being amalgamated with youth custody centres to become young offender institutions (YOIs). Courts were given the power to decide on the length of sentence though the location where the sentence was to be served was to be determined by the Home Office. Detention in a YOI is available for people aged 15 and above.

Before moving on it is important to mention the existence, and demise, of the s. 7(7) care order. This was an order created by the Children and

Young Persons Act 1969, which could be used by the juvenile court in criminal proceedings to place a juvenile in the care of the local authority. The local authority then placed the juvenile where it thought most appropriate, including back in the parental home. During the 1970s, practice in relation to care orders was criticised by magistrates, on the one hand, for tending to undermine the intentions of the court by failing to place offenders where they could be controlled and, on the other, by academic critics concerned at the potential criminogenic consequences of using a care order early on in an offender's 'career' (see, for example, Thorpe et al., 1980). Significant claims have been made about the impact of this academic critique (Cavadino and Dignan, 1992) though, whatever the reality, the use of s. 7(7) care orders declined rapidly during the 1980s and they were eventually abolished (from October 1991) by the Children Act 1989.

For the purposes of this discussion here, there is one final significant change that has taken place in juvenile justice since that point. The Criminal Justice Act 1991 changed the name of the Juvenile Court to the Youth Court and extended its jurisdiction to include 17-year-olds. The clear aim was to extend the gains made with the younger age group to 17-year-olds and, indeed, as early as 1988 in the Green Paper, *Punishment, Custody and the Community*, the Home Office signalled its intention to transfer the lessons learnt in juvenile justice to policies in relation to offenders more generally, though it recognised that modifications would need to be made (Home Office, 1988b, paras 2.17–2.19). It did, however, emphasise the reasons for seeking to restrict the use of custodial sentences for young offenders:

> most young offenders grow out of crime as they become more mature and responsible. They need encouragement and help to become law abiding. Even a short period of custody is quite likely to confirm them as criminals, particularly as they acquire new criminal skills from the more sophisticated offenders. They see themselves labelled as criminals and behave accordingly.

The Criminal Justice Act 1991, in tandem with the Children Act 1989 which was part of the same general development (Faulkner, 1992), continued the by now well-established twin-track approach of punishment and welfare. The Children Act 1989 gave statutory recognition to the need to avoid prosecution, and the 1991 Act and subsequent Home Office Circular (30/92) explaining the changes brought about by the legislation reminded sentencers of s. 44 of the Children and Young Persons Act 1933, which states that 'all courts must have regard to the welfare of children and young people who appear before them'. The Act extended this consideration to 17-year-olds. The legislation also gave magistrates new sentencing powers within the overall framework created by the 1991 Act (including unit fines, community sentences and custody) along with a new scheme of post-custody supervision. The Act reduced the maximum term of detention in a YOI to 12 months, and brought 17-year-olds within the ambit of s. 53 of the Children and Young Persons Act 1933, which gives the Crown Court the power to order longer terms of detention in respect of certain 'grave crimes'. Finally, again reinforcing lessons learnt from developments in practice over the past decade, the 1991 Act signalled the importance of inter-agency and joint working by giving chief probation officers and directors of social services joint responsibility for making local arrangements to provide services to the Youth Court.

The history of juvenile justice, though relatively short, is an extremely complicated one. It has been characterised by the co-existing approaches of 'welfare' and 'punishment': a tendency, on the one hand, to wish to support and protect those children who for a variety of reasons may find themselves on the wrong side of the law and, on the other, a determination to ensure that those who continually offend despite efforts to stop them receive a punishment that makes clear that their behaviour is unacceptable. The tension between these two approaches is seen at its starkest in the debates over how best to respond to that 'hardcore' of young people whose offending, it is believed, continues unchecked irrespective of the interventions of criminal justice agencies.

The rediscovery of populist punitiveness

From 1991 onwards, there was a noticeable change in the tenor of official concern about juvenile offending. Concerns were fuelled by one or two very specific factors. The first was the well-publicised urban disturbances of 1991. Though different in scale, causes and style from the inner-city riots involving black and marginalised white youth in the early 1980s, the disturbances at Blackbird Leys (Oxford), Ely (Cardiff) and on the Meadowell estate in Tyneside focused attention on young men in large-scale violent confrontations with the police. In many cases, these were a consequence of attempts by the police to put a stop to the very public displays of 'joyriding' so popular with young men and with the journalists who increasingly turned up to record their activities (Campbell, 1993).

What these public disturbances did was allow long-standing concerns about young or very young offenders to be dusted down, distorted, sometimes exaggerated, and then served up in symbolic form via the mass media. Within much of the reporting of these events it was increasingly suggested that the greatest scourge of inner-city life was the young criminal, who was so prolific in his activities that almost alone he was terrorising local communities. Furthermore, it was then claimed, first by the police, but closely followed by politicians, that the police and the courts were powerless to deal with such offenders. The issue was taken up in a speech to the Federated Ranks of the Metropolitan Police in October 1992 by the then Home Secretary, Kenneth Clarke. A small number of children, he suggested: 'are committing a large number of crimes. There is a case for increasing court powers to lock up, educate and train them for their own and everyone else's interest. We will certainly be taking a long hard look at the options which are available to the courts in dealing with serious offenders of this age. If court powers need to be strengthened or new institutions created, then they will be.'

Clarke's speech was widely reported and stories of 'persistent juvenile offenders', as they were generally referred to, started to appear on a regular basis in the press. Thus, for example, the *Daily Mail* on 10 September 1992 under the headline 'One-boy crime wave', began its story, 'He was only 11 when his life of crime began with the theft of chocolate bars from a corner shop . . . within two years he had become a one-boy crime wave'. The *Daily Express* (9 September 1992) summed up the police view with the headline 'Mini-gangster is beyond our control'. The *Daily Star* (30 November 1992) following its report of a case involving an 11-year-old offender, headlined its editorial 'We've got too soft', and went on: 'CHILDREN are supposed to be little innocents – not crooks in short trousers. But much of Britain is now facing a truly frightening explosion of kiddie crime. As we reveal today, too many youngsters are turning into hardened hoods almost as soon as they've climbed out of their prams.'

In the Autumn of 1992, the House of Commons Home Affairs Committee announced an inquiry into issues affecting juvenile offenders and the particular problems of persistent offenders. The Committee received conflicting evidence about trends in juvenile crime and suggested that: 'one possible explanation for the apparent discrepancy between ACPO's picture of greater juvenile offending and the decline in the number of juvenile offenders is a growth in the numbers of *persistent* offenders. . . . If there is a small but growing number of juvenile offenders responsible for many offences (some of which they may be convicted or cautioned for and some of which may go undetected) it is possible to reconcile the indisputable fact that the number (and rate, to a lesser extent) of known juvenile offenders has fallen over time with the more speculative assertion that the number of offences committed by juveniles has risen (Home Affairs Committee, 1993: para. 15). Moreover, the majority of witnesses lent support to the suggestion that the most pressing problem was what the Committee described as 'persistent juvenile trouble makers'. It remains the case, however, that there are no British empirical data which can establish whether or not the number of persistent offenders has increased in recent years.

The Home Secretary, Kenneth Clarke, acted quickly. In March 1993, he announced that the government proposed to introduce legislation that would make a new disposal available to the courts. These 'secure training orders', were to be aimed at 'that comparatively small group of very persistent juvenile offenders whose repeated offending makes them a menace to the community' (*Hansard*, HC Deb, col. 139, 2 March 1993). The new order would apply to 12–15-year-olds (though this was later amended to 12–14-year-olds) who had been convicted of three imprisonable offences and who had proved 'unwilling or unable to comply with the requirements of supervision in the community while on remand or under sentence'. The order was to be a custodial one and would be served in a 'secure training unit' which, he suggested, would provide 'high standards of care and discipline'. Regimes would include provision for education and training for inmates; after release individuals would be subject to 'rigorous, consistent and firmly delivered' supervision until their supervising social worker or probation officer felt that he or she was no longer a threat to society.

The public concern about juvenile crime which the Home Affairs Committee made reference to, and which had been stoked by the press, might not have reached the pitch it eventually did were it not for the tragic events of 12 February 1993 and their highly publicised aftermath. It was at approximately 3.30 that afternoon that two-year-old James Bulger was abducted from the Strand shopping centre in Bootle, Liverpool. As time passed, and the young boy remained missing, the search spread and intensified. Enhanced still-photographic images from the CCTVs at the shopping centre were broadcast on national television. These showed James walking with, or being led by, one of two young people with whom witnesses had seen him leaving the shopping centre; pictures which appeared to convey both innocence and, because of what was then already suspected and later confirmed, something much more sinister. Eventually, two days later, James Bulger's battered body was found near a railway line in Liverpool, some two miles from the shopping centre. The abduction and murder of such a young child would always have had a significant public impact; in this case, however, the arrest and charging of two ten-year-old boys 'inspired a kind of national collective agony' (Young 1996: 113), and provided the strongest possible evidence to an already worried public that something new and particularly malevolent was afoot.

The trial of the two youngsters accused of James Bulger's murder took place at Preston Crown Court in November 1993 amidst massive national and international media interest. On the day after the verdict, 25 November, the *Daily Mail* carried 24 stories about the case, and a total of almost 40 stories in the three days after the trial. The broadsheets gave it similar space: the *Guardian* including 22 articles and the *Daily Telegraph* 23 articles and two editorials (Franklin and Petley, 1996). The tone of most of the coverage – despite the age of the offenders – was harshly punitive. Though for some commentators the sheer horror of the crime made it inexplicable in any terms other than 'evil', within days of the end of the trial some of the 'usual suspects' were being rounded up to help explain how it could have happened. Somewhat unexpectedly, for there had been no mention during the trial, one of these was video films. In his summing-up, the trial judge made reference to a film that, it was implied, one of the offenders, Jon Venables, might have watched. The judge said he felt that there ought to be an informed public debate about 'exposure to violent video films, including possibly *Childs Play 3*, which has some striking similarities to the manner of the attack on James Bulger' (*Guardian*, 27 November 1993). The response to this was swift. Questions were tabled in the House, David Alton MP put down an amendment to the Criminal Justice and Public Order Bill to further restrict access to video films, the Home Affairs Committee conducted an inquiry (Home Affairs Committee, 1993) and a group of academic psychologists came out firmly in favour of regulation (Newson, 1994).

Public discourse about the murder of James Bulger was particularly contradictory. On the one hand, for example, the police officer leading the murder inquiry reflected one fairly typical set of beliefs when he described the case as 'unique'. Though highly unusual, the case clearly was by no means unique (Boswell, 1996). On the other hand, there was also the pervasive view – as frequently expressed in the media – that despite the highly unusual nature of the case, it somehow illustrated that there was something wrong with society generally, and youth crime and youth justice more particularly. Indeed, in some public/political discourse this most unusual and horrific of crimes became confused with the whole issue of persistent, yet less serious offending. The Bulger case was the 'flashpoint' which ignited a new moral panic and led to further demonisation of young people and, increasingly in the 1990s, also of lone mothers who were increasing in number and, in right-wing underclass theory (Murray, 1990), were perceived to be a key part of the 'problem'. With politicians of all parties becoming increasingly punitive in their pronouncements, and the Labour Party's clichéd but resonant soundbite 'tough on crime, tough on the causes of crime' apparently meeting with some success, the new Home Secretary, Michael Howard, used his speech at the Conservative Party conference to announce yet another new 'law and order' package. The choice that Howard made in seeking to bolster his party's and his own fortunes was to employ a strategy of 'populist punitiveness' (Bottoms, 1995).

The package of measures that Howard announced was punitive, involving a reassertion of the central position of custody in a range of sanctions he interpreted as having deterrence as their primary aim (see Ashworth, 2002). Most famously, he announced that previous approaches which involved attempts to limit prison numbers were henceforward to be eschewed. The new package of measures would be likely to result in an increase in prison numbers, an increase which he appeared to welcome: 'I do not flinch from that. We shall no longer judge the success of our system of justice by a fall in our prison population. . . . Let us be clear. *Prison works*. It ensures that we are protected from murderers, muggers and rapists – and it makes many who are tempted to commit crime think twice' (emphasis added) (quoted in Gibson et al., 1994: 83). The Criminal Justice and Public Order Act 1994 doubled the maximum sentence in a young offenders institution for 15–17-year-olds from one year to two. It introduced the possibility that parents of young offenders could be bound over to ensure that their children carried out their community sentences, and it provided for the introduction of a new 'secure training order' for 12–14-year-olds. The proposal was that five new secure training centres would be built, each housing approximately 40 inmates. The new sentences would be determinate, of a maximum of two years, half of which would be served in custody and half under supervision in the community. There was widespread criticism of, and resistance to, the new provisions for dealing with 12–14-year-olds. Home Office-funded research cast doubt on the likely efficacy of such a policy (Hagell and Newburn, 1994), the main voluntary organisations in the field refused to consider becoming involved in the management of the new centres (NACRO, 1994), and planning permission for the building of them was consistently refused by local councils. Though it was originally anticipated that the centres would be up and running in 1995, by the end of 1996 only one of the five contracts had been let and building of the centre had yet to begin.

The resistance to secure training centres, however, came mainly from professionals working with young offenders, rather than opposition politicians. By and large, the secure training order met with relatively little political hostility within Parliament. After the passage of the Act, the battle between the Home Secretary and his Shadow for the law and order 'high ground' escalated. A series of leaks from the Home Office announced numerous proposed initiatives. In February 1995, a leaked Prison Service document suggested that the government wished to introduce United States-style 'boot camps' for young offenders. Both the Director General of the Prison Service and the Home Secretary had visited the United States to inspect the high impact incarceration programmes being run on Rikers Island and in other parts of the country. A report written by prison service officials after a visit to a number of United States boot camps concluded that 'there is little point in devoting time and resources to considering an initiative which seems to have little to offer us'. More specifically, it said that 'there is no basis for this type of approach in terms of reducing offending, and its potential popular appeal would be undermined by the fact that we have tried this approach before with detention centres and abandoned it as a failure. . . . The question what advantage boot camps offer over detention centres is bound to be asked, and would not be easy to answer' (quoted in Nathan, 1995). Nonetheless, by August 1995 further leaks revealed that the government were to press ahead with the idea of boot camps – the first to be instituted at Thorn Cross near Warrington, though with a far more progressive regime than those associated with United States boot camps. The same month, again via a leak, it became apparent that there had been correspondence between the Home Secretary and the Defence Secretary, Michael Portillo, exploring the possibility of using the Military Corrective Training Centre at Colchester for young offenders aged 18 and above. This opened in 1997 and closed after only a short period. Nonetheless, the predictable consequence of such punitive rhetoric was visible in the

increasing numbers of children and young people in prison establishments, and a projected rise of a further one third in the number of young
males in custody by 2004 (Home Office, 1996a).

At the other end of the scale from custody, the cautioning system also
came in for increased scrutiny and criticism, and Home Office Circular
18/1994 (Home Office, 1994b) sought to place further limits on its use.
The 1990 Circular had stated that 'a previous conviction or caution
should not rule out a subsequent one if other factors suggest it might be
suitable'. At the launch of the new Circular, the then Home Secretary outlined the new approach. He said: 'From now on your first chance is your
last chance. Criminals should know that they will be punished. Giving
cautions to serious offenders, or to the same person time and again, sends
the wrong message to criminals and the public' (quoted in Evans, 1994).
A similar message was also contained in Labour Party proposals on the
future of youth justice (Labour Party, 1996) in which it was proposed that
the formal caution be replaced by a 'Final Warning'.

New Labour and youth justice

New Labour, under the banner of 'tough on crime, tough on the causes
of crime',[7] sought to redefine itself in the law and order landscape – in
order to rid itself of another of its 'hostages to fortune' (Downes and
Morgan, 1997). In using what was to become the most famous of New
Labour soundbites, Blair and colleagues sought to move the argument
about crime away from 'the choice between personal and social responsibility, the notion that there are only two sides to the "law and order"
debate – those who want to punish the criminal and those who point to
the poor social conditions in which crime breeds' (Blair, 1993).
'Responsibilities as well as rights' became the cornerstone of Tony Blair's
new agenda. In his first speech on taking over as Shadow Home Secretary,
Jack Straw took up the refrain. He described the party's aim as being to
create 'the better society ... [that] is one that fosters and celebrates
strong British values: decency; reward for hard work; tolerance and
respect for others. . . . It is one in which rights for everyone are matched
by responsibilities for all'.

In Opposition, New Labour began to develop a new approach to
criminal justice policy that combined elements of communitarianism,
managerialism and populist punitiveness. There followed a series of
speeches from the Shadow Home Secretary designed to illustrate his willingness to be 'tough'. In his speech at the launch of the London Borough
of Lewisham's new community safety strategy in September 1995, Straw
was critical of the 'aggressive begging of winos and addicts' and the
'squeegee merchants who wait at large road junctions to force on reticent
motorists their windscreen cleaning service'. 'Even where graffiti is not

comprehensible or racialist in message', he went on, 'it is often violent and uncontrolled in its violent image, and correctly gives the impression of a lack of law and order on the streets.' The speech reflected part of the thinking taken from Wilson and Kelling's 'Broken Windows' thesis (Wilson and Kelling, 1982), and contained some of the language and style that, it was believed, characterised the 'zero tolerance' approach to policing in vogue in New York at the time.

Reaction to Straw's speech was heated and undoubtedly more negative than he had anticipated. Although he quickly released briefings offering a 'tough on the causes of crime' message to counterbalance his speech, in the main his stance remained unchanged. Before long, he had floated the idea of curfews for young children (and, indeed, 'approved bedtimes' for children in care), and opposition support was generally provided for the increasingly punitive set of measures introduced by Michael Howard in the dying days of the Conservative government. It would be wrong, however, to present the Labour position simply as attempting to 'out-tough' the incumbent government. Though both parties appeared to share an obsession with punitive rhetoric, in reality there were some significant differences in their criminal justice policies – particularly in the area of youth justice. In this area, the influence of Jack Straw's advisor, Norman Warner, was vital. An ex-Director of Social Services, but also a hard-headed pragmatist, his hand can clearly be seen on the major Labour Party discussion documents of the time. Indeed, pragmatism was the glue that held the disparate strands of New Labour's initial youth justice reforms together.

In May 1996, the Labour Party published its plans, in outline, for reform of the youth justice system and for preventing youth crime (Labour Party, 1996). Entitled *Tackling Youth Crime, Reforming Youth Justice* (TYCRYJ), the document made it clear that, once elected, this was to be a priority area for government. Launching the document, Jack Straw argued that:

> The criminal justice system should work best where it could be most effective – in turning youngsters away from crime, teaching them the difference between right and wrong before it is too late. However, in England and Wales, this system is in a state of advanced decay. It does not work. It can scarcely be called a system at all. It lacks coherent objectives. It satisfies neither those whose prime concern is crime control, nor those whose principal priority is the welfare of the young offender. . . . The system needs a radical overhaul. . . . A Labour Government will act on youth crime and youth justice as an urgent priority. . . . Our proposals represent the most significant overhaul of the youth justice system since the war.[8]

The Shadow Home Secretary made clear the opposition's view was that the 'heart of the crisis' in youth justice was 'confusion and conflict between welfare and punishment' (Labour Party, 1996: 9), and resolving this confusion was stated to be a central plank of future Labour youth justice policy. The proposals in TYCRYJ were far-reaching. They included: reforming the cautioning system which, it was argued, was losing public confidence; 'modernising' the principle of *doli incapax*; action to speed up the youth justice system, especially for so-called persistent offenders was proposed (and, indeed, this was to become one of the Party's key manifesto commitments in its 1997 manifesto); the introduction of new court orders (parental responsibility orders and reparation orders); and the introduction of multi-agency youth justice teams. The central plank of TYCRYJ was a proposal to 'provide national leadership on youth crime and justice' through the creation of a National Youth Justice Board. Its aim would be to remove the 'mixed messages' and 'different approaches' of the Home Office and the Department of Health towards young offenders. In attempting to find a new balance between punishment and welfare, the proposals made it clear where priorities were in future to lie. First, it was proposed that responsibility for policy on young offenders would be located in the Home Office and that, via the Youth Justice Board, it would be the Home Office that would issue national standards and guidance on other changes to youth justice. TYCRYJ made the bottom line clear. In removing the confusion between punishment and welfare, it said, 'ultimately the welfare needs of the individual young offender cannot outweigh the needs of the community to be protected from the adverse consequences of his or her behaviour' (Labour Party, 1996: 9).

In addition to the strands of communitarianism and populist punitiveness, there was one further element that had a profound impact on the development of New Labour youth justice policy: 'managerialism'. (In relation to other areas of criminal justice policy see Atkinson and Cope, 1994; McLaughlin and Muncie, 1994; Newburn, 1995.) *Systemic managerialism* within criminal justice, Bottoms (1995: 25) argues, tends to contain some or all of the following features:

- An emphasis on inter-agency co-operation in order to fulfil the overall goals of the system.
- An emphasis on creating an overall strategic plan for criminal policy.
- The creation of key performance indicators, related to the overall 'mission statement' of each agency.
- Active monitoring of aggregate information about the system and its functioning.

At the same time that the Opposition Home Affairs team had been preparing TYCRYJ, the Audit Commission was engaged in its first major inquiry into young people and crime. Beginning in early 1995, the Audit Commission began reviewing the arrangements for young offenders provided by public services and in November 1996 published its hugely influential report, *Misspent Youth* (Audit Commission, 1996a). The parallels between the Labour Party's consultation document and the Audit Commission's eventual report are striking – both in terms of the issues covered and the proposals each contained. Both documents are split into two main parts: one focusing on the youth justice system; the other examining means of preventing or reducing youth crime.

In relation to the youth justice system, the Audit Commission had little of a positive nature to say and a number of biting criticisms. Its overall conclusion was that:

> The current system for dealing with youth crime is inefficient and expensive, while little is being done to deal effectively with juvenile nuisance. The present arrangements are failing young people who are not being guided away from offending to constructive activities. . . . Resources need to be shifted from processing young offenders to dealing with their behaviour. At the same time, efforts to prevent offending and other anti-social behaviour by young people need to be co-ordinated between the different agencies involved.
>
> (Audit Commission, 1996a: 96)

According to the Audit Commission, the youth justice system was both expensive and was becoming less and less efficient. In its most damning indictment it suggested that 'overall, less is done now than a decade ago to address offending by young people. Fewer young people are now convicted by the courts, even allowing for the fall in the number of people aged 10–17 years, and an increasing proportion of those who are found guilty are discharged'. The system needed to be streamlined and speeded up, they argued. Moreover, the Commission noted, 'surprisingly, the effectiveness of different kinds of sentence on re-offending by young people is not assessed on a regular basis in most areas of England and Wales' and, consequently, recommended that information on the *outcome* of sentencing should be passed regularly by youth justice teams to their local courts.

Many of the Audit Commission's central recommendations were, predictably given its remit, managerialist in nature. They emphasised the need for consistency of aims and objectives in youth justice, for improved inter-agency co-operation to meet these aims and objectives, for the creation of appropriate performance indicators for all agencies involved in youth justice and for better monitoring of performance so as to improve the functioning of the system. This approach chimed closely with much of the Opposition's emergent policy proposals in this area and, subsequently, were of great importance in influencing the eventual shape of the new government's legislation.

In the first few months of taking office, the Labour government published six consultation documents on the subject of youth crime (Home Office, 1997a, 1997b, 1997c, 1997d, 1997e, 1997f, 1997g). Each contained considerable discussion of various proposals first fully mooted in TYCRYJ and all made detailed reference to the analysis and conclusions drawn by the Audit Commission. The proposals contained in this and the other five consultation papers eventually found their way, largely unchanged, into the government's flagship legislation, the Crime and Disorder Act 1998.

The Act (first published as a Bill in November 1997) was, for New Labour, a very significant piece of legislation. It was very sizeable, running to some 119 clauses and ten Schedules. The Act set out an explicit principal aim for the youth justice system and imposed requirements on local authorities, in consultation with others, for formulating 'youth justice plans'. It provided for the replacement of cautions with reprimands and final warnings, introduced six new court orders, amended the conditions that may be attached to a supervision order and abolished the legal presumption of *doli incapax.*

Historically, juvenile justice had a 'broad church' in which considerable variation in service delivery at the local level had existed. Inspired in part by the excoriating criticisms of the extant system by the Audit Commission (1996a), New Labour sought, as in so many areas, to impose order from the centre. With an enormous legislative programme envisaged, the new Home Secretary established a Youth Justice task force in June 1997. Its aims were to maintain the momentum developed in opposition and to provide a continuing formal link with the major agencies involved with young offenders (Windlesham, 2001). The Chair of the Task Force was Norman Warner, who had been adviser to Jack Straw in opposition, and its secretary was one of the authors of the Audit Commission report. When as a result of s. 41 of the Crime and Disorder Act 1998, the Youth Justice Board (YJB) became a non-departmental public body sponsored by the Home Office, Warner became its Chairman, and the Audit Commission author its first Chief Executive.

The YJB's principal function was to monitor the operation of the youth justice system and the provision of youth justice services, together with monitoring national standards, and establishing appropriate performance measures. The 1998 Act also allowed the Home Secretary to expand the Board's role and, from April 2000, the YJB also became the commissioning body for all placements of under-18s in secure establishments on remand or sentence from a criminal court. The Comprehensive Spending Review of the secure estate (Home Office, 1998a) had concluded that there was 'little positive to say about the current arrangements. . . . Regime standards are inconsistent and often poor. Costs vary considerably. There is no effective oversight or long term planning'. The YJB's role was therefore expanded to include commissioning places from Prison Service Young Offender Institutions (YOIs), local authority secure units and Secure Training Centres (STCs). In this connection, the Board advises the Home Secretary, is responsible for planning and setting standards, and accredits establishments that operate according to those standards.

Prior to the 1998 Act, youth justice teams, comprised mainly of social workers, had had primary responsibility for working with young offenders subject to non-custodial penalties, and for liaising with other criminal justice and treatment agencies in connection with that work. Stimulated by a concern with efficiency and consistency, on the one hand, and by a pragmatic belief in multi-agency working, on the other, New Labour's new model YOTs had to include a probation officer, a local authority social worker, a police officer, a representative of the local health authority and someone nominated by the chief education officer. YOTs have been in operation in all 154 local authority areas since April 2000. Social services remain the major player in local youth justice, contributing 55 per cent to YOTs. They are followed by the police (13 per cent), probation (10 per cent), Local Authority Chief Executives (9 per cent), education (7 per cent) and health (6 per cent) (Renshaw and Powell, 2001).

As Pitts (2001) notes, the constitution of these new teams had echoes of the Multi-Agency Diversion Panels of the 1980s and of the Northampton Diversion Scheme; the latter having been subject to particularly good press by the Audit Commission (Audit Commission, 1996a). However, whereas the Diversion Schemes were the child of an earlier era – a product of the 1980s 'corporatism' in juvenile justice (Pratt, 1989) – YOTs were established not to divert but to intervene. The two primary functions of YOTs are to co-ordinate the provision of youth justice services for all those in the local authority's area who need them, and to carry out such functions as are assigned to the team in the youth justice plan formulated by the local authority. The Home Office-funded evaluation of the YOT pilots outlined the key assumptions about offending that informed the development of the new structures:

> [The Crime and Disorder Act 1998] has a central objective to prevent
> offending by children and young people and is concerned with addressing
> offending behaviour; with early interventions on the basis of risk
> assessments related to known criminogenic factors; with the systematic use of
> evidence-based practice; with reparation and, therefore, the needs of victims;
> and with the promotion of crime prevention measures.
>
> (Holdaway et al., 2001)

As implied above, the Crime and Disorder Act 1998 places a duty on local authorities to formulate and implement annual youth justice plans. In doing this, the authority must consult with the senior officers of the major agencies (police, probation, health) that make up YOTs. Such reports are published and submitted to the YJB, which monitors local provision and advises the Home Secretary. It was originally suggested that there be some further inspection of YOTs, either jointly by the Inspectorates of Constabulary, Probation and Social Services along with Ofsted, or by the YJB itself (Leng et al., 1998). In practice, neither of these has yet occurred and the work of YOTs (and arguably the YJB itself) remains one of the significant gaps in performance management in the criminal justice system – an odd situation for bodies that are the product of managerialism.

The creation of youth offending teams (YOTs) is, however, by no means the end of the change to the structure of local youth justice. In addition to requiring local authorities to set up such teams, the Act also requires them to publish, annually, a youth justice plan. This must set out how youth justice services are to be provided and funded, how YOTs locally are to operate and to be funded and what functions they are to carry out. Assessment of the operation of youth justice locally and, more particularly, scrutiny of local youth justice plans is to be undertaken by a newly created Youth Justice Board, the principal function of which will be to monitor the operation of the youth justice system and the provision of youth justice services, together with the monitoring of national standards, and establishing appropriate performance measures.

In addition to restructuring youth justice nationally and locally, the Act also radically reforms the non-custodial penalties faced by young offenders. Responding to the problems identified in opposition and reinforced by the findings of the Audit Commission study, the Act revamps the cautioning system, introduces a broad range of new court orders and reinforces the conditions attached to supervision orders. The clearest illustrations of the influence of the Audit Commission was New Labour's critique and reform of the cautioning system. The Crime and Disorder Act 1998 scrapped the caution (informal and formal) and replaced it with a reprimand (for less serious offences) and a Final Warning. As the name implies, one of the crucial characteristics of the Final Warning is that, except in unusual circumstances, it may only be used once. In addition to the change of nomenclature, and the more sparing manner of usage, the new system of reprimands and Final Warnings also set in motion a set of other activities – such as those previously associated with 'caution plus' – more frequently, and often earlier, than previously had been the case. Under the Act, all young offenders receiving a final warning are referred to a YOT. Offenders are then expected, 'unless they consider it inappropriate to do so' to participate in a rehabilitation programme (in which reparation is expected generally to be present). According to one informed commentator (Dignan, 1999: 52) 'this new approach represents a considerable improvement on Michael Howard's much more restrictive plans simply to crack down on repeat cautioning'.

The Criminal Justice and Court Services Act 2000 removed the requirement that a police reprimand or final warning be given to a young offender only at a police station. This introduced the possibility of 'conferences' at which parents, victims and other adults could be present – what has sometimes been referred to as 'restorative cautioning' (Young and Goold, 1999). Though one of the intentions behind the new warnings system may have been to encourage more restorative practices with young offenders, to date there is little evidence that the new system is experienced as a more participative one by young people. Indeed, the Home Office evaluation of the Crime and Disorder Pilots (Holdaway et al., 2001) raised questions about the appropriateness of some of the change programmes attached to Warnings, and the most recent research, conducted in the North West of England (Evans and Puech, 2001: 804), concluded that many young offenders and YOT workers saw 'the warning system as arbitrary, unfair and disproportionate'.

The Crime and Disorder Act 1998 provided the basis for earlier interventions in the lives of young offenders, and for interventions in the lives and the families of those 'at risk'. In doing so it became 'the first piece of criminal justice legislation in England and Wales (at least since the Vagrancy Statutes of the early nineteenth century) to act explicitly against legal *and* moral/social transgressions' (Muncie, 2001). Adopting the new 'what works' paradigm and using the language of risk factors, New Labour introduced a range of new orders, covering both criminal and civil penalties, that focused not only on criminal activity but 'anti-social behaviour' and 'poor parenting'. It contained a range of orders – the child safety order, the anti-social behaviour order, the local child curfew and the sex offender order – where there is no necessity for either the prosecution or the commission of a criminal offence. These, together with the abolition of *doli incapax*, represent the most controversial aspects of the 'new youth justice'.

The Labour Party in opposition had been much influenced by the 'Broken Windows' thesis (Wilson and Kelling, 1982) and sought to introduce a range of measures that would enable local agencies to tackle 'low-level disorder' or 'anti-social behaviour'. One of these new measures, the child safety order, relates to children under ten (i.e. below the age of criminal responsibility). In fact the order, made in a family proceedings court, is aimed at controlling anti-social behaviour rather than protecting a child's welfare and involves placing a child under supervision, usually for a period of three months, though up to a maximum of 12 months. Though the child safety order was subject to criticism in some quarters (Family Policy Studies Centre, 1998) it was the anti-social behaviour order which drew the greatest ire. Originally termed the 'Community Safety Order' in Labour's consultation documents, the order was renamed because of the potential for confusion with the proposed 'Community Protection Order' (which became the 'Sex Offender Order') and because the original was felt not to capture the purpose of the order.

The order was designed specifically to tackle 'anti-social behaviour' defined as 'a manner that caused or was likely to cause harassment, alarm or distress to one or more persons not of the same household'. Prior to the Crime and Disorder Act 1998 much of this behaviour had been dealt with, if at all, under the provisions of the Housing Act 1996, the Noise Act 1996, the Environmental Protection Act 1990 or the Protection from Harassment Act 1997. However, proceedings against juveniles were often problematic under such legislation (Nixon et al., 1999). By contrast, anti-social behaviour orders (ASBOs) were clearly designed with juvenile 'anti-social behaviour' in mind.

Applications for an ASBO can be made by the police or the local authority. The orders are formally civil – requiring a civil burden of proof.[9] The order itself consists of prohibitions deemed necessary to protect people – within the relevant local authority area – from further anti-social conduct. What is most controversial about the order, however, is that non-compliance is a criminal matter, triable either way and carrying a maximum sentence in the magistrates' court of six months imprisonment, or five years imprisonment plus a fine in the Crown Court. This led some of the most distinguished critics of the new order (Gardner et al., 1998) to observe that it was strange: 'that a government which purports to be interested in tackling social exclusion at the same time promotes a legislative measure destined to create a whole new breed of outcasts'.

Though it initially appeared that there was some reluctance on the ground to use ASBOs, the most recently published information suggests that they are now being sought with increasing regularity. The take-up varies greatly across police force areas, although 39 of the 43 police forces in England and Wales have now applied for and been granted orders. The numbers of ASBOs applied for by police forces and local authorities have been more or less equal (49 versus 51 per cent). In the first 18 months of operation (April 1999–September 2000) a total of 466 ASBOs were made and 18 were refused (Campbell, 2002). Just under three-fifths (58 per cent) were made against juveniles. Three-quarters of those given ASBOs were aged 21 or under. Home Office research identified a broad range of behaviours in the files of cases resulting in ASBOs, with the average case citing six different forms of anti-social behaviour. 'Threats' were most commonly cited – occurring in just under half of cases – followed by 'intimidation' in over a third.

Concerns similar to those voiced about the ASBO were also aimed at the provisions in the Act that allowed local authorities to introduce 'local child curfew schemes'. The introduction of curfews in the United Kingdom had been foreshadowed by proposals in the consultation paper, *Tackling Youth Crime* (Home Office, 1997g) and the White Paper, *No More Excuses* (Home Office, 1997d). The former described the problem thus: 'unsupervised children gathered in public places can cause real alarm and misery to local communities and can encourage one another into anti-social and criminal habits' (Home Office, 1997g: para. 114). The provisions in the Crime and Disorder Act 1998 enabled local authorities, after consultation with the police and with support of the Home Secretary, to introduce a ban on children of specified ages (though under ten) in specified places for a period of up to 90 days. Children breaking the curfew were to be taken home by the police, and breach of the curfew constitutes sufficient grounds for the imposition of a child safety order. In practice, there has been remarkable reluctance on the ground to use such powers and no child curfew orders were made in the first two years of operation. Despite such reluctance, and sustained criticism of curfews from some quarters, government has remained keen on the idea of curfews. Armed with what appeared to be some positive results from an evaluation of a scheme in Hamilton in Scotland (McGallagly et al., 1998), new legislation was introduced to extend the reach of curfew powers. The Criminal Justice and Police Act 2001 extends the maximum age at which children can be subject to a curfew up from ten to 'under 16', and also makes provision for a local authority or the police to make a curfew on an area and not just an individual.

The final element of the Act that drew sustained criticism (*inter alia*, Wilkinson, 1995) was the abolition of the presumption – rebuttable in court – that a child aged between ten and 13 is incapable of committing a criminal offence (generally known as *doli incapax*). Whilst the United Kingdom has long been out of step with much of the rest of Western Europe with its significantly lower age of criminal responsibility, the principle of *doli incapax* has traditionally protected at least a proportion of children under 14 from the full weight of the criminal law. However, during the course of the 1990s, spurred in part by the Bulger case, pressure had built up to abolish the principle and politicians from both major parties were vocal in their criticism of it. In fact, the doctrine very nearly disappeared in 1996 when the Divisional Court ruled that *doli incapax* was no longer part of the criminal law. This was, however, later overturned by the House of Lords (C (A Minor) *v* DPP [1996] 1 A.C. 1, HL), although it took the view that the law in this area was in need of reform. New Labour worked hard to appear a convincing party of 'law and order' and 'responsibilisation – of parents, of young offenders and of those below the age of criminal responsibility – was a key part of their approach. The Home Secretary was vehemently critical of the doctrine of *doli incapax* arguing that it was archaic, illogical and unfair (Leng et al., 1998). He stated his reasons for the reform robustly: 'The presumption that children aged ten to thirteen do not know the difference between serious wrongdoing and simple naughtiness flies in the face of common-sense and is long overdue for reform' (Straw, 1998). Though much of New Labour's discourse may have concerned 'what works', this hardly applied to the abolition of *doli incapax*, which had more to do with the government's 'remoralising' mission and its focus on individual and parental responsibility (Muncie, 2000).

Those concerned about the trajectory of New Labour's youth justice have also pointed to its perceived failure to tackle the problem of increasing use of custodial sentences for young offenders. Indeed, in its first term, Labour also continued with the previous administration's Secure Training Centre building programme – even arguing that they might be expanded – and introduced a new, generic custodial sentence: the detention and training order (DTO). Available to the courts from April 2000, in a DTO half of the sentence is served in custody and half in the community. Over 500 such orders have been made per month on average since they were introduced. The DTO is a single sentence replacing the Secure Training Order (available for 12–14-year-olds) and detention in a young offender institution (available for 15–17-year-olds). Long-term detention under s. 53 of the Children and Young Persons Act 1933 for 'grave offences' remains an available sentence in the Crown Court. The intention behind the DTO was to create a more 'constructive sentence' (Home Office, 1997d) in which a training plan would be drawn up for the custodial phase and where the subsequent period of supervision in the community would be considered an integral part of the sentence.

As such, the DTO represents something of an increase in the powers of the Youth Court to impose custodial sentences. Thus, whereas the maximum period of detention in a YOI for 15–17-year-olds had been six months for a single offence, the DTO has a maximum of two years. Similarly, although the Secure Training Order for 12–14-year-olds already provided for a 24-month maximum, the DTO has the potential to be extended to young offenders below the age of 12. In practice, the introduction of the DTO has if anything heightened the existing trend towards increased use of custodial penalties for young offenders. In the first year (April 2000–March 2001) a total of 6,058 DTOs were made. Of these, 617 (10 per cent) involved 12–14-year-olds, and 455 (7.5 per cent), young women. The numbers increased steadily during the first year of operation, from 1,235 in the first quarter to 1,799 in the fourth quarter. During this period the juvenile sentenced population in secure establishments rose by 15 per cent though the remand population fell by 21 per cent. The total number in secure facilities was higher during the course of the year than it was during the previous year. The average daily population was 2,807, compared with 2,611 in 1999 – an increase of 7.5 per cent (Renshaw and Powell, 2001).

The influence of restorative justice

> Young offenders are spectators at legalistic, adversarial court proceedings and often hear lawyers making excuses for their offending. With the restorative approach there is no way for youngsters – or their parents – to hide from their personal responsibilities.
>
> (Alun Michael, 1998)

The influence of communitarian thinking, which was very visible in the Home Office's consultation documents published immediately after the 1997 General Election, found form in the central place accorded to restorative justice in New Labour's youth justice. Initially, this was most visible in the place given to reparation in the Crime and Disorder Act 1998, and to the support given to experiments such as that with restorative cautioning in Thames Valley (Young and Goold, 1999).

There were a number of aspects of the Crime and Disorder Act 1998 that were based, at least in part, on ideas influenced by restorative justice. In particular, the reformed cautioning system, action plan orders and reparation orders all sought to promote the idea of reparation and, wherever possible, to seek victims' views. The action plan order was designed to be the first option for young offenders whose offending is serious enough to warrant a community sentence. *No More Excuses* (Home Office, 1997d) described the order as 'a short, intensive programme of community intervention combining punishment, rehabilitation and reparation to change offending behaviour and prevent further crime'. The evaluation of the Crime and Disorder pilots found that many YOTs developed standard programmes in order to meet the reparative requirements of the order and that 'it is common for the same reparative activity to be built in final warning programmes, reparation orders, action plan orders and supervision orders' (Holdaway et al., 2001: 42).

The 'reparation order' requires young offenders to make reparation – specified in the order – either to a specified person or persons or 'to the community at large'. The language of responsibilisation was once again central to the underlying rationale. According to the Minister of State at the time (Michael, 1998): 'With the restorative approach there is no way for youngsters – or their parents – to hide from their personal responsibilities.' The White Paper (Home Office, 1997d) explained the order in the following terms:

> Courts will have to consider imposing [this penalty] on young offenders in all cases where they do not impose a compensation order. The order will require reparation to be made in kind, up to a maximum of 24 hours work within a period of three months. . . . Of course not all victims would want reparation. The government's proposals will ensure that the victim's views will be sought before an order is made. Where a victim does not want direct reparation, the reparation may be made to the community at large.

There can be little doubt that there was a concerted effort by New Labour to make both victims' views and reparation more central aspects of youth justice than previously had been the case. However, Dignan (1999: 58) was undoubtedly right when he argued that these 'reforms hardly amount to a "restorative justice revolution", let alone the "paradigm shift" that some restorative justice advocates have called for'. Following the implementation of the 1998 Act, the YJB also committed considerable funds to the stimulation of restorative justice projects for young offenders and, together with Crime Concern, issued guidance on the establishment of victim-offender mediation and family group conferencing programmes. Of all New Labour's restorative youth justice initiatives, arguably the most significant, however, has been the creation of referral orders as part of the Youth Justice and Criminal Evidence Act 1999.

The referral order is available in the Youth Court and adult magistrates' courts and may be made for a minimum of three and a maximum of 12 months, depending on the seriousness of the crime (as determined by the court). The order is mandatory for 10–17-year-olds pleading guilty and convicted for the first time by the courts, unless the crime is serious enough to warrant custody or the court orders an absolute discharge. The disposal involves referring the young offender to a youth offender panel (YOP). The intention is that the panel will provide a forum away from the formality of the court. As Crawford (2003) argues, the panels draw on at least three sources: the Scottish Children's Hearings system (Whyte, 2000); the experience of family group conferencing (Morris and Maxwell, 2000); and the history of victim-offender mediation in England and Wales (Marshall and Merry, 1990) and restorative cautioning (Young, 2000). The referral order constitutes the entire sentence for the offence and, as such, substitutes for action plan orders, reparation orders and supervision orders.[10]

The Act extends the statutory responsibility of YOTs to include the recruitment and training of YOP volunteers, administering panel meetings and implementing referral orders. Panels consist of one YOT member and (at least) two community panel members, one of whom leads the panel. A parent or both parents of a young offender aged under 16 are expected to attend all panel meetings in all but exceptional cases. The offender can also nominate an adult to support them. It is not intended that legal representatives acting in a professional capacity be included in panel meetings, either directly or as an offender's supporter. To encourage the restorative nature of the process, a variety of other people may be invited to attend given panel meetings (any participation is strictly voluntary). Those who may attend include: the victim or a representative of the community at large; a victim supporter; a supporter of the young person and/or anyone else that the panel considers to be capable of having a 'good influence' on the offender; and signers and interpreters for any of the participants in the process who require them.

The aim of the initial panel meeting is to devise a 'contract' and, where the victim chooses to attend, for them to meet and talk about the offence with the offender. It is intended that negotiations between the panel and the offender about the content of the contract should be led by the community panel members. The contract should always include reparation to the victim or wider community and a programme of activity designed primarily to prevent further offending. Where possible, it is recommended that reparation should have some relation to the offence itself. Early reports from the evaluation of the referral order pilots indicated mixed success. On the positive side, the youth offender panels appeared to have established themselves within a year of operation as deliberative and participatory forums in which a young person's offending behaviour can be addressed (Newburn et al., 2001b). The informal setting of youth offender panels appeared to allow young people, their parents/carers, community panel members and YOT advisers opportunities to discuss the nature and consequences of a young person's offending, as well as how to respond to this in ways which seek to repair the harm done and to address the causes of the young person's offending behaviour. In addition, the successful integration of a large number of volunteers within the youth justice process provides an opportunity for a potentially powerful new exterior voice to participate and influence this arena.

The major difficulty encountered so far, as in other restorative justice developments (Dignan, 2000; Miers et al., 2001), concerns the involvement of victims (Newburn et al., 2002). During the period of the referral order pilots, the level of victim involvement in panels was very low. There were a number of reasons for this though, in essence, they appeared to concern issues of implementation rather than problems with the general principles underlying referral orders. The response of all the major participants in the process to date has been largely supportive of the general principles underlying referral orders. The introduction of referral orders and youth offender panels and, more especially, the involvement of community panel members, represents a fairly radical departure in youth justice in England and Wales (Crawford and Newburn, 2002). However, as a number of authors have noted (Dignan, 1999; Crawford, 2003; Crawford and Newburn, 2002) there are some important tensions between attempts to extend the reach of restorative justice and other aspects of New Labour's approach to youth justice. First, as we have seen, apparent promotion of restorative justice exists alongside the continuing 'incarceration spiral' (Dignan, 1999). Second, despite the more inclusionary tone associated with restorative justice, much contemporary youth justice discourse remains profoundly punitive. Third, there is a tension between the managerialism at the heart of New Labour's reforms – and its concern with speed, efficiency, cost reductions and performance measurement – and communitarian appeals to local justice in which there is an expectation that local people will play a central role in the handling of cases in their own local area (Crawford and Newburn, 2002). Thus, the growing emphasis on output and outcome measurement puts at risk restorative justice processes which place greater emphasis on providing a secure forum in which there is room for emotions to be expressed and for sometimes complex negotiations to take place. Most fundamentally, the greatest danger, perhaps as a result of a combination of the above, is that the very idea of restorative justice, 'and the mainly positive image which it has enjoyed thus far, might become subordinated to the more traditional and punitive approaches of the past' (Dignan, 1999: 54).

Conclusion

It was always likely that youth justice would be the main focus of New Labour criminal justice policy in its first term of office. Understanding this part of the justice system is by no means straightforward, however, and under New Labour, the 'mélange of measures' (Muncie, 2001) that is youth justice has become even more complicated than previously. Is the 'new youth justice' really new, or should we regard the policies of the Labour government on youth justice 'as simply a continuation, and in some ways a more radical extension, of the policies of its immediate Conservative predecessor' (Smith, 2000)?

Regarding it simply as a radical extension of previous approaches is too simplistic and, indeed, to be fair to Smith (2000), he recognises that though there are clear continuities between New Labour and previous administrations, not least in some of their punitive rhetoric, there are also clear differences. Indeed, even in relation to populist rhetoric there have been changes, for some of the populist punitiveness of the pre-1997 period has been toned down or jettisoned altogether. Though New Labour came to power using the language of 'zero tolerance', this was largely abandoned in the latter stages of the first administration, and has only been deployed sporadically since then. Similarly, the corporatist modernising agenda, though clearly a descendant of the 1980s version, is also radically different from it. In particular, the rise to prominence of the 'What Works' paradigm, and the centralising managerialist initiatives embodied in the creation of the Youth Justice Board and YOTs, signal a major departure from previous arrangements.

On the positive side, the increased profile of restorative approaches in youth justice has generally been welcomed. In particular, the introduction of referral orders appears to offer both a different way of working with 'first time' offenders as well as offering a somewhat different vision of how the justice system might operate. A few words of caution in relation to this are called for, however. First, despite ministerial assertions that this represents the replacement of old-style adversarial youth justice with a system now attuned to restorative principles, there must be some doubt about this. The adversarial system is deeply embedded and resistant to change. Previous research on reparation within criminal justice found it to be fairly easily marginalised by courts, police and lawyers and, moreover, in implementation to suffer from a lack of coherence and from ambiguity of objectives and process (Davis, 1992). Second, one of the issues perennially raised in relation to reparation is whether it should be entirely voluntary or whether, under some circumstances, it may be coerced. Although reparation as part of a court order will undoubtedly require acquiescence on the part of an offender, in practice the majority of the Crime and Disorder Act 1998 provisions are coercive (as potentially, of course, are referral orders). Whilst there are elements of coercion which may be useful in facilitating reparative work on the part of an offender, it is important not to lose sight of Davis' (1992: 213) important conclusion that 'non-material reparation delivered in the shadow of a pending court appearance will generally fail to convince'.

The question of the appropriateness of coercion has also be raised in connection with parenting orders, child curfews and anti-social behaviour orders. Thus, whilst there is considerable evidence that poor parenting and inconsistent parental discipline are key risk factors (among many others) in offending, is it really the case that these can be dealt with via a court order and coerced attendance at parenting classes? There are many working in the field who remain strongly of the opinion that counselling and guidance sessions must be delivered on a voluntary basis if they are to work (see, for example, McGlone, 1998). Coercion, it is suggested, may exacerbate existing tensions in relationships and families. Moreover, given current governmental emphasis on tackling the roots of social exclusion, it is perhaps surprising that poor parenting should be viewed as the consequence of wilfulness – requiring parents to be disciplined – rather than the product of multiple social disadvantage.

Similar questions have been raised in connection with child curfews and anti-social behaviour orders. Again, there is considerable empirical evidence which shows that 'childhood conduct problems predict later offending' (Farrington, 1997: 378). Early intervention therefore makes sense. However, the governmental response has been, in part, to use the blunt instrument of legislation. Youthful 'anti-social behaviour' is to be tackled by introducing curfews, by placing 10–14-year-olds at significantly greater risk of involvement in the criminal justice system, and by extending the supervisory net of local agencies to include those below the age of criminal responsibility. This is part of the 'no more excuses'[11] approach to crime and anti-social behaviour – the 'tough on crime' part of the famous mantra. Curfews, the abolition of *doli incapax*, the decision to proceed with the building of secure training centres for 12–14-year-olds, and the desire to 'name and shame' young offenders, all fall into this category. Moreover, they provide clear evidence that populist punitiveness is alive and well.

Whilst the 'tough on crime, tough on the causes of crime' approach was generally presented by New Labour as an unproblematic pairing of mutually compatible approaches to tackling crime, in practice, there was often considerable tension between the two. One of the ways in which this has sometimes been played out is in the use of punitive rhetoric to emphasise approaches that could be presented to the public as evidence of the government's 'toughness', whilst diverting attention from reforms that contained a greater 'tough on the causes of crime' element to them. Nowhere were the effects of this clearer than in relation to the reforms in the youth justice system. Despite the shortcomings of, and inherent dangers in, some of the youth justice reforms, they nonetheless represent some of the more far-reaching and important changes introduced by New Labour. The refashioning of youth justice teams into YOTs, the emphasis on restorative justice, the provision of major new resources were part of a long overdue overhaul of youth justice. They were, in intention at least, something that the government could have made a centrepiece of its rhetoric and not just its legislative programme in its first term. In the event, however, as in so much else, the government lost its nerve. At the heart of New Labour there lies a 'confidence deficit'. The electorate – or at least that part of the electorate that is fought over – is perceived by New

Labour as being both morally and fiscally conservative as well as being punitive. As a consequence, in public statements the major youth justice reforms have largely been invisible, blocked from view by the tough talk that is considered to be *de rigueur*. Both the message and the performance have been mixed, and further significant reform in the next five years cannot be ruled out.

Notes

1. Recommendations originally contained in the *Young Offenders Report* (1927), and later in the 1938 Criminal Justice Bill.
2. Provision for (Senior) Attendance Centres was also included in the 1948 Act, but it was a full decade before they came into being. For a full history see Mair, G. (1991) *Part-Time Punishment: The Origins and Development of Senior Attendance Centres.* London: HMSO.
3. These authors who, themselves, advocated an approach to juvenile justice known as 'systems management', 'can claim a substantial degree of success' according to Cavadino and Dignan (1992). The authors were critical of traditional welfarism which, they argued, failed, despite its best efforts, to limit the degree of state social control over juvenile offenders.
4. Rutherford (1986a) quotes two further members of the Association expressing similar views; 'Sir William Addison talked of "the hard core of young offenders – that is to say, the offenders in the youngest age group – that is now resulting in the very serious increase in the incidence of crime in the 15 to 17 age groups". Mr R.C. Stranger added: "the hard core of sophisticated young criminals hitherto considered and spoken of as small in number but which one fears [is] increasing".'
5. Section 1(4) of the Criminal Justice Act 1982 laid down that a young offender could only be sentenced to custody if the court was satisfied that one of the following three conditions was met: (a) that the offender was unable or unwilling to respond to non-custodial penalties; (b) that custody was necessary for the protection of the public; or (c) that the offence was so serious that a non-custodial penalty could not be justified. (The criteria were subsequently amended by the Criminal Justice Act 1988 and eventually superseded by the new criteria in the Criminal Justice Act 1991, which also apply to adults).
6. This is not to ignore the quite extended debate that has taken place about the possibility that some of these changes – increased use of cautioning and non-custodial penalties, for example – may have resulted in a degree of 'net-widening', i.e. bringing into the criminal justice process children who would not otherwise have been there (cf. Ditchfield, 1976; Farrington and Bennett, 1981; Tutt and Giller, 1983).
7. The phrase was first used by Tony Blair on Radio 4's *The World This Weekend*, 10 January 1993.
8. Jack Straw speaking at the launch of *Tackling Youth Crime, Reforming Youth Justice*, 20 May 1996.
9. That this is the case was confirmed by the Court of Appeal (R *v* Manchester Crown Court, *Ex Parte* McCann (2001)).

10. However, the referral order may be accompanied by certain ancillary orders such as orders for costs, compensation, forfeiture of items used in committing an offence, exclusion from football matches, etc. (s. 4(2) and (3)).
11. Interestingly, a phrase that was resonant of John Major's injunction to 'understand a little less and condemn more'.

Chapter 9

Victims and criminal justice policy

The bulk of this text so far has focused upon offenders and the agencies tasked with detecting and recording their offences, together with those that have the job of administering punishment. Little has been said about victims, and this reflects the offence and offender-centred nature of British criminal justice. One consequence of such a focus is that it has long been suggested that 'the victim' is the forgotten party in the criminal justice process. However, the development of a variety of victim services over the past two or three decades have begun, albeit slightly, to address this oversight. In fact, a veritable industry of 'services' has developed and so strong has this growth been, that a number of authors have referred to the emergence of an all-encompassing 'victims movement' (*inter alia*, Pointing and Maguire, 1988).

Nevertheless, it would still be a mistake to describe the criminal justice system as victim-friendly. The victim of crime is by no means the central focus of the criminal justice system, and a variety of studies have shown in some detail how victims are often poorly treated by criminal justice agencies, sometimes to the point where it is suggested they may suffer some form of secondary victimisation. There is evidence from the late 1970s, for example (Berger, 1977; Katz and Mazur, 1979), and early 1980s (Chambers and Millar, 1983) that women who reported sexual assault to the police often had their character and morality questioned in such a way as to imply some responsibility for their victimisation. The treatment of rape and sexual assault victims has changed in many respects in recent years and this reflects a growing recognition of the needs if not the rights of victims. The position of the victim in the modern criminal justice system is the focus of this chapter.

At this stage it is worth saying something briefly about 'victimology' (the sub-discipline of criminology devoted to the study of victims) as it has, in part, been responsible for the increasing attention that has been devoted to victims in recent years. The term 'victimology' was first used in the late 1940s by Frederick Wertham, and the classic early studies in the genre appeared at about the same time. Beginning with Von Hentig in the late 1940s and Marvin Wolfgang in the 1950s, early studies concentrated on the role of the victim in the causes of crime. At this point, criminologists were still searching for 'grand theories' that would explain crime, and victims of crime became, in part, another focus of that concern. For Von Hentig and others, the specific focus was upon the role of the victim in the precipitation or perpetration of the crime.

It was not until the mid-1960s and the early 1970s, however, that victims 'attracted any serious public attention' (Pointing and Maguire, 1988). The mid to late 1960s saw the first murmurings of the nascent victims movement and in its wake academic victimology, which was about to be radically transformed by the utilisation of large-scale survey techniques, moved its focus to the victim population in general rather than the individual (Fattah, 1992). This gave rise to what one author has characterised as a 'lifestyle' approach to victimology or, alternatively, as 'conventional victimology' (Walklate, 1989). In this approach, it is argued that there is a link between routine daily activities and exposure to circumstances in which the risk of victimisation is high. Whilst this constituted a significant advance on the work of Von Hentig, it tended to fail to take account of those structural constraints which were not easily observable or measurable. Furthermore, in its concentration on the public domain and its avoidance of the private, it merely reinforced conventional views of victimisation (that is, for example, it paid relatively little attention to domestic violence) and through its policy emphasis on individual lifestyle engaged in, at least implicit, victim-blaming once more.

The shortcomings of 'conventional' victimology were thrown into sharp relief, however, by the re-emergence of feminism and its impact on criminology generally. Feminists were critical of both the theory and methodology associated with the lifestyle approach, and they stressed the importance of the experience of victimisation. Focusing in particular on rape and domestic violence, a number of authors were able to illustrate the limitations of the social survey as a method of uncovering either the incidence of these forms of victimisation or the reality of the experience of victimisation. Central to their account was the issue of power for as Stanko (1988: 46), for example, has argued 'unless policing and crime survey researchers lend credence to the concept and reality of gender stratification, violence against women will, on many levels, remain a hidden, but all too real part of women's lives'.

The work of feminists, and particularly activists rather than academics, was crucial to the transformation in understanding about the frequency and impact of rape, sexual assault and domestic violence. One simple but important historical lesson, therefore, is that certain forms of victimisation only become visible when they do, because of campaigning work of representative groups.

In a short essay on the 'victims' movement', van Dijk (1988) has, for the sake of clarity if not always historical accuracy, identified three waves in its development which he distinguishes chronologically: first, state compensation and initiatives by probation officers, 1965–75; second, rape crisis centres, shelter homes and the first victim support schemes, 1975–80; and, third, institutionalisation of victims support and the call for justice, 1980 onwards. These general distinctions provide a useful structure for considering victims and criminal justice policy. This chapter will follow a roughly similar course, beginning by considering the introduction not only of the state compensation scheme, but also court-based compensation. It will then focus on the re-emergence of the feminist movement and services for victims of rape, sexual assault, domestic violence and child abuse and, finally, will consider the history of victim support.

It is worth bearing in mind at this stage, and we will return to this point on a number of occasions below, that there has been no reference so far in this chapter to a 'victims policy'. The reason for this is that for the bulk of the period under discussion here, neither of the major political parties – whether in government or not – has had a particularly coherent policy on crime victims. Indeed, it is probably true to say that victims have for the most part been used by government as means of justifying or, occasionally, even diverting attention from broader criminal justice policies or trends in crime. It is rare for much consideration to be given to victims of crime in their own right.

Compensation by the offender and the state

Compensation by the state

In many respects, the story of the 'victims movement' in the United Kingdom begins with the introduction of criminal injuries compensation, for it was through the introduction of that scheme that the needs of victims were first formally recognised. Rock (1990)[1] suggests that two groups of people were influential in the campaign that eventually led to the development of the criminal injuries compensation scheme (CICS). The first were what he calls a group of 'general reformers' drawn from the major political parties; the second a narrower group of penal reformers drawn from bodies like the Howard League and Justice. More particularly, however, the development of the CICS is associated with the penal reformer, Margery Fry.

A Quaker, Margery Fry had been the first secretary of the Howard League for Penal Reform, a magistrate, the Chairman of a juvenile court bench, Vice-President of the Magistrates' Association, and a member of the Advisory Council on the Treatment of Offenders. Fry became convinced of the idea that restitution and reconciliation was preferable and more constructive than the more punitive process of arrest, charge, prosecution and punishment that tended to characterise the criminal justice system. However, the range of problems associated with a system based on restitution and reconciliation – the large proportion of cases in which no offender is apprehended; the limited financial circumstances of the majority that are arrested and prosecuted; and the difficulties associated with enforcing some form of restitution order – convinced her that compensation from the state was a more realistic option. Furthermore Fry and others made the assumption that compensation was what victims wanted: 'In the absence of a demand from victims, without any knowledge of what victims might want, compensation was in effect a solution devised to solve the imagined ills of an imagined population' (Rock, 1990: 52).

In 1958, before her campaigning could bear fruit, Margery Fry died. In the year prior to her death, she had made contact with Justice – the British section of the International Commission of Jurists – and it was they that took up the campaign from then on. In 1959, Reg Prentice introduced a Private Members' Bill – the Criminal Injuries (Compensation) Bill – which, though it made no progress, did help keep the subject on the table. Another identical Bill was introduced a year later with the same effect. Also in 1959, the government published *Penal Practice in a Changing Society*, which although focusing primarily on the penal measures did consider obligations to the victims of crime and resulted in the setting up of a working party to examine the proposal to introduce a scheme for the payment of compensation to victims of crimes of violence. Although in its report it actually considered two possible methods of making compensation available, as far as reformers were concerned, there appeared to be a lack of appetite for any such ideas within the Home Office.

One result was that Justice set up its own working party to consider the Home Office report. Once again, Justice, like other organisations before it, did not feel it important to consult victims – the assumption was that their needs and desires were predictable. The report (Justice, 1961) proposed that compensation should be available for a specified range of offences. Importantly, the notion of victim culpability was introduced, the effect of which would be to reduce the size of any awards made. A little after this time, a committee set up by the Conservative Political Centre also produced a report recommending the introduction of a compensation scheme – this time to be based on common law damages (Conservative Political Centre, 1962). Pressure was kept up and in 1964 a second White Paper was published (Home Office, 1964) which made reference to the flurry of reports that had come out in the previous few years, but also to the criminal injuries scheme that had been introduced in New Zealand in 1963. The White Paper advocated an 'experimental and non-statutory' scheme be introduced in Britain, that payments be *ex gratia*, and that the scheme be administered by an independent board. There was to be a minimum payment of £50.

Two elements of the subsequent debate in Parliament are worth briefly mentioning. First, the proposed scheme was justified by reference to the argument that for too long the criminal justice system had ignored the needs of victims and that such a scheme would begin to right this imbalance. Second, there was much discussion of the idea of victim culpability and therefore of the process of attempting to make the distinction between deserving and undeserving victims. There was virtual consensus around these issues. Rock (1990: 83) notes: 'No one inside or outside Parliament was reported to have dissented from those arguments. There was such an overwhelming agreement about principle that debate centred entirely on practical matters of costings, definitions, and applications. Within that consensus, the authority and assumptions of the groups that had championed compensation were never examined.' The criminal injuries compensation scheme came into operation on 1 August 1964 and in its first year of operation received over 500 applications for an award. In its first full year of operation, the scheme paid out almost half a million pounds in compensation.

As soon as the scheme had been successfully set up, those campaigners who had been most centrally involved in bringing about the change turned their attentions to other matters. Rock (1990) suggests that even Margery Fry, had she lived, would most likely have moved on to other things once the scheme was underway. The crucial point here is that the campaigns to bring in criminal injuries compensation never once involved victims themselves – such a thing does not seem to have been considered – nor did it presage the beginnings of a more concerted campaign on behalf of victims of crime more generally: 'No organization of victims had emerged. None had been sponsored. On the contrary, compensation was designed precisely to prevent such a coalescence' (Rock, 1990: 86).

The reform that had taken place had come about as part of a process of penal reform; it was perceived to be the righting of a wrong in the criminal justice system, not as the start of a long-term programme on behalf of victims. At this time, doing things for the victim was, as Rock remarks, an oblique way of doing something for the offender: '[Victims] were to become a working projection of the politics of penal reform, a figment of the reforming imagination, shaped by the concerns and purposes of their creators. Their character never seemed to be a problem, a thing to be investigated and considered. It was invented and bestowed, and the result was a contradictory creature' (Rock, 1990: 88). This schizophrenic creature was, on the one hand, desirous of retribution and therefore to be placated by compensation and was, on the other hand, considered to be helpless, innocent and, therefore, *deserving* (Newburn, 1990). As the Home Office White Paper (1964) itself described:

> Compensation will be paid ex gratia. The Government do not accept that the State is liable for injuries caused to people by the acts of others. The public does, however, feel a sense of responsibility for and sympathy with the *innocent victim*, and it is right that this feeling should find practical expression in the provision of compensation on behalf of the community [emphasis added].

The new scheme operated on the basis that compensation should only be paid to the 'deserving', and there should be safeguards to ensure that public money would not be wasted on fraudulent or unmerited applications. In particular, this referred to those who failed to report crimes to the police, who provoked the crime or were in some way related to the offender.

The scheme was amended five years later in 1969, and again in 1979 following a review by an Interdepartmental Working Party. In December 1983, during a debate in the House of Lords, Lord Allen called attention to the need to put the scheme on a statutory footing, and the government conveyed its intention to introduce legislation for precisely such a purpose. Following another Working Party, provision for placing the scheme on a statutory footing was included in the next Criminal Justice Bill, but this was halted by a General Election. The Criminal Justice Act 1988 eventually provided the means for amending the status of the scheme but, as yet, this has not been acted upon. Meanwhile, the number of applications for compensation and the cost of the scheme increases year on year. There were, for example, approximately 26,000 applications in 1981–82 and this had risen to just under 66,000 by 1992–93 (Home Office, 1993a). The amount of compensation paid out rose from approximately £22 million in 1981–82 to over £152 million in 1992–93.

Over the years, a number of means of limiting the increase in the cost of the scheme have been introduced. One of the most frequently used tactics has been to increase the financial minimum below which awards are not made. When the scheme was introduced in 1964, the lower limit for payments was £50. This was raised to £150 in 1977, £250 in 1981, £400 in 1983, £550 in 1987 and then to £1,000 in the early 1990s. In 1994, a much more severe set of restrictions was put forward by the Home Secretary, Michael Howard, who proposed to introduce a tariff which would have severely limited payments, particularly to victims of especially violent crimes. However, a legal action brought by ten trade unions and the TUC resulted in the Court of Appeal ruling that the Home Secretary had 'acted unlawfully and abused his prerogative and common law powers' in flouting the will of Parliament (*Guardian*, 10 November 1994) and that he was under a duty to put the old scheme on a statutory footing. Further reviews of the scheme took place in 1995 and 2001, primarily in an attempt to restrict rising costs and encourage administrative efficiency. The number of applications has continued to rise and the amount paid out to victims has all but doubled in the last 10 years (Zedner, 2002).

Compensation by the offender

Compensation via the courts has quite a long history in England and Wales. The Larceny Act and the Malicious Damage Act of 1861 gave magistrates' courts the powers to order compensation for loss or damage to property, and the Forfeiture Act 1870 provided further powers to the courts to order convicted felons to pay for loss of property. The Probation of Offenders Act 1907 enabled courts discharging an offender or releasing him on probation to award damages for injury or compensation for loss.

It was, however, the Criminal Justice Act 1972 which broadened the circumstances under which compensation could be ordered and which forms the basis for court-ordered compensation which still exists today. Section 1 of the Act gave magistrates' courts and the Crown Court a general power to order offenders to pay compensation for loss, damage or personal injury resulting from a criminal offence. Crucially, it dispensed with the need for an application for compensation to be made to the court and it introduced powers to order compensation for offences taken into consideration.

The changes made by the Act resulted in large part from the recommendations of a report of the Advisory Council on the Penal System chaired by Lord Justice Widgery (Home Office, 1970). Very much like the case of criminal injuries compensation in the 1960s, the impetus behind the introduction of the compensation order was cast in terms of the potential effect on the offender rather than the victim. As Mawby and Gill (1987: 51) note: 'The context within which the working party operated is notable. While compensation orders could be justified as having an intrinsic moral value, or as a means of reform, their main appeal to the committee was as a means of preventing the offender enjoying the fruits of his crime; reparation was thus "an essential element in the punishment of crime"' (Home Office, 1970: 3).

At this point the compensation order was an ancillary order which had to be made in conjunction with another penalty. Furthermore, there was a certain lack of clarity about how such orders were to be used, and Viscount Colville in the House of Lords debate on the Criminal Justice Bill had stated that the circumstances for compensation should not be made overly precise (Wasik, 1978; Shapland et al., 1985). In 1975, Lord Widgery had pronounced that 'A compensation order made by the [criminal] court can be extremely beneficial as long as it is confined to simple, straightforward cases and generally cases where no great amount is at stake' (quoted in Davies, 1992: 23). Because of the restricted nature of the order, the lack of clarity about how it was to be used, the inherent limitations in imposing financial penalties on offenders (the majority of offenders do not come before the courts; many do not have sufficient means to pay compensation; some will be incarcerated and therefore not be in a position to pay any financial penalty) and the fact that many victims continued to remain ignorant of their 'right' to compensation, meant that orders were only made in a minority of cases in which, in theory, they might have been made (Softley, 1978; Newburn, 1988).

In an effort to overcome some of these problems, the Criminal Justice Act 1982 modified the position of the compensation order so that it could be used either as an ancillary order or as a penalty in its own right. The 1982 Act also required courts to give preference to the compensation order where it considered both compensation and a fine to be appropriate sentences. In reality these changes only had a limited impact on the way such orders were used by the courts, and magistrates (compensation orders are used very infrequently in the Crown Court) retained a degree of unease about using compensation in preference to fines or other non-custodial measures, largely because of the continuing confusion about the reparative and punitive elements in the order. Research at the time concluded: 'magistrates are generally unwilling to use compensation as a sole penalty, preferring to combine it with a fine, probation or, in some cases, absolute or conditional discharge. The rationale for this is that compensation, they feel, is not in itself a sufficient punishment, returning one only to the *status quo ante*' (Newburn, 1988: 48).

The system remained in need of overhaul and a further attempt at improvement was made in the Criminal Justice Act 1988. This required courts to give reasons whenever compensation was not ordered in cases involving damage, loss or injury (Miers, 1990). Although this had the effect of dramatically increasing the proportion of cases involving personal injury in which compensation was ordered – it doubled in the magistrates courts to 46 per cent (Moxon, 1993) – it still did not overcome magistrates' reluctance to use compensation as a sole penalty.

In short, the delivery of compensation via the courts was, and most likely remains, haphazard. Only a minority of victims will ever receive compensation from an offender via the court system, and fewer still will receive anything from the Criminal Injuries Compensation Scheme (CICS). In addition, the two systems of compensation do not mesh (Newburn, 1990) and, indeed, are not intended to fit together. This is an important point for it illustrates the absence of an overall strategy in relation to the needs of victims of crime. The two compensation systems cover predominantly different offences, operate at different financial levels and have quite distinct threshold criteria. Even in the area of criminal injury there appears to be little correspondence between the court system and the CICS. As it stands at the moment, victims of crime tend to receive sums of compensation from magistrates' courts which, because, in practice, claims are generally small and many offenders have limited means, are generally far below the lower limit operated by the CICS. Although theoretically compensation orders should cover injuries up to and over the minimum threshold at CICS, in practice, there exists a considerable gulf between awards from the scheme and awards from the court.

Whilst much is made of the need to do things for victims of crime, financial reparation remains at best an expensive symbolic exercise with confused aims. At least in part, the confusion stems from the fact that these initiatives which are ostensibly about victims of crime were, in reality, introduced because of a paucity of ideas in relation to dealing with offenders. As Mawby (1988: 130) concludes: 'Of course, it would be naive to suggest that deterrence was the only pressure behind the introduction of compensation orders. Nevertheless, they, like the Criminal Injuries

Compensation Scheme, clearly fail to address either the needs or the rights of crime victims. While they may, *post hoc*, be justified in terms of such principles, it makes more sense to view them as an integral part of Conservative penal philosophy of the 1960s and 1970s, representing one aspect of concern over the crime problem and balancing punishment of offenders with a carefully constrained demonstration of response to the needs of *some* victims.'

Duff (1988) argues that there are two discernible trends which illustrate the worldwide impact the 'victim movement' has had on the criminal justice process: the first is the introduction of state-funded compensation schemes (with the aim of strengthening the relationship between the offender and the state) and, second, the adoption of compensation by the offender to the victim into the criminal justice system (thereby increasing the importance attached to the victim-offender relationship). However, in respect of the relationship between victim and offender, it was actually the case for some time that many reformers were keener on the idea of mediation and reparation (whether material or not) than they were on financial compensation.

In part, this had much to do with the fact that reparation fitted much more neatly into contemporary penal thought. Although it involved victims, it was, strictly speaking, in many ways not really about victims. Many of those who were most in favour of the introduction of some form of new reparation order were primarily more interested in introducing something which offenders would find challenging than they were in finding something which victims would find beneficial. This was by no means true of all commentators and campaigners of course (see, for example, the work of Marshall, 1985; Marshall and Merry, 1990; and Wright, 1982; 1991). Early developments in mediation and reparation in the United Kingdom were heavily influenced by practice in the United States, and a large number of the early projects were either court or probation service-based (Marshall and Walpole, 1985). Although reparation was often discussed, it appeared to be relatively low on the political agenda until, in 1984, the then Home Secretary, Leon Brittan, made a highly publicised speech at the Holborn Law Society in which he advocated the idea of reparation. Brittan said:

> The idea of reparation appeals to me for three reasons. First, through reparation, the criminal justice system can concentrate its attention on the individual victim whose interests must never be ignored. Secondly, the principle of reparation can be used to ensure that the wider interests of society are better served, and thirdly, nothing is more likely to induce remorse and reduce recidivism among a certain, all too numerous, kind of offender than being brought face to face with the human consequences of crime.
>
> (quoted in Reeves, 1989: 44)

He later supported requests for the funding of a number of experimental reparation projects, each of which was to be independently evaluated. In 1986, a discussion paper was issued (Home Office, 1986) which, in its concentration on the possibility of a new court penalty – the 'reparation order' – proved to be 'a watershed in the development of reparation in the UK' (Davies, 1992: 34). The idea of a reparation order was not popular with practitioners and, indeed, the split between the policy-makers' emphasis on reparation as a sentencing option, and practitioners' emphasis on somewhat less criminal justice-centred priorities led to a fairly full and fairly quick withdrawal of interest by government. By 1988, reparation had, as Davies (1992: 39) puts it, 'resumed its place at the margins of criminal justice', and there it looked set to remain.

The emergence of restorative justice

As Johnstone (2002: ix) points out, 'during the past decade, restorative justice has been promoted – often with evangelistic fervour – as the way forward for criminal justice, which is allegedly failing to prevent crime and provide victims and communities with a satisfactory experience of justice'. Despite the relatively recent revival of interest, according to its major proponents 'restorative justice has been the dominant model of criminal justice throughout most of human history for all the world's peoples' (Braithwaite, 1998: 323). Reflecting on the trend away from restorative and towards retributive models in state punishment, in a now famous essay, Nils Christie (1977) commented on the way in which conflict had been appropriated. Criminal conflicts, he argued, have progressively either become other people's property, usually lawyers, or have been defined away by those in whose interest it is valuable to do so.

Restorative justice quite clearly means different things to different people; it is a broad rubric under which many linked, but differentiable practices can be housed. One now established definition of restorative justice, at least in the United Kingdom, is of a 'process whereby the parties with a stake in a particular offence come together to resolve collectively how to deal with the aftermath of the offence and its implications for the future' (Marshall 1996: 37). In recent policy debates in England and Wales, restorative justice has been summarised as the '3Rs' of restoration, reintegration and responsibility (Home Office 1997d: para. 9.21). In the *No More Excuses* White Paper, this was defined as:

restoration: → young offenders apologising to their victims and making amends for the harm they have done;

reintegration: → young offenders paying their debt to society, putting their crime behind them and rejoining the law abiding community; and

responsibility: → young offenders – and their parents – facing the consequences of their offending behaviour and taking responsibility for preventing further offending.

The subsequent Crime and Disorder Act 1998 contained numerous elements that were based, at least in part, on ideas influenced by restorative justice. In particular, the reformed cautioning system, action plan orders and reparation orders all sought to promote the idea of reparation and, wherever possible, to seek victims' views. The action plan order was designed to be the first option for young offenders whose offending is serious enough to warrant a community sentence. *No More Excuses* (Home Office, 1997d) described the order as, 'a short, intensive programme of community intervention combining punishment, rehabilitation and reparation to change offending behaviour and prevent further crime'.

Of all of New Labour's restorative justice-influenced initiatives, as was suggested in the last chapter, it is the referral order that is arguably the most significant. The order was flagged up in *No More Excuses* (Home Office, 1997d), although it was not called a referral order at that point. It is mandatory for 10–17-year-olds pleading guilty and convicted for the first time by the courts, unless the crime is serious enough to warrant custody or the court orders an absolute discharge. The disposal involves referring the young offender to a youth offender panel. The intention is that the panel will provide a forum away from the formality of the court. As Crawford (2003) argues, the panels draw on at least three sources: the Scottish Children's Hearings system (Whyte, 2000); the experience of family group conferencing (Morris and Maxwell, 2000); and the history of victim-offender mediation in England and Wales (Marshall and Merry, 1990) and restorative cautioning (Young, 2000). The referral order is available in the Youth Court and adult magistrates' courts and may be made for a minimum of three and a maximum of 12 months, depending on the seriousness of the crime (as determined by the court). The referral order constitutes the entire sentence for the offence and, as such, substitutes for action plan orders, reparation orders and supervision orders.

As with many restorative justice initiatives, however, there have been major difficulties in securing high levels of involvement among victims. The evaluation of referral orders, in particular, showing extremely low levels of involvement and participation (Newburn et al., 2002), though the authors argued that this was at least as much a problem of implementation as it was a problem of principle. There can be little doubt that there has been a concerted effort by New Labour to make both victims' views and reparation more central aspects of youth justice than previously had been the case. In addition, there are increasing signs that such principles are to be extended to the adult system to a greater degree than has previously been the case. Most recently, the Auld Review of criminal justice has recommended that a national strategy for including restorative justice within criminal matters be developed so as to ensure its 'consistent, appropriate and effective use' (2001: 391, para. 69). Nonetheless, Dignan's (1999: 58) observation that these 'reforms hardly amount to a "restorative justice revolution", let alone the "paradigm shift" that some restorative justice advocates have called for' remains largely correct.

The re-emergence of feminism

The last 20 years have seen a marked increase in awareness of issues surrounding the role and status of women in society. Whilst a major focus has been on sexual discrimination and disadvantage in the labour market, there is also a substantial body of research on women's experiences of the criminal justice system (Gelsthorpe and Morris, 1990). An important part of this has concerned the way that the criminal justice system deals with crimes of sexual violence against women. The same period has also witnessed increasing recognition of the vulnerability of children to criminal victimisation (Morgan and Zedner, 1991). During the 1980s, there were a series of public scandals involving incidents of child sexual abuse. One in Cleveland, perhaps the best known of all, led to a major public inquiry and an official report which provided a number of recommendations for procedures to be adopted by the agencies involved in such cases (Butler-Sloss, 1988).

Rape and domestic violence

The increasing recognition of women victims of sexual assault or domestic violence and the changes this has brought about have their roots in the re-emergence of the feminist movement in the 1970s (Coote and Campbell, 1987). It has been argued, for example, that the agents of the criminal justice system tend to treat women complainants in a way that amounts to 'secondary victimisation', especially in the case of sexual assault. As was suggested above, there is evidence from the late 1970s (see, for example, Berger, 1977; Katz and Mazur, 1979) and early 1980s (Chambers and Miller, 1983) that women reporting sexual assault to the police were, on occasion, treated as if they were responsible for their own victimisation. Public attention was focused sharply on such issues in early 1982, when a judge imposed a fine rather than a prison sentence on a man convicted of rape on the grounds that the victim was guilty of what he called 'contributory negligence'. This was followed shortly after by a BBC television 'fly-on-the-wall' documentary about Thames Valley Police, one episode of which concerned the interview of a woman who was reporting that she had been raped. So intimidating was the investigating officer's approach that a considerable public furore followed the broadcast. Much concern was voiced about the lack of sensitivity and sympathy being given to the victim's rights and feelings. As Adler (1987) put it some time later: 'All but the most transparently flawless victim was liable to be bullied by interrogators and prosecutors, exposing her to a form of secondary victimisation.' The process is summed up by one practitioner (Anna, 1988: 62–3) who said:

> Barristers play upon the sexist prejudices of society in order to undermine what the woman is saying as a witness. She is often cross-questioned in an

aggressive or accusatory way . . . There is a rule that women should not be questioned about their sexual relations with anyone except the accused, but judges often waive that rule at the request of defence barristers, who then use these kinds of questions to discredit women.

The Women's Movement has been particularly influential in changing this situation. A campaigning body, Women Against Rape (WAR), was established in 1976, roughly coinciding with the importation into the United Kingdom from the United States of Rape Crisis Centres (RCCs). Reinforcing the point about the unattractiveness of the criminal justice as an option for women who had been assaulted, the first of these Centres took over 600 referrals in its first two years of operation, of which under a third involved incidents that had been reported to the police.

The following year, a governmental advisory group, the Women's National Commission (WNC), set up a working party to examine the issue of violence against women. Smith (1989a) suggests that the major concern of the WNC: 'was to try to effect certain practical changes – for example, to help ensure that female victims receive the legal, medical, social and psychological help which they need and that their role as court witnesses be made as tolerable as possible. But it was also concerned to offer practical advice to the police and to court personnel on their procedures and to bring home to them that these procedures could be contributing to a lack of effectiveness.' The working party also reflected on broader criminal justice issues. Its report, *Violence Against Women*, criticised the police for 'reluctance to interfere in domestic disputes, and in particular, for their reluctance to arrest and prosecute the perpetrators of the violence' (Womens' National Commission, 1985). Further guidelines were issued In October 1986 by the Home Office via Circular 69/1986, which dealt with victims of both rape and domestic violence. This made a number of suggestions, including the proposal that police forces should consider setting up special victim examination suites, more advice and information for rape victims, follow-up visits and enhanced training for officers who deal with rape victims.

An increasing body of research during the 1970s and 1980s questioned the role of criminal justice agencies in relation to women victims of crime. Studies, for example, suggested that the effect of arrest in domestic violence cases may be to exacerbate the violence experienced by women rather than reduce it (Sherman et al., 1992). Research in the United Kingdom context has also provided support for a more active arrest policy in the police response to domestic violence (Edwards, 1989). It has also been argued that inadequate police responses result in only a very low proportion of incidents of sexual assault and domestic violence being reported to the police. This is supported by evidence from victim surveys, which suggest very low levels of reporting for these crimes (Hough and Mayhew, 1985).

There have been a number of practical developments in response to these issues. The Women's Movement has been instrumental in setting up rape crisis centres and women's refuges in many towns and cities in the United Kingdom. The first refuge was set up in 1971 (Pizzey, 1974) and there were over 150 by 1978 (Binney et al., 1981). The centres operate telephone counselling services and offer emergency and, to some extent, continuing support and advice for any woman or girl who has been raped or sexually assaulted – irrespective of whether or not the offence is reported to the police. Although referrals are taken from a number of agencies, most women refer themselves to RCCs and on the whole the centres rely on volunteers although there are a small number of full-time posts (Anna, 1988).

It was, however, the Parliamentary Select Committee on Violence in Marriage that heralded the beginnings of change in public policy and the Committee's Report, according to Dobash and Dobash (1992), signalled government support for refuges. The Working Party's survey of police forces found that domestic violence was not perceived by them as an area where their procedures fell down or where new measures were necessary or important. However, 'despite criticism of law enforcement stressed by activists and some fairly pressing questioning of the police by MPs when taking oral evidence', this concern virtually disappeared in the text of the Report and from the recommendations.

The ineffectiveness of the criminal justice system – and especially the police – was one of the major focuses of the women's movement in this area. The central and most often voiced criticism of the police was that they remained reluctant to intervene in domestic incidents, and that this reluctance was underpinned on the one hand by the perception that the threat to officer's personal safety was high (Parnas, 1972) and on the other the widespread belief that such work was not 'real' police work (Pahl, 1982; Smith, 1989b).

Pressure for change remained high and, as far as the police were concerned, it was the Metropolitan Police that led the way. During 1985, they set up a working party to look into the problems of policing domestic violence. Reporting in 1986, it recommended a more active arrest and prosecution policy, better collection of statistics on the nature and extent of domestic violence, and the introduction of improved training for the police officers who deal with such incidents. It was particularly critical of existing training which, it said, 'perpetuate[d] current terminology ("domestic dispute") which . . . trivialise[d] marital violence rather than treating it as an allegation of crime'. A Force Order encouraging arrest was issued in 1987, and the Metropolitan Police quickly set up a number of specialist domestic violence units, being followed in later years by a small number of provincial forces. The Home Office issued further guidance to police forces about domestic violence in 1990, and senior ministers made a number of public statements drawing attention to the seriousness of the problem and the need for action to address it.

Child abuse

This issue of child abuse, in particular child sexual abuse, is one in which the criminal justice agencies have been required to review policies and practices over recent years. Early work on child abuse focused its attention upon physical assaults or neglect of children. In 1962, C. Henry Kempe, a United States-based paediatrician and his associates coined the term 'battered child syndrome'. This described the process leading to physical assaults by parents on their young children. Kempe went on to argue both that the abuse was more common than was generally recognised and that professionals had been turning a blind eye to the phenomenon. His view was that child abuse stemmed from emotional or psychological problems with the parent(s) and the response should involve therapy for the parent(s) combined with temporary protection for the child. This model of child abuse was extremely influential in the United States during the 1960s and 1970s and, largely thanks to the efforts of Kempe and his colleagues to publicise the subject, it became a major social issue there. Developments in the United Kingdom were strongly influenced by those in the United States. During the 1960s, the two main groupings involved in dealing with child abuse were the NSPCC and GPs. During the late 1960s and early 1970s, the NSPCC published a large number of studies on the subject of child abuse (Parton, 1985).

However, as well as the actions of bodies working in the area of child abuse, it is the repercussions of specific highly publicised incidents of abuse which have done as much as anything to raise the profile of the issue in Britain. A key example, and the first major case, is that of Maria Colwell in 1973. Maria was seven years old when she was killed by her stepfather. She had previously been removed from home by social services for fostering, but had later been returned and had been both beaten and starved before eventually being murdered. It was this case, and the ensuing public outcry, which led to the acceptance of the term 'child abuse' and to the establishment of a new system of child protection in the United Kingdom – involving area child protection committees, interagency case conferences, the development of specific training and so forth. The legal framework for the treatment of children who had been abused was set out in two Acts of Parliament – the Children and Young Persons Acts of 1933 and 1969.

Certainly, it was not until the early 1980s that the idea of *sexual* abuse of children, as opposed to physical abuse, gained any sort of real recognition. In 1984, a further notorious case involving the abuse and later murder of a young girl by her stepfather was crucial in bringing the issue to public attention. Jasmine Beckford and her sister were placed in care soon after their births because of evidence of physical abuse. They were later returned and Jasmine died, aged four, in 1984. The case led to a public inquiry, chaired by Louis Blom-Cooper, which produced clear conclusions that the primary role of social work was to protect the child, rather than keep the family together.

The pressure on the police around this time to introduce more sympathetic means of dealing with adult victims of sexual violence was quickly extended to children. Once again, the Metropolitan Police were at the forefront, and in 1984 established a pilot project in the Borough of Bexleyheath, where training of officers was undertaken jointly with that of social workers and, subsequently, investigations of allegations of abuse were also handled jointly (Metropolitan Police and the London Borough of Bexley, 1987; for a critique see Kelly and Regan, 1990). Following the end of the pilot project, the general approach was endorsed and efforts were made to introduce it universally. Home Office Circular 52/1988, for example, encouraged joint investigations by the police and social services.

Two other crucial developments in 1986 and 1987, however, did more to frame the issue of child abuse in the United Kingdom at this time than perhaps any others. The first of these was the setting up of 'Childline' in 1986. The television programme *That's Life* later on in the year had embarked upon a special investigation of child abuse. The response was huge and it prompted the programme's host, Esther Rantzen, to launch a telephone helpline for any child wanting to report abuse or seek help. Tens of thousands of calls were made on the first day of Childline, and although the service was not without its critics, the publicity that surrounded its operation did as much as anything to draw public attention to the issue of sexual abuse of children.

It was, however, the 'Cleveland affair' in the summer of 1987 which brought the issue of sexual abuse to the forefront of public debate. The scandal involved two local paediatricians who had over a period of months been instrumental in bringing over 100 children into care on place of safety orders. On the basis of a particular physical test – the anal dilatation test, which later came under question – the doctors argued that many of the children had been anally abused. Before long, stories of large numbers of children being taken into care in Cleveland began to surface in the national press, and parents in the area began to mobilise. The parents of the children gained the support of the MP for Cleveland, Stuart Bell, who raised the matter in Parliament and campaigned vigorously on their behalf (Bell, 1988; Campbell, 1988). The eventual outcome was the establishment of another public inquiry.

The Inquiry, chaired by Judge Elizabeth Butler-Sloss, was surrounded by massive media and public attention. The report (Butler-Sloss, 1988) made a number of detailed recommendations for the agencies involved in dealing with child abuse. These included procedures for joint investigation of child abuse cases by police officers and social workers, joint training of police and social workers, new interview techniques and a network of communication between all the involved agencies. In contrast to the above cases of physical abuse, the main criticism of social workers in the Cleveland case was that they had been over-zealous in their desire to take action to protect children. Crucially, the Report recommended that it was the interests of the child that should form the primary focus of any policies established to deal with the problem. Indeed, it is this general philosophy that found expression in the Children Act 1989.

This has been far from the end of the story. From 1990 onwards stories of 'ritual abuse' have appeared in the media and a number of social services departments have become involved in dealing with cases in which highly ritualised and organised abuse of children has been alleged – the most notorious of which were those in Nottingham (where police and social services disagreed publicly over an investigation of alleged 'satanic' abuse); in the Orkneys (where police and social workers had to return a number of children they had taken into care because there appeared to be little evidence of child abuse); and the more recent investigation of a large number of allegations involving childrens' homes in North Wales and Leicester (Jenkins, 1992).

Much of the focus on child victims of crime has been upon the potentially traumatic consequences for those that have to give evidence in court. Powerful arguments have been advanced in favour of limiting the range of cases that come to court and thereby protecting the child (Criminal Law Revision Committee, 1984) and in favour of prosecution (Adler, 1988). Inquiries in 1989 (Home Office, 1989) and 1990 (Scottish Law Commission, 1990) highlighted the needs of child witnesses and 'cast doubt on the belief that children are more highly suggestible and less able to differentiate fantasy from reality than adults' (Morgan and Zedner, 1991: 117). The Criminal Justice Act 1988 has abolished the requirement that unsworn evidence from a child be corroborated and the Criminal Justice Act 1991 introduced the use of video recordings of testimony and, more recently, screens and video links in court have been established to prevent direct contact between child witnesses and the accused. The protection of children has now become a priority for police and social services and support for child victims is now provided by Victim Support. Court procedures have been amended to take the needs of young victims and witnesses into account and, subject to reviewing how these procedures are working in practice, the Royal Commission on Criminal Justice (RCCJ, 1993) recommended that such safeguards should be extended to other vulnerable witnesses coming before the courts.

The rise of Victim Support

In the introduction to this chapter, it was noted that recent decades have seen the development of a victims' movement in the United Kingdom. This movement did not, however, come about as a result of the successful campaigns for the introduction of criminal injuries compensation. It is only later with the development of victim support schemes and other forms of support or self-help groups that something approximating a movement emerged. Not only did the victims movement emerge after the introduction of state compensation, but as has already been suggested, the campaign which resulted in the CICS must properly be described as a reform of penal policy, not the emergence of a victims policy.

The absence of a movement, or even a recognisable pressure group, meant that further change was very slow in coming. When it did, it was supported by a relatively new organisation whose primary focus was, once again, offenders: the National Association for the Care and Resettlement of Offenders (NACRO). Rock (1990) identifies three people: Christopher Holtom, Philip Priestly and Charles Irving, respectively Deputy Chairman, Regional Organiser and Chairman of NACRO's first regional committee, and suggests that they in their activities between 1969 and 1978 'rediscovered the victim' (1990: 95).

In setting up a meeting of concerned parties in Bristol, where they were based, to discuss offenders and offending, they decided that it would be interesting to have victims take part, and the result was the setting up of a victim-offender group in 1970. What, of course, distinguished what they decided to do from what had gone on before was that on this occasion they actually involved victims rather than assuming that they already knew what it was that victims wanted. What they found was that the emotional pain of victimisation was often as great if not greater than the physical injury or financial loss; that even supposedly trivial events might lead to trauma; that not only was the victim largely ignored by the criminal justice system, but almost any form of reparation was precluded; that victims often found that relatives and neighbours were sometimes less helpful that they imagined they might be; and that there appeared to be no statutory or voluntary body that took responsibility for looking after victims of crime (Holtom and Raynor, 1988).

Out of this work, there were two main developments. A study day was organised to look at the work of the victim-offender group and, eventually, a working party was set up to look into the setting up of a pilot project providing a service for victims of crime. The second development was the establishment of the National Victims Association (NVA), whose aim was to promote services for victims and to encourage experiments in conciliation between victims and offenders. In relation to the latter development at least, the driving force once again was penal reform. Priestly, the secretary of the NVA said in 1974: 'purely political reform, although it can achieve significant specific victories such as the abolition of hanging, can never lead to real penal reform since it leaves untouched the bedrock attitudes from which resistance to change draws its profound yet subtle strength' (quoted in Rock, 1990: 113).

The NVA never really took off. Its membership remained small and it was largely unsuccessful at raising funds. Within a couple of years of its establishment, it abandoned the idea of becoming a large-scale national organisation. It was not that its officers were in any way inexperienced at raising money and getting new enterprises off the ground, indeed, they were extremely successful, it was simply that there was little apparent sympathy and support for groups that attempted to work in this area (Rock, 1990). In the first half of the 1970s, victims of crime were not a subject designed to attract sponsors. What the NVA did do, however, was keep the issue in the public domain while others deliberated and established other initiatives.

Priestly summed up the work of the NVA in the following way:

> We have been in existence since the end of 1972 and operate principally as a pressure group trying to get a better deal for the people on the receiving end of crime. We have campaigned for a drastic revision of the current Criminal Injuries Compensation scheme; for better treatment of the victims of meter thefts; . . . and to get recognition of the principle of victim-offender conciliation as a saner and more effective way of dealing with offence behaviour. We also set up the first Victim Counselling Service in this country at Kingswood and have conducted pilot conciliation sessions between violent offenders and victims. The nett effect of all this activity, I am afraid to say is rather small.
>
> (quoted in Rock, 1990: 128–9)

The study group and the subsequent working party that had been set up in Bristol, on the other hand, gave birth to the Bristol Victims Support Scheme (BVSS) and, eventually, to a national movement. In designing the new service, a number of the working party's findings were acted upon and, indeed, continue to inform the work of Victim Support to this day. First of all, in recognising that although police records were significantly incomplete, they were the best source of information available about victims of crime, it was obvious that the service was only likely to work if it proved to be acceptable to the police. 'This meant that in some respects a cautious and "conventional" approach was adopted as a positive policy decision' (Holtom and Raynor, 1988: 19). Before he agreed to co-operate, the Chief Constable had to be assured that volunteers would be selected with care, and that the scheme would be run by responsible people (Rock, 1990).

Second, an 'outreach' service was planned as a way of overcoming resistance or reticence on the part of potential 'clients' of the service, and as facilitating approaches to those likely to be most traumatised by their experiences. Third, there was the question of staffing. It was felt that using volunteers from the local community would be an effective method of counteracting the feeling of ostracisation or alienation often felt by crime victims as a result of their experiences. These volunteers would be given some training in order to ensure that they were prepared to deal with the problems they would face. Finally, influenced by the crisis intervention model, the feeling was that a brief intervention by volunteers would be sufficient in the vast majority of cases, though referral on to professional help would be considered. The idea was the project should be run on a trial basis for the first six months.

The scheme started visiting victims in January 1974 and 'within a month it was clear that a large proportion of victims faced quite severe problems and almost without exception welcomed the offer of help' (Holtom and Raynor, 1988: 20). In addition those running the scheme also found that the number of referrals was greater than they had been expecting, and the voluntary visitors couldn't cope with all the work. Seven to ten referrals a week had been anticipated. In the event, the scheme received over 500 in its first three months. If anything, 'the scheme was too successful' (Rock, 1990: 143) and it was forced to recruit more volunteers. In addition, they decided to send letters to victims of thefts of or from motor vehicles offering help, rather than visiting in the first instance. This tension, between outreach and limited resources continues to characterise the work of Victim Support. Perhaps more importantly, the police had already started to 'filter out' domestic violence incidents and fights in which it was not clear who the victim was, thereby reinforcing the gatekeeping role which they continued to occupy in relation to victim support schemes for some years.

The problem that had affected the NVA then began to trouble the BVSS. It had been assumed that such a good and worthy cause would have few difficulties in attracting sponsors. After the first six months, work had to be temporarily halted in order to allow time to concentrate on fund-raising. In the interim, the opportunity arose to become involved in the making of a BBC *Open Door* programme. The role of the media in the development of social policy is rarely commented upon, though there are a small number of instances – even in criminal justice – of television in particular having an important influence on the direction of policy. In the event, the programme, entitled *Once every twenty seconds*, played a key part in ensuring the future of BVSS. The programme resulted in a flood of inquiries and even some small financial donations. Crucially, what it did do was lead to the setting up of a day conference attended by like-minded people and thereafter to the establishment of a number of other victim support schemes. Some of the money that was forthcoming from charitable sources at this time was given in order to support and to co-ordinate the development of schemes nationwide.

By May 1977, there were 13 schemes in England and Wales, and two years later when a National Association was set up there were 30. Thereafter, the movement expanded rapidly. A national committee had been established in 1978, with Holtom as Chair, and both ACPO and ACOP were invited to join. At around this time NACRO, which was still providing support for the developing organisation in a number of ways, approached the Home Office with a view to securing some financial backing for a national association for the victim support movement. In mid-1979, this was successful, and the Home Office promised £10,000 a year for three years. More important than the money, Rock argues, was what it represented for the future of the organisation:

> The Home Office's decision was a gesture whose significance reached far beyond the granting of a few thousand pounds a year. It was a major step for the Home Office to do something of this kind for the first time. It signalled government endorsement of the character and ends of the National Association, an acceptance of the duties of patronage, and the possibility of an indefinite commitment.
>
> (1990: 171)

A national development officer was appointed and work began to turn the fledgling movement into a fully operational national body. When the National Association (known originally as the National Association of Victims Support Schemes or NAVSS) was officially launched in 1979, there had been approximately 30 schemes. By the end of the following year, there were 79. This increased to 159 by September 1983 and to over 300 by 1987. Referrals increased at a faster rate than did the schemes: from 18,000 in 1979 to 65,000 in 1983 and 257,000 in 1986–87 (Rock, 1990). The work increased not only in quantity, but also in range, taking on, for example, victims of rape and sexual assault, and of serious assault and even murder.[2]

Much of the energy of the Director of National Association was taken up at this time in trying to secure funding, not only to maintain the national body, but to ensure that local schemes continued to operate. Not surprisingly, much of this fund-raising effort was directed at the Home Office. Just as those running BVSS in the early 1970s had realised that the public face of their scheme was crucial in securing co-operation with their activities and funding for their work, so the national organisation worked hard at creating an acceptable and appropriate image. There were a number of key elements to this image.

First, it was crucial that the movement was, and was seen to be, non-party political. As Holtom summarised it: 'We'd obviously run a mile from the "hang 'em and flog 'em" wing of the Tories. Similarly, we don't want to get involved with the "let's control the police" Left-wing bit' (quoted in Rock, 1990: 223). Second, from the outset, the organisation decided against getting involved in penal politics of any sort. It steadfastly refused to comment on criminal justice issues unless they directly affected victims or victim services. 'This single issue approach was a deliberate device to avoid distractions and to guard against co-option by the developing political theme of "law and order"; particularly, we wanted to avoid reinforcing illusions that victims benefit from tougher sentencing' (Holtom and Raynor, 1988: 24).

Third, in many respects it fought shy of publicity. It certainly avoided sensationalist accounts of victimisation at all costs. Doing so was perhaps less easy than it sounds. As has already been suggested, despite the general worthiness of the work, it was extremely difficult to get funding bodies interested in supporting the organisation. One of the most effective ways of galvanising support, however – as all charities know – is to seek and exploit publicity in the mass media. Because of its policy of avoiding publicity, which might bring distress to victims, the National Association was therefore faced with having to turn down many opportunities for coverage which might have heightened its profile at a time when it was desperately in need of further financial support. In relation to its goal of securing funding from the state, however, this was to prove a very important strategy.

Fourth, the National Association followed the lead established by BVSS and encouraged very close ties with the police. The fact that schemes relied upon the police for referrals meant that without their co-operation the organisation simply could not function. In addition, being a very powerful and influential body, the police also carried great weight with other agencies and bodies that NAVSS wished to influence. Early on, ACPO had insisted on a policy of what were called 'indirect referrals', that is the police would act as formal gatekeepers, only passing on the names and addresses of people where they had their permission to do so. In many cases, this led to a very significant lack of referrals and put the futures of schemes at risk. In the end, the Home Office, which was concerned about the drop in referrals resulting from the policy, persuaded ACPO to reconsider, and the stricture requiring local constabularies to operate such a policy was removed. The early 1980s saw the development of a relationship of increasing trust between NAVSS and the police, to the point where victim support schemes were regarded 'as a reliable client and adjunct' by the middle of the decade (Rock, 1990: 247).

By the mid-1980s, with the developing penal crisis, increasing scepticism about the effectiveness of the crime control role of the police, politicians and administrators in the Home Office were looking for innovative policies with which to freshen the penal landscape. The Home Office had published a 'working document' – *Criminal Justice: A Working Paper* (Home Office, 1984a) – in which the possibility of finding a new role for victims was flagged up. As Rock (1990: 258) summarises: 'It was thought that little could be done to curb crime, and that increased expenditure could not be justified indefinitely. Yet the problem of crime remained, people were worried, and a public lessening of effort was politically impossible.' Into this impasse, among other things, entered 'the victim'. Some of this attention was devoted to the subjects of compensation and reparation; increasingly, however, it was the victim support movement which dominated the scene. Unfortunately for NAVSS, this was the point at which the FMI was really beginning to bite and new expenditure within the criminal justice system was vigorously resisted. Rock (1990: 330) quotes the Deputy Under-Secretary in the Home Office at the time telling NAVSS:

> The present Government [will not] contemplate developing a victims' support system which would in effect be a new paid social service. The Government's view is that victim support is essentially a local responsibility, ideally suited for voluntary action, and not one which should be professionalized or bureaucratized in the way which would become inevitable if it came to rely on large numbers of full-time paid staff.

Funding was, however, a major problem. The Home Office had been supporting the National Office since 1978, and local schemes had been relying on the Manpower Services Commission, on local authorities, Urban Aid and a variety of other sources of income to pay for their co-ordinators and other expenses. By the mid-1980s, it was becoming increasingly clear that some local schemes were going to fold unless more secure funding could be found. In effect the whole future of the organisation rested on how the question of funding local schemes was resolved.

The Home Affairs Select Committee, which published a report on *Compensation and Support for Victims of Crime* at the end of 1984, had praised victim support schemes and had recommended that the government consider providing some financial support for co-ordinators for local schemes. For as long as Leon Brittan was Home Secretary, however, the Home Office seemed more interested in pursuing the possibility of reparation schemes than it was in putting victim support on a sounder financial footing. By this stage, however, the Home Office had commissioned research which had illustrated in graphic detail the disadvantaged position of the victim in the criminal justice system (Shapland et al., 1985) and a further study was underway investigating the work and impact of victim support schemes (eventually published as Maguire and Corbett, 1987). The research painted a positive picture of the victims support, illustrated in detail the effects of crime on a wide variety of victims, and provided further impetus to substantial central funding. The decision finally came in 1986, when £9 million was set aside over a period of three years 'to strengthen the work of these local victims support schemes', said Douglas Hurd, the new Home Secretary (quoted in Rock, 1990: 405). One former Home Office minister, commenting on this development, described it as 'a clear and welcome departure from the previous policy of making contributions to headquarters' expenses, backed up by periodic hand-outs to schemes in financial difficulty. Central government has now indicated a readiness to maintain victims' support as a regular and specific commitment, rather than on an incidental or exceptional basis' (Windlesham, 1987: 56).

In the first years of the organisation, the work of victim support schemes reflected the rather apolitical, unproblematic model of victimisation that was so popular with the major political parties. The schemes tended to focus their attention on the victims of 'conventional' crimes such as burglary and theft (Zedner, 1994). During the 1980s, however, they have become progressively more involved in providing support for a wider variety of victims, including victims of racial harassment, families of murder victims and victims of rape and serious sexual assault. By the time of their research in the mid-1980s, Maguire and Corbett (1987) found that over half of all VSSs had taken one or more referrals in this last area, and by 1988 over 900 cases of rape were referred to VSSs. Undoubtedly one of the reasons for the development of the VSS service to rape victims, alongside and in addition to the already established Rape Crisis Centres (RCCs), was the fact that as Corbett and Hobdell (1988) have argued, the former 'tend to be more palatable to the police in style and philosophy'.

In relation to RCCs, Maguire and Corbett (1987) have argued that their great strengths are, first, that their existence is widely known and, second, that some form of help is available to any woman who requests it, 24 hours a day, whenever the offence occurred and irrespective of whether the offence was reported to the police. The major problem with the RCC model Maguire and Corbett (1987) argue, is that victims are not always willing to come forward and request help (cf. also King and Webb, 1981). Maguire and Corbett (1987) argue that the major advantage of the Victim Support model for some women is that contact is not left to the victim, as it is the scheme itself that takes the first initiative.

'Victims Support, women's refuges, and rape crisis centres are far from enjoying coherence of outlook, organization, or method', Zedner argues (1994: 1229). She continues: 'The "victim movement" is ideologically heterogeneous. Relations between the various agencies range from close cooperation to barely concealed hostility. . . . Despite, or perhaps because of this heterogeneity, the combined impact of these endeavours has been enormous.'

In recent years, the work of Victim Support has broadened out in a variety of new areas. One area that was identified by researchers (Shapland et al., 1985; Shapland and Cohen, 1987) in which victims required support was that of the court process itself. A longitudinal study undertaken by Shapland and colleagues charted a continuous decline in levels of satisfaction reported by victims as they passed through the criminal justice system. Crucially, they found that facilities in the courts were sadly lacking, with victims and defendants frequently having to share the same waiting spaces in court and little information available to victims or witnesses about court dates (see also Raine and Walker, 1990; Newburn and Merry, 1990).

A working party set up by NAVSS (as it then was) in 1988 to consider the role of the victim/witness in court recommended that courts should reconsider their practices with regard to the treatment of victims (NAVSS, 1988) and, in addition, issued a Circular (20/1988) to Chief Police Officers pointing out the benefits 'both for the welfare of the victim and for the police-public relationship, from making a purposeful effort to provide victims with information about progress'. One recommendation made by the working party, that a leaflet explaining court procedures should be available, and sent routinely to prosecution witnesses, was accepted and acted upon by the Home Office. Indeed, the Victims'

Charter, published by the government in 1990, further encouraged this process: 'The Home Office produces a leaflet called "Witness in Court" which tells witnesses who may not have been to court before something about the procedure and what to expect. Witnesses should always receive this with the notice which tells them that they may be needed to give evidence and should attend. ... Many magistrates' courts also distribute their own leaflets showing exactly where they are, how to get there, where there is parking and so on. This is an excellent practice, to be encouraged' (Home Office, 1990b: 14).

By 1990, Victim Support were running a series of pilot victim/witness support programmes in seven Crown Court centres. Even getting this far was fraught with difficulties. Rock (1993: 328–9) describes the process as follows: 'With some wariness, government departments had consented to mounting a trial project to assist victims and prosecution witnesses attending the Crown Court. The Home Office was to fund the project's staffing costs but not the evaluation research, which would establish its effectiveness. The Lord Chancellor's Department was to afford access to the Crown Court, but it did so only with some nervousness. ... There should be no victim impact statements, statements of the kind that had become accepted in a number of courts in North America and which listed the suffering and injuries inflicted on the victim as matters to be considered by the judge in sentencing.'

Gains such as this were limited and hard fought. They appear, however, to have been successful. The evaluation conducted as part of the pilot recommended that the system should be expanded, and this expansion is now well underway. This is potentially a particularly important development in the work of Victim Support. In many respects, the work of Victim Support volunteers has been largely hidden from view, and certainly not open to scrutiny from other criminal justice professionals (Mawby and Walklate, 1994). Not only did the development of the Crown Court experiment mark a recognition of the negative experiences of many victims and witnesses in the criminal justice system, but it also signified the emergence of Victim Support as a significant 'player' in the system.

Progress since the 1990s

By the early 1990s, as even this brief overview illustrates, there had been no shortage of initiatives undertaken 'on behalf of' victims of crime. In addition, there could be no doubt that the changes brought about as a result of some of those initiatives had improved, often markedly, the situation of the victim in the criminal justice system. By 1990, there was even a Victim's Charter, subtitled 'A Statement of the Rights of Victims of Crime'. Despite this commendable progress, however, it remained the case at that time that the United Kingdom still lacked a coherent victims policy.

Despite the subtitle of the original Charter, victims of crime continued to occupy a position which was much more likely to be defined by needs or deserts than by rights. While the Charter was valuable in staking out much of the territory in which victims' needs have to be addressed and, no doubt, provided useful leverage for those organisations attempting to respond to those needs, it fell somewhat short of guaranteeing rights. As Mawby (1988) has pointed out, acceptance of the idea of victims' rights leads to the necessity of recognising that these rights exist irrespective of need: 'victims who have not been caused serious hardship or lasting anguish still have a right to redress' (Mawby, 1988: 135). Rights in relation to the four areas that he and Martin Gill identified in earlier work: the right to play an active part in the criminal justice process; the right to knowledge; the right to financial help; and the right to support and help, remain limited in important respects.

First, the various 'fiefs' (Shapland, 1988) in the criminal justice system are quick to guard their own territory and thereby limit the extent to which victims might make incursions into decision-making processes (Mawby and Walklate, 1994). Second, despite the considerable body of research that has been conducted into victims' informational needs (Shapland et al., 1985; Maguire and Corbett, 1987; Newburn and Merry, 1990), the police and courts are often still slow to inform and inconsistent in keeping victims and witnesses up-to-date. Crucially, formal responsibility for such work together with sanctions for failure had at that stage not been imposed.

Third, access to financial recompense remained still extremely limited: compensation orders, though more effectively administered, still only reach a minority of victims; the CICS still only compensates a narrow range of crime victims and continues to operate on the basis of compensating the 'deserving victim' (Newburn, 1989). Furthermore, had it not been for the Court of Appeal in November 1994, the then Home Secretary, Michael Howard, would have instituted changes to the CICS which would have resulted in cutbacks in payments to victims of violence by up to £250 million a year. Finally, although the available services were continually bringing a greater number of victims within their ambit, the possibility of 'blanket coverage' remained some way off. As with most if not all areas of criminal justice, financial considerations are perhaps the greatest inhibitor to fundamental change. Mawby and Walklate (1994: 198) in reviewing criminal justice policy in relation to victims recognise this key factor:

> To put it bluntly, *crime costs*, in both a personal and a financial sense. At the moment too much of that cost is borne by the victim of crime. In a just system it is appropriate for the state, through all its citizens, to take over that burden.

Underpinning the failures in relation to the development of a 'victims policy' was the continuing overriding concern with crime and with offenders rather than with victims. The Conservative Party – which, at least in terms of its manifestoes, had shown interest in victims since the early 1960s – nevertheless resisted all calls to provide significant funding for victim services for many years, and when in power still sought to cut back on expenditure when it could. As Phipps (1988: 180) argues, 'in a rather paradoxical way, victims in Conservative thinking are transformed from injured individuals into symbols of injured order'. The main purpose of the techniques they use in arousing sympathy or outrage of victims of crime 'is to excite hostility against the offender or to discredit the "softness" of the criminal justice system . . . [and] . . . to promote support for deterrence and retribution'. Much of victims policy has in many ways therefore been a means to an end rather than end in itself.

The discussion above of the process by which the decision about funding of local victim support schemes was made, however, perhaps paints a rather too apolitical picture of the context in which it was actually taken. As has been suggested above, up until the point at which the decision about full-scale funding was finally taken, the government had shown little interest in getting involved in a major way with the 'victims movement'. The Thatcher government's financial contribution had been to invest heavily in policing in the hope that this would have some impact upon crime rates. By the mid-1980s, the law and order policies upon which successive Conservative administrations had been elected were beginning to look more than a little threadbare. With the criminal justice policy cupboard also looking a little bare, the announcement of £9 million of funding for NAVSS was an attractive proposition, particularly with a General Election approaching. As Phipps (1988: 178) has argued, 'the change in policy remains open to the charge of political opportunism and only *seems on the surface* to be a major advance'. In addition, Phipps also points out that the expenditure on victims represents a very small investment when set alongside the £3 billion spent annually on criminal justice at that time.

The charge of opportunism might also quite reasonably be levelled at the then Labour opposition as well. In all their manifestoes up to and including that in 1983, the Labour Party had singularly failed to show any major interest in victims of crime. By 1987, however, victims having become an established political football in Home Affairs debates, the Labour Party had developed a fully fledged set of policies on victim support (which it promised to fund), criminal injuries compensation (which it wished to extend) and police treatment of victims and witnesses (which it wished to improve). Furthermore, although much was made in the manifesto about issues such as racism and sexism, there was an absence of policies which might have had any significant impact on the victims of racial harassment or domestic violence. What was being promised was extra cash for some of the more visible initiatives, rather than the development of a coherent and forward-looking victims policy.

During the 1980s and early 1990s, both of the major political parties pursued half-formed and in many ways half-hearted, policies in relation to victims of crime and there was little indication that major change was likely in this area, though a new version of the Victims' Charter was promised. In fact, the pace of change has probably been somewhat quicker and more extensive than would have been anticipated at the time. In 1995, Victim Support published *The Rights of Victims of Crime* (Victim Support, 1995), in which it set out its agenda for the future of victims policy. Since its publication, Victim Support are of the view that 'the status of victims in the UK has dramatically improved' (Reeves and Mulley, 2000: 131). In particular, the publication of the second Victim's Charter in 1996 (Home Office, 1996b) made a significant impact on the status of victims. The Charter covered police responsibilities for providing information to victims and familiarisation visits to courts, together with details of complaints procedures if the standards set out were not met. The Charter suggested that victims of crime could in future expect:

- To be given the name and phone number of a police officer or 'crime desk' responsible for their case.
- To be given a leaflet, 'Victims of Crime', as soon as they report a crime in person at a police station.
- To be told if someone has been caught, cautioned or charged, and to be asked if they require further information. If so, they will be told of any decision to drop charges, the date of the trial and the final result.
- To have the chance to explain how they have been affected by the crime.
- To be told when an offender serving a sentence of life imprisonment, or a custodial sentence for a serious sexual or violent crime, is likely to be released.
- To be treated with sensitivity when attending court as a witness, and to receive support from the Witness Service before, during and after the trial.
- To be paid travel and other expenses for attending court.
- (In the case of child witnesses) to have special arrangements made, including the provision of a TV link.
- To be offered emotional and practical support by Victim Support and, where appropriate, the CICS.

As part of the process of developing the services outlined by the revised Charter, two pilot projects were launched by the Home Office. The first, generally referred to as the 'One Stop Shop', covered the new procedures within which the police were to collect, collate and disseminate information on the progress of cases to victims of crime. This was the latest in a series of initiatives attempting to improve the experience of crime victims, long shown by research to have considerable difficulty in eliciting information about 'their' cases from criminal justice agencies (Maguire, 1982; Shapland et al., 1985; Newburn and Merry, 1990).

The second pilot project was the victim statement scheme, in which victims may opt to make written statements about the impact of a crime or crimes upon them and, in principle, to have these read out in court. Although what are often referred to as 'victim impact statements' are permitted in certain jurisdictions (South Australia, Canada and many States of the United States), there has been considerable scepticism about, and resistance to, them in the United Kingdom. Their function is generally seen as being 'to inform a decision-maker of any physical or emotional harm, or any loss of or damage to property, suffered by the victim through or by means of the offence, and any other effects on the victim' (Ashworth, 1993). In a seminal article, Ashworth outlines a number of potential problems with victim impact statements, including a number of procedural problems together with the possibility that unfounded or excessive claims might be made by victims, and victims' hopes might be raised unduly by their introduction. In addition, Ashworth distinguishes between *rights to services* and *procedural rights*. The One Stop Shop concerns the former, whereas the introduction of the victim statement 'hints at procedural rights' (Hoyle et al., 1998). As Hoyle et al. (1998: 6) explain, 'even if in the victim statement schemes victims are seen purely as providing information to decision makers (the police, prosecutors and the courts) it is hard to deny that this could, and some would argue should, influence decision-making'.

The One Stop Shop and victim statement initiatives were linked. The pilot projects involved an opt-in element; victims were asked whether they wished to opt-in to receiving further information after their initial contact with the police. The police were to write to victims after charge and before papers were passed to the CPS inviting them to opt-in. For those that did, the police then had a responsibility to see that certain information was passed to them. In addition, a combined compensation/victim statement form was also sent. There was no obligation to make a statement, but victims were told that if they did it would be added to the case papers and that they could, potentially, be cross-examined on it at court.

The pilots raised a number of interesting issues. First, and in line with previous research, they suggested that citizens have rather imprecise expectations when they become victims and make a report to the police. They generally are keen to receive information, but are rather unclear as to what this might mean. The pilots, however, suggested that expectations appeared to have been raised, sometimes beyond what services could offer. The researchers concluded that the receipt of information from one point only 'may create as many problems as it solves' (Hoyle et al., 1998: 45). The victim statement pilot also raised a number of issues. The evaluation found that police officers, when outlining reasons for making a victim statement, though tending to do so in procedural terms, often also outlined *expressive* and *instrumental* terms – in particular, the possibility of the use of the statement in sentencing considerations. Perhaps tellingly, only a small minority of victims later had any idea what use had been made subsequently of their statement.

As this chapter suggests, much victims policy up until this point had been concerned with the provision of information, the issuance of compensation and the offer of emotional and practical support. Relatively little attention had been paid to the protection of victims and witnesses. This was another area of change in the late 1990s. New Labour, in its 1997 election manifesto, had promised that 'greater protection will be provided for victims in rape and serious sexual offence trials and those subject to intimidation including witnesses'. Soon after taking office, an inter-departmental group was established to view the treatment of such witnesses and its report, *Speaking Up For Justice*, was published in June 1998 (Home Office, 1998b). A further inter-departmental steering group was then established to oversee implementation of the report. The major proposals in *Speaking Up For Justice* included:

- Greater protection for rape victims, with a ban on victims being cross-examined by the defendant in person and further restrictions on the cross-examination on the victim's sexual history.
- New measures to help child witnesses, including videoed pre-trial cross-examination and the use of intermediaries to help children give evidence.
- A range of measures to assist vulnerable or intimidated witnesses give their evidence such as the use of screens, live TV links, video-recorded interviews of witnesses and assistance with communication where this is needed.

Underpinning such recommendations was the assumption that the traditional system of justice, involving cross-examination in court by trained advocates in an adversarial style, may limit the ability of some witnesses to give their best evidence. Previous reforms, introduced by the Criminal Justice Acts of 1988 and 1991, had introduced a range of measures to allow for greater flexibility in the treatment of child witnesses in court. The Youth Justice and Criminal Evidence Act 1999 sought to extend this flexibility. Introducing the Bill in the House of Commons, Paul Boateng said that:

> The Government recognise that in the past the criminal law and the criminal justice system have not always got it right. All too often, witnesses have not been able to give of their best in court, for a variety of reasons. The measure is designed to protect the public interest and thus the interests of justice, striking a proper balance between the interests and rights of the defendant and those of the victim. That demands that the best evidence possible be laid before the jury. Fear, intimidation and the vulnerability of age or incapacity can militate against witnesses giving their best evidence. The [Act] will ensure that the best evidence comes before the jury.
>
> (*Hansard*, HC Deb, 17 June 1999)

These provisions introduced by the 1999 Act included: screening the witness from the accused (s. 23); giving evidence by live link (s. 24); ordering the removal of wigs and gowns when the witness testifies (s. 25); giving evidence in private (in sexual cases involving intimidation – s. 26); video-recording of evidence in chief (s. 27); video-recording of cross-examination and re-examination (s. 28); examination through intermediary (s. 29); and the provision of aids to communication for young or incapacitated witnesses (s. 30). Such measures are intended to provide special treatment not only to child witnesses, but also to those with learning disabilities or a mental illness, to those that have suffered intimidation and for complainants in sexual cases. In the statement in Parliament quoted above, the Minister of State makes explicit reference to the 'balance' between the 'rights' of defendants and victims. Given that victims' 'rights' are a relatively new development in the British justice system – and whether they really are rights is contestable[3] – this flurry of activity inevitably raises questions about the impact on the protections afforded suspects in criminal trials. As one commentator notes, 'the criminal trial is potentially a terrifying ordeal for an accused person . . . [yet] curiously there does not appear to be much pressure to introduce measures to assist defendants to give evidence, whatever their communication difficulties might be. . . . Nevertheless, the emphasis on witness protection risk the possibility of miscarriages of justice' (McEwan, 2002: 250–1).

The question of victims' rights was raised specifically in the Home Office's review of the Charter (Home Office, 2001). The consultation document asked:

- Whether the 'service standard' approach in the current Charter should be continued in the new Charter or be replaced by a 'rights' approach?
- If the 'rights' approach is taken, should the rights be put on a statutory basis?
- Should the rights be enforceable?

In the event, and perhaps predictably given the problems in this area, the latest proposals steer something of a middle course between greater recognition of victims' 'rights' and continuing to use the 'charter language' of standards of service and codes of practice. In this regard, the language of the White Paper, *Justice For All* (Home Office, 2002a), is interesting. It proposes to (emphasis added):

- Appoint an independent Commissioner for Victims and Witnesses, supported by a National Victims' Advisory Panel, to champion their *interests*.
- Appoint victim liaison officers to join Youth Offending Teams.
- Introduce more measures for vulnerable and intimidated witnesses.
- Extend specialist support to the victims of road traffic accidents and their families.

- Legislate to produce a Victims' *Code of Practice* setting out what protection, practical support and information every victim of a crime has a *right* to expect from the criminal justice agencies.
- Publish a national strategy for victims and witnesses. . . . setting out how we propose to better meet their *needs* by changing the way the CJS works.
- Introduce a *right* of complaint to the Parliamentary Ombudsman for victims and witnesses who are not satisfied the Code has been followed.

Many of the proposals concern criminal procedure and aim to enhance victims' experiences of the criminal justice system. Research undertaken by the Institute of Public Policy Research (Spencer and Stern, 2002) found that almost two-fifths of witnesses interviewed would not wish to give evidence again because of their experience of intimidation or of cross-examination in court. The establishment of a formal complaints system, together with an independent commissioner to champion victims' and witnesses' interests, should, in principle, further enhance the role of the victim in the criminal justice process.

Conclusion

In a recent essay, Andrew Ashworth (2000b) noted that we find ourselves in 'a confusing time for criminal justice'. More particularly, he suggested that this is because of two, not necessarily compatible, processes that are visible in many jurisdictions. On the one hand, there is a movement towards penal severity as evidenced most particularly in the United States over the past 30 years (see Garland, 2001). On the other hand, there is the greater attention being paid to the "victim's perspective" (Crawford and Goodey, 2000). There are different political relationships between these two movements. They go hand in hand in some jurisdictions – the United States again being the prototype. In others they appear to develop simultaneously but separately – and sometimes in considerable tension and even opposition – the United Kingdom might be taken as one example. As a consequence, he suggests, we are faced, at least potentially, by two different dangers: 'victims in the service of severity' and 'victims in the service of offenders' each of which can be seen as a form of 'victim prostitution' (Ashworth, 2000b: 186).

Very significant changes have been introduced during the last decade. These include the introduction and expansion of the Witness Service, new protections for vulnerable and intimidated witnesses, increasing financial support for Victim Support and, perhaps most importantly, significant engagement since 1997 with some of the ideas and principles of restorative justice – most particularly in the youth justice arena. As with the general issue of incorporating the views of victims in the criminal justice process, the attempt to incorporate restorative justice practices within current penal arrangements is fraught with difficulty. This includes endangering the rights of suspects, the potential disempowerment of particular members or sections of communities – including victims, undermining attempts to develop 'principled sentencing' as well as the potential prospect of 'net-widening' and 'mesh-thinning' (see Johnstone, 2002 for a discussion). Thus, whilst there is much that is positive in developments in criminal justice policy in this area in recent years, the extension of victims' 'rights' is by no means an unproblematic good. Perhaps the final word here should be left with Andrew Ashworth, who wisely notes that the twin dangers of 'victims in the service of severity' and 'victims in the service of offenders' – to which can be added Crawford's (2000: 292) 'victims in the service of system efficiency' – should 'remind us of the need to ensure that the growing interest in promoting the victim perspective should not reduce our vigilance about proper standards and safeguards in criminal justice' (Ashworth, 2000b: 186).

Notes

1. Paul Rock's book, *Helping Victims of Crime*, is one of the few explorations of the development of a particular area of British criminal justice policy. It is a most comprehensive account and much of what is contained in this chapter – especially in relation to victims support – is drawn from or informed by Paul Rock's work.
2. In the last case, of course, this meant the families of murder victims.
3. The Home Office, in its review of the Victim's Charter (Home Office, 2001), notes: 'The first Charter had a secondary heading "A statement of the rights of victims of crime". But any actual rights within the document were hard to find. The 1996 Charter avoided mention of rights and talked the then Charter language of "standards of service".'

Chapter 10

Conclusion: the future of criminal justice policy

Crime and criminal justice policy is now accepted as being a major political issue. That is, not only do we expect politicians to spend a lot of their time talking about crime and criminal justice, but we expect them to disagree. It was not always thus. As many commentators have noted (*inter alia*, Brake and Hale, 1992; Rawlings, 1992; Downes and Morgan, 1994), for many years there existed something approximating a bipartisan consensus on issues to do with policing, crime and punishment. Although it is often assumed that 1979 marked the point at which all this ended (see Nash and Savage, 1994), as Downes and Morgan (1994: 187) have pointed out, this was merely 'the heightening of a trend in relation to law and order' that had existed since the election of 1970 (see also Hall et al., 1978). From that point onwards, the major political parties began to blame each other for what was happening in relation to crime, and began to look to make political capital out of their criminal justice policies.

The end of the bipartisan consensus coincided (in very rough terms) with the death-throes of the rehabilitative ideal, the emergence of penal pessimism, and a significant ratcheting up of the prison crisis. In addition, of course, the period 1979–97 saw only one party in power. The Conservative Party therefore had a significant opportunity to leave its imprint on the criminal justice system in England and Wales. Subsequently, the arrival of New Labour, with two consecutive landslide election victories, has had a similar, if not yet similarly long, opportunity. Although the focus of this book has been on a longer time-frame than merely the last two decades or so, these closing reflections are confined in the main to this most recent historical period.

The Conservatives were elected in 1979 on a ticket that not only suggested that the Labour Party were responsible for the increases in crime in the latter half of the 1970s, but maintained that the extra expenditure that was promised by their opponents for criminal justice would have a significant impact on crime levels; 'never, ever, have you heard me say that we will economise on law and order' said Margaret Thatcher in 1985 (quoted in Nash and Savage, 1994: 142–3). However, as we saw, for example, in Chapter 4, the hugely increased expenditure on the police in the first half of the 1980s did not lead to the hoped-for reductions in recorded offences. Far from it. Crime continued to rise, and rise at a dramatic rate, as, in general, did people's fear of crime. Indeed, this was in some respects recognised by the Conservative administration itself. Certainly, the 'spend, spend, spend' strategy was experimented with and then, fairly quickly, abandoned. Partly as a consequence of the dismay politicians felt at the perceived ineffectiveness of criminal justice agencies, especially given the sums of public money being used, crime-control strategies have been dominated since by increasing managerialism, including greater participation by the private sector, together with ever-increasing centralisation of control. Of all the elements of the approach to managing crime that emerged in the late 1970s, the one that has remained visible consistently since that period has been a fairly naked form of penal populism. Arguably, these three major features have dominated the criminal justice landscape throughout that period.

Managerialism and financial control

The continued rise in crime despite the doubling of police expenditure between 1979 and 1984 led to the ending of the apparent immunity the police had enjoyed from the financial stringencies being applied to all the other public services. From the mid-1980s onwards, a policy of 'tight-resourcing' was applied not only to the police, but also to the probation service and to the courts system (Raine and Willson, 1993). Thus, although the major criminal justice agencies were not cash-limited in the way that, say, the health and social services were, other limiting factors quickly came into play. One of the difficulties for criminal justice agencies is that available resources are not necessarily linked to levels of demand.

The policy solution to the combination of tight resourcing and increasing demand was in essence managerialist (Atkinson and Cope, 1994). The public services were encouraged to change their management styles. Through the application of the Financial Management Initiative, the construction of performance indicators, the use of management information systems and, from later in the 1980s, scrutiny by the Audit Commission and the National Audit Office, radical changes in the management of criminal justice agencies were encouraged.

In relation to prisons, there were initially two principal foci: the managerialist 'Fresh Start' package and the increasing emphasis upon and use of privatisation. Announcing the publication of a joint report by the

Prison Department and a group of management consultants in 1986, the Home Secretary said that it presented 'a telling indictment of the present shift and complementing systems in the Prison Service and the working practices that surround them'. Furthermore, the report also included 'recommendations for new systems which would release large amounts of now unproductive capacity which ought to be used for other purposes' (McDermott and King, 1989: 161). It was as a result of this report that the 'Fresh Start' package came into being. As part of the process of implementation of the package, new management structures were introduced which reduced prison governors' autonomy by making them answerable to area managers – indeed, the new management structures were designed so that 'everybody was accountable to somebody'. Fresh Start, it is suggested, 'involved some of the most far-reaching changes to the prison system since it was nationalised in 1878' (King and McDermott, 1992: 153).

No doubt a similarly radical set of changes was in the Home Secretary's mind when he set Sir Patrick Sheehy the task of inquiring into police rank structures and remuneration. Although much of what Sheehy recommended was successfully resisted by the police, many of the cumbersome managerial structures once visible in the service – many of which were identified by Sheehy – are now being dismantled. In much the same way, the professional skills of the probation service have been increasingly subject to the new managerialism (McLaughlin and Muncie, 1994).

Although privatisation was resisted for some years, and the policy has only been pursued in earnest relatively recently, major changes have nevertheless taken place. The first major announcement came in April 1992, when Group 4 Security won the contract to manage a new purpose-built institution for remand prisoners, the Wolds. A second prison, Blakenhurst, opened in 1993 under the management of UK Detention Services, and later that year tenders were invited for the running of existing as well as new prisons, including Strangeways. In April 1993, the Prison Service itself became an executive agency under the 'Next Steps' programme. It was suggested by some commentators that this move, including the appointment of ex-Granada TV boss, Derek Lewis, as Chief Executive of the Prison Service, would lead to further privatisation. This appeared to be confirmed by the Home Secretary who on announcing the change said the 'Chief Executive . . . will be personally responsible for the day-to-day running of the Service and will be my chief policy advisor on all prison issues. I will be looking to him to improve the performance of directly managed prisons and to increase private sector imvolvement to provide competition [and] a fresh stimulus for innovation'. Though privately run prisons remain very much a minority of penal estate, they are very clearly now a central part of it. We now live in times in which there is no question but that private prisons are here to stay – and for the foreseeable future all new prisons will be privately run.

In relation to policing, the encouragement of the private sector has taken place with a greater degree of stealth. Until recently, Britain was one of the few Western European countries not to have statutory licensing or some other form of vetting of its private security industry. There is evidence that the private security industry is expanding particularly quickly (Jones and Newburn, 1998) and is increasingly moving into areas of work like patrol – which is considered to be one of the primary functions of public constabularies. The passage of the Crime and Disorder Act 1998, the increasing emphasis on best value testing, and the acknowledgement and stimulation of the 'extended police family' via the Police Reform Act 2002, are all likely to lead to further private sector expansion in this area.

One of the solutions that the government has pursued in relation to the problems it has faced in crime and criminal justice has been to seek to make criminal justice agencies more business-like. 'The perceived attributes of the well-run private sector company (of high efficiency, of explicit accountabilities, of clear objectives, and of measured performance)' are increasingly applied to management in the police, prison and probation services and other agencies (Raine and Willson, 1993: 23). New Public Management (NPM) has had a significant impact on all criminal justice agencies. There is some dispute as to the key characteristics of NPM but, in brief, in the criminal justice arena it would appear to involve some or all of the following (McLaughlin et al., 2001):

- increased emphasis on achieving results rather than administering processes;
- the setting of explicit targets and performance indicators to enable the auditing of efficiency and effectiveness;
- the publication of league tables illustrating comparative performance;
- the identification of core competencies;
- the costing and market testing of all activities to ensure value for money;
- the externalisation of non-essential responsibilities;
- the establishment of a purchaser-provider split;
- the encouragement of inter-agency co-operation; and
- the redesignation of clients as 'customers'.

Part of this new management creed involves a devolution of decision-making and of budgetary control and, indeed, there have been moves – particularly within the prison and police services – to provide local managers with considerably enhanced powers. All too often, however, it appears that lip-service is being paid to such devolution of responsibility, rather than any significant reorientation of power and influence. More than anything else, the reason for this has been a continual, and by no means always gradual, accretion of power to the centre. Here lies one of the fundamental and continuing tensions in contemporary criminal justice policy and practice.

Local autonomy or state control?

Although the new managerialism has involved a great deal of talk about devolution, one author has argued that this is merely a front behind which the state is increasing its control over the various criminal justice agencies (Jones, 1993). This is visible across the criminal justice spectrum. As we saw in relation to both the long-term and more recent history of the probation service, the overriding feature of change in this area has been the increasing power and control exercised by the centre. Home Office Circulars, Green Papers, White Papers, consultation documents, decision documents, SNOP followed by national standards, suggest in combination that the Home Office now occupies the key role in the tripartite structure of probation governance. When all else 'failed' in terms of delivery, New Labour made the service a national one, and further reduced local control. The recognition of the importance of local delivery of services, combined with an apparently insatiable desire to control from the centre, is also visible in youth justice. The creation of multi-agency YOTs, with significantly increased resources, has been matched with the establishment of the YJB and a raft of national monitoring and auditing practices that have run counter to the localising intentions of the new teams.

In relation to the police, a similar process has been taking place. Indeed, the entire history of the police service can, in part, be read as a continual process of centralisation of control (see, for example, Emsley, 2003, on this process in the nineteenth and early twentieth centuries). Despite the intentions of the Police Act 1964, local police authorities have always occupied a relatively powerless position when compared with the other players in the tripartite structure. Since the early 1990s, several reformist and interventionist Home Secretaries, notably Ken Clarke and David Blunkett, have sought to impose their own vision on policing and to ensure that messages emanating from the Home Office are unquestionably the ones that chief constables should pay greatest attention to. Ken Clarke's intention behind the original Police and Magistrates' Courts Bill was to take influence away from locally elected officials, who he felt were ineffective and, via Home Office appointments, to install 'independent members' who would be better placed to offer advice to, and to question, chief constables. Though Parliament, and the House of Lords in particular, diluted his reforms, the result at least in part still strengthened the hand of the Home Secretary. More recently, David Blunkett's first act as Home Secretary was to establish the Police Standards Unit, under the direction of a private sector manager, to impose further centrally determined performance measures on local police forces and Basic Command Units. In addition, the newly published national policing plan and, perhaps most significantly, the Downing Street-driven street crime initiative, made plain the New Labour administration's lack of patience with, and trust in, locally driven services.

A return to penal populism?

The 1979 General Election was the first in which 'law and order' was a central plank. It was also the last in which a government pinned faith in the apparently simple equation of spending more as a solution to crime problems. The Thatcher government's brief flirtation in the early 1980s with 'money no object' law and order policies was quickly abandoned and, though expenditure has continued to rise, and often rapidly in the criminal justice arena, neo-liberal managerialist concerns and centralising tendencies have become more pronounced since that period.

More particularly, from the 1980s on, increasing attention was paid to the notion that (the by now better-resourced) criminal justice agencies could not tackle crime alone. They were encouraged to form partnerships and inter-agency groupings and, more importantly, the wider 'community' was itself encouraged to take responsibility for the fight against crime (Garland, 2001). Towards the end of the decade, there was increasing recognition that the problem of crime and the 'crisis of containment' needed to be tackled in a rational manner and the eventual result, after a series of Green and White Papers, was the reinforcement of the policy of bifurcation via the passage of the Criminal Justice Act 1991. The Act sought to impose on the sentencing process a framework which would encourage a 'coherent approach to non-custodial sentencing' (Ashworth, 1992: 245), would bring about greater use of punishments in the community and reduce prison numbers. The general spirit of optimism which greeted the passage of the 1991 Act was reinforced by nature of the Report produced by Lord Woolf (1991) in the aftermath of the worst prison disturbances in the twentieth century.

Furthermore, this sense of optimism was furthered by the initial period after the passing of the legislation and the publication of the Report. Prison numbers began to fall, there was some respite from the problems of overcrowding that had bedevilled prisons for many years, there was some evidence of increasing use of certain community-based penalties and the government, though it by no means made across-the-board promises with regard to Woolf's proposals, nevertheless produced a White Paper which was perhaps more progressive than many expected. The greatest of all U-turns, however, was just around the corner.

At the Conservative Party conference in 1993, the new Home Secretary, Michael Howard, announced a new 'law and order' package. The description is not a loose one, for the approach taken by Howard flew directly in the face of all the major trends in criminal justice since the late 1980s. The government were by this stage under pressure from a Labour Party that was interested in appearing to be just as 'tough on crime' as the traditional party of law and order claimed to be, whilst simultaneously implementing social policies that, as in Tony Blair's famous soundbite, would make them 'tough on the causes of crime' as well. The choice that

Howard made in seeking to bolster his party's and his own fortunes was to return to the strident tones reminiscent of Margaret Thatcher's 'authoritarian populism'.

The package of measures that Howard announced were punitive, involving a reassertion of the central position of custody in a range of sanctions he interpreted as having deterrence as their primary aim. Most famously, he announced that previous approaches which involved attempts to limit prison numbers were henceforward to be eschewed. The new package of measures would be likely to result in an increase in prison numbers, an increase which he appeared to welcome: 'I do not flinch from that. We shall no longer judge the success of our system of justice by a fall in our prison population. . . . Let us be clear. *Prison works.* It ensures that we are protected from murderers, muggers and rapists – and it makes many who are tempted to commit crime think twice' (emphasis added). Elements of this speech have been quoted in several chapters in this book. Without doubt, the speech was a pivotal moment in recent British law and order politics, ushering in three years of almost uninterrupted bidding wars by the two main parties for occupation of the punitive 'high ground'. The Labour Party, led by Blair on law and order, was, in this period, rarely more than mildly critical of government proposals to increase penalties, whilst seeking to advance its own harshly punitive credentials.

The short-term decline in the prison population that had occurred after the introduction of the 1991 Act was quickly reversed; numbers quickly returned to record levels and, despite the biggest prison-building programme in the twentieth century, again quickly exceeded the overall capacity of the estate. The recent history of criminal justice policy makes depressing reading. Just over a decade ago, albeit for what now seems a relatively short period of time, the outlook appeared more optimistic. It is not, therefore, that lessons cannot be learnt, or that once learnt they cannot be put into practice. It is that with the politicisation of criminal justice issues comes the likelihood that long-term benefits will continually be sacrificed on the altar of short-term expediency. This turned out to be an important element of the story in the 1990s, especially the mid-1990s during Michael Howard's tenure at the Home Office (with Blair and subsequently Straw as his Shadow). With the front bench Home Affairs spokesmen battling to 'out-tough' each other, there appeared little prospect of coherent and forward-thinking policy-making. Whilst the Criminal Justice Act 1991 may not by any means have been an ideal piece of legislation, it was at least formulated in a constructive manner. It was the product of considerable thought, debate and consultation. A decade on, the prospects of there being new criminal justice legislation in the near future that is a product of a similar process, despite the rhetoric of evidence-based policy, seem slim. Short-term electoral advantage (whether imagined or real) remains a key driving force in criminal justice policy-making.

Crime, government and image management

In discussing the politics of crime control, Jonathon Simon (1997) has described the strategy of 'governing through crime'. Simon's central argument is that advanced industrial societies are experiencing a crisis of governance (rather than a crisis of crime) and that the response to this has been to prioritise crime and punishment as the preferred contexts for governance. Though the argument is undoubtedly overstated in some respects, it is certainly possible to agree with Simon that crime currently casts a 'disproportionate shadow over what we primarily identify with governance, i.e., politicians and the electoral process of democracy' (1997: 174). This has been true for much of the last decade and has perhaps been particularly the case under New Labour administrations in the United Kingdom. This is visible in many ways, not the least of which has been the centrality of crime and punishment to New Labour's image and news management.

In the criminal justice arena, politicians' concern about how they are likely to be perceived has had a profound effect on policy making in recent years. The past two decades have seen a progressively intensifying battle by the two main political parties to be seen as the party of law and order. This struggle was at its clearest in the five years after Labour's 1992 election defeat. In this period, as the Democratic Party in the United States had done before it (Baer, 2000), Labour sought to reinvent itself and, particularly, to relocate itself as a party more in tune with what were perceived to be 'middle England's' concerns about crime. The most visible sign of change was Blair's famous soundbite, 'tough on crime and tough on the causes of crime'. It was important not simply because it signalled a 'third way' in law and order, but because it allowed the then Shadow Home Secretary to utter a New Labour 'keyword' (Fairclough, 2000) – tough – twice in the space of ten words.

A preoccupation with language – particularly the language of toughness and punitiveness – has frequently distracted attention from (often by design), and sometimes seemingly undermined, some of New Labour's more thoughtful and more constructive approaches to crime and punishment. In the lead-up to the 1997 general election, this manifested itself in a wholesale importation of United States crime control rhetoric, including both the idea of 'zero tolerance' (Newburn, 2002b) and the manifesto proposal, later acted upon, to create a 'drugs czar' (Quayle, 1998). This concern with image is the source of much of the ambiguity and tension in the New Labour project. As two influential New Labour architects put it in the early 1990s, 'the lessons which the British left can learn [from the United States] are not so much about *content* – although there is valuable intellectual exchange already underway – as about *process*' (Hewitt and Gould, 1993). It is here that the tensions between short-termism and the longer-term modernisation project have perhaps been clearest. Thus, against a background of progressive and sometimes impressive reforms in the first three years of the first term, with a huge parliamentary majority and continuing falls in recorded crime, the Labour government rarely looked like it was confident in the face of even relatively minor 'bad news' stories. As one example, not long after the case of the Norfolk farmer, Tony Martin, the Prime Minister still felt compelled to write a memo to his Director of Communications in which he sought to regain the apparently lost ground. In the memo, dated 29 April 2000, but leaked in July, Blair said:

> On crime, we need to highlight the *tough* measures: compulsory tests for drugs before bail . . . the extra number of burglars jailed under 'three strikes and you're out'. Above all, we must deal *now* with street crime, especially in London. When the figures are published for the six months to April, they will show a small – 4 per cent – rise in crime. But this will almost entirely be due to the rise in levels of street crime – mobile phones, bags being snatched. This will be worst in London. The Met Police are putting in place measures to deal with it; but as ever, we lack a tough *public* message along with the strategy. We should think now of an initiative, e.g. locking up street muggers. Something tough, with immediate bite that sends a message through the system. Maybe, the driving licence penalty for young offenders. But this should be done soon and I, personally, should be associated with it.
>
> (the full text was printed in the *Sun*, 17 July 2000)

There are numerous other examples from the past five years. The timing of the activation of the third of the 'three strikes' provisions in the Crime (Sentences) Act 1997 was dictated not by criminal justice concerns but by the desire to bury a particularly bad news story. There followed the Prime Minister's speech in Germany, to a bemused audience, in which he outlined, apparently to the surprise of the Home Office, plans to introduce fixed penalties and raised the spectre of police officers marching young offenders to cash-point machines on a rowdy Saturday night to pay their on-the-spot fines. The more recent, again Prime Ministerial, announcement that the new co-ordinated street crime initiative would crack the problem by September 2002 ('Prime Time', *Police Review*, 26 July 2002), distracted attention almost entirely from the White Paper and led to widespread concern within the police service about the possibility of operational control of policing from Whitehall. Though the Prime Minister may be the main culprit in this regard, New Labour Home Secretaries have been far from immune. David Blunkett, in particular, has at various points issued statements that appear highly critical of the 'prison works' approach adopted by Michael Howard and then made highly punitive public speeches within days of each other.[1] Neither Straw nor Blunkett have appeared unequivocal on what they feel should be happening to the prison population. Both have seemed uncomfortable with continuing rises in the numbers incarcerated, but neither has acted in a way that might have significantly altered the situation (with the rather limited exception of the home detention curfew).[2]

Though there are clear continuities between New Labour and previous administrations (Smith, 2000), not least in some of their punitive rhetoric, there are also clear differences. Indeed, even in that regard there have been changes, for some of the populist punitiveness of the pre-1997 period has been toned down or jettisoned altogether. Similarly, the modernising agenda, though clearly of a piece with earlier Conservative approaches to service management, is also radically different from it. In particular, the rise to prominence of the 'what works' paradigm, and the centralising managerialist initiatives under New Labour, signal something of a departure from previous arrangements.

Nonetheless, given the circumstances outlined above, it should be no surprise that New Labour's record, like its public pronouncements, is a mixed one. The modernisation project has diverse tributaries and, at heart, has contained an uneasy mix in which the desire to produce technically competent, well-resourced and publicly responsive local systems of delivery has continually been in tension with an apparent strong desire to manage and control from the centre. An uneasy mixture is the consequence. The radical reform of youth justice, which contained a genuine attempt to empower local youth justice practitioners, was accompanied by the establishment of a powerful and controlling bureaucracy in the centre in the form of the YJB. The rationalisation of the geographical boundaries of local criminal justice agencies, and the creation of potentially powerful new local partnerships and responsibilities, was accompanied by the release of increasing numbers of central directives and performance measures. To date, New Labour appears to be an administration that believes in the importance of local services and local delivery, but does not yet quite trust those responsible to provide such services in a consistent or an effective manner.

In parallel, and perhaps equally importantly, the modernisation project, which included a full-scale overhaul of the Labour Party itself and its communications strategies (Gould, 1998), has been characterised by a *confidence deficit.* Successive New Labour administrations, underpinned by overwhelming parliamentary majorities, and faced by a disorganised and toothless Opposition, have rarely looked like having the confidence to take advantage of this unparalleled position of power. Electoral success in recent times has undoubtedly been partly contingent on the ability of politicians to persuade voters that they will be 'tough' on crime (Downes and Morgan, 2002). Once elected in 1997, and established in an impregnable position in Parliament, it should have been possible for the 'tough on the causes of crime' elements of New Labour's message to be as visible as its more punitive counterpart. This has rarely been the case. In practice, the undoubted achievements of New Labour in the arena of home affairs – the reform of the youth justice system, the gradual embracing of restorative justice ideas (Crawford and Newburn, 2003), the establishment of Crime and Disorder partnerships, changes in the treatment of cannabis possession, and elements of police reform – have tended to be masked by, and occasionally undermined by, knee-jerk policy-making and populist, short-term rhetoric. Quite apart from the erosion of civil liberties and the continued increasing use of incarceration and other forms of punishment that parts of the New Labour project have entailed, the danger is that the opportunity to break out of the punitive policy-making cycle of the last decade will be lost.

Notes

1. For example, in a speech to the Prison Service on 4 February 2002, David Blunkett said: 'Prison is an expensive way of denying people liberty. A new intermediate option could reduce costs dramatically, giving us more money to spend on crime reduction.' Then, on 20 March 2002, in a speech on street crime, he said: 'What we need is practical action on the streets at local level to tackle the thugs that are striking fear into our communities. What I want to do is to put the fear back where it belongs, with those that seek to break the law and terrorise others.' Both speeches are available at www.nds.coi.gov.uk/coi/coipress.nsf
2. At the time of writing, the prison population has reached 72,502. When Labour came to power in 1997, the figure was just over 61,000.

Bibliography

ACOP (1988) *More Demanding Than Prison.* Wakefield: ACOP.

ACOP (1994) *Finance and Resource Newsbrief.* Wakefield: ACOP, March.

Adam Smith Institute (1984) *The Omega Justice Report.* London: Adam Smith Institute.

Adler, Z. (1987) *Rape on Trial.* London: Routledge & Kegan Paul.

Adler, Z. (1988) 'Prosecuting child sexual abuse: A challenge to the status quo', in Maguire, M. and Pointing, J. (eds) *Victims of Crime: A New Deal?* Milton Keynes: Open University Press.

Advisory Council on the Penal System (1968) *The Regime for Long-term Prisoners in Conditions of Maximum Security.* London: HMSO.

Alderson, J. (1979) *Policing Freedom.* Plymouth: McDonald and Evans.

Allen, F. (1981) *The Decline of the Rehabilitative Ideal.* New Haven: Yale University Press.

Allen, R. (1991) 'Out of jail: The reduction in the use of penal custody for male juveniles 1981–88', *Howard Journal* 30 (1).

Anderson, P. and Mann, N. (1997) *Safety First: The making of New Labour.* London: Granta.

Andrews, D., Zinger, I., Hoge, R. et al. (1990) 'Does correctional treatment work? A clinically relevant and psychologically informed meta-analysis'. *Criminology* 28: 369–404.

Anna, T. (1988) 'Feminist responses to sexual abuse: The work of the Birmingham Rape Crisis Centre', in Maguire, M. and Pointing, J. (eds) *Victims of Crime: A New Deal?* Milton Keynes: Open University Press.

Aries, P. (1962) *Centuries of Childhood.* London: Jonathan Cape.

Ashworth, A. (1983) *Sentencing and Penal Policy.* London: Weidenfeld & Nicolson.

Ashworth, A. (1984) *Sentencing in the Crown Court*, Occasional Paper No. 10, Centre for Criminological Research, University of Oxford.

Ashworth, A. (1990) 'The White Paper on Criminal Justice Policy and Sentencing', *Criminal Law Review*, April.

Ashworth, A. (1992) *Sentencing and Criminal Justice.* London: Weidenfeld & Nicolson.

Ashworth, A. (1993) 'Victim impact statements and sentencing', *Criminal Law Review.* 498–509.

Ashworth, A. (1994a) *The Criminal Process.* Oxford: Oxford University Press.

Ashworth, A. (1994b) 'Sentencing', in Maguire, M., Morgan, R. and Reiner, R. (eds) *The Oxford Handbook of Criminology.* Oxford: Oxford University Press.

Ashworth, A. (1995) *Sentencing and Criminal Justice*, 2nd edn. London: Butterworths.

Ashworth, A. (2000a) *Sentencing and Criminal Justice*, 3rd edn. London: Butterworths.

Ashworth, A. (2000b) 'Victims' rights, defendants' rights and criminal procedure', in Crawford, A. and Goodey, J. (eds) *Integrating a Victim Perspective Within Criminal Justice: International Debates.* Aldershot: Ashgate.

Ashworth, A. (2002) 'Sentencing', in Maguire, M., Morgan, R. and Reiner, R. (eds) *The Oxford Handbook of Criminology.* Oxford: Clarendon Press.

Association of Metropolitan Authorities (1990) *Crime Reduction – A framework for the 1990s.* London: AMA.

Association of Metropolitan Authorities (1994) *Changing the Face of Quangos: A discussion document.* London: AMA.

Atkinson, R. and Cope, S. (1994) 'Changing styles of governance since 1979', in Savage, S., Atkinson, R. and Robins, L. (eds) *Public Policy in Britain.* Basingstoke: Macmillan.

Audit Commission (1989) *The Probation Service: Promoting Value for Money.* London: HMSO.

Audit Commission (1994) *Cheques and Balances: A Management Handbook on Police Planning and Financial Delegation.* London: Audit Commission.

Audit Commission (1996a) *Misspent Youth.* London: Audit Commission.

Audit Commission (1996b) *Streetwise.* London: Audit Commission.

Audit Commission (1999) *Safety in Numbers: Promoting Community Safety.* London: Audit Commission.

Auld, Lord Justice (2001) *Review of the Criminal Courts of England and Wales.* London: The Stationery Office.

Baer, K. (2000) *Reinventing the Democrats.* Lawrence, K.S: Kansas University Press.

Bailey, V. (1987) *Delinquency and Citizenship: Reclaiming the Young Offender 1914–48.* Oxford: Clarendon Press.

Baker, E. and Clarkson, C.M.V. (2002) 'Making Punishments Work? An evaluation of the Halliday Report on Sentencing in England and Wales', *Criminal Law Review.* 81.

Bayley, D. and Shearing, C. (1996) 'The future of policing', *Law and Society Review* 30 (3): 585–606.

Beattie, J.M. (1986) *Crime and the Courts in England 1660–1800.* Oxford: Clarendon Press.

Bell, S. (1988) *When Salem Came to the Boro: The True Story of the Cleveland Child Abuse Crisis.* London: Pan.

Bellamy, J.G. (1973) *Crime and Public Order in the Later Middle Ages.* London: Routledge & Kegan Paul.

Belson, W. (1975) *Juvenile Theft: The Causal Factors.* London: Harper & Row.

Bennett, T. (1989) 'The neighbourhood watch experience', in Morgan, R. and Smith, D. (eds) *Coming to Terms with Policing.* London: Routledge.

Bennett, T. (1990) *Evaluating Neighbourhood Watch.* Aldershot: Gower.

Benyon, J. and Bourn, C. (eds) (1986) *The Police, Powers, Procedures and Proprieties.* Oxford: Pergamon.

Berger, V. (1977) 'Man's trial, women's tribulation: Rape cases in the court room', *Columbia Law Review* 77: 1.

Binney, V., Harekell, G. and Nixon, J. (1981) *Leaving Violent Men: A Study of Refuges and Housing for Battered Women.* Leeds: Women's Aid Federation England.

Blair, I. (1998) 'Where do the Police fit into policing?' Speech to the ACPO conference (unpublished).

Blair, T. (1993) 'Why crime is a socialist issue', *New Statesman and Society*, 29 January.

Bochel, D. (1976) *Probation and After-Care. Its Development in England and Wales.* Edinburgh: Scottish Academic Press.

Boswell, G. (1996) *Young and Dangerous: The backgrounds and careers of section 53 offenders.* Aldershot: Avebury.

Bottomley, A.K. (1984) 'Dilemmmas of parole in a penal crisis', *Howard Journal* 25 (1): 24–40.

Bottomley, A.K. (1994) 'Long-term prisoners', in Player, E. and Jenkins, M. (eds) *Prisons After Woolf: Reform through riot.* London: Routledge.

Bottomley, A.K. and Pease, K. (1986) *Crime and Punishment: Interpreting the Data.* Buckingham: Open University Press.

Bottoms, A.E. (1974) 'On the decriminalization of English juvenile courts', in Hood, R. (ed.) *Crime, Criminology and Public Policy.* London: Heinemann.

Bottoms, A.E. (1977) 'Reflections on the renaissance of dangerousness', *Howard Journal* 16: 70–96.

Bottoms, A.E. (1980) 'The suspended sentence after ten years: A review and assessment', University of Leeds: Centre for Social Work and Applied Social Studies, Occasional Paper No. 2.

Bottoms, A.E. (1981) 'The suspended sentence in England 1967–78', *British Journal of Criminology* 21: 1.

Bottoms, A.E. (1983) 'Neglected topics in contemporary penal systems', in Garland, D. and Young, P. (eds) *The Power to Punish.* Aldershot: Gower.

Bottoms, A.E. (1987) 'Limiting prison use: Experience in England and Wales', *Howard Journal* 26 (3): 177–202.

Bottoms, A.E. (1990a) 'Crime Prevention: Facing the 1990s', *Policing and Society* 1 (1): 3–22.

Bottoms, A.E. (1990b) 'The aims of imprisonment', in Garland, D. (ed.) *Justice, Guilt and Forgiveness in the Penal System.* Centre for Theology and Public Issues: University of Edinburgh.

Bottoms, A.E. (1995) 'The philosophy and politics of punishment and sentencing', in Clarkson, C. and Morgan, R. (eds) *The Politics of Sentencing Reform.* Oxford: Oxford University Press.

Bottoms, A.E. and Light, R. (eds) (1987) *Problems of Long-Term Imprisonment.* Aldershot: Gower.

Bottoms, A.E. and McWilliams, W. (1979) 'A non-treatment paradigm for probation practice', *British Journal of Social Work* 9 (2): 159–202.

Bottoms, A.E. and Stevenson, S. (1992) 'What went wrong? Criminal Justice policy in England and Wales, 1945–70', in Downes, D. (ed.) *Unravelling Criminal Justice.* Basingstoke: Macmillan.

Bowling, B. (1999) *Violent Racism.* Oxford: Clarendon Press.

Bowling, B. and Phillips, C. (2002) *Racism, Crime and Justice.* Harlow: Pearson.

Braithwaite, J. (1998) 'Restorative justice', in Tonry, M. (ed.) *The Handbook of Crime and Punishment.* New York: Oxford University Press.

Braithwaite, J. (2003) 'What's wrong with the sociology of punishment?', *Theoretical Criminology* 7 (1): 5–28.

Brake, M. and Hale, C. (1992) *Public Order and Private Lives.* London: Routledge.

Brantingham, P.J. and Faust, L. (1976) 'A conceptual model of crime prevention', *Crime and Delinquency* 22: 284–96.

Bratton, W.J. (1997) 'Crime is Down in New York City: Blame the Police', in Dennis, N. (ed.) *Zero Tolerance: Policing a free society.* London: Institute of Economic Affairs.

Brody, S.R. (1976) *The Effectiveness of Sentencing*, Home Office Research Study No. 35. London: HMSO.

Brogden, M. (1982) *The Police: Autonomy and Consent*. London: Academic Press.

Brown, D. (1989) *Detention at the Police Station under the Police and Criminal Evidence Act 1984*. London: HMSO.

Brown, D., Ellis, T. and Larcombe, K. (1992) *Changing the Code: Police Detention under the Revised PACE Codes of Practice*. London: HMSO.

Brown, D. and Iles, S. (1985) *Community Constables: A Study of a Policing Initiative*, Research and Planning Unit Paper 30. London: Home Office.

Brownlee, I. (1998) *Community Punishment: A critical introduction*. Harlow: Longman.

Burrows, J. and Lewis, H. (1988) *Directing Patrolwork: A Study of Uniformed Policing*, Home Office Research Study No. 99. London: HMSO.

Butler-Sloss, E. (1988) *Report of the Inquiry into Child Abuse in Cleveland, 1987*, Cm 412. London: HMSO.

Campbell, B. (1988) *Unofficial Secrets: Child Sexual Abuse – The Cleveland Case*. London: Virago.

Campbell, B. (1993) *Goliath: Britain's Dangerous Places*. London: Methuen.

Campbell, S. (2002) *A Review of Anti-Social Behaviour Orders*. London: Home Office.

Casale, S. (1984) *Minimum Standards for Prison Establishments*. London: NACRO.

Casale, S. (1994) 'Conditions and standards', in Player, E. and Jenkins, M. (eds) *Prisons After Woolf: Reform through riot*. London: Routledge.

Cavadino, M. and Dignan, J. (1992) *The Penal System: An Introduction*. London: Sage.

Cavadino, P. (1992) 'Reflections on the Criminal Justice Act 1991', *Criminal Justice Matters* 9, Autumn.

Central Statistical Office (1994) *Social Trends*. London: HMSO.

Chambers, G. and Miller, A. (1983) *Investigating Sexual Assault*. Scottish Office Central Research Unit, Edinburgh: HMSO.

Chatterton, M. and Rogers, M. (1989) 'Focused policing', in Morgan, R. and Smith, D. (eds) *Coming to Terms With Policing*. London: Routledge.

Cheney, D., Dickson, L., Skilbeck, R. and Uglow, S., with Fitzpatrick, J. (2001) *Criminal Justice and the Human Rights Act 1998*. London: Jordans.

Chibnall, S. (1977) *Law and Order News*. London: Tavistock.

Christie, N. (1977) 'Conflicts as Property', *British Journal of Criminology* 17 (1): 1–15.

Clarke, J. (1980) 'Social democratic delinquents and Fabian families', in National Deviancy Conference (ed.) *Permissiveness and Control: The Fate of Sixties Legislation*. London: Macmillan.

Clarke, R.V.G. (1981) *The prospects for controlling crime*, Research Bulletin No. 12. London: Home Office.

Clarke, R.V.G. (ed.) (1992) *Situational Crime Prevention*. New York: Harrow & Heston.

Clarke, R.V.G. and Mayhew, P. (eds) (1980) *Designing Out Crime*. London: HMSO.

Clarkson, C.M.V. and Morgan, R. (1994) 'Sentencing Reform: Lessons from abroad', *Journal of Crime, Criminal Law and Criminal Justice* 2 (2): 105–19.

Coggan, G. and Walker, M. (1982) *Frightened for my Life*. London: Fontana.

Cohen, S. (1979) 'The punitive city: Notes on the dispersal of social control', *Contemporary Crises* 3: 339–63.

Cohen, S. (1985) *Visions of Social Control*. Oxford: Polity Press.

Cohen, S. and Taylor, L. (1972) *Psychological Survival: The Experience of Long-term Imprisonment*. Harmondsworth: Penguin.

Conservative Central Office (1987) *The Conservative Manifesto 1987*. London: Conservative Party.

Conservative Political Centre (1962) *A Report on Compensation for Injuries through Crimes of Violence.* London: Conservative Political Centre.

Coote, A. and Campbell, B. (1987) *Sweet Freedom: The Struggle for Women's Liberation,* 2nd edn. Oxford: Blackwell.

Corbett, C. and Hobdell, K. (1988) 'Volunteer-based services to rape victims: Some recent developments', in Maguire, M. and Pointing, J. (eds) *Victims of Crime: A New Deal?* Milton Keynes: Open University Press.

Councell, R. and Simes, J. (2002) *Projections of long-term trends in the prison population to 2009,* Statistical Bulletin 14/02. London: Home Office.

Cox, B., Shirley, J. and Short, M. (1977) *The Fall of Scotland Yard.* Harmondsworth: Penguin.

Crawford, A. (1997) *The Local Governance of Crime: Appeals to community and partnerships.* Oxford: Clarendon Press.

Crawford, A. (1998) *Crime Prevention and Community Safety: Politics, Policies and Practices.* Harlow: Longman.

Crawford, A. (2000) 'Salient themes and the limitations of restorative justice', in Crawford, A. and Goodey, J. (eds) *Integrating a Victim Perspective Within Criminal Justice: International Debates.* Aldershot: Ashgate.

Crawford, A. (2003) 'The prospects of restorative justice for young offenders in England and Wales: A tale of two Acts', in McEvoy, K. and Newburn, T. (eds) *Criminology, Conflict Resolution and Restorative Justice.* Basingtoke: Palgrave.

Crawford, A. and Goodey, J. (eds) (2000) *Integrating a Victim Perspective Within Criminal Justice: International Debates.* Aldershot: Ashgate.

Crawford, A. and Newburn, T. (2002) 'Recent developments in restorative justice for young people in England and Wales: Community Participation and Restoration', *British Journal of Criminology* 45 (2): 476–95.

Crawford, A. and Newburn, T. (2003) *Youth Offending and Restorative Justice: Implementing reform in youth justice.* Cullompton: Willan Publishing.

Criminal Law Revision Committee (1984) *Fifteenth Report: Sexual Offences,* Cmnd 9213. London: HMSO.

Critchley, T.A. (1978) *A History of the Police in England and Wales.* London: Constable.

Davies, G. (1992) *Making Amends: Mediation and Reparation in Criminal Justice.* London: Routledge.

Dignan, J. (1999) 'The Crime and Disorder Act and Prospects for Restorative Justice', *Criminal Law Review.* 48–60.

Dignan, J. (2000) *Youth Justice Pilots Evaluation: Interim Report on Reparative Work and Youth Offending Teams.* London: Home Office.

Ditchfield, J. (1976) *Police Cautioning in England and Wales,* Home Office Research Study No. 37. London: HMSO.

Dobash, R.E. and Dobash, R.P. (1992) *Women, Violence and Social Change.* London: Routledge.

Dodgson, K., Goodwin, P., Howard, P., Llewelyn-Thomas, S., Mortimer, E., Russell, N. and Weiner, M. (2001) *Electronic monitoring of released prisoners: an evaluation of the Home Detention Curfew Scheme,* Home Office Research Study No. 222. London: Home Office.

Downes, D. and Morgan, R. (1994) 'Hostages to fortune? The politics of law and order in post-war Britain', in Maguire, M., Morgan, R. and Reiner, R. (eds) *The Oxford Handbook of Criminology.* Oxford: Oxford University Press.

Downes, D. and Morgan, R. (1997) 'Dumping the hostages to fortune? The politics of law and order in post-war Britain', in Maguire, M., Morgan, R. and Reiner, R. (eds) *The Oxford Handbook of Criminology*. Oxford: Clarendon Press.

Downes, D. and Morgan, R. (2002) 'The skeletons in the cupboard: the politics of law and order at the millennium', in Maguire, M., Morgan, R., and Reiner, R. (eds) *The Oxford Handbook of Criminology*. Oxford: Oxford University Press.

Duff, P. (1988) 'The "victim movement" and legal reform', in Maguire, M. and Pointing, J. (eds) *Victims of Crime: A New Deal?* Milton Keynes: Open University Press.

Dunbar, I. (1985) *A Sense of Direction*. London: Home Office.

Dunbar, I. and Langdon, A. (1998) *Tough Justice: Sentencing and Penal Policies in the 1990s*. London: Blackstone Press.

Dunlop, A. and McCabe, S. (1965) *Young Men in Detention Centres*. London: Routledge & Kegan Paul.

Edwards, S. (1989) *Policing 'Domestic' Violence: Women, Law and the State*. London: Sage.

Ekblom, P., Sutton, M. and Law, H. (1997) *Safer Cities and Residential Burglary: A summary of evaluation results*. London: Home Office.

Elliot, R. and Nicholls, J. (1996) *It's Good to Talk: Lessons in public consultation and feedback*, Police Research Series Paper 22. London: Home Office.

Emsley, C. (1983) *Policing and its Context 1750–1870*. London: Macmillan.

Emsley, C. (1987) *Crime and Society in England, 1750–1900*. London: Longman.

Emsley, C. (1991) *The English Police: A Political and Social History*. Hemel Hempstead: Harvester Wheatsheaf.

Emsley, C. (2003) 'The introduction of the new police', in Newburn, T. (ed.) *The Handbook of Policing*. Cullompton: Willan Publishing.

Evans, R. (1994) 'Cautioning: Counting the cost of retrenchment', *Criminal Law Review*. 566–75.

Evans, R. and Puech, K. (2001) 'Reprimands and Warnings: populist punitiveness or restorative Justice?', *Criminal Law Review*. 794–805.

Evans, R. and Wilkinson, C. (1990) 'Variations in police cautioning policy and practice in England and Wales', *Howard Journal of Criminal Justice* 29.

Fairclough, N. (2000) *New Labour, New Language?* London: Routledge.

Family Policy Studies Centre (1998) *The Crime and Disorder Bill and the Family*. London: FPSC.

Farrington, D. (1984) 'England and Wales', in Klein, M. (ed.) *Western Systems of Juvenile Justice*. Beverly Hills: Sage.

Farrington, D. (1986) 'Age and crime', in Tonry, M. and Morris, N. (eds) *Crime and Justice*, Vol. 7. Chicago: University of Chicago Press.

Farrington, D. (1990) 'Age, period, cohort and offending', in Gottfredson, D.M. and Clarke, R.V. (eds) *Policy and Theory in Criminal Justice*. Aldershot: Avebury.

Farrington, D. (1996) *Understanding and Preventing Youth Crime*, York: Joseph Rowntree Foundation.

Farrington, D. (1997) 'Human development and criminal careers', in Maguire, M., Morgan, R. and Reiner, R. (eds) *The Oxford Handbook of Criminology*. Oxford: Clarendon Press, 361–408.

Farrington, D. and Bennett, T. (1981) 'Police cautioning of juveniles in London', *British Journal of Criminology* 21: 123–35.

Fattah, E.A. (1992) 'Victims and victimology: The facts and the rhetoric', in Fattah, E.A. (ed.) *Towards a Critical Victimology*. Basingstoke: Macmillan.

Feldman, D. (1990) 'Regulating treatment of suspects in police stations: judicial interpretations of detention provisions in the Police and Criminal Evidence Act 1984', *Criminal Law Review.* 452–71.

Faulkner, D. (1992) 'Magistrates in the Youth Court', *The Magistrate*, September.

Faulkner, D. (1998) 'A Principled Response', *Criminal Justice Matters* 31, Spring: 3–4.

Fitzgerald, M. and Sim, J. (1980) 'Legitimating the prison crisis: A critical review of the May Report', *Howard Journal* XIX: 73–84.

Fitzgerald, M. and Sim, J. (1982) *British Prisons.* Oxford: Blackwell.

Fitzmaurice, C. and Pease, K. (1982) 'Prison sentences and population: A comparison of some European countries', *Justice of the Peace* 148: 575–9.

Fitzmaurice, C. and Pease, K. (1986) *The Psychology of Judicial Sentencing.* Manchester: Manchester University Press.

Folkard, M.S., Fowles, A.J., McWilliams, B.C., McWilliams, W., Smith, D.D., Smith, D.E. and Walmsley, G.R. (1974) *IMPACT* Vol. 1 *The Design of the Probation Experiment and an Interim Evaluation,* Home Office Research Study No. 24. London: HMSO.

Folkard, M.S., Smith, D.D. and Smith, D.E. (1976) *IMPACT* Vol. 2 *The Results of the Experiment,* Home Office Research Study No. 36. London: HMSO.

Fowles, A. (1990) 'Monitoring expenditure in the criminal justice system', *Howard Journal* 29 (2): 82–100.

Fox, L. (1952) *The English Prison and Borstal Systems,* London: Routledge & Kegan Paul.

Franklin, B. and Petley, J. (1996) 'Killing the Age of Innocence: Newspaper reporting of the death of James Bulger', in Pilcher, J. and Wagg, S. (eds) *Thatcher's Children: Politics, childhood and society in the 1980s and 1990s.* Brighton: Falmer Press.

Gardner, J., von Hirsch, A., Smith, A.T.H., Morgan, R., Ashworth, A. and Wasik, M. (1998) 'Clause 1 – the hybrid law from hell?', *Criminal Justice Matters* 31, Spring.

Garland, D. (1985) *Punishment and Welfare: A History of Penal Strategies.* Aldershot: Gower.

Garland, D. (1990) *Punishment and Modern Society.* Oxford: Clarendon Press.

Garland, D. (1995) 'Penal modernism and postmodernism', in Cohen, S. and Blomberg, T.G. (eds) *Punishment and Social Control: Essays in Honor of Sheldon L. Messinger.* New York: Aldine de Gruyter.

Garland, D. (1996) 'The Limits of the Sovereign State: Strategies of crime control in contemporary society', *British Journal of Criminology* 35 (4): 445–71.

Garland, D. (2001) *The Culture of Control.* Oxford: Oxford University Press.

Gatrell, V.A.C. (1980) 'The decline of theft and violence in Victorian and Edwardian England', in Gatrell, V.A.C., Lenman, B. and Parker, G. (eds) *Crime and the Law: the Social History of Crime since 1500.* London: Europa.

Gelsthorpe, L. and Morris, A. (1990) *Feminist Perspectives in Criminology.* Milton Keynes: Open University Press.

Gelsthorpe, L. and Morris, A. (1994) 'Juvenile justice 1945–1992', in Maguire, M., Morgan, R. and Reiner, R. (eds) *The Oxford Handbook of Criminology.* Oxford: Oxford University Press.

Gibson, B., Cavadino, P., Rutherford, A., Ashworth, A. and Harding, J. (1994) *Criminal Justice in Transition.* Winchester: Waterside Press.

Gilling, D. (1997) *Crime Prevention: Theory, Policy and Politics.* London: UCL Press.

Gladstone, F.J. (1980) *Coordinating Crime Prevention Efforts,* Home Office Research Study No. 62. London: HMSO.

Gottfredson, M.R. and Hirschi, T. (1990) *A General Theory of Crime*. Stanford: Stanford University Press.

Gould, P. (1998) *The Unfinished Revolution*. London: Abacus.

Graef, R. (1989) *Talking Blues*. London: Collins.

Graham, J. and Bennett, T. (1995) *Crime Prevention Strategies in Europe and North America*. Helsinki: HEUNI.

Graham, J. and Moxon, D. (1986) *Some trends in juvenile justice*, Home Office Research Bulletin 22: 10–13.

Gurr, T.R. (1976) *Rogues, Rebels and Reformers*. London: Sage.

Gusfield, J. (1963) *Symbolic Crusade: Status Politics and the American Temperance Movement*. Urbana: University of Illinois Press.

Hagell, A. and Newburn, T. (1994) *Persistent Young Offenders*. London: Policy Studies Institute.

Hall, S. (1979) 'The great moving-right show', *Marxism Today* 23.

Hall, S., Critcher, C., Jefferson, T., Clarke, J. and Roberts, B. (1978) *Policing the Crisis. Mugging, the State and Law and Order*. London: Macmillan.

Harding, C., Hines, B., Ireland, R. and Rawlings, P. (1985) *Imprisonment in England and Wales: A Concise History*. Beckenham: Croom Helm.

Harris, R. (1992) *Crime, Criminal Justice and the Probation Service*. London: Routledge.

Harris, R. (1994) 'Continuity and Change: probation and politics in contemporary Britain', *International Journal of Offenders Therapy and Comparative Criminology* 31 (1).

Harris, R. and Webb, D. (1987) *Welfare, Power and Juvenile Justice*. London: Tavistock.

Harvey, L., Grimshaw, P. and Pease, K. (1989) 'Crime Prevention delivery: the work of crime prevention officers', in Morgan, R. and Smith, D. (eds) *Coming to Terms with Policing*. London: Routledge.

Harwin, J. (1982) 'The battle for the delinquent', in Jones, C. and Stevenson, J. (eds) *The Yearbook of Social Policy in Britain, 1980–81*. London: Routledge & Kegan Paul.

Haxby, D. (1978) *Probation: A Changing Service*. London: Constable.

Heal, K. (1991) Changing perspectives on crime prevention: the role of information and structure, in Evans, D., Fyfe, N. and Herbert, D. (eds) *Crime, Policing and Place*, London: Routledge.

Her Majesty's Inspectorate of Constabulary (1996) *A Review of Crime Recording Procedures*. London: Home Office.

Her Majesty's Inspectorate of Constabulary (1999a) *Thematic Inspection on Police and Community Relations*. London: Home Office.

Her Majesty's Inspectorate of Constabulary (1999b) *Winning the Race Revisited: Policing Plural Communities*. London: Home Office.

Her Majesty's Inspectorate of Constabulary (2000) *Calling Time on Crime: A thematic inspection of crime and disorder conducted by HMIC in collaboration with the Home Office, Audit Commission, Local Government Association, Office for Standards in Education and the Social Services Inspectorate*. London: Home Office.

Hewitt, P. and Gould, P. (1993) 'Lessons from America: Learning from success – Labour and Clinton's New Democrats', *Renewal* 1 (1): 45–51.

Hirschi, T. and Gottfredson, M.R. (1983) 'Age and the explanation of crime', *American Journal of Sociology* 89.

Holdaway, S. (1983) *Inside the British Police*. Oxford: Basil Blackwell.

Holdaway, S., Davidson, N., Dignan, J., Hammersley, R., Hine, J. and Marsh, P. (2001) *New Strategies to Address Youth Offending: The national evaluation of the pilot youth offending teams*. London: Home Office.

Holtom, C. and Raynor, P. (1988) 'Origins of victims support philosophy and practice', in Maguire, M. and Pointing, J. (eds) *Victims of Crime: A New Deal?* Milton Keynes: Open University Press.

Home Affairs Committee (1993) *Juvenile Offenders*, Sixth Report. London: HMSO.

Home Affairs Committee (1998) *Alternatives to Prison Sentences*, Vol. 1. London: The Stationery Office.

Home Office (1936) *Report of the Departmental Committee on the Social Services in the Courts of Summary Jurisdiction.* London: Home Office.

Home Office (1961a) *Compensation for Victims of Crimes of Violence*, Cmnd 1406. London: HMSO.

Home Office (1961b) *Report of the Interdepartmental Committee on the Business of the Criminal Courts* (The Streatfield Committee), Cmnd 1289. London: HMSO.

Home Office (1962) *Report of the Departmental Committee on the Probation Service* (The Morison Report), Cmnd 1650. London: HMSO.

Home Office (1964) *Compensation for Victims of Crimes of Violence*, Cmnd 2323. London: HMSO.

Home Office (1965a) *The Adult Offender*, Cmnd 2582. London: HMSO.

Home Office (1965b) *Report of the Committee on the Prevention and Detection of Crime.* London: HMSO.

Home Office (1969) *People in Prison.* London: HMSO.

Home Office (1970) *Reparation by the Offender: Report of the Advisory Council on the Penal System.* London: HMSO.

Home Office (1971) *Crime Prevention Panels*, Home Office Circular 48/1971. London: HMSO.

Home Office (1979) *Committee of Inquiry into the United Kingdom Prison Services* (The May Inquiry), Cmnd 7673. London: HMSO.

Home Office (1984a) *Criminal Justice: A Working Paper.* London: HMSO.

Home Office (1984b) *Managing the Long-Term Prison System: The Report of the Control Review Committee.* London: HMSO.

Home Office (1984c) *Probation Service in England and Wales: Statement of National Objectives and Priorities.* London: Home Office.

Home Office (1984d) *Tougher Regimes in Detention Centres: Report of an Evaluation by the Young Offender Psychology Unit.* London: HMSO.

Home Office (1985) *New Directions in Prison Design, Report of a Home Office Study of New Generation Prisons in the USA.* London: HMSO.

Home Office (1986) *Reparation: A Discussion Document.* London: HMSO.

Home Office (1987) *Efficiency Scrutiny of Her Majesty's Probation Inspectorate.* London: Home Office.

Home Office (1988a) *National Standards for Community Service Orders.* London: Home Office.

Home Office (1988b) *Punishment, Custody and the Community*, Cm 424. London: HMSO.

Home Office (1988c) *Tackling Offending: An Action Plan.* London: HMSO.

Home Office (1989) *Report of the Advisory Group on Video Evidence.* London: HMSO.

Home Office (1990a) *Supervision and Punishment in the Community: A Framework for Action.* London: Home Office.

Home Office (1990b) *Victims' Charter.* London: Home Office.

Home Office (1990c) *Crime, Justice and Protecting the Public*, Cm 965. London: HMSO.

Home Office (1991) *Custody, Care and Justice: The Way Ahead for the Prison Service in England and Wales*, Cm 1647. London: HMSO.

Home Office (1992) *Projection of long-term trends in the prison population to 2000,* Home Office Statistical Bulletin 10/92. London: Home Office.

Home Office (1993a) *Compensating Victims of Violent Crime: Changes to the Criminal Injuries Compensation Scheme,* Cm 2434. London: HMSO.

Home Office (1993b) *Partnership in Dealing with Offenders in the Community.* London: Home Office.

Home Office (1993c) *H.M. Inspectorate of Probation Annual Report 1992–3.* London: Home Office.

Home Office (1993d) *White Paper on Police Reform.* London: Home Office.

Home Office (1994a) *Monitoring of the Criminal Justice Acts 1991 and 1993 – Results from a Special Data Collection Exercise,* Home Office Statistical Bulletin 20/94. London: Home Office.

Home Office (1994b) *Core and Ancilliary Tasks Review: Interim Report.* London: Home Office.

Home Office (1995a) *Review of Core and Ancillary Tasks.* London: HMSO.

Home Office (1995b) *Strengthening Punishment in the Community.* London: HMSO.

Home Office (1996a) *Protecting the Public.* London: HMSO.

Home Office (1996b) *The Victim's Charter: A statement of rights of victims of crime.* London: Home Office.

Home Office (1997a) *Community Safety Order. A consultation paper.* London: Home Office.

Home Office (1997b) *Getting to Grips with Crime: A New Framework for Local Action. A consultation document.* London: Home Office.

Home Office (1997c) *Now National and Local Focus on Youth Crime: A Consultation Paper.* London: Home Office.

Home Office (1997d) *No More Excuses – A New Approach to Tackling Youth Crime in England and Wales,* Cm 3809. London: Home Office.

Home Office (1997e) *Preventing Children Offending: A Consultation Document.* London: Home Office.

Home Office (1997f) *Tackling Delays in the Youth Justice System: A Consultation Paper.* London: Home Office.

Home Office (1997g) *Tackling Youth Crime: A Consultation Paper.* London: Home Office.

Home Office (1998a) *Joining Forces to Protect the Public. Prisons-Probation: A Consultation Document.* London: Home Office.

Home Office (1998b) *Speaking Up For Justice.* Report of the Interdepartmental Working Group on the Treatment of Vulnerable or Intimidated Witnesses in the Criminal Justice System. London: Home Office.

Home Office (1998c) *The Prison Population in 1997.* London: Home Office.

Home Office (1999) *The Correctional Policy Framework: Effective execution of the sentences of the courts so as to reduce re-offending and protect the public.* London: Home Office.

Home Office (2000a) *A Review of the Sentencing Framework.* London: Home Office.

Home Office (2000b) *National Standards for Supervision of Offenders in the Community.* London: Home Office.

Home Office (2001) *A Review of the Victim's Charter.* London: Home Office.

Home Office (2002a) *Justice For All.* London: Home Office.

Home Office (2002b) *National Policing Plan 2003–2006.* London: Home Office.

Home Office and others (1976) *Children and Young Persons Act 1969: Observations on the Eleventh Report of the Expenditure Committee,* Cmnd 6494. London: HMSO.

Home Office and others (1984) *Crime Prevention*, Home Office Circular 8/84. London: Home Office.

Home Office Advisory Council on the Treatment of Offenders (1963) *The Organisation of After-Care*. London: Home Office.

Home Office Statistical Department (1985) *Criminal Careers of those born in 1953, 1958, 1963*, Statistical Bulletin No. 5/85. London: Home Office Statistical Department.

Hood, C. (1991) 'A public management for all seasons?', *Public Administration* 69, Spring: 3–19.

Hope, T. (1985) *Implementing Crime Prevention Measures*, Home Office Research Study No. 86. London: HMSO.

Hope, T. and Murphy, D. (1983) 'Problems of implementing crime prevention: the experience of a demonstration project', *Howard Journal* 22 (1): 38–50.

Hope, T. and Shaw, M. (1998) *Communities and Crime Reduction*. London: HMSO.

Hopley, K. (2002) 'National Standards: Defining the Service', in Ward, D., Scott, J. and Lacey, M. (eds) *Probation: Working for Justice*. Oxford: Oxford University Press.

Hough, J.M. and Mayhew, P. (1985) *Taking Account of Crime: Key Findings from the 1984 British Crime Survey*. London: HMSO.

Hoyle, C., Cape, E., Morgan, R. and Sanders, A. (1998) *Evaluation of the 'One Stop Shop' and Victim Statement Pilot Projects*, Home Office Occasional Paper. London: Home Office.

Hudson, B. (1993) *Penal Policy and Social Justice*. Basingstoke: Macmillan.

Humphries, S. (1981) *Hooligans or Rebels? An Oral History of Working Class Childhood and Youth 1889–1939*. Oxford: Basil Blackwell.

Husain, S. (1988) *Neighbourhood Watch in England and Wales: a locational analysis*, Crime Prevention Unit Paper No. 12. London: Home Office.

Ignatieff, M. (1978) *A Just Measure of Pain: The Penitentiary in the Industrial Revolution 1750–1850*. Harmondsworth: Penguin.

Irving, B., Bird, C., Hibberd, M. and Willmore, J. (1989) *Neighbourhood Policing: The Natural History of a Policing Experiment*. London: Police Foundation.

James, A., Bottomley, K., Clave, E. and Leibling, A. (1997) *Privatizing Prisons: Rhetoric and Reality*. London: Sage.

Jarvis, F.V. (1972) *Advise, Assist and Befriend. A History of the Probation and After-care Service*. London: National Association of Probation Officers.

Jefferson, T. (1990) *The Case Against Paramilitary Policing*. Milton Keynes: Open University Press.

Jefferson, T. and Grimshaw, R. (1984) *Controlling the Constable: Police Accountability in England and Wales*. London: Muller.

Jeffrey, C. (1971) *Crime Prevention Through Environmental Design*. Thousand Oaks, CA: Sage.

Jenkins, P. (1992) *Intimate Enemies: Moral Panics in Contemporary Great Britain*. New York: Walter de Gruyter.

Johnson, L. (2000) *Policing Britain: Risk, security and governance*. Harlow: Pearson.

Johnston, V., Shapland, J. and Wiles, P. (1993) *Developing Police Crime Prevention: Management and Organisational Change*, Police Research Group Crime Prevention Unit Series Paper No. 41. London: Home Office Police Department.

Johnstone, G. (2002) *Restorative Justice: Ideas, values, debates*. Cullompton: Willan Publishing.

Joint Prison/Probation Accreditation Panel (2000) *What Works: First report from the Joint Prison/Probation Accreditation Panel 1999–2000*. London: Home Office.

Jones, C. (1993) 'Auditing criminal justice' *British Journal of Criminology* 33: 3.

Jones, T. and Newburn, T. (1995a) 'How big is the private security sector?', *Policing and Society* 5.

Jones, T. and Newburn, T. (1995b) 'Local government and policing: arresting the decline of local influence', *Local Government Studies* 21 (3): 448–60.

Jones, T. and Newburn, T. (1997) *Policing After the Act: Police governance after the Police and Magistrates' Courts Act 1994*. London: PSI.

Jones, T. and Newburn, T. (1998) *Public Policing and Private Security*. Oxford: Clarendon Press.

Jones, T. and Newburn, T. (2002) 'The Transformation of Policing?', *British Journal of Criminology* 42: 129–46.

Jones, T., Newburn, T. and Smith, D.J. (1994) *Democracy and Policing*. London: PSI.

Justice (1961) *Compensation for Victims of Crimes of Violence*. London: Stevens.

Katz, S. and Mazur, M. (1979) *Understanding the Rape Victim*. London: John Wiley and Sons.

Kelly, L. and Regan, L. (1990) 'Flawed Protection', *Social Work Today*, 19 April.

Kemp, C. and Morgan, R. (1990) *Lay Visitors to Police Stations*. Bristol Centre for Criminal Justice, University of Bath.

King, H.E. and Webb, C. (1981) 'Rape crisis centers: Progress and problems', *Journal of Social Issues* 37 (4): 93–104.

King, M. (1991) 'The political construction of crime prevention', in Stenson, K. and Cowell, D. (eds) *The Politics of Crime Control*. London: Sage.

King, R.D. (1985) 'Control in prisons', in Maguire, M., Vagg, J. and Morgan, R. (eds) *Accountability in Prisons: Opening up a Closed World*. London: Tavistock.

King, R.D. (1994) 'Order, disorder and the regimes in the prison services of Scotland, and England and Wales', in Player, E. and Jenkins, M. (eds) *Prisons After Woolf: Reform through riot*. London: Routledge.

King, R.D. and McDermott, K. (1989) 'British Prisons 1970–1987: The ever deepening crisis', *British Journal of Criminology* 29 (2): 107–28.

King, R.D. and McDermott, K. (1992) 'A fresh start: managing the prison service', in Renier, R. and Cross, M. (eds) *Beyond Law and Order: Criminal Justice Policy and Politics into the 1990s*. London: Macmillan.

King, R.D. and McDermott, K. (1995) *The State of Our Prisons*. Oxford: Clarendon Press.

King, R.D. and Morgan, R. (1976) *A Taste of Prison: Custodial Conditions for Trial and Remand Prisoners*. London: Routledge & Kegan Paul.

King, R.D. and Morgan, R., with Martin, J.P. and Thomas, J.E. (1980) *The Future of the Prison System*. Farnborough: Gower.

Koch, B.C.M. (1998) *The Politics of Crime Prevention*. Aldershot: Ashgate.

Labour Party (1996) *Tackling Youth Crime, Reforming Youth Justice*. London: Labour Party.

Labour Party (1997) *New Labour – Because Britain Deserves Better*. London: Labour Party.

Laycock, G. and Heal, K. (1989) 'Crime prevention: The British experience', in Evans, D.J. and Herbert, D.T. (eds) *The Geography of Crime*. London: Routledge.

Laycock, G. and Tarling, R. (1985) 'Police force cautioning policy and practice in England and Wales', *Howard Journal of Criminal Justice* 24.

Le Mesurier, L. (1935) *A Handbook of Probation and Social Work of the Courts.* London: NAPO.

Leng, R., Taylor, R. and Wasik, M. (1998) *Blackstone's Guide to the Crime and Disorder Act 1998.* London: Blackstone Press.

Letwin, O. (2002) *Beyond the causes of crime,* The Sixth Keith Joseph Memorial Lecture. London: Centre for Policy Studies.

Lewis, D. (1997) *Hidden Agendas: Politics, law and disorder.* London: Hamish Hamilton.

Lipsey, M. (1992) Juvenile delinquency treatment: a meta-analytic enquiry into the variability of effects, in T. Cook, H. Cooper, D.S. Cordray, H. Hartmann, L.V. Hedges, R.L. Light, T.A. Louis and F. Mosteller, (eds) *Meta-Analysis for Explanation: A Case Book,* New York: Russell Sage.

Lipton, D., Martinson, R. and Wilks, J. (1975) *Effectiveness of Treatment Evaluation Studies.* New York: Praeger.

Livingstone, S. (1994) 'The changing face of prison discipline', in Player, E. and Jenkins, M. (eds) *Prisons After Woolf: Reform through riot.* London: Routledge.

Lloyd, C. (1986) *Response to SNOP.* Cambridge: Cambridge Institute of Criminology.

Loader, I. (1997) 'Policing and the social: questions of symbolic power', *British Journal of Sociology* 48 (1): 1–18.

Loader, I. (2001) 'Plural policing and democratic governance' *Social and Legal Studies* 9 (3): 323–45.

Loveday, B. (1987) 'Joint boards for police in Metropolitan areas – a preliminary assessment', *Local Government Studies* 13 (3): 85–101.

Loveday, B. (1991) 'The new police authorities', *Policing and Society* 1 (3): 193–212.

Lustgarten, L. (1986) *The Governance of Police.* London: Sweet & Maxwell.

McConville, M., Sanders, A. and Leng, R. (1991) *The Case for the Prosecution.* London: Routledge.

McConville, M. and Shepherd, D. (1992) *Watching Police, Watching Communities.* London: Routledge.

McConville, S. and Hall Williams, J.E. (1985) *Crime and Punishment: A Radical Rethink.* London: Tawney Society.

McDermott, K. and King, R.D. (1989) 'A fresh start: The enhancement of prison regimes', *Howard Journal* 28 (3): 161–76.

McEvoy, K., Gormally, B. and Mika, H. (2002) 'Conflict, crime control and the "re"-constitution of state-community relations in Northern Ireland', in Hughes, G., McLaughlin, E. and Muncie, J. (eds) *Crime Prevention and Community Safety: New Directions.* London: Sage.

McEwan, J. (2002) 'Special measures for witnesses and victims', in McConville, M. and Wilson, G. (eds) *The Handbook of the Criminal Justice Process.* Oxford: Oxford University Press.

McGallagly, J., Power, K., Littlewood, P. and Meikle, J. (1998) *Evaluation of the Hamilton Child Safety Initiative.* Edinburgh: Scottish Office.

McIvor, G. (1992) *Sentenced to Serve.* Aldershot: Avebury.

McLaughlin, E. and Muncie, J. (1993) 'The silent revolution: Market-based criminal justice in England', *Socio-Legal Bulletin.* Australia: La Trobe University.

McLaughlin, E. and Muncie, J. (1994) 'Managing the criminal justice system', in Clarke, J., Cochrane, A. and McLaughlin, E. (eds) *Managing Social Policy.* London: Sage.

McLaughlin, E., Muncie, J. and Hughes, G. (2001) 'The permanent revolution: New Labour, new public management and the modernization of criminal justice', *Criminal Justice* 1 (3): 301–18.

McLaughlin, E. and Murji. K. (1998) 'Resistance through Representation: "Storylines", advertising and Police Federation campaigns', *Policing and Society* 8 (4): 367–99.

McLaughlin, E. and Murji, K. (2001) 'Lost connections and new directions: neo-liberalism, new public managerialism and the "modernization" of the British police', in Stenson, K. and Sullivan, R.R. (eds) *Crime, Risk and Justice: The politics of crime control in liberal democracies*. Cullompton: Willan Publishing.

Macpherson, Sir William (1999) *The Stephen Lawrence Inquiry: Report of an Inquiry by Sir William Macpherson of Cluny*, Cm 4262–1. London: HMSO.

McWilliams, W. (1981) 'The probation officer at court: From friend to acquaintance', *Howard Journal* XX: 97–116.

McWilliams, W. (1983) 'The mission to the English Police Courts 1876–1936', *Howard Journal* XXII: 129–47.

McWilliams, W. (1985) 'The mission transformed: professionalisation of probation between the wars', *Howard Journal* 24 (4): 257–74.

McWilliams, W. (1986) 'The English probation system and the diagnostic ideal', *Howard Journal* 25 (4): 241–60.

McWilliams, W. (1987) 'Probation, pragmatism and policy', *Howard Journal* 26 (2): 97–121.

Maguire, M. (1982) *Burglary in a Dwelling: The offence, the offender and the victim*. London: Heinemann Educational Books.

Maguire, M. (1992) 'Parole', in Stockdale, E. and Casale, S. (eds) *Criminal Justice Under Stress*. London: Blackstone Press.

Maguire, M. (1994) 'Crime statistics, patterns, and trends', in Maguire, M., Morgan, R. and Reiner, R. (eds) *The Oxford Handbook of Criminology*. Oxford: Oxford University Press.

Maguire, M. and Corbett, C. (1987) *The Effects of Crime and the Work of Victims Support Schemes*. Aldershot: Gower.

Maguire, M. and Corbett, C. (1991) *A Study of the Police Complaints System*. London: HMSO.

Mair, G. (1989) *Some developments in probation in the 1980s*, Home Office Research Bulletin No. 27. London: Home Office.

Mair, G. (1991) *Part-Time Punishment: The Origins and Development of Senior Attendance Centres*. London: HMSO.

Mair, G. (1995) 'Developments in probation in England and Wales 1984–1993', in McIvor, G. (ed.) *Working with Offenders: Research Highlights in Social Work*. London: Jessica Kingsley.

Mair, G. (2000) 'Creditable accreditation?', *Probation Journal* 47: 688–71.

Mair, G. and Nee, C. (1990) *Electronic Monitoring: The Trials and their Results*, Home Office Research Study No. 120. London: HMSO.

Malik, M. (1999) '"Racist crime": Racially aggravated offences in the Crime and Disorder Act 1998 Part II', *Modern Law Review* 62 (3): 409–24.

Mannheim, H. and Wilkins, L. (1955) *Prediction Methods in Relation to Borstal Training*, Home Office Study in Causes of Delinquency and the Treatment of Offenders No. 1. London: Home Office.

Manwaring-White, … (1983) …

Marshall, G. (1973) 'The government of the police since 1963', in Alderson, J. and Stead, P. *The Police We Deserve*. London: Wolfe.

Marshall, G. (1978) 'Police accountability revisited', in Butler, D. and Halsey, A. (eds) *Policy and Politics*. London: Macmillan.

Marshall, T. (1996) 'The evolution of restorative justice in Britain', *European Journal of Criminal Policy and Research* 4 (4): 21–43.

Marshall, T.F. (1985) *Alternatives to Criminal Courts*. Aldershot: Gower.

Marshall, T.F. and Merry, S. (1990) *Crime and Accountability: Victim/Offender Mediation in Practice*. London: HMSO.

Marshall, T.F. and Walpole, M. (1985) *Bringing People Together: Mediation and Reparation Projects in Great Britain*, Research and Planning Unit Paper No. 33. London: Home Office.

Marx, G. (1995) 'The engineering of social control: The search for the silver bullets', in Hagan, J. and Peterson, R. (eds) *Crime and Inequality*. Stanford: Stanford University Press.

Mathieson, D. (1992) 'The Probation Service', in Stockdale, E. and Casale, S. (eds) *Criminal Justice Under Stress*. London: Blackstone Press.

Mawby, R.I. (1988) 'Victims' needs or victims' rights?', in Maguire, M. and Pointing, J. (eds) *Victims of Crime: A New Deal?* Milton Keynes: Open University Press.

Mawby, R.I. and Gill, M. (1987) *Crime Victims: Needs, Services and the Voluntary Sector*. London: Tavistock.

Mawby, R.I. and Walklate, S. (1994) *Critical Victimology*. London: Sage.

May, M. (1973) 'Innocence and experience: the evolution of the concept of juvenile delinquency in the mid-nineteenth century', *Victorian Studies* 17: 1.

May, T. (1991) *Probation: Politics, Policy and Practice*. Milton Keynes: Open University Press.

May, T. (1994) 'Probation and community sanctions', in Maguire, M., Morgan, R. and Reiner, R. (eds) *The Oxford Handbook of Criminology*. Oxford: Oxford University Press.

Mayhew, P., Elliott, D. and Dowds, E.A. (1989) *The 1988 British Crime Survey*, Home Office Research Study No. 111. London: HMSO.

Melossi, D. and Pavarini, M. (1981) *The Prison and the Factory*. London: Macmillan.

Merrington, S. and Stanley, S. (2000) 'Doubts about the what works initiative', *Probation Journal* 47: 272–5.

Metropolitan Police and the London Borough of Bexley (1987) *Child Sexual Abuse Joint Investigative Project: Final Report*. London: HMSO.

Michael, A. (1998) Speech to the crime concern Parliamentary Discussion Group. London, 7 July.

Miers, D. (1990) *Compensation for Criminal Injuries*. London: Butterworths.

Miers, D., Maguire, M., Goldie, S., Sharpe, K., Hale, C., Netten, A., Uglow, S., Doolin, K., Hallam, A., Enterkin, J. and Newburn, T. (2001) *An Exploratory Evaluation of Restorative Justice Schemes*, Crime Reduction Research Series Paper 9. London: Home Office.

Morgan, J. (1987) *Conflict and Order: The police and labour disputes in England and Wales 1900–1939*. Oxford: Oxford University Press.

Morgan, J. and Zedner, L. (1991) *Child Victims*. Oxford: Oxford University Press.

Morgan, N. (1983) 'The shaping of parole in England and Wales', *Criminal Law Review* 137.

Morgan, R. (1987) 'The local determinants of policing policy', in Willmott, P. (ed.) *Policing and the Community*. London: Policy Studies Institute.

Morgan, R. (1989) 'Policing by consent: legitimating the doctrine', in Morgan, R. and Smith, D. (eds) *Coming to Terms with Policing*. London: Routledge.

Morgan, R. (1991) 'Woolf: In retrospect and prospect', *Modern Law Review* 54 (5): 713–25.

Morgan, R. (1992a) 'Following Woolf: The prospects for prisons policy', *Journal of Law and Society* 19 (2): 231–50.

Morgan, R. (1992b) 'Not just prisons: Reflections on prison disturbances', *Policy Studies* 13: 2.

Morgan, R. (1992c) 'Talking about policing', in Downes, D. (ed.) *Unravelling Criminal Justice*. London: Macmillan.

Morgan, R. (1994a) 'An awkward anomaly: Remand prisoners', in Player, E. and Jenkins, M. (eds) *Prisons After Woolf: Reform through riot*. London: Routledge.

Morgan, R. (1994b) 'Imprisonment', in Maguire, M., Morgan, R. and Reiner, R. (eds) *The Oxford Handbook of Criminology*. Oxford: Oxford University Press.

Morgan, R. (1994c) 'Justice and responsibility in prisons', in Gwynedd Jones, I. and Williams, G. (eds) *Social Policy, Crime and Punishment: Essays in Memory of Jane Morgan*. Cardiff: University of Wales Press.

Morgan, R. (2002) 'Imprisonment: A brief history, the contemporary scene, and likely prospects', in Maguire, M., Morgan, R. and Reiner, R. (eds) *The Oxford Handbook of Criminology*, 3rd edn. Oxford: Clarendon Press.

Morgan, R. and Jones, S. (1991) 'Prison discipline: The case for implementing Woolf', *British Journal of Criminology* 31: 280–91.

Morgan, R. and Jones, S. (1992) 'Bail or jail?', in Stockdale, E. and Casale, S. (eds) *Criminal Justice Under Stress*. London: Blackstone.

Morgan, R. and Maggs, C. (1985) 'Police community dialogues: consultative groups in action', in Brown, J. (ed.) *Models of Public/Police Consultation in Europe*, Cranfield-Wolfson Colloquium Papers.

Morgan, R. and Newburn, T. (1997) *The Future of Policing*. Oxford: Oxford University Press.

Morgan, R. and Smith, D.J. (1989) 'Opening the debate', in Morgan, R. and Smith, D. (eds) *Coming To Terms With Policing*. London: Routledge.

Morris, A. and Giller, H. (1987) *Understanding Juvenile Justice*. Beckenham: Croom Helm.

Morris, A. and McIsaac, M. (1978) *Juvenile Justice?* London: Heinemann.

Morris, A. and Maxwell, G. (2000) 'The practice of family group conferences in New Zealand: Assessing the place, potential and pitfalls of restorative justice', in Crawford, A. and Goodey, J. (eds) *Integrating a Victim Perspective Within Criminal Justice*. Aldershot: Ashgate.

Morris, T. (1989) *Crime and Criminal Justice since 1945*. Oxford: Blackwell.

Mountbatten Report (1966) *Report of the Inquiry into Prison Escapes and Security*, Cmnd 3175, London: HMSO.

Moxon, D. (1993) *Use of Compensation Orders in Magistrates' Courts*, Home Office Research and Statistics Department Research Bulletin No. 33. London: Home Office.

Moxon, D., Sutton, M. and Hedderman, C. (1990) *Unit Fines: Experiments in Four Courts*, Research and Planning Unit Paper No. 59. London: Home Office.

Muncie, J. (1984) *The Trouble with Kids Today*. London: Hutchinson.

Muncie, J. (2000) 'Pragmatic realism? Searching for criminology in the new youth justice', in Goldson, B. (ed.) *The New Youth Justice*. Lyme Regis: Russell House.

Muncie, J. (2001) 'A new deal for youth? Early interventions and correctionalism', in Hughes, G., McLaughlin, E. and Muncie, J. (eds) *Crime Prevention and Community Safety: New Directions*. London: Sage.

Murray, C. (1990) *The Emerging Underclass*. London: Institute of Economic Affairs.

NACRO (1987) *Diverting Juveniles from Custody: Findings from the Fourth Census of the Projects Funded under the DHSS Intermediate Treatment Initiative.* London: NACRO Juvenile Crime Section.

NACRO (1989) *Progress Through Partnership.* London: NACRO.

NACRO (1992) 'Expenditure on the criminal justice system', *Criminal Justice Digest* 73: 21.

NACRO (1993) *Evidence to the Home Affairs Committee.* London: NACRO.

NACRO (1994) *The Criminal Justice and Public Order Bill and Young Offenders.* London: NACRO, May.

Nash, M. and Savage, S. (1994) 'A criminal record? Law, order and Conservative Policy', in Savage, S., Atkinson, R. and Robins, L. (eds) *Public Policy in Britain.* Basingstoke: Macmillan.

Nathan, S. (1995) *Boot Camps: Return of the short, sharp shock.* London: Prison Reform Trust.

Nathan, S. (1998) 'Prison Privatization Factfile 21', *Prison Report* 42: 13–16.

National Association of Victim Support Schemes (1988) *The Victim in Court: Report of a Working Party.* London: NAVSS.

National Audit Office (1989) *Home Office: Control and Management of Probation Services in England and Wales.* London: HMSO.

NCH (1993) *Setting the Record Straight: Juvenile Crime in Perspective.* London: NCH.

Newburn, T. (1988) *The Use and Enforcement of Compensation Orders in Magistrates' Courts,* Home Office Research Study No. 102. London: HMSO.

Newburn, T. (1989) *The Settlement of Claims at the Criminal Injuries Compensation Board,* Home Office Research Study No. 112. London: HMSO.

Newburn, T. (1990) 'Compensation by the offender and the state', in Viano, E. (ed.) *The Victimology Research Handbook.* New York: Garland.

Newburn, T. (1991) *Permission and Regulation: Law and Morals in Post-war Britain.* London/New York: Routledge.

Newburn, T. (1995) 'The politics of sentencing reform and the Criminal Justice Act 1991', *Policy Studies* 16: 3.

Newburn, T. (2001) 'The Commodification of policing: Security networks in the late modern city', *Urban Studies* 38 (5–6): 829–48.

Newburn, T. (2002a) 'Atlantic Crossings: Policy transfer and crime control in England and Wales', *Punishment and Society* 4 (2): 165–94.

Newburn, T. (2002b) 'Community safety and policing: some implications of the Crime and Disorder Act 1998', in Hughes, G., McLaughlin, E. and Muncie, J. (eds) *Crime Prevention and Community Safety: New Directions.* London: Sage.

Newburn, T., Crawford, A., Earl, R., Goldie, S., Hale, C., Masters, G., Netten, A., Saunders, R., Sharpe, K. and Uglow, S. (2001a) *The Introduction of Referral Orders into the Youth Justice System,* RDS Occasional Paper No. 70. London: Home Office.

Newburn, T., Crawford, A., Earl, R., Goldie, S., Hale, C., Masters, G., Netten, A., Saunders, R., Sharpe, K., Uglow, S. and Campbell, A. (2001b) *The Introduction of Referral Orders into the Youth Justice System: Second Interim Report,* RDS Occasional Paper No. 73. London: Home Office.

Newburn, T., Crawford, A., Earle, R., Goldie, S., Hale, C., Masters, G., Netten, A., Saunders, R., Sharpe, K., and Uglow, S. (2002) *The Introduction of Referral Orders into the Youth Justice System,* Home Office Research Study No. 242. London: Home Office.

Newburn, T. and Jones, T. (2000) 'The Police and the New Magistracy: Independent members and the new police authorities' *Liverpool Law Review* 21: 241–59.

Newburn, T. and Merry, S. (1990) *Keeping in Touch: Police-Victim Communication in Two Areas*, Home Office Research Study No. 116. London: HMSO.

Newburn, T. and Stanko, E.A. (eds) (1994) *Just Boys Doing Business? Men, Masculinities and Crime*. London: Routledge.

Newman, O. (1972) *Defensible Space: People and design in the violent city*. London: Architectural Press.

Newson, E. (1994) *Video violence and the protection of children*. Nottingham: Nottingham University Press.

Nixon, J., Hunter, H. and Shayer, S. (1999) *The use of legal remedies by social landlords to deal with neighbourhood nuisance: Survey report*. Sheffield: Sheffield Hallam University.

Norris, C., Moran, J. and Armstrong, G. (1998) 'Algorithmic surveillance: the future of automated visual surveillance', in Norris, C., Moran, J. and Armstrong, G. (eds) *Surveillance, Closed Circuit Television and Social Control*. Aldershot: Ashgate.

Northam, G. (1989) *Shooting in the Dark*. London: Faber & Faber.

Pahl, J. (1982) 'Police response to battered women', *Journal of Social Welfare Law*, November.

Parnas, R.I. (1972) 'The police response to domestic disturbance', in Radnowitz, L. and Wolfgang, M.E. (eds) *The Criminal in the Arms of the Law*. New York: Basic Books.

Parton, N. (1985) *The Politics of Child Abuse*. London: Macmillan.

Patten, C. (1999) *A New Beginning: Policing in Northern Ireland: The report of the Independent Commission on policing for Northern Ireland*. London: The Stationery Office.

Pearson, G. (1975) *The Deviant Imagination*. London: Macmillan.

Pearson, G. (1983) *Hooligan: A History of Respectable Fears*. London: Macmillan.

Pease, K. (1980) 'Community Service and prison: Are they alternatives?', in Pease, K. and McWilliams, W. (eds) *Community Service by Order*. Edinburgh: Scottish Academic Press.

Pease, K. (1985) 'Community Service Orders', in Tonry, M. and Morris, N. (eds) *Crime and Justice: An Annual Review of Research*. Chicago: University of Chicago Press.

Pease, K. (1997) 'Crime Prevention', in Maguire, M., Morgan, R. and Reiner, R. (eds) *The Oxford Handbook of Criminology*. Oxford: Clarendon Press.

Pease, K., Billingham, S. and Eamshaw, I. (1977) *Community Service Assessed in 1976*. London: Home Office.

Phillips, C. (2002) 'From voluntary to statutory status', in Hughes, G., McLaughlin, E. and Muncie, J. (eds) *Crime Prevention and Community Safety: New Directions*. London: Sage.

Phipps, A. (1988) 'Ideologies, political parties, and victims of crime', in Maguire, M. and Pointing, J. (eds) *Victims of Crime: A New Deal?* Milton Keynes: Open University Press.

Pitts, J. (1992) 'Juvenile justice policy in England and Wales', in Coleman, J.C. and Warren-Adamson, C. (eds) *Youth Policy in the 1990s*. London: Routledge.

Pitts, J. (2001) 'The new correctionalism: young people, youth justice and New Labour', in Matthews, R. and Pitts, J. (eds) *Crime, Disorder and Community Safety*. London: Routledge.

Pizzey, E. (1974) *Scream Quietly or the Neighbours Will Hear*. Harmondsworth: Penguin.

Platt, A. (1969) *The Child Savers*. Chicago: University of Chicago Press.

Player, E. and Jenkins, M. (1994) *Prisons After Woolf: Reform through riot*. London: Routledge.

Pointing, J. and Maguire, M. (1988) 'The rediscovery of the crime victim', in Maguire, M. and Pointing, J. (eds) *Victims of Crime: A New Deal?* Milton Keynes: Open University Press.

Police Foundation/Policy Studies Institute (1996) *Final Report of the Independent Inquiry into the Role and Responsibilities of the Police*. London: Police Foundation/PSI.

Pollard, C. (1997) 'Zero tolerance: short term fix, long term liability?', in Dennis, N. (ed.) *Zero Tolerance: Policing a free society*. London: Institute of Economic Affairs.

Pratt, J. (1989) 'Corporatism: The third model of juvenile justice', *British Journal of Criminology* 29 (3): 236–54.

Quayle, S. (1998) 'The "drug Czar": A triumph of presentation over substance?', *Talking Politics*, Winter: 87–92.

Radzinowicz, L. (1948) *A History of English Criminal Law and its Administration*, Vol. 1, *The Movement for Reform*. London: Stevens & Stevens.

Radzinowicz, L. and Hood, R. (1990) *The Emergence of Penal Policy in Victorian and Edwardian England*. Oxford: Clarendon Press.

Raine, J.W. and Walker, B. (1990) *Quality of Service in the Magistrates' Courts*, Home Office Research Bulletin No. 28. London: Home Office.

Raine, J.W. and Willson, M.J. (1993) *Managing Criminal Justice*. Hemel Hempstead: Harvester Wheatsheaf.

Raine, J.W. and Willson, M.J. (1995) 'New public management and criminal justice', *Public Money and Management*, January–March.

Rawlings, P. (1992) 'Creeping privatization? The police, the Conservative government and policing in the late 1980s', in Reiner, R. and Cross, M. (eds) *Beyond Law and Order: Criminal Justice Policy and Politics into the 1990s*. London: Macmillan.

Raynor, P. (2002) 'What Works: Have we moved on?', in Ward, D., Scott, J. and Lacey, M. (eds) *Probation: Working for Justice*. Oxford: Oxford University Press.

Raynor, P. and Vanstone, M. (2002) *Understanding Community Penalties: Probation, policy and social changes*. Buckingham: Open University Press.

Reeves, H. (1989) 'The victim support perspective', in Wright, M. and Galaway, B. (eds) *Mediation and Criminal Justice*. London: Sage.

Reeves, H. and Mulley, K. (2000) 'The new status of victims in the UK: opportunities and threats', in Crawford, A. and Goodey, J. (eds) *Integrating a Victim Perspective Within Criminal Justice: International Debates*. Aldershot: Ashgate.

Reiner, R. (1985) *The Politics of the Police*. Brighton: Harvester.

Reiner, R. (1991) *Chief Constables*. Oxford: Oxford University Press.

Reiner, R. (1992) *The Politics of the Police*, 2nd edn. Brighton: Harvester.

Reiner, R. (1993) 'Police accountability: Principles, patterns and practices', in Reiner, R. and Spencer, S. (eds) *Accountable Policing: Effectiveness, Empowerment and Equity*. London: Institute for Public Policy Research.

Reiner, R. (2000) *The Politics of the Police*, 3rd edn. Oxford: Oxford University Press.

Reith, C. (1938) *The Police Idea*. Oxford: Oxford University Press.

Renshaw, J. and Powell, H. (2001) *The Story So Far: Emerging evidence of the impact of the reformed youth justice system*. London: Youth Justice Board.

Roberts, J. (1994) 'The relationship between the community and the prison', in Player, E. and Jenkins, M. (eds) *Prisons After Woolf: Reform through riot*. London: Routledge.

Rock, P. (1990) *Helping Victims of Crime*. Oxford: Clarendon Press.

Rock, P. (1993) *The Social World of an English Crown Court.* Oxford: Clarendon Press.

Rosenbaum, D.P. (1988) 'Community crime prevention: A review and synthesis of the literature', *Justice Quarterly* 5 (3): 323–96.

Rosenbaum, D.P. (ed.) (1994) *The Challenge of Community Policing.* London: Sage.

Royal Commission on Criminal Justice (1993) *Report.* London: HMSO.

Royal Commission on the Police (1962) *Final Report,* Cmnd 1728. London: HMSO.

Rutherford, A. (1986a) *Growing Out of Crime: Society and Young People in Trouble.* Harmondsworth: Penguin.

Rutherford, A. (1986b) *Prisons and the Process of Justice.* Oxford: Oxford University Press.

Rutherford, A. (1990) 'British penal policy and the idea of prison privatization', in McDonald, D.C. (ed.) *Private Prisons and the Public Interest.* New Brunswick: Rutgers University Press.

Rutherford, A. (1993) 'Penal policy and prison management', *Prison Service Journal* 90.

Rutter, M. and Giller, H. (1983) *Juvenile Delinquency: Trends and Perspectives.* Harmondsworth: Penguin.

Ryan, M. (1983) *The Politics of Penal Reform.* Harlow: Longman.

Ryan, M. (1992) 'The Woolf Report: on the treadmill of prison reform?', *Political Quarterly* 63 (1), January–March: 50–6.

Ryan, M. and Ward, T. (1989) 'Privatisation and penal politics', in Matthews, R. (ed.) *Privatising Criminal Justice.* London: Sage.

Sampson, A., Stubbs, P., Smith, D., Pearson, G. and Blagg, H. (1988) 'Crime, localities and the multi-agency approach', *British Journal of Criminology* 28: 478–93.

Sanders, A. and Young, R. (1994) *Criminal Justice.* London: Butterworths.

Savage, S., Charman, S. and Cope, S. (2000) 'The Policy Context', in Leishman, F., Loveday, B. and Savage, S. (eds) *Core Issues in Policing.* Harlow: Pearson.

Scarman, Lord (1982) *The Scarman Report.* Harmondsworth: Penguin.

Scott, J. and Ward, D. (2002) 'Introduction', in Ward, D., Scott, J. and Lacey, M. (eds) *Probation: Working for Justice.* Oxford: Oxford University Press.

Scottish Law Commission (1990) *Report on the Evidence of Children and Other Potentially Vulnerable Witnesses,* Scottish Law Commission Study No. 125. Edinburgh: Scottish Law Commission.

Scraton, P., Sim, J. and Skidmore, P. (1991) *Prisons Under Protest.* Milton Keynes: Open University Press.

Shapland, J. (1988) 'Fiefs and peasants: accomplishing change for victims in the criminal justice system', in Maguire, M. and Pointing, J. (eds) *Victims of Crime: A New Deal?* Milton Keynes: Open University Press.

Shapland, J. and Cohen, D. (1987) 'Facilities for victims: the role of the police and the courts', *Criminal Law Review,* January.

Shapland, J., Willmore, J. and Duff, P. (1985) *Victims in the Criminal Justice System.* Aldershot: Gower.

Sharpe, J.A. (1988) 'A history of crime in England c.1300–1924', in Rock, P. (ed.) *A History of British Criminology. British Journal of Criminology* 28 (2), special edn, Spring.

Sharpe, J.A. (1990) *Judicial Punishment in England.* London: Faber & Faber.

Shaw, S. (1992) 'Prisons', in Stockdale, E. and Casale, S. (eds) *Criminal Justice Under Stress.* London: Blackstone Press.

Shearing, C. (1996) 'Public and private policing', in Saulsbury, W., Mott, J. and Newburn, T. (eds) *Themes in Contemporary Policing*. London: Police Foundation/Policy Studies Institute.

Sheerman, B. (1991) 'What Labour wants', *Policing* 7 (3).

Sherman, L. (1992) 'The variable effects of arrest on criminal careers: the Milwaukee Domestic Violence Experiment', *Journal of Criminal Law and Criminology* 83, Spring: 1.

Silver, A. (1967) 'The demand for order in a civil society', in Bordua, D. (ed.) *The Police*. New York: Wiley.

Sim, J. (1987) 'Working for the clampdown: Prisons and politics in England and Wales', in Scraton, P. (ed.) *Law, Order and the Authoritarian State*. Milton Keynes: Open University Press.

Sim, J. (1991) '"We are not animals, we are human beings": Prisons, protest and politics in England and Wales, 1969–90', *Social Justice* 18 (3).

Sim, J. (1994) 'Reforming the penal wasteland? A critical review of the Woolf Report', in Player, E. and Jenkins, M. (eds) *Prisons After Woolf: Reform through riot*. London: Routledge.

Simon, J. (1997) 'Governing through crime', in Friedman, L.M. and Fisher, G. (eds) *The Crime Conundrum*. Boulder, CO: Westview Press.

Skogan, W.G. (1990) *The Police and Public in England and Wales: A British Crime Survey Report*, Home Office Research Study No. 117. London: HMSO.

Smith, D. (2000) 'Corporatism and the new youth justice', in Goldson, B. (ed.) *The New Youth Justice*. Lyme Regis: Russell House.

Smith, D.J. (1987) 'Research, the community and the police', in Willmott, P. (ed.) *Policing and the Community*. London: PSI.

Smith, L.J.F. (1989a) *Concerns About Rape*, Home Office Research Study No. 106. London: HMSO.

Smith, L.J.F. (1989b) *Domestic Violence: An Overview of the Literature*. London: HMSO.

Softley, P. (1978) *Compensation Orders in Magistrates' Courts*, Home Office Research Study No. 43. London: HMSO.

Spencer, S. (1985) *Called to Account: The Case for Police Accountability in England and Wales*. London: NCCL.

Spencer, S. and Stern, B. (2002) *Reluctant Witness*. London: IPPR.

Standing Conference on Crime Prevention (1991) *Safer Communities: The Local Delivery of Crime Prevention through the Partnership Approach* (The Morgan Report). London: Home Office.

Stanko, E.A. (1988) 'Hidden violence against women', in Maguire, M. and Pointing, J. (eds) *Victims of Crime: A New Deal?* Milton Keynes: Open University Press.

Stern, V. (1989) *Bricks of Shame: Britain's Prisons*. 2nd edn. Harmondsworth: Penguin.

Stevenson, S. (1989) 'Some social and political tides affecting the development of juvenile justice 1938–64', in Gorst, A., Johnman, L. and Lucas, W.S. (eds) *Post-War Britain: Themes and Perspectives, 1945–64*. London: Pinter Press and the Institute of Contemporary British History.

Stevenson, S. and Bottoms, A.E. (1989) 'The politics of the police 1955–1964: A Royal Commission in a decade of transition', in Morgan, R. (ed.) *Policing Organised Crime and Crime Prevention*. British Criminology Conference, Vol. 4.

Straw, J. (1998) Speech to Magistrates' Association, Blackburn, 25 June.

Taylor, I., Walton, P. and Young, J. (1973) *The New Criminology: For a Social Theory of Deviance*. London: Routledge & Kegan Paul.

Taylor, Lord Justice (1996) 'Continuity and Change in the Criminal Law', Public Lecture delivered at King's College, University of London, 6 March 1996, available at www.kcl.ac.uk/depsta/law/kclj/articles/taylor_fn.html.

Thane, P. (1981) 'Childhood in history', in King, M. (ed.) *Childhood, Welfare and Justice.* London: Bedford.

Thomas, J.E. (1972) *The English Prison Officer since 1850: A Study in Conflict.* London: Routledge & Kegan Paul.

Thomas, J.E. (1994) 'Woolf and prison staff: Still looking for "good gaolers"', in Player, E. and Jenkins, M. (eds) *Prisons After Woolf: Reform through riot.* London: Routledge.

Thomas, J.E. and Pooley, R. (1980) *The Exploding Prison: Prison Riots and the Case of Hull.* London: Junction Books.

Thorpe, D., Smith, D., Green, C. and Paley, J. (1980) *Out of Care.* London: Allen & Unwin.

Tilley, N. (2002) 'Crime prevention in Britain 1975–2010', in Hughes, G., McLaughlin, E. and Muncie, J. (eds) *Crime Prevention and Community Safety: New Directions.* London: Sage.

Tobias, J.J. (1972) *Crime and Industrial Society in the Nineteenth Century.* Harmondsworth: Penguin.

Tonry, M. and Rex, S. (2002) 'Reconsidering sentencing and punishment in England and Wales', in Rex, S. and Tonry, M. (eds) *Reform and Punishment: The future of sentencing.* Cullompton: Willan Publishing.

Tuck, M. (1988) *Crime Prevention: A shift in concept,* Home Office Research Bulletin No. 24. London: Home Office.

Tuck, M. (1989) *Drinking and Disorder: A Study of Non-Metropolitan Violence,* Home Office Research Study No. 108. London: HMSO.

Tutt, N. (1981) 'A decade of policy', *British Journal of Criminology* 21: 4.

Tutt, N. and Giller, H. (1983) 'Manifesto for management – the elimination of custody', *Justice of the Peace* 151: 200–2.

Uglow, S. and Trelford, V. (1997) *The Police Act 1997.* London: Jordans.

van Dijk, J.J.M. (1988) 'Ideological trends within the victims movement: an international perspective', in Maguire, M. and Pointing, J. (eds) *Victims of Crime: A New Deal?* Milton Keynes: Open University Press.

Victim Support (1995) *The Rights of Victims of Crime: A policy paper.* London: Victim Support.

Waddington, D. (1992) *Contemporary Issues in Public Disorder.* London: Routledge.

Waddington, D., Jones, K. and Critcher, C. (1989) *Flashpoints: Studies in Public Disorder.* London: Routledge.

Waddington, P.A.J. (1991) *The Strong Arm of the Law.* Oxford: Oxford University Press.

Waddington, P.A.J. (1993) 'The case of the hidden agenda', *Independent,* 1 July.

Walklate, S. (1989) *Victimology: The Victim and the Criminal Justice Process.* London: Unwin Hyman.

Wall, D. (1998) *The Chief Constables of England and Wales.* Aldershot: Dartmouth.

Waller, I. (1989) *Current Trends in European Crime Prevention: Implications for Canada.* Ottawa: Department of Justice.

Wargent, M. (2002) 'The new governance of probation', *Howard Journal* 41 (2): 182–200.

Wasik, M. (1978) 'The place of compensation in the penal system', *Criminal Law Review.* 599–611.

Wasik, M. (1992) 'Sentencing: A fresh look at the aims and objectives', in Stockdale, E. and Casale, S. (eds) *Criminal Justice under Stress*. London: Blackstone Press.

Wasik, M. and von Hirsch, A. (1990) 'Statutory sentencing principles: The 1990 White Paper', *Modern Law Review* 53: 4.

Weatheritt, M. (1986) *Innovations in Policing*. London: Croom Helm.

West, D. (1982) *Delinquency: Its roots, Careers and Prospects*. London: Heinemann Educational.

Whyte, B. (2000) 'Between two stools: Youth justice in Scotland', *Probation Journal* 47 (2): 119–25.

Wilkinson, T. (1995) '*Doli Incapax* Revisited', *Solicitors Journal*, 14 April: 338–9.

Willmott, P. (ed.) (1987) *Policing and the Community*. London: PSI.

Wilson, J. and Kelling, G. (1982) 'Broken Windows', *Atlantic Monthly*, March.

Windlesham, Lord (1987) *Responses to Crime*. Oxford: Oxford University Press.

Windlesham, Lord (1993) *Responses to Crime*, Vol. 2, *Penal Policy in the Making*. Oxford: Oxford University Press.

Windlesham, Lord (2001) *Dispensing Justice: Responses to Crime*, Vol. 4, *Penal Policy in the Making*. Oxford: Oxford University Press.

Women's National Commission (1985) *Violence Against Women*. London: Cabinet Office.

Woolf, Lord Justice (1991) *Prison Disturbances April 1990: Report of an Inquiry by the Rt. Hon. Lord Justice Woolf (Parts I and II) and His Honour Judge Stephen Tumin (Part II)*, Cm 1456. London: HMSO.

Wright, M. (1982) *Making Good: Prisons, Punishment and Beyond*. London: Unwin Hyman.

Wright, M. (1991) *Justice for Victims and Offenders*. Milton Keynes: Open University Press.

Young, A. (1996) *Imagining Crime*. London: Routledge.

Young, R. (2000) 'Integrating a multi-victim perspective into criminal justice through restorative justice conferences', in Crawford, A. and Goodey, J. (eds) *Integrating a Victim Perspective Within Criminal Justice*. Aldershot: Ashgate.

Young, R. and Goold, B. (1999) 'Restorative youth cautioning in Aylesbury – from degrading to reintegrative shaming ceremonies?', *Criminal Law Review*. 126–38.

Young, W. (1979) *Community Service Orders: The Development and Use of a New Penal Measure*. London: Heinemann.

Zedner, L. (1994) 'Victims', in Maguire, M., Morgan, R. and Reiner, R. (eds) *The Oxford Handbook of Criminology*. Oxford: Oxford University Press.

Zedner, L. (2002) 'Victims', in Maguire, M., Morgan, R. and Reiner, R. (eds) *The Oxford Handbook of Criminology*, 3rd edn. Oxford: Clarendon Press.

Index